Consolidating the Third Wave Democracies

Themes and Perspectives

A *Journal of Democracy* Book

•

BOOKS IN THE SERIES

Edited by Larry Diamond and Marc F. Plattner

The Global Resurgence of Democracy (1993)

Capitalism, Socialism, and Democracy Revisited (1993)

Nationalism, Ethnic Conflict, and Democracy (1994)

Economic Reform and Democracy (1995)

The Global Resurgence of Democracy, 2d ed. *(1996)*

Civil-Military Relations and Democracy (1996)

Consolidating the Third Wave Democracies (1997)
(with Yun-han Chu and Hung-mao Tien)

Published under the auspices of

the International Forum for Democratic Studies

Consolidating the Third Wave Democracies
edited by Larry Diamond, Marc F. Plattner, Yun-han Chu,
and Hung-mao Tien

Available in separate paperback editions:

Consolidating the Third Wave Democracies: Themes and Perspectives
edited by Larry Diamond, Marc F. Plattner, Yun-han Chu,
and Hung-mao Tien

Consolidating the Third Wave Democracies: Regional Challenges
edited by Larry Diamond, Marc F. Plattner, Yun-han Chu,
and Hung-mao Tien

Consolidating the Third Wave Democracies

Themes and Perspectives

Edited by Larry Diamond, Marc F. Plattner,
Yun-han Chu, and Hung-mao Tien

The Johns Hopkins University Press
Baltimore and London

The Johns Hopkins University Press
2715 North Charles Street, Baltimore, Maryland 21218-4319
The Johns Hopkins Press Ltd., London

Library of Congress Catalog Card Number 97-72775

A catalog record for this book is available from the British Library.

ISBN 0-8018-5794-5 (pbk.)

CONTENTS

IV. Civil Society

V. Economic Development

ACKNOWLEDGMENTS

This book is the offspring of the most memorable conference that any of us has ever attended—a four-day event held in Taipei on 27–30 August 1995. Cosponsored by the National Endowment for Democracy's International Forum for Democratic Studies and Taiwan's Institute for National Policy Research (INPR), the conference brought to Taiwan some 60 leading scholars and practitioners of democracy from 25 countries to discuss the issue of consolidating the new "third wave" democracies that have emerged over the past two decades.

Among the political leaders who participated were Edgardo Boeninger, former minister of the presidency in Chile; Yegor Gaidar, a member of the Duma and former acting prime minister of Russia; Mart Laar, former prime minister of Estonia; and José María Maravall, former minister of education and science in Spain. The scholars included such luminaries in political science as Robert A. Dahl, Francis Fukuyama, Samuel P. Huntington, Juan J. Linz, Abraham Lowenthal, Guillermo O'Donnell, Adam Przeworski, Robert Scalapino, Philippe C. Schmitter, and Alfred Stepan. Among the heads of major civil society organizations present were Sadikou Alao (GERDDES-Afrique), Wilmot James (Institute for Democracy in South Africa), Ghia Nodia (Caucasian Institute for Peace, Democracy, and Development, Georgia); Aleksander Smolar (Stefan Batory Foundation, Poland); and Chai-Anan Samudavanija (Institute of Public Policy Studies, Thailand). In addition to those whose essays appear in these two volumes, other prominent democratic scholars and practitioners who participated in the conference included Vincent Maphai (South Africa); Yasmeen Murshed (Bangladesh); Anthony Bing-leung Cheung (Hong Kong); Hyug-baeg Im and Sung Chul Yang (South Korea); Hulan Hashbat (Mongolia); Carolina Hernandez and Haydee Yorac (Philippines); Ergun Özbudun (Turkey); Rudolf Joo (Hungary); Nina Belyaeva, Vladimir Mau, and Lilia Shevtsova (Russia); Serhiy Holovaty (Ukraine); Patricia Valdez (Argentina); Bolívar Lamounier (Brazil); Denise Dresser (Mexico); Juan Arias (Panama); and Carl Gershman, Gordon Hein, Ramon Myers, and Marc F. Plattner (United States).

The conference was remarkable not only for bringing together leading figures from so many third wave democracies, but also for the role it played in the democratic evolution of Taiwan. Not long after the conference's conclusion, Taiwan held the parliamentary elections (in December 1995) and the presidential elections (in March 1996) that are regarded by most analysts as having completed its transition to democracy. In the importance that they accorded our conference, and the strong statements that they made there, the top political leaders of Taiwan made clear in a very public way their determination to follow through with their transition and to join the ranks of the world's democracies.

The attendees were privileged to hear major addresses from four of Taiwan's most important officials: President Lee Teng-hui; Premier Lien Chan (who was elected vice-president in March 1996); James C.Y. Soong, the elected governor of Taiwan province; and Chen Shui-bien, the elected mayor of Taipei (and a member of the opposition Democratic Progressive Party). We are very pleased to be able to publish here revised versions of the presentations by the first three of these, and regret that circumstances did not allow Mayor Chen Shui-bien to provide us with a revised version of his remarks in time for publication. In this context, we also wish to take special note of the key role played by Jason Hu, then the director of Taiwan's Government Information Office, whose encouragement and assistance were vital to the success of this project. Another important contribution was made by Hui-cheng Huang, then executive director of INPR.

With the completion of its democratic transition, Taiwan can lay claim to being one of the most notable of the third wave democracies. It is remarkable not only for its extraordinary economic success, but also for embodying the first freely elected government in the history of the Chinese people—and thereby disproving the contention of those who claim that democracy is incompatible with Chinese culture. Given the venue of our conference, we gave special attention in this project to Taiwan's emerging democracy, and to the prospects for democratization in the neighboring People's Republic of China. We believe that the importance of China for the future of democracy in the world more than justifies this emphasis.

A project of this scope requires the contributions of many people. We were blessed to have the assistance of a considerable number of dedicated staff members at both the International Forum and INPR. The conference arrangements were handled primarily by INPR, with invaluable administrative support provided by Chih-peng Lin, Chia-ching Lu, Pei-ling Lin, Mamie Barrett, and Trevor Sponagle. A report on the conference was prepared by You-ming Yang and Mamie Barrett and was produced and printed by the Cultural Development Division, Evergreen International Corporation. Debra Liang-Fenton of the International Forum provided important assistance at the conference, and she and Art Kaufman efficiently took charge of communications with overseas participants.

The work on this book was performed primarily by the International Forum. The enormous task of coordinating and supervising the editorial and production process on these two volumes was superbly handled by Annette Theuring. She received help on various administrative matters from Debra Liang-Fenton and from Jennifer Alstad and Bo Tedards of INPR. The essays by Samuel P. Huntington, Juan J. Linz and Alfred Stepan, Guillermo O'Donnell, Aleksander Smolar, E. Gyimah-Boadi, Adam Przeworski et al., Lee Teng-hui, Minxin Pei, and Andrew J. Nathan were first published in the *Journal of Democracy;* these reflect the skillful manuscript editing of Phil Costopoulos and Annette Theuring, along with other editorial contributions by Miriam Kramer, Zerxes Spencer, and David Ratigan. The remaining essays were edited with care by Amy Blitz and Megan Klose. The index was ably compiled by David Ratigan. Henry Tom at the Johns Hopkins University Press was once more an unfailing source of useful advice and encouragement.

Finally, we wish to express our thanks to Carl Gershman, the president of the National Endowment for Democracy, for his valuable participation at the conference in Taipei and for his enthusiastic support for this project.

INTRODUCTION:
IN SEARCH OF CONSOLIDATION

Larry Diamond

World politics have changed radically in the past two decades. At the beginning of 1975, there were only some 40 democracies in the world, and they were predominantly the rich, industrialized nations of the West.[1] Few states in what was then termed the Third World had democratic systems of government. Communist dictatorships were firmly entrenched—or so it seemed—in the Soviet Union, Eastern Europe, Cuba, China, North Korea, and North Vietnam. In 1975, communist forces took control of South Vietnam, Cambodia, and Laos as well. That year, Marxist governments also came to power in the former Portuguese colonies of Angola and Mozambique and, soon thereafter, in Ethiopia. Military or one-party dictatorships held sway in most of Latin America, Africa, and Asia; only three countries in Central and South America had democratically elected leaders. Indeed, the mid-to-late 1970s seemed a low-water mark for democracy in the world, and the empirical trends were reified by intellectual fashions dismissing democracy as an artifice, a cultural construct of the West, or a "luxury" that poor states could not afford.

Yet even as authoritarian trends were expanding and deepening in most parts of the world, a countertrend was taking shape. In 1974, the 48-year-old dictatorial regime in Portugal was deposed by a military coup, and three months later the Greek military dictatorship collapsed. Elected, civilian democratic government took hold in Greece first, but by late 1975 democrats had bested radical forces at the polls in Portugal as well. That same month of November 1975, the 36-year-old dictatorship of Francisco Franco in Spain ended with his death, and a transition to democracy ensued. Over the following three years, Spain crafted a new democratic regime while the process of military withdrawal began in Latin America and military regimes gave way to civilian, elected governments in Ghana and Nigeria.

The latter two democracies did not last long, but in a grand process that Samuel P. Huntington has dubbed the "third wave" of global democratization, a democratic *Zeitgeist* swept the globe.[2] As the return to at least formally democratic, civilian rule was becoming the norm in Central and South America, democracy was restored in Turkey in 1983, in the Philippines in 1986, in South Korea in 1987, and in Pakistan in 1988. By then, Hungary was already in transition to a multiparty system. In 1989, communism collapsed in Eastern Europe, and a regional wave of democratic transitions ensued there, followed in 1990 by the beginning of a "second liberation" on the African continent. By the end of 1994, 38 of the (then) 47 countries in sub-Saharan Africa had held competitive multiparty elections for at least the national legislature,[3] and the number of electoral democracies in Africa had increased to 18 from just 3 in 1988.[4] Communism collapsed in the Soviet Union as well, and new democracies emerged in many of the former Soviet states, including, most significantly, Russia.

In two decades, the third wave of democratization has transformed the balance of political regimes in the world. This transformation has been especially dramatic since the end of the Cold War and the collapse of communism in the former East bloc. Between 1990 and 1996, the number of electoral democracies in the world increased from 76 to 118. Even with the increase in the total number of countries in the world during this period, this trend established democracy as the typical form of government. The percentage of countries with at least an electoral form of democracy—in which multiple political parties regularly compete for power through (relatively) free and fair elections—increased from 27.5 percent in 1974 to 46 percent in 1990 and to 61 percent in 1996.

On closer examination, however, the scope of democratic progress in the world is partly illusory, for regular, free, and fair elections do not ensure the presence of other important dimensions of democracy. A more comprehensive conception—what I have elsewhere termed "liberal democracy"—encompasses extensive protections for individual and group freedoms, inclusive pluralism in civil society as well as party politics, civilian control over the military, institutions to hold officeholders accountable, and thus a strong rule of law secured through an independent, impartial judiciary.[5] Although it is not articulated in these precise terms, the distinction between the minimal framework of electoral democracy and the deeper institutional structure of liberal democracy figures prominently in many of the theoretical and empirical chapters in our two volumes, entitled *Themes and Perspectives* and *Regional Challenges*. Indeed, as Juan J. Linz and Alfred Stepan insist in their contribution to *Themes and Perspectives,* "If freely elected executives (no matter what the magnitude of their majority) infringe the constitution, violate the rights of individuals and minorities, impinge upon the legitimate functions of the legislature, and thus fail to rule within the bounds of a state of law, their regimes are not democracies."

The number of "liberal" democracies has also increased during the third wave, although not nearly as sharply as the number of electoral democracies. Taking the Freedom House rating of "free" as a rough indicator of liberal democracy, the number of such states jumped from 39 at the start of the third wave to 52 in 1980 and then to 76 in 1990.[6] In proportional terms, the increase is even more moderate, from 27.5 percent of all states in 1974 to 41.5 percent in 1990. Moreover, in recent years the number of free states has more or less stagnated (as have freedom levels in general). In fact, the number of free states dipped slightly in 1992 and 1993, edging back up to 76 in the following two years and increasing to 79 in 1996. In proportional terms, liberal democracies were no more common in 1996 (41.4 percent of the world's regimes) than in 1991.[7]

The juxtaposition of these two trends—steady expansion in the number of electoral democracies, but recent stagnation in levels of political and civil freedom in the world—signals a growing gap between the two standards. In 1990, 86 percent of all the formally democratic states in the world were "free," or liberal democracies. Since 1993, only about two-thirds have been. And over the past decade, freedom levels have actually declined in many third wave democracies, such as Turkey, Pakistan, Peru, Brazil, Ecuador, and Zambia, as well as in some older democracies, including India, Sri Lanka, Colombia, and Venezuela.

Regional differences are also much more apparent in the prevalence of liberal democracy than of electoral democracy. By the end of 1996, all 24 West European countries were "free" (with most of them well above the threshold dividing "free" from "partly free"). By contrast, only 57 percent of the countries in the Americas, a third of those in East Central Europe and the former Soviet Union, 42 percent in the Asia-Pacific region, 17 percent in Africa, and one (Israel) of 14 states in the Middle East were free.[8] In the proportion of states that are electoral democracies, however, other regions came much closer to the West European standard of 100 percent: 89 percent in the Americas, 69 percent in the former East bloc, 63 percent in the Asia-Pacific region, and 34 percent in Africa.

Clearly, the third wave of democratization has had much greater breadth than depth. As a number of the essays in this two-volume collection demonstrate, democracy may be the most common form of government in the world, but outside of the wealthy industrialized nations it tends to be shallow, illiberal, and poorly institutionalized. If there are no immediate threats of democratic collapse in most of those countries, neither are there clear signs that democracy has become consolidated and stable, truly the only viable political system and method for the foreseeable future. In fact, of the more than 70 new democracies that have come into being since the start of the third wave, only a small number are generally considered to be deeply rooted and secure. The remainder appear for now "'condemned' to remain democratic" while they "muddle through as 'unconsolidated democracies,'"[9] with militaries unwilling to seize power even in the classic circumstances of political stalemate and crisis that were used to justify past coups.[10] But there are clear signs of erosion of the quality and stability of democracy in many of these third wave regimes—abuses of power and even "self-coups" by domineering executives, constraints on the press and independent organizations, assassinations of crusading journalists, and mounting corruption, criminality, political violence, and civil strife. There are even growing doubts, reflected in some of our chapters, about how long the constitutional structures of democracy can survive amid prolonged economic suffering, severe inequality, rampant crime, venal and feeble judicial systems, growing vigilante movements, and chronically weak and ineffectual political institutions. From this perspective, the greatest challenge still lies ahead: to consolidate and make permanent the extraordinary democratic gains of the past two decades.

There is more at stake here than the quality and stability of new (and, in countries like Sri Lanka and Colombia, old) democracies. The future status of democracy in the world could itself be in question. As Huntington emphasizes in his book *The Third Wave*, each of the previous two waves of global democratization ended in a "reverse wave" of democratic breakdown. And each of these reverse waves was a traumatic time for human freedom, international peace, and liberal values, giving rise to fascist and communist regimes in the interwar period and to numerous insurgencies and brutal military dictatorships in the 1960s and early 1970s. Today, human rights abuses, genocide, aggression, warfare, and insecurity are still generated by nondemocratic states; generally, the more repressive these states are, the more they threaten their neighbors as well as their own people.

As Huntington observes in the opening chapter of *Themes and Perspectives,* the euphoria generated by the collapse of communism has long since worn off, and we must now recognize that "this great third wave of democratization . . . may be losing its outward dynamic" of expansion, and even that "a new reverse wave may be gathering which could lead to the erosion of some third wave gains." It is vitally important to preempt this third reverse wave. And this can be done only if the third wave democracies become consolidated.

What Is Democratic Consolidation?

Our two companion volumes, and the 1995 conference that spawned them, were organized in the belief that consolidation is an important concept in the study of democracy, and a vital political goal for new democracies. This view is not without its critics, one of whom, Guillermo O'Donnell, offers a thoughtful challenge here. Yet the bulk of our contributors have converged on an understanding of democratic consolidation as a discernible process by which the rules, institutions, and constraints of democracy come to constitute "the only game in town," the one legitimate framework for seeking and exercising political power.

In *Themes and Perspectives,* Linz and Stepan offer a conceptual framework for consolidation that has already become widely influential and that informs many of the other chapters in this collection. They posit overlapping behavioral, attitudinal, and constitutional dimensions of consolidation, through which "democracy becomes routinized and deeply internalized in social, institutional, and even psychological life, as well as in political calculations for achieving success." In consolidated democracies, they argue, there may be intense conflict, but no significant political or social actors attempt to achieve their objectives by illegal, unconstitutional, or antidemocratic means. Further, though there may be severe problems of governance and widespread disapproval of the government of the day, elites and the public at large overwhelmingly believe "that democratic procedures and institutions are the most appropriate way to govern collective life." At bottom, then, the consolidation of democracy represents a kind of mirror image of the process of democratic breakdown that Linz and Stepan studied a generation ago.[11] While democratic breakdowns feature the erosion of democratic legitimacy and the rise of disloyal and semi-loyal political actors, consolidation is buttressed by a deep and widespread legitimation of democracy. And this legitimation—internalized, practiced, and transmitted across political generations—involves more than a commitment to democracy in the abstract; it also entails adherence to the specific rules and constraints of the country's constitutional system.[12]

It is this broad, unquestioning embrace of democratic procedures that produces a crucial element of consolidation—a reduction in the uncertainty of democracy, regarding not so much the outcomes as the rules and methods of political competition. As P. Nikiforos Diamandouros observes in his case study of Southern Europe in *Regional Challenges,* this regularization of politics promotes democratic stability by safeguarding the rights of political oppositions and minorities, containing conflict within institutional channels, and thus reducing the intensity of conflict. As consolidation advances, "there is a widening of the range of political actors who come to assume democratic conduct [and democratic loyalty] on the part of their adversaries," a transition from "instrumental" to "principled" commitments to the democratic framework, an increase in trust and cooperation among political competitors, and a socialization of the general population (through both deliberate efforts and the practice of democracy in politics and civil society).[13] As Robert A. Dahl notes in *Themes and Perspectives,* the consolidation of democracy thus implies, and indeed requires, the emergence of a democratic political culture. Democratic cultures may vary across countries in many of their particulars, but unless democratic institutions are braced by such broadly shared norms as political trust, tolerance, willingness to compromise, and, most of all, belief in democratic legitimacy, those institutions will be vulnerable to breakdown in times of crisis.[14] In the cases examined in this study, progress toward democratic consolidation is closely correlated with the growth of democratic culture. In this respect, our Southern European cases are the most advanced; Poland, Hungary, and the Czech Republic have seen the rapid emergence of democratic values; and such value change has been significant but uneven in Latin America, East Asia, and especially Russia (where Michael McFaul notes some recent slippage in support for democracy).

Democratic consolidation is fostered by a number of institutional, policy, and behavioral changes. Many of these improve governance directly by strengthening state capacity; liberalizing and rationalizing economic structures; securing social and political order while maintaining basic freedoms; improving horizontal accountability and the rule of law; and controlling corruption. Others improve the representative functions of democratic governance by strengthening political parties and their linkages to social groups, reducing fragmentation in the party system, enhancing the autonomous capacity and public accountability of legislatures and local governments, and invigorating civil society. Most new democracies need these types of institutional reform and strengthening, especially those that O'Donnell has labeled "delegative democracies" precisely because of their particularism, lack of horizontal accountability, and hence tendency toward corruption.[15] Some also require steady efforts to reduce military involvement in nonmilitary issues and subject the military and intelligence establishments to civilian control and oversight. And some require legal and institutional innovations to foster accommodation and mutual security among different ethnic and nationality groups.

Underlying all of these specific challenges, however, is an intimate connection between the deepening of democracy and its consolidation. Some new democracies have become consolidated during the third wave (and there are also some older consolidated democracies in the "Third World"), but none of the "nonliberal" electoral democracies that have emerged during the third wave has yet achieved consolidation. To do so, they must become *more* democratic, making more progress in protecting individual rights, ensuring a rule of law, representing citizen interests, incorporating marginalized groups, institutionalizing "horizontal accountability" of different branches of officeholders to one another, and eliminating the "reserved domains of power" enjoyed by the military and other social and political forces that are not accountable (directly or indirectly) to the electorate.[16] Put in slightly different terms, as Abraham Lowenthal does in his contribution to *Themes and Perspectives,* before democratic institutions can become consolidated, they must first fully exist. From this perspective, "talk of consolidating democracy is premature and misleading" in much of Latin America and the Caribbean because so many of the essential institutions of democratic governance remain to be "solidly constructed."[17]

In some cases, becoming more democratic may involve completing the transition from authoritarian to democratic rule. Linz and Stepan argue in their essay here (and at greater length in their *Problems of Democratic Transition and Consolidation*) that a democratic transition is completed only when the freely elected government has full authority to generate new policies, and thus when the executive, legislative, and judicial powers generated by the new democracy are not constrained or compelled by law to share power with other actors, such as the military. Chile's interlocking system of prerogatives for the military and its civilian appointees, embedded in the 1980 Constitution that General Augusto Pinochet left to the new civilian regime, so constrains the authority of elected governments and so insulates the military from democratic control that until it "is removed or greatly diminished, the Chilean transition cannot be completed, and, by definition, Chilean democracy cannot be consolidated."[18]

An important issue in the conceptual debate on consolidation is: How do we recognize it? Certainly no single indicator will do. And it is easier to recognize the phenomenon in its absence: the signs of fragility, instability, and nonconsolidation (or *de*consolidation). These include all the manifestations of "disloyalty" that Linz has noted: explicit rejection of the legitimacy of the democratic system—or of the nation-state and its boundaries—by (significant) parties, movements, or organizations; willingness by political competitors to use force, fraud, or other illegal means to acquire power or influence policies; "knocking at the barracks door" for military support in a political struggle; refusal to honor the right to govern of duly elected leaders and parties; abuse of constitutional liberties and opposition rights by ruling elites; and blatantly false depiction of democratically loyal opponents as disloyal ("instruments of outside secret and conspiratorial groups"). Fragility may be further indicated by "semi-loyalty": intermittent or attenuated disloyal behaviors; a willingness to form governments and alliances with disloyal groups; or a readiness to encourage, tolerate, or cover up such groups' antidemocratic actions.[19]

At the elite level, consolidation may be discerned from the behavioral patterns (and mutual interactions), symbolic gestures, public rhetoric, official documents, and ideological declarations of leaders, parties, and organizations.[20] At the mass level, public-opinion survey data are needed, not only to assess the degree of support for the legitimacy of democracy (in principle and in the regime's specific form), but also to determine its depth and its resilience over time. In Spain, support for democracy remained high and even increased during the late 1970s and early 1980s, even as unemployment rose dramatically. This durability of public support, fostered by effective "political crafting" on the part of political elites, was surely evidence of democratic consolidation, and most scholars consider that Spain became a consolidated democracy by 1982, only seven years after the start of its transition.[21] Yet in South America, democratic regimes have persisted for a decade and longer, through much more crushing economic depressions that have dramatically lowered living standards and increased rates of urban poverty, as Edgardo Boeninger notes in his chapter in *Regional Challenges*. These developments have (in most cases) generated no new antisystem parties or movements, yet regional and country specialists still regard most of these regimes (with the exception of Uruguay) as unconsolidated. Why?

One could point to pervasively weak political institutions (parties, legislatures, judiciaries, and so on); a general lack of horizontal accountability; and the prevalence of delegative democracy. But this may be to confuse the phenomenon (nonconsolidation) with some of its causes (or facilitating factors). In fact, it is precisely because these third wave democracies—particularly Brazil, Argentina, Bolivia, and Ecuador—have persisted for some time now in the face of weak institutionalization of formal democratic structures that O'Donnell, in his contribution to *Themes and Perspectives,* vigorously questions the utility of the concept of "democratic consolidation": "All we can say at present is that, as long as [competitive] elections are institutionalized [as they are in the above countries], polyarchies are likely to endure."

O'Donnell challenges the equation of consolidation with political institutionalization in general. In principle, countries can have weak, volatile party systems but highly stable and legitimate democracies (though some degree of political institutionalization appears to be important for democratic consolidation). Or established party systems can dissolve into considerable turbulence (as in Italy today) with no visible sign that democracy itself is losing legitimacy and becoming less viable. The strength of formal democratic institutions and rules—as opposed to the informal practices of clientelism, vote buying, rule-bending, and executive domination—no doubt facilitates the endurance (and consolidation) of democracy, but as O'Donnell notes, the two are not the same, and other factors "have strong independent effects on the survival chances of polyarchies."

To respond to O'Donnell's important challenge, it is necessary to step back and ask: If these South American (and other third wave) democracies have persisted through serious adversity for a decade or more, why are they not considered consolidated? How can we tell when consolidation occurs? And what does it matter, if the democracies continue to persist? Without satisfactory answers to these questions, the concept of consolidation does indeed lose its utility.

The key factor may be the pattern of behavior (and beliefs, if we could find a reliable way to measure them) of major players in these systems. There may be no significant, explicit antisystem players, but there are military and police establishments that remain, or have again become, unaccountable to civilian authority and contemptuous of legal and constitutional norms. There are presidents—a rather extraordinary succession of them across the South American continent in recent years—who are not just "delegative" but have so openly abused the laws and constitution that they have been driven from office, or have done so with such political cunning and economic success that (as with Alberto Fujimori in Peru and Carlos Menem in Argentina) they have thrived politically. There are corrupt and oligarchical local bosses, and deeply corrupted legislatures and judiciaries. There is, in short, precisely what O'Donnell observes—"another," very different, institutionalization, of informal, indeed illegal and even unconstitutional, practices, especially between elections. Of course, the degree and distribution of these "informalities" vary across countries. Where such departures from the democratic framework are not just one feature of the system (as they are to some degree in virtually every complex democracy) but a recurring and defining feature, they signal a lack of commitment to the basic procedural framework of democracy: democratic disloyalty, semi-loyalty, frailty, in other words, *nonconsolidation.*

The implications of these behavioral signs of uneven, ambivalent, or deteriorating democratic commitment are twofold. First, in those cases where powerful officials (elected and unelected) and powerful persons and groups outside the state behave in this way, civil liberties get abused, opposition forces get harassed, elections may get violent (and even fraudulent), and democracy gets hollowed out. The second implication is more speculative, but follows logically. If these abusive elites do not act against the constitutional form of democracy, their commitment to it nevertheless appears to remain contingent and instrumental rather than routinized, internalized, and principled. And a good deal of the instrumental value they derive from sustaining the democratic form (or facade), one may speculate, owes to the international system, which imposes costs on countries that overturn democracy. If this international pressure (or the perception of it) ever recedes, the viability of frail democracies will also diminish. International, and especially European regional, constraints ultimately helped to consolidate democracy in Southern Europe, and are doing so today in some countries in East Central Europe, because they quickened and reinforced enduring changes in elite and mass political culture. Such cultural changes are not occurring among key elites in many third wave democracies, even though those democracies have persisted.

Political Institutions and Institutional Design

As summarized above, the first part of *Themes and Perspectives* traces the evolution and character of the new democracies of the third wave and advances the theoretical debate about the meaning and importance of democratic consolidation. The rest of our two-volume study pursues two additional goals: to identify and explore the factors that facilitate (or obstruct) democratic consolidation, and to assess the progress made toward consolidation by some of the principal countries and regions in the third wave.

Increasing scholarly attention has been paid in recent years to the strength and character of political institutions as a key factor affecting the viability and stability of democracy. If democracy is to be consolidated, it must garner broad and deep legitimacy among all significant political actors and the citizenry at large. Such legitimacy may accrue in part in reaction to the failures and abuses of the authoritarian past, or it may derive from a historic cultural commitment to democratic values and norms that—as in the Czech Republic—has been revived after a long period of authoritarian rule. It may be stimulated or reinforced by incorporation into regional and international networks dominated by democratic states (such as the European Union) and liberal values. But legitimation is unlikely to be fully and lastingly achieved without some degree of effective governance on the part of the new democratic institutions.

As several of our chapters demonstrate, economic performance remains an important part of the governance challenge. But it has tended to be overemphasized, to the neglect of other, more political, dimensions of governance. Citizens of new democracies form judgments about their political systems based not only on what they deliver economically, but also on the degree to which they deliver valued political goals: freedom, order, a rule of law, accountability, representativeness, and overall efficacy. In other words, citizens expect their democracies to govern democratically, in compliance with the constitution and the laws, and to govern efficaciously, in terms of choosing and implementing policies that address the most important problems the society confronts. Among the most frequent causes of democratic alienation, delegitimation, and breakdown have been the abuse of democratic procedures and norms by government officials and political leaders themselves, so that democracy comes to be seen as a sham; the turn toward political violence on the part of significant actors who are either marginalized from the democratic process or impatient with its procedures; and the incapacity of governments to decide and act as a result of political fragmentation, polarization, and stalemate.[22]

Sometimes democracy seems simply overwhelmed by the weight of insoluble problems, or is destroyed by the incompetence, venality, and stubbornness of failed political leaders. Yet, at some point in their lives, most democracies confront crises that appear (at least for a time) overwhelming and insoluble. And a key challenge for democratic constitutions is to anticipate the flaws and foibles of potential leaders.

If democracies are to weather the storms of history and limit the self-aggrandizing impulses of human actors, they need strong and well-designed political institutions.

The most basic institution is the state itself. In their chapter in this collection, Linz and Stepan argue that a state of law—a *Rechtsstaat*—is vital to the consolidation of any democracy. Unless the behavior of public officials is effectively constrained by "a network of laws, courts, semiautonomous review and control agencies, and civil-society norms" of transparency and accountability, democracy will be diminished by political abuse and cynicism, and actors will fail to commit themselves to a consensus on the rules of the game. Beyond this, however, a consolidated democracy also requires what they term "a usable bureaucracy," a state that has the administrative capacity to perform the essential functions of government: to maintain order, adjudicate disputes, construct infrastructure, facilitate economic exchange, defend the national borders, and collect the taxes necessary to fund these activities. Where state structures have been historically weak, or state decay has accompanied the decomposition of the authoritarian regime, state-building emerges as a central challenge for democratic consolidation. In particular, McFaul shows in *Regional Challenges* how Russia's dual transition—from communism and from empire—left a huge vacuum in state political authority, administrative capacity, and judicial efficacy. The result has been a sense of anarchy, which poses one of the most formidable threats to democracy in Russia in the near term. Where the state-building challenge is compounded by significant ethnic or nationality divisions (as in many postcommunist and African states), democratic consolidation is also fostered by the construction of an inclusive state that gives all citizens political equality, with "a common 'roof' of state-mandated and state-enforced individual rights," as Linz and Stepan explain.

One of the most important institutional arenas for democracy is the party system. Even with the growing prominence of civil society, political parties remain important if not essential instruments for representing political constituencies and interests, aggregating demands and preferences, recruiting and socializing new candidates for office, organizing the electoral competition for power, crafting policy alternatives, setting the policy-making agenda, forming effective governments, and integrating groups and individuals into the democratic process. Institutionalized party systems thus increase democratic governability and legitimacy by facilitating legislative support for government policies; by channeling demands and conflicts through established procedures; by reducing the scope for populist demagogues to win power; and by making the democratic process more inclusive, accessible, representative, and effective.[23]

Many of our chapters demonstrate the obstacle to democratic

consolidation presented by institutionally weak party systems, in which parties lack clear programmatic identities, autonomous organizations, strong linkages to social groups, and durable bases of electoral support, and in which parties may proliferate in number and flit across the national stage, never lasting long enough to build up strong structures, identities, and ties. These problems are particularly apparent in McFaul's analysis of Russia and the discussions of South Korea by Teh-fu Huang and James Cotton. As Boeninger observes, weak and fragmented party systems are also a problem for many of Latin America's third wave democracies. By contrast, as Diamandouros stresses, democratic consolidation was greatly facilitated in the Southern European cases, especially Greece, by the emergence of relatively strong and effective political parties.[24]

Diamandouros acknowledges that "the consolidation of a party system is not a necessary condition for the consolidation of democracy," but shows that the importance of the former for the latter increases with the weakness of other political institutions and facilitating conditions. This generalization helps to explain the puzzle that Gábor Tóka presents in his study of the emerging party systems in the Czech Republic, Hungary, Poland, and Slovakia. In the first half of the 1990s, each of these party systems exhibited considerably greater electoral volatility than did the party systems of the West European democracies in their first decade, or even the new party systems of Latin America's third wave democracies. In their durability, in their levels of actual voter support, and in surveys of voter preferences, political parties in East Central Europe have appeared highly unstable. Yet, Tóka argues, by the criteria of Linz and Stepan, democratic consolidation has now clearly been achieved in each of these countries, except possibly Slovakia. Among politicians as well as overwhelming majorities of the public, there is now deep commitment to the norms and institutions of the democratic order. This democratic consolidation, Tóka persuasively argues, "could hardly have been the result of strongly institutionalized party systems."

Does this conclusion challenge the prevailing wisdom about the importance for democracy of effective parties and party systems? Not exactly. As Tóka argues, Poland, Hungary, and the Czech Republic were able to achieve rapid consolidation despite unfavorable party structures because of other factors that were overwhelmingly favorable, especially their close proximity to Western Europe (the most strongly democratic region of the world) and political cultures that in each country generated widespread initial commitment to democracy and tempered the extreme uncertainty that typically surrounds institutionally shallow party systems. Thus political culture and the incipient or anticipated integration into a larger Europe produced the political predictability, trust, and willingness to compromise that typically derive in part from strong and settled party systems. Where, as in Russia and Belarus, these other variables have been far less favorable, the consequences of shallow, inchoate party systems have been much more damaging. Moreover, though East Central European party systems have exhibited high volatility, they have also featured levels of programmatic structuring typical of much more institutionalized party systems. And finally, Tóka reminds us, stable and effective parties and party systems may improve the quality of democracy, even if they are not necessary for its consolidation.[25]

The challenge of institutional performance and design involves a number of dilemmas. One is the tension between the "durability" features of institutional strength (coherence around principles, programs, and policies; unified action in the legislature and political process; and elaborate, well-ordered vertical and horizontal structures) on the one hand, and the capacity to adapt to changing social and political circumstances on the other. From this perspective, stronger is not necessarily better; political parties and party systems can be "overinstitutionalized" as well as "underinstitutionalized." In the former instance, structural coherence, discipline, and regularity may turn into rigidity and underrepresentation of important new (or newly salient) generational, regional, ethnic, or class groups; and extremely low electoral volatility may signify a lack of competitiveness, meaningfulness, or civic engagement in the party system.[26]

Similar dilemmas confront the choice or design of democratic institutions. Representativeness and inclusiveness, secured through highly proportional systems of representation, foster broad commitments to democratic legitimacy by incorporating ethnic and political minorities into the democratic process. In addition, as McFaul shows in his chapter on Russia, party-list proportional representation (PR) provides a greater stimulus to the emergence of coherent parties than does the single-member-district (SMD) plurality method of electing legislators. The more purely proportional the electoral system, however, the more parties it tends to produce; the resulting political fragmentation undermines governability. Majoritarian electoral systems for the parliament, in particular SMD plurality, may enhance governability, but at the cost of producing a disjunction between vote shares and seat shares that may leave many groups feeling poorly represented or even voiceless. The top-down party control over nominations that is often found in party-list PR systems produces more coherent, disciplined parties, but deprives voters of choice in the selection of individual representatives, and if carried too far, may produce a brittle system.

"Democraticness" and governability may also be seen as competing in the choice of an executive structure. Advocates of presidentialism argue that a directly elected chief executive is closer to the people and offers more direct personal accountability for governance than the indirectly chosen prime minister in a parliamentary system. But several studies maintain that parliamentary democracy is more conducive to democratic stability, a view confirmed by the statistical analysis of Adam Przeworski and his colleagues in their contribution to *Themes and Perspectives*. They find (as have other empirical studies) that presidential democracy is particularly vulnerable to breakdown when it is joined to a fragmented party system, and most of all under conditions of "legislative deadlock" (in which the largest party has between one-third and one-half of the seats in parliament).[27]

In *Themes and Perspectives,* John M. Carey assesses some of these issues and trade-offs in institutional design that affect the quality and stability of democracy, and hence the prospects for consolidation. But he does so by examining finer-grained issues than the choice between PR and SMD plurality or parliamentary versus presidential government. Carey focuses on two key factors affecting regime support and governability: the degree of fragmentation in the party system and the degree of cohesion within each major political party. In a presidential system, the degree of party fragmentation in parliament, he shows, can be heavily influenced by the formula used to elect the president and the timing of presidential and legislative elections. Where a candidate must win an absolute majority to be elected (rather than a simple plurality in a single-round election), many more parties compete for the presidency, since they expect to secure more bargaining strength by forming coalitions after the first round. Where such a presidential election is held concurrently with legislative elections, the greater party fragmentation in the presidential election carries over into the legislature. A plurality rule can produce a less fragmented legislature. Carey shows (and our case studies of Russia and Latin America confirm) that, independent of whether a majority is required, legislatures also tend to be more fragmented when their elections are not fully synchronized with presidential ones, but occur either at mid-term or on an entirely different timetable.

The importance of holding elections concurrently is also emphasized by Emerson M.S. Niou and Peter C. Ordeshook, but for a rather different reason. For them, democratic governance is most stable and effective within an *integrated* political system in which politicians of different branches and levels are dependent on one another and therefore inclined to cooperate and coordinate—rather than incessantly compete and bargain—on jurisdictional and other issues. Such interdependence is fostered, argue Niou and Ordeshook, by the presence of large numbers of elective offices, at various levels of governmental authority, all of which are contested simultaneously. In such systems, autonomous local party structures mobilize crucial support for the national party ticket but in turn depend on the national party label (and the coattails of the national party leader) to help elect their local candidates. Where elections for different levels of authority are not concurrent, as in Russia and Taiwan (and many other third wave democracies), and where relatively few offices are filled through elections, politicians in the various branches and levels of government have far fewer incentives to cooperate. Russian president Boris Yeltsin's 1991 decision to postpone elections for governors, mayors, and regional legislatures stifled party-system development and democratic consolidation in Russia, McFaul concludes. In Taiwan, the centralization of internal party politics further complicates the quest for an integrated polity.

Like Niou and Ordeshook, Carey considers party coherence a crucial dimension of governability, but his concern is with the extent to which legislators are encouraged to support their party's program rather than cultivate an independent, personal constituency (with all of its implications for wasteful pork-barrel politics). A key factor is whether electoral rules require candidates of the same party to compete against one another; this can be the case under presidential or parliamentary, and SMD or PR, systems. In closed-list PR systems, the higher the district size, the greater the tendency toward party coherence; however, in open-list systems like that of Brazil or in the single nonstranferable vote (SNTV) system in Taiwan, where voters choose a single candidate among many, the more candidates per district, the more intense the competition. Overall, the incentives for party cohesion in the legislature are shaped to a great degree by a complex mix of institutional factors: district size, the number and types of votes citizens cast, party leaders' control over nominations, and the degree to which the votes for one candidate may help other candidates of her party (vote-pooling).[28]

The fragmenting effect of the SNTV electoral system is emphasized both by Teh-fu Huang in his contribution to *Themes and Perspectives* and by Hung-mao Tien in his case study of Taiwan in *Regional Challenges*. The SNTV system has produced a fairly proportional distribution of seats among parties in Taiwan, but within the two principal parties, the Kuomintang (KMT) and the Democratic Progressive Party (DPP), it has fostered severe factionalism that has undermined the governing effectiveness of the KMT, hampered the competitiveness of the DPP, and facilitated the birth of new splinter parties. In South Korea, the problem—as Huang shows—has been excessive top-down organization of parties, but on the very shallow institutional basis of personal loyalty to an individual leader. This extreme personalization of both the ruling and opposition parties has combined with powerful regional ties, frequent changes in electoral rules and constitutional structure, and the long disruption of democratic politics by authoritarian rule to produce breathtaking instability and weakness in the Korean party system, with parties constantly changing names and identities. (These same problems have plagued democracy in Thailand and the Philippines.) Huang thus concludes that democratic consolidation would be advanced by implementing electoral reforms: in Taiwan, terminating SNTV by increasing the currently small proportion of seats elected through PR and converting the remaining seats into single-member districts (a reform now under discussion); in South Korea, by increasing the number of PR seats while decreasing or eliminating the proportion of seats automatically awarded as a premium to the leading party.

Our contributors do not entirely agree on the most desirable institutional designs. But their analyses do suggest that, because major institutional decisions (especially that of presidentialism versus parliamentarism), once made, are very difficult to change, a democracy seeking consolidation is probably best off pursuing specific institutional reforms that address specific problems. Stronger, more effective party systems could be fostered by reforms that increase the number of elected officials, enhance the autonomy of local party branches (and of local and regional government more generally), and synchronize the timing of elections for most offices. In particular, if a country is to have an elected president with significant executive authority, it makes sense, as Carey argues, to synchronize presidential and legislative elections and to make it more likely for a president to be elected on a first ballot—if not by plurality, then by a "double complement rule" that requires the leading candidate to have a substantial margin over his or her closest competitor.

Civil-Military Relations

By definition, democracy cannot be consolidated until the military becomes firmly subordinated to civilian control and solidly committed to the democratic constitutional order. More specifically, as Felipe Agüero puts it in *Themes and Perspectives,* "civilian supremacy" gives democratically elected governments unquestioned authority over all policy arenas, including defining the goals and overseeing the organization and implementation of national defense. In such a system, the military role is limited to matters of national defense and international security—with the military relieved of all responsibility for internal security—and governmental structures (such as a civilian ministry of defense) are put in place to enable civilians to exercise effective oversight and control of the military (as well as the intelligence services). A key element in the rapid progress toward consolidation of the new democracies of Spain, Portugal, and Greece was the establishment (facilitated in part by integration into NATO) of such norms and structures.

One reason why several new democracies of East Central Europe have been able to make such rapid progress toward consolidation is that they inherited and maintained traditions of firm civilian control over the military. This, ironically, has been one of the few positive legacies of their communist past. Many Latin American and Asian third wave democracies have not been so fortunate. As Agüero details for South America and Harold Crouch for Thailand and the Philippines, most of these new regimes have had to struggle to overcome deeply entrenched structures and traditions of military autonomy and even impunity. So has South Korea, where President Kim Young Sam's initiatives to enhance civilian control and purge the dominant military faction may rank among his more important accomplishments. Like the new democracies of postcommunist Europe, those in Spain, Portugal, and Taiwan benefited from the military's lack of direct involvement in authoritarian governance (although the extensive penetration of the military by Taiwan's long-dominant party, the KMT, does complicate democratic consolidation there).[29] As Diamandouros argues, the nature of prior military rule also matters: where, as in Greece, the military as a hierarchical institution did not administer the regime and the military did not rule for long, the consequences for future civil-military relations are less serious.

Where the military as an institution has a long tradition of political intervention and where it retains extensive political and economic prrogatives, democracies face a particularly difficult and dangerous challenge. In such circumstances, as Agüero and Crouch show, establishing civilian supremacy is a complex and typically protracted process, requiring many of the factors that promote democratic consolidation in general: skilled political leadership, unity among civilian political forces (across partisan and other divides), and civilian expertise (both within and outside of government) on national-security matters, as well as luck (in the form of divisions within the military and the failure of military rebellions). Successful reform also requires a long-term policy vision. Typically this involves gradually reducing the size of the military (and hence its capacity to seize and exercise political power) while increasing the military's capacity to perform its defense mission, keeping salaries at a respectable level, and preserving the honor of the military as an institution.[30]

Good leadership involves knowing when and how far to push reform, as well as how to forge proreform coalitions both in the legislature and among rising military officers. Presidents Fidel Ramos in the Philippines and Carlos Menem in Argentina were able to implement reforms in part because of their political skills (in sharp contrast to their predecessors, Corazon Aquino and Raul Alfonsín). Yet Ramos benefited considerably from his prestige and connections as the former head of the military, and Menem purchased military acceptance of reforms at the cost of sweeping immunity for past human rights abuses. Unfortunately, civilian supremacy can rarely be achieved through systematic punishment of human rights abuses under military rule. Most cases in which those abuses were serious and recent are precisely the ones in which the military retains too much power for civilians to risk a polarizing confrontation over the issue. Still, as Agüero stresses, immunity for past crimes need not and should not carry over into the current and future conduct of security forces.

The strength and legitimacy of civilian political institutions—the president, the legislature, and political parties in general—can also greatly affect the ability to narrow military prerogatives and restructure military commands without inviting resistance or rebellion. As Crouch emphasizes, one reason the Thai military was able to seize power again in 1991 was that the massive corruption of the civilian politicians had broadly discredited them in the eyes of the public. In Latin America, weakened and discredited presidents have been unable to achieve policy reforms of any kind, including those involving civil-military relations.[31]

Finally, civilian supremacy requires the wisdom and the will to remove the military fully from matters of domestic policy. As Agüero notes, the growing demand for participation in international peacekeeping activities opens up a new, appropriate mission for the armed forces. But the growing pressure on Latin American militaries to go to war against drug production and trafficking takes them in the wrong direction, toward a new involvement in internal security and in the corruption that invariably surrounds the drug trade.

Civil Society

Perhaps no single factor more readily evokes the romance, excitement, and heady possibilities of democracy's third wave than the image of resurgent civil societies mobilizing peacefully to resist, discredit, and ultimately overturn authoritarian rule. Although democratic transitions are typically inaugurated and negotiated by political elites in both the regime and the opposition, civil society has played a crucial role in building pressure for democratic transition and pushing it through to completion. This is an important and sometimes neglected insight of a famous work on democratic transitions by Guillermo O'Donnell and Philippe C. Schmitter, reiterated by Schmitter in his contribution to *Themes and Perspectives*.[32] The role of civil society in bringing down authoritarian rule was seminal in the democratic transitions in East Central Europe and sub-Saharan Africa, as Aleksander Smolar and E. Gyimah-Boadi show here. Social movements and organizations were also among the leading forces behind democratization in South Korea and Taiwan, as Hsin-Huang Michael Hsiao and Hagen Koo explain. Yet as all these contributors emphasize, the democratic spirit and capacity of civil society may decline precipitously after the transition.

Civil society—the realm of organized intermediary groups that are voluntary, self-generating, independent of the state and the family, and bound by a legal order or set of shared rules—may contribute to democratic consolidation in numerous ways: by stabilizing expectations and social bargaining, generating a more civic normative environment, bringing actors closer to the political process, reducing the burdens of governance, and checking potential abuses of power. Yet as Schmitter notes, civil society can also impede consolidation by making political majorities more difficult to form, exacerbating ethnic divisions and pork-barrel politics, and entrenching socioeconomic biases in the distribution of influence. Civil society can contribute to democratic consolidation only if other institutions are also favorable, and if actors in civil society behave in a "civil" way, respecting the law and other social and political actors while accepting and not seeking to usurp or conquer democratic political authority.

Viewing democracy as a composite of "partial regimes," Schmitter is particularly concerned with the *way* in which the interests of various social groups are politically articulated and represented, and how their conflicts with one another and with the state are resolved. A key dimension is the degree to which interest associations have encompassing scope, strategic capacity, and broad authority to speak and bargain for an entire class or sector. Civil society will tend to advance democratic consolidation more under such corporatist arrangements, he believes, than under pluralist ones, "where a great multiplicity of narrowly specialized and overlapping organizations emerge with close dependencies upon their members or interlocutors."

A key post-transition dilemma, Schmitter notes, is that the "primacy" of social movements and other democratizing civil society actors inevitably declines after the transition, as the authoritarian state disappears, political parties and more established interest groups take center stage, and people turn to more private concerns. Civil society must adapt after the transition, writes Smolar of postcommunist Europe, because "revolutionary civil society is by definition a transient phenomenon, even though it remains deeply embedded in the minds of its participants as a myth and an ideal." As McFaul's chapter on Russia also shows, democratic adaptation is especially difficult for postcommunist civil societies, because the all-encompassing nature of state control over (and penetration of) society under communism precludes the smoother passage from authoritarian state corporatism to democratic societal corporatism that has occurred in Southern Europe and is now in progress in Taiwan.

What has followed the democratic revolutions in East Central Europe, Russia, and Africa has not been adaptation so much as retreat and dissipation of civic energy. The broad fronts of religious, professional, student, labor, and other associations broke up once their common goal of bringing down a despised regime had been achieved. Class and ethnic divisions once again fragmented society, and the leadership ranks (and thus operational capacities) of civil society organizations were rapidly depleted as activists were drawn into politics, government, or business. The social inheritances of communism in Europe and neopatrimonial statism in Africa also reasserted themselves in the forms of renewed dependence on the state, co-optation, mistrust, and societal atomization, revealing the paucity of social capital and, in Smolar's words, "the lack of a culture of free collective activity." In fact, "preliberal," illiberal, and uncivic cultural orientations constitute a major obstacle to democratic consolidation in much of Africa and the postcommunist world. In both regions as well, civil society has been further hampered after the transition by the harsh economic conditions of the 1990s, which have driven people to preoccupation with the exigencies of daily survival, and have rendered African associations in particular much more vulnerable to the compromising blandishments of domineering states.

A rich, dense, vibrant, institutionalized, and highly "civic" civil society is not strictly necessary for democratic consolidation, but democracy will be more likely to achieve consolidation, and will undoubtedly be of higher quality, to the extent that such a society emerges. Thus in a great many third wave democracies, and especially in Africa and the postcommunist world, a great task of social construction and civic empowerment lies ahead. Precisely because of the financial and political weakness of civil society in these countries, direct international assistance to nongovernmental organizations (NGOs) and the cooperative linkages that Schmitter terms "transnational civil society" loom increasingly large in the quest for democratic consolidation. Such international support and linkages have been especially important in encouraging new types of NGOs (and critical media) that seek to reform and deepen democracy as they "foster group and individual autonomy from the state," in Gyimah-Boadi's words. This underscores the importance of the types of initiatives Michael Pinto-Duschinsky discusses in his contribution to *Regional Challenges*.

Socioeconomic Development

The contributors to this collection are more or less unified in rejecting structurally deterministic explanations of democratic consolidation and persistence. Democratic consolidation is largely a matter of political crafting, the design and maturation of political institutions, and the spread of democratic norms and values. The opportunity for democratic development and consolidation is not ruled out for any country, however poor. Yet the comprehensive statistical analysis of Adam Przeworski and his colleagues does show the powerful impact of economic development and economic performance.

Like O'Donnell, Przeworski and colleagues diverge from the consensus that consolidation is a discernible process and a useful concept. Because older democracies (when economic development is controlled for) do not enjoy any immunity against democratic breakdown, they conclude that consolidation is "an empty term" and that it is more useful simply to examine "what makes democracies endure."[33] Their findings are striking. Confirming the classic thesis of Seymour

Martin Lipset, they demonstrate a strongly positive relationship between the affluence of a nation and the likelihood of democratic persistence. During the period of their study (1950–90) democracy (understood simply as electoral democracy) had a 12 percent chance of breakdown in any given year among the lowest-income countries. The expected life of democracy increases with per-capita income up to the highest income level of over $6,000 (in 1985 purchasing-power-parity U.S. dollars). At that level of affluence—now exceeded not only by Spain, Portugal, and Greece, but by South Korea and Taiwan (and probably Argentina and Chile) as well—"democracies are impregnable and can be expected to live forever."

In less affluent countries, and especially in the poorest ones, annual economic performance becomes critical. Democracies are significantly more likely to persist when they experience real economic growth (especially rapid growth, in excess of 5 percent annually). High inflation—above 30 percent annually—is also toxic to democracy (though moderate inflation is associated with somewhat improved prospects for democratic survival). And, despite the scantiness of data on inequality, Przeworski and colleagues find that democracy is much more likely to endure in countries where income inequality declines over time than where it increases. It appears that the ability to meet popular expectations for better income distribution improves the prospects for democracy.

One major way that socioeconomic development has been thought to increase the likelihood and stability of democracy is through changes in the class structure. From Aristotle to Lipset, a large middle class has been considered conducive to political moderation and democracy. Major historical analyses of class actors have pointed either to the bourgeoisie or to the organized working class as the driving force behind democratization.[34] Hsiao and Koo show instead the need for a more disaggregated class analysis. In the cases of South Korea and, especially, Taiwan, the most important social force for democratization has been the "new middle class" of professional, technical, and white-collar workers and especially its intellectual elements (writers, professors, journalists, lawyers, religious leaders, and so on). Organized labor played an important role as well, but—especially in South Korea, where it was very strong—this role cut both ways, provoking a conservative reaction when labor mobilization became too intense. The "old middle class" of small entrepreneurs and the self-employed was less active on behalf of democracy, and has been more inclined (again, especially in Korea) to support the status quo. As the quest for democratic consolidation unfolds in each country, it is the middle class in general and its professional and intellectual elements in particular that are leading civil society movements for democratic deepening and reform. Their economic, political, and demographic weight in the body politic—the product of three decades of rapid economic development—is one of the most important positive factors for democratic consolidation in these two very promising East Asian third wave democracies.

In Diamandouros's analysis of the three success stories of Southern Europe, we find an important additional reason why socioeconomic development facilitates democratic consolidation. Rapid economic development (particularly in Spain and Greece) in the two decades before 1975 transformed not only social structures but values as well. As these societies became more secularized and educated, and as class, gender, and urban-rural inequalities attenuated, values and belief systems became more "open-ended and positive-sum," more flexible, moderate, conciliatory, and tolerant of different interests. This in turn facilitated an essential feature of consolidated and stable democracy, the predominance "of dialogue and compromise in the daily practices, tactics, and strategies of both individual and collective actors." Here again we see the centrality of change in political culture to the consolidation of democracy.

International Factors

One of the distinguishing features of the third wave of democratization has been the salience of international influences. As Huntington emphasizes in *The Third Wave,* international and especially regional demonstration effects played a crucial role in stimulating and providing models for subsequent democratic transitions. No less influential were a variety of more tangible international pressures and inducements, including the growth of governmental and nongovernmental forms of assistance to democratic actors, and the increasing emphasis on human rights and democracy promotion in the foreign policies of established democracies, especially the United States. As Diamandouros shows, regional and international assistance efforts (especially through the West German party foundations) were particularly crucial in bolstering democratic forces in Portugal during the first 18 months after the April 1974 revolution, when the authoritarian Left threatened to prevail.

International factors also figure as never before in the quest to consolidate the third wave democracies, as the two concluding chapters of *Regional Challenges* make clear. Yun-han Chu, Fu Hu, and Chung-in Moon explore how regional and international factors fueled the transitions and now shape the prospects and challenges for consolidation in two of the third wave's more externally threatened new democracies, South Korea and Taiwan. With the reunification of Germany, these two democracies are now unique in their status as divided countries, facing threats to their very existence from communist regimes of the same nationality that claim sovereignty over them. It is only on the Korean peninsula and across the Taiwan Strait that the Cold War continues. The resulting threats to the national security of the two democracies have slowed efforts to democratize civil-military relations and to dismantle the vestiges of authoritarian national-security laws and structures. At the same time, the quest for international legitimacy and Western (especially U.S.) support has driven forward the process of democratization in many other respects, including most recently Taiwan's presidential elections in 1996. As Chu, Hu, and Moon stress, the dilemma is particularly acute for Taiwan, given mainland China's economic dynamism and substantially greater size and power. Yet precisely because Taiwan is so threatened—and by one of the world's most authoritarian states—democracy has become a resource and a legitimating symbol in its quest for an accepted place in world affairs, and democratic procedures have forged a growing pragmatic consensus on the national-identity question that is beginning to bridge the old divides.[35]

Chu, Hu, and Moon also show how the export dependence of Korea and Taiwan has pushed political development in a democratic direction. Closer economic and political integration with the advanced industrial democracies—which has become an ever more valued goal as Korea and Taiwan have crossed the threshold of national affluence themselves, and have grown culturally closer to the democratic West—will become virtually impossible if these two countries cannot implement and maintain democratic systems. At the same time, however, middle classes aware of the need for socioeconomic stability to maintain international competitiveness have not been sympathetic to militant mobilization by labor and other organized groups. Thus the high degree of involvement in the world economy also generates a bias for stability and moderation that tends to limit the potential for polarizing conflict over socioeconomic issues (to which South Korea, with its strong labor unions and "hyperactive" civil society, is particularly prone).

At somewhat earlier stages of their development, Korea and Taiwan also benefited from various forms of private and semipublic assistance to their nascent civil societies. As Pinto-Duschinsky shows in the final chapter of *Regional Challenges,* such democracy-promotion efforts have expanded dramatically in scope and scale during the third wave and now constitute an important factor in democratic consolidation, even though their impact is difficult to measure precisely and their effects can only complement and reinforce favorable domestic factors. Following the model of the West German party foundations—which since the early 1960s have received public funding to support democratic parties, trade unions, and civic activities around the world—the United States and seven additional European countries have by now established party foundations to promote democracy abroad using public funds. In a few countries, these efforts are part of a larger program of nongovernmental but publicly funded assistance, as exemplified by the U.S. National Endowment for Democracy, created in 1983. The growing international-ization of democracy-building efforts has had numerous other institutional manifestations discussed by Pinto-Duschinsky: the redirection of many official development-assistance agencies toward goals and programs concerned with democracy, human rights, and "good governance"; increasingly explicit conditionality of official aid on standards of human rights and democracy; an expanding architecture of formal declarations and conventions entrenching international standards of democracy and human rights; and growing involvement of the United Nations and various regional bodies (such as the European Union, the Commonwealth, the Organization for Security and Cooperation in Europe, and the Organization of American States) in election monitoring and other forms of democratic assistance, especially to transitional regimes.

These external influences have probably contributed greatly to the scope and dynamism of the third wave. As Pinto-Duschinsky cautions, however, excessive zeal, inflated ambitions, and "unwise triumphalism" can undermine the effectiveness of democratic-assistance programs. If such programs are to work, he argues, they must have circumscribed goals that are consistently pursued. At the same time, they cannot rest content with the role of midwife in the birth of a new electoral democracy, but must address with equal vigor problems of human rights and democratic governance after the transition. They need to share and disseminate information about their activities and coordinate their programs and strategies more effectively. And they need to appreciate the inherent uncertainties of trying to foster democratic institutions. As Pinto-Duschinsky states, "Democracy promotion should be a process of sowing a considerable number of seeds in the hope that a small proportion of them will take root."

Democratic Consolidation: Progress and Prospects

The third wave democracies examined in this study display considerable variety in their progress toward consolidation, and in the factors that have inclined them toward or away from it. As Diamandouros shows, Southern Europe represents the most unambiguous (and rapid) instance of democratic consolidation in the third wave. Many of the factors that facilitated consolidation in the three Southern European cases have been noted above: the preceding decades of rapid development, the consequent transformation of class structure and values, the lack of highly politicized militaries, the favorable regional context, and timely international assistance. In addition, Diamandouros calls attention to the nature of the transition itself and the vital role of political leadership. Democratic consolidation in Spain and Greece was facilitated by the absence of extensive mass mobilization and violence during the transition. In Spain it was also helped by the centrality of elite negotiations in the transition, and, in Greece, by the weakness of the military as it withdrew from power. The more violent and revolutionary nature of the Portuguese transition "severely complicated democratization . . . and significantly retarded the advent of consolidation."[36] In contrast to most postcommunist regimes (especially in the former Soviet Union), the emergence of limited political and social pluralism in the later, softer phase of the Spanish dictatorship helped (as in Taiwan) make for a less disruptive and conflictual transition to democracy. Political learning from the mistakes of previous democratic attempts, and resurrection of their positive legacies and memories, enabled political actors to adjust more quickly and effectively to the give-and-take of democratic politics. Finally, in all three Southern European cases, democratic consolidation was clearly advanced by the "vision and tactical acumen" of strong, democratically committed leaders like Mário Soares, Adolfo Suárez, and Constantine Karamanlis.

In many respects, the Russian case stands as a mirror image of the Southern European ones. As McFaul shows, Russia inherited at its rebirth as a state in 1991 a sweeping array of "major impediments to democratic consolidation from the Soviet era, including an ambiguous set of constitutional rules, a weak state, a collapsing economy, a lack of political parties, and virtually no rule of law." Almost every aspect of the political and economic system—including the territorial boundaries and federal structure of the Russian state—remained to be defined or transformed. In addition, Russia's sharply confrontational and revolutionary mode of transition generated acute polarization and uncertainty, with "many of the rules of the game ambiguous, uncodified, and subject to constant manipulation." In contrast to Portugal, political-leadership choices in Russia—particularly President Boris Yeltsin's fateful decision to defer constitutional reform and founding elections—further confounded these inherited problems. Only with the adoption of a new constitution in 1993 and the subsequent holding of legislative, presidential, and then regional elections has the political framework of democracy begun to gel. As McFaul emphasizes, the new constitutional structure is flawed in important respects, but it at least clarifies institutional powers and provides a framework in which elections can become institutionalized and parties can begin to take shape. Thus while democracy remains endangered, Russia may now have a chance to make progress toward consolidation if it can meet the other challenges that McFaul identifies: building a state that can control crime and corruption while generating new social classes and civil society organizations that are independent of the state and capable of articulating and aggregating their interests. These tasks require further progress in market reforms to create the economic foundations for a modern system of interests and interest intermediation. But all of this hinges, finally, on the establishment of a "rule-of-law state."

The picture that Boeninger paints locates Latin America's new democracies somewhere between the extremes of Southern Europe's rapid consolidation and Russia's torturous path. Progress toward democratic consolidation has been tentative and uneven in Latin America (with the exception of Uruguay and, to some extent, Chile, where the reserved powers of the military now seem the chief obstacle). As O'Donnell also emphasizes in his contribution to *Themes and Perspectives,* Latin America's renewed democracies have persisted for well over a decade now, and they have at least institutionalized the principle of electoral competition for power. This is rather limited progress, Boeninger concedes, but for countries like El Salvador, Nicaragua, Ecuador, and Paraguay, it is nevertheless a historic breakthrough. Throughout Latin America, polarization has eased greatly and political culture has been transformed as the Left has recognized the necessity of democracy's political procedures and more or less resigned itself to capitalism. Economic culture has also changed profoundly in other ways, as free-spending populism has been discredited, privatization programs (and other liberalizing reforms) have gained momentum in many countries, and all sectors have come to appreciate the necessity of permanently controlling inflation. Militaries remain powerful in many countries, but in most cases—even in Chile—their prerogatives have been reduced.[37] And U.S. policy and the entire regional context have never been more favorable. As a result of these sweeping and probably enduring changes, Boeninger concludes, Latin America's prospects for democracy and development "look indisputably better than ever before."

Yet democracy is far from complete—much less secure—in the Americas. Three diffuse challenges lie ahead; they can be effectively addressed only through far more extensive reforms. At bottom lie the interrelated economic and social challenges. No region touched by the third wave has more massive and embedded social and economic inequalities. And while economic growth has been rekindled in most Latin American countries, it is still typically far from producing the level of prosperity of, say, Southern Europe. Thus much remains to be done to improve social equity and the structural foundations of economic growth. As the East Asian miracles have taught, the two are not unrelated: raising the level of human capital, especially through expanding mass access to high-quality education, extending social insurance (especially through social-security reform), and expanding the tax base are clear imperatives for growth and equity. These will in turn entrench the fragile and fraying social consensus around market-oriented policies. Yet economic and social progress in turn require major reforms of political institutions. Most Latin American party systems need to become less fragmented and more institutionalized. Boeninger believes that higher electoral thresholds (of at least 5 percent) or even more majoritarian electoral systems would help, as would simultaneous election of presidents and parliaments and public financing of election campaigns. Further devolution of power to state and local government and the private (or nonprofit) sector is also called for, but Boeninger warns of the corruption and fiscal chaos that can result when power is devolved hastily and excessively, as with Brazil's "regional feudalism." Moreover, the state needs to be reformed in many other ways, through comprehensive modernization and professionalization of judicial systems, greater autonomy for legislatures, stronger central banks, greater technical competence in macroeconomic management, and institutionalized mechanisms of the kind that the administration of Patricio Aylwin implemented in Chile for consultation among government leaders, party and legislative leaders, and top-level economic technocrats. The key, stresses Boeninger, is to accelerate the pace of state-building and institutional reform.

Positive trends may be discerned in East Asia as well, but, again, progress toward democratic consolidation has been tentative and mixed. Among the four third wave democracies that Cotton examines (the Philippines, South Korea, Taiwan, and Thailand), only the Philippine regime failed to inherit a dynamic economy and a strong state bureaucracy. Yet it has the benefit of a more substantial prior democratic history than the other three regimes have. While problems of inequality are significant in the Philippines and to a lesser extent in Thailand (and are growing in Taiwan), the key challenges are political and institutional. As Cotton stresses, a distinctive feature of East Asian democracies is the weakness of political opposition. All four regimes may be considered at least electoral democracies, but democracy is "contained" by the dominance of ruling parties and by controls on civil society and the mass media. The Philippines and Thailand have more competitive party systems, but they are fragmented to a degree that renders political opposition a rather fluid and shallow phenomenon. Moreover, personalism, clientelism, vote buying, and scant linkages of parties to issues and organized interests contribute to the weak, inchoate character of party systems, which are dominated in all four regimes by "money politics." Only in Taiwan are parties substantially defined, and, as Hung-mao Tien shows (as does Huang in *Themes and Perspectives*), its party system is still evolving. Democracy in East Asia requires political and institutional reforms to strengthen parties, streamline party systems, and reduce the role of money in politics. Prospects for consolidation appear brightest in Korea and Taiwan, given their economic dynamism and recent political reforms aimed at controlling corruption and increasing judicial independence. But political liberalization must go further to dismantle the legal architecture of the national-security state and provide more space for dissent and independent organization. If the reform process continues and democracy survives without interruption, political parties seem likely to develop institutional strength, and electoral politics to become more competitive.

For Cotton, the weakness of political opposition and constraints on democracy prevalent in East and Southeast Asia derive in large part from the collectivist, elitist, and uncompromising features of "Asian values" (whether of Confucian or other origin). But this interpretation—which has been more forcefully asserted by some Asian political leaders, and accepted by many intellectuals in both Asia and the West—is largely rejected by other contributors to this study, including the elected political leaders on Taiwan. In *Regional Challenges,* the president of the Republic of China (ROC) on Taiwan, Lee Teng-hui, notes the considerable political pluralism and freedom that have emerged in Taiwan during its gradual and peaceful political transformation. Independent observers agree: Taiwan is now counted among the 40 percent of the world's regimes that Freedom House rates as "free." Rather than viewing Taiwan's Confucian cultural heritage as an obstacle to democracy, President Lee identifies its significant continuities with basic democratic principles. These include benevolent (rather than corrupt and abusive) governance and responsiveness to the will of the people—and thus popular sovereignty. He argues that classical Chinese civilization, untainted by the monarchical politics of later centuries, can actually be a resource and inspiration for the development of democracy.

The compatibility of democracy and Confucian culture is echoed here by the vice-president of the ROC, Lien Chan. Stressing the widespread support for democracy among the Taiwanese people, Lien suggests that the "experience with democratic reform in Taiwan could be called a Confucian cultural renaissance, in that it involves remolding and refining an ancient Oriental civilization, while extending Western thought and institutions." Ying-shih Yü takes a similar approach in rebutting the culturalist argument that Confucianism limits democracy in Asia: "Confucian education often inculcated in the minds of the young a sense of justice, social responsibility, human equality, and the well-being of people, which are some of the closest Confucian equivalents to Western civic virtues. It was this Confucian public-spiritedness that disposed many Chinese intellectuals [such as Sun Yat-sen] to Western democratic ideas at the turn of the century."

Neither of our case studies of Taiwan, by Hung-mao Tien and Thomas B. Gold, views traditional political culture as a significant obstacle to democratic consolidation. Gold does see in Confucian Chinese cultural traditions a largely unfavorable legacy, featuring a "zero-sum, moralistic view of political disagreements," a heavy stress on "obedience to distant authority," and suspicion of autonomous organizations. But these cultural constraints on democracy have been heavily eroded by the breathtaking pace of socioeconomic development, which has produced a host of more powerful favorable conditions: widespread affluence, relatively low inequality, growing opportunities for women, high educational levels, increasing political sophistication, a greater disposition to compromise, a burgeoning civil society full of issue-based movements and think tanks, and a flourishing pluralism in the mass media. The latter trends have been further facilitated by the liberalizing reforms of political leaders such as presidents Chiang Ching-kuo and Lee Teng-hui, who have transcended cultural traditions to embrace accommodation and initiate reform at decisive moments in the country's political evolution.

As Tien demonstrates, the obstacles to democratic consolidation in Taiwan are primarily institutional and geopolitical in nature: the extensive vestiges of the KMT's longtime hegemony over politics, society, the military, and even the economy; the profoundly contrasting visions of national identity and the related ethnic divisions between "mainlanders" and "native Taiwanese"; the continuing threat of force from the People's Republic of China (PRC); the factionalism and the increasingly large role of money in party and electoral politics; and the long shadow that the party and state have cast over civil society. Yet each of these factors contains or is balanced by positive elements. The KMT's unquestioned dominance permitted a gradual and elite-centered mode of transition that fostered stability and the growth of democratic practices and norms. The impressive degree of negotiation and consensus-building underlying this transition is detailed here by one of its key architects, James C.Y. Soong. The threat of aggression—which surfaced anew with the PRC's offshore firing of missiles in the preludes to the 1995 and 1996 elections—has fostered moderation on the national-identity question, undermining support for advocates of both overt independence and near-term reunification. The political disenfranchisement of trade unionism has weakened civil society but checked an important source of political instability and economic vulnerability (as seen in Korea). And, for all its problems, factionalism did generate a new splinter party from the KMT that has helped to produce a more competitive and less polarized party system, as well as a legislature that is more independent of the government.

Taiwan's 1996 presidential election—by all accounts a victory for the democratic process and for the political center on the national-identity question—marked an important step on the road to democratic consolidation. Completing that journey will require, as in so many other third wave democracies, further institutional reforms to modernize political structures, alter the electoral system, control organized crime and its infiltration of electoral politics, and complete the extrication of the ruling party from the state, society, and economy. Even with such reforms, consolidation may not be clearly achieved until control of government passes smoothly to the political opposition through the electoral process. Yet in such key respects as its economic prosperity, sizeable middle class, favorable mode of transition, civilian supremacy over the military, pragmatic and competitive politics, and visionary national leadership,

Taiwan now bears a striking resemblance to the Southern European cases of successful consolidation. Clearly, these parallels augur well for its prospects for consolidation. Yet, more than any other third wave democracy, Taiwan finds its political future still clouded by the escalating power and increasingly unpredictable behavior of the authoritarian colossus on the other side of the Taiwan Strait.

A Fourth Wave?

Even if the third wave is drawing to a close, a democratic recession is not inevitable. The chapters in these two volumes paint a sober but largely hopeful picture of the prospects for consolidating the extraordinary democratic gains of the past two decades. Some new democracies are clearly entrenched, and many more (especially in East Asia and Latin America) should achieve consolidation soon as long as the necessary institutional changes and growth-inducing economic reforms are implemented. If the democratic expansion of the third wave is deepened and secured in this way, the first decades of the next century could bring a political reality that seemed virtually unimaginable just a decade ago: a world composed mainly of stable democracies.

But "mainly" would still refer to states rather than population. According to Freedom House at the start of 1997, 40 percent of the world's people still live in the most authoritarian class of regimes: "not free." And half of these 2.2 billion people live in one country: mainland China. In the first decades of the twenty-first century, no other country's politics will more heavily determine the scope for democratic expansion in the world. If a "third reverse wave" does not ensue but is instead preempted by widespread democratic consolidation, the development of a fourth wave of global democratization will hinge primarily on events in one country: China.

Is the democratization of China a wildly distant and implausible dream? In the years of political freeze that have followed the June 1989 massacre at Tiananmen Square, the conventional assumption has been yes. But in *Regional Challenges* Minxin Pei and Andrew J. Nathan give us empirical grounds for questioning that assumption. Ying-shih Yü stresses the shallow and very tentative nature of the trends Pei and Nathan identify. Still, the latter two show that political liberalization has at least begun, and that thinking about political reform in China has advanced significantly.

The kinds of incremental and endogenous institutional changes that initiated regime opening in other East Asian autocracies (notably Taiwan) are now taking place in China (and, to different degrees, in Indonesia and Vietnam as well), Pei argues. A system of law is gradually taking shape to buttress economic reform, protect property rights, and constrain the arbitrary power of the state. The community of private legal practitioners is growing in size and becoming more assertive. Both the National People's Congress (NPC) and the local people's congresses are exhibiting more autonomy and initiative. Power is becoming more decentralized in "a nascent federalist structure," allowing economic and political reforms to advance more rapidly in some regions and then diffuse to others. A growing number of villages are experimenting with direct and sometimes vigorously competitive elections. A key part of the Chinese Communist Party's structure of domination—its grassroots organizations in the countryside—is crumbling, while peasant political awareness and activism mount. In addition to these political changes, China's rapid economic development and integration with its Asian neighbors are producing a more sophisticated, open, secular, and aware society, as David S.G. Goodman observes here.[38] China's political reforms have been modest to date and carry risks, not least of which is the danger, in Pei's words, of "an accelerating crisis of governability" if the old system collapses "before the new institutions take root." Thus, Pei warns, China's leaders in the post–Deng Xiaoping era are in a race against time.

A key imperative, writes Pei, is for China to adopt a new constitutional framework to codify and clarify the evolving boundaries of political authority. This, argues Nathan, is not a far-fetched prospect. He notes numerous calls for constitutional revitalization and reform under Deng, and a growing need of Communist Party leaders to "limit government by law" for two reasons: to reinforce their sagging popular legitimacy and to "institutionalize power relations among agencies and levels of the vast party-state." Gradually, an agenda for "transition from lawlessness to constitutionalism" is taking shape, focusing on four broad goals: professionalizing and empowering the NPC while reducing Communist Party authority over it; instituting direct and meaningfully competitive (even possibly multiparty) elections for the national and provincial people's congresses (the two highest levels); establishing a specialized body (perhaps even a constitutional court) to interpret the Constitution and supervise its implementation; and increasing the independence of judges while improving their professional capacity. All of these changes (and others that are being discussed) entail a progressive separation of party and state. Such a program of "constitutionalization" would not make China a democracy, but it would greatly diminish the central obstacle to democratization, the pervasive, Leninist hegemony of the Communist Party.

As communist politicians jockey for power in the post-Deng era, some are likely to promote constitutional reforms in order to advance their own political influence. Elsewhere in the world, precisely such divisions, calculations, and functional needs for regime adaptation have spawned real political liberalization—and ultimately transitions to democracy. Nathan's scenario of an incremental, smooth, regime-led

transition from a Leninist party-state "to a Chinese brand of constitutional democracy" is striking in its parallels with the Taiwan experience. It would be ironic and fitting if what Gold calls "the great
imponderable" for Taiwan's democratic consolidation—Beijing's potential
for belligerence—were neutralized by the "creeping democratization" of
China itself. For the future of democracy and peace in the world, there
is no higher long-term priority than to encourage this trend.

NOTES

1. See Freedom House's annual survey of political rights and civil liberties, as
reported in the January–February 1975 issue of *Freedom in the World.* Freedom House
classified only 39 countries as "free" at the end of 1974; that is a reasonable measure
of the number of democracies at the time. Today, there are many political systems that
are not "free," or liberal (in the sense of enforcing a rule of law and protecting
individual rights) but are nevertheless formally democratic in that they have reasonably
open and competitive elections involving multiple political parties. In 1975, however,
there were few if any countries that met the latter standard but not the former. The
distinction between electoral and liberal democracy is elaborated later in the body of this
introduction.

2. Samuel P. Huntington, *The Third Wave: Democratization in the Late Twentieth
Century* (Norman: University of Oklahoma Press, 1991).

3. Michael Bratton and Nicolas van de Walle, *Democratic Experiments in Africa:
Regime Transitions in Comparative Perspective* (New York: Cambridge University Press,
1997).

4. Larry Diamond, *Prospects for Democratic Development in Africa* (Hoover Institution
Essays in Public Policy No. 74) (Stanford, Calif.: Hoover Institution Press, 1997),
Appendix.

5. On the distinction between liberal and electoral democracy, see Larry Diamond, "Is
the Third Wave Over?" *Journal of Democracy* 7 (July 1996): 20–37.

6. "Free" states are those with an average score of 2.5 or less on the twin Freedom
House scales of political rights and civil liberties. Each scale ranges from 1 to 7, with 1
indicating the most free and 7 the least free. The methodology of the survey is described
in the annual Freedom House publication *Freedom in the World: The Annual Survey of
Political Rights and Civil Liberties* (New York: Freedom House) and in the January–February issue each year of the Freedom House periodical *Freedom Review* (formerly
Freedom in the World).

7. See Diamond, "Is the Third Wave Over?" 27–28, Tables 2 and 3; and *Freedom
Review*, January–February 1997.

8. *Freedom Review*, January–February 1997.

9. Philippe C. Schmitter, "Democracy's Future: More Liberal, Preliberal, or Postlib-
eral?" *Journal of Democracy* 6 (January 1995): 17.

10. A classic example was the political crisis in Ecuador in February 1997, when the
Congress declared the recently elected president, Abdalá Bucaram, "mentally unstable," and
three different officials claimed the presidency. Instead of seizing power, the military
persuaded Bucaram to step aside, with the vice-president assuming power briefly, followed
by the president of Congress. Similarly, during two other recent political crises—in
Guatemala in 1993 following the attempted *autogolpe* ("self-coup") of President Jorge
Serrano and in Pakistan in 1996–97 following the ouster (for corruption) of the
government of Benazir Bhutto—the military remained on the sidelines and constitutional
procedures, however controversial, were observed.

11. Juan J. Linz and Alfred Stepan, eds., *The Breakdown of Democratic Regimes* (Baltimore: Johns Hopkins University Press, 1978).

12. This theoretical perspective on consolidation is elaborated and applied in Juan J. Linz and Alfred Stepan, *Problems of Democratic Transition and Consolidation: Southern Europe, South America, and Post-Communist Europe* (Baltimore: Johns Hopkins University Press, 1996); and Richard Gunther, Hans-Jürgen Puhle, and P. Nikiforos Diamandouros, "Introduction," in Gunther, Diamandouros, and Puhle, eds., *The Politics of Democratic Consolidation: Southern Europe in Comparative Perspective* (Baltimore: Johns Hopkins University Press, 1995).

13. Laurence Whitehead, "The Consolidation of Fragile Democracies: A Discussion with Illustrations," in Robert Pastor, ed., *Democracy in the Americas: Stopping the Pendulum* (New York: Holmes and Meier, 1989), 79; on the contributions of civil society in this process, see Larry Diamond, "Rethinking Civil Society: Toward Democratic Consolidation," *Journal of Democracy* 5 (July 1994): 4–17. In a seminal formulation, Dankwart Rustow gave the name "habituation" to this process, in which contingent and instrumental elite commitments to democracy become rooted in values and beliefs at both the elite and mass levels through the continuous, successful practice of democracy. See his "Transitions to Democracy: Toward a Dynamic Model," *Comparative Politics* 2 (April 1970): 357.

14. For further elaboration of the relationship between political culture and democratic stability, see, for example, Gabriel A. Almond and Sidney Verba, *The Civic Culture: Political Attitudes and Democracy in Five Nations* (Princeton: Princeton University Press, 1963); Robert A. Dahl, *Polyarchy: Participation and Opposition* (New Haven, Conn.: Yale University Press, 1971), 124–62; J. Roland Pennock, *Democratic Political Theory* (Princeton: Princeton University Press, 1979), 236–59; and Larry Diamond, "Political Culture and Democracy," in Diamond, ed., *Political Culture and Democracy in Developing Countries* (Boulder, Colo.: Lynne Rienner, 1993), 1–15.

15. Guillermo O'Donnell, "Delegative Democracy," *Journal of Democracy* 5 (January 1994): 55–69. See also O'Donnell's essay in *Themes and Perspectives.*

16. A seminal discussion of reserved domains appears in J. Samuel Valenzuela, "Democratic Consolidation in Post-transitional Settings: Notion, Process, and Facilitating Conditions," in Scott Mainwaring, Guillermo O'Donnell, and J. Samuel Valenzuela, eds., *Issues in Democratic Consolidation: The New South American Democracies in Comparative Perspective* (Notre Dame, Ind.: University of Notre Dame Press, 1992), 64–66. See also Huntington, *The Third Wave*, 10; Philippe C. Schmitter and Terry Lynn Karl, "What Democracy Is . . . and Is Not," *Journal of Democracy* 2 (Summer 1991): 81; and O'Donnell's essay in *Themes and Perspectives.*

17. Indeed, as Lowenthal observes, even the electoral process has been "marred by gross irregularities" in such formally democratic systems as those of the Dominican Republic and Paraguay. For more comprehensive assessments of the status of democracy in the region and the challenges confronting consolidation, see Larry Diamond, "Democracy in Latin America: Degrees, Illusions, and Directions for Consolidation," in Tom Farer, ed., *Beyond Sovereignty: Collectively Defending Democracy in the Americas* (Baltimore: Johns Hopkins University Press, 1996), 52–104; and the various essays in Jorge I. Domínguez and Abraham F. Lowenthal, eds., *Constructing Democratic Governance: Latin America and the Caribbean in the 1990s* (Baltimore: Johns Hopkins University Press, 1996).

18. Linz and Stepan, *Problems of Democratic Transition and Consolidation*, 210. For their conceptual treatment of the problem, see 3–5 and 207–11. On Chile, see also Felipe Agüero's chapter in *Themes and Perspectives.*

19. Juan J. Linz, *The Breakdown of Democratic Regimes: Crisis, Breakdown, and Reequilibration* (Baltimore: Johns Hopkins University Press, 1978), 28–38.

20. Gunther, Puhle, and Diamandouros, "Introduction," in Gunther, Diamandouros, and Puhle, eds., *The Politics of Democratic Consolidation*, 13.

21. Juan J. Linz and Alfred Stepan, "Political Crafting of Democratic Consolidation or Destruction: European and South American Comparisons," in Pastor, ed., *Democracy in the Americas*, 41–61, and *Problems of Democratic Transition and Consolidation*, ch. 6.

22. See the essays in Linz and Stepan, eds., *The Breakdown of Democratic Regimes*, and particularly Linz, *The Breakdown of Democratic Regimes: Crisis, Breakdown, and Reequilibration*.

23. Scott Mainwaring and Timothy R. Scully, "Introduction: Party Systems in Latin America," in Mainwaring and Scully, eds., *Building Democratic Institutions: Party Systems in Latin America* (Stanford, Calif.: Stanford University Press, 1995), 1–34; *Political Parties and Democracy* (report of a conference sponsored by the International Forum for Democratic Studies in Washington, D.C., on 18–19 November 1996) (Washington, D.C.: International Forum for Democratic Studies, 1997).

24. See also Leonardo Morlino, "Political Parties and Democratic Consolidation in Southern Europe," in Gunther, Diamandouros, and Puhle, eds., *The Politics of Democratic Consolidation*, 315–88.

25. Although Tóka finds no evidence among his four cases of a relationship between party-system strength and policy effectiveness, or between support for parties and support for democracy among the populace, other evidence does identify features of the party system (in particular, fragmentation and polarization) as having an important relationship to policy effectiveness. With respect to economic reform, see Stephan Haggard and Robert R. Kaufman, *The Political Economy of Democratic Transitions* (Princeton: Princeton University Press, 1995).

26. Andreas Schedler, "Under- and Overinstitutionalization: Some Ideal Typical Propositions Concerning New and Old Party Systems" (Working Paper No. 213, Helen Kellogg Institute for International Studies, Notre Dame, Ind., March 1995).

27. On the debate over presidentialism versus parliamentarism, see (in addition to the sources cited by Przeworski et al.) Matthew Soberg Shugart and John M. Carey, *Presidents and Assemblies: Constitutional Design and Electoral Dynamics* (Cambridge: Cambridge University Press, 1992); Juan J. Linz and Arturo Valenzuela, eds., *The Failure of Presidential Democracy* (Baltimore: Johns Hopkins University Press, 1994); and Larry Diamond and Marc F. Plattner, eds., *The Global Resurgence of Democracy*, 2nd ed. (Baltimore: Johns Hopkins University Press, 1996), pt. 2.

28. Niou and Ordeshook do not differ as sharply from Carey on the structural inducements to party coherence as it may appear at first glance. Carey's concern is for coherence (or integration) among a party's *national* legislators, and among those legislators and their national leadership (or president) outside of parliament. For Niou and Ordeshook, the key issue is vertical autonomy of party branches at subnational levels of power—their freedom to choose their own candidates and craft their own campaigns. Both hypotheses may be right; party coherence may be maximized when different levels of party organization (e.g., state and local branches) have the freedom to choose their own nominees, but, within each level, party officials exercise some top-down control over who those nominees will be. Here again, democratic effectiveness implies a certain balance, in this case between undercentralization and overcentralization.

29. In both Taiwan and South Korea, the legacy of divided nationhood—which poses grave threats to national security—complicates the quest to develop more democratic and institutionalized control over the military. See the essay by Yun-han Chu, Fu Hu, and Chung-in Moon in *Regional Challenges*.

30. With the disastrous decline in the physical and economic conditions of the armed forces in Russia—as military readiness collapses and salaries plummet to below-poverty levels, if they are paid at all—it may seem a wonder that no military coup has been attempted. On the other hand, when military capacity collapses almost entirely, the ability to stage a successful coup may go down with it. On strategies and conditions for democratizing civil-military relations, see Alfred Stepan, *Rethinking Military Politics: Brazil*

and the Southern Cone (Princeton: Princeton University Press, 1988), chs. 6–8; Huntington, *The Third Wave*, 231–53; Diamond, "Democracy in Latin America," 86–91; and Larry Diamond and Marc F. Plattner, eds., *Civil-Military Relations and Democracy* (Baltimore: Johns Hopkins University Press, 1996).

31. In part, this underscores the importance of the design of political institutions. As Agüero notes, where political institutions incline democracy toward fragmentation and stalemate (as in Brazil), structural improvements in civil-military relations are difficult to achieve.

32. See Guillermo O'Donnell and Philippe C. Schmitter, *Transitions from Authoritarian Rule: Tentative Conclusions About Uncertain Democracies* (Baltimore: Johns Hopkins University Press, 1986), 48–56.

33. They do acknowledge that consolidation is not "just a matter of time." Indeed, theorists of consolidation, in this study and elsewhere, do not argue that consolidated democracies will last indefinitely, but only that their breakdown (as Linz and Stepan put it here) "would be related not to weaknesses or problems specific to the historic process of democratic consolidation, but to a new dynamic" of insoluble problems and shifts to disloyal or semi-loyal norms and behavior on the part of key political actors. Neither do theorists of consolidation rule out the possibility that unconsolidated democracies may persist for some time, but usually in a state of lower-quality democracy.

34. See, respectively, Barrington Moore, *Social Origins of Dictatorship and Democracy: Lord and Peasant in the Making of the Modern World* (Boston: Beacon, 1966); and Dietrich Rueschemeyer, Evelyne Huber Stephens, and John D. Stephens, *Capitalist Development and Democracy* (Chicago: University of Chicago Press, 1992).

35. In fact, as party politics and democratic elections gather momentum, a new line of cleavage relating to the issue of socioeconomic justice is beginning to cross-cut and soften the longstanding national-policy divide of reunification versus independence and the once-polarizing ethnic divide of mainlander versus Taiwanese. On this important trend, see Tse-min Lin, Yun-han Chu, and Melvin J. Hinich, "Conflict Displacement and Regime Transition in Taiwan: A Spatial Analysis," *World Politics* 48 (July 1996): 453–81.

36. For seminal statements of the relationship between the mode of transition and the subsequent nature and stability of democracy, see Terry Lynn Karl, "Dilemmas of Democratization in Latin America," *Comparative Politics* 23 (October 1990): 1–21; and Terry Lynn Karl and Philippe C. Schmitter, "Modes of Transition in Latin America, Southern and Eastern Europe," *International Social Science Journal* 128 (May 1991): 269–84. Both Diamandouros and Karl and Schmitter recognize that elite-pacted transitions that excessively marginalize mass actors run the risk of generating their own "birth defects" by narrowing the base of democracy.

37. An important step in Chile, Boeninger notes, has been the transfer of domestic-intelligence functions to civilian bodies accountable to the executive. The improvement in civilian control and the declining scope for military coups appear to be part of a broader global trend. See Samuel P. Huntington, "Reforming Civil-Military Relations," in Diamond and Plattner, eds., *Civil-Military Relations and Democracy,* 3–12.

38. Goodman sees these various economic, social, and political changes in China as probably leading to a much more controlled and authoritarian form of Asian "democracy," perhaps on the model of Singapore. For a view that sees rising income and educational levels impelling China more strongly toward democracy in the next quarter-century, see Henry S. Rowen, "The Short March: China's Road to Democracy," *The National Interest* 45 (Fall 1996): 61–70.

I

Theoretical and Conceptual Perspectives

1

DEMOCRACY
FOR THE LONG HAUL

Samuel P. Huntington

Samuel P. Huntington is Albert J. Weatherhead III University Professor at Harvard University, where he is also director of the John M. Olin Institute for Strategic Studies and chairman of the Harvard Academy for International and Area Studies. He has served in the White House as coordinator of security planning for the National Security Council. His most recent books are The Third Wave: Democratization in the Late Twentieth Century *(1991) and* The Clash of Civilizations and the Remaking of World Order *(1996).*

I was last in Taipei in January 1989, participating in a conference on political change in Taiwan cosponsored by the Institute of International Relations of National Chengchi University and the Harvard Center for International Affairs. At that time, as a result of the leadership of President Lee Teng-hui, the process of political change was well under way and was becoming a process of democratization. Martial law had been lifted; the Democratic Progressive Party (DPP) had been formed; electoral competition was expanding; legislative debates had become vigorous; press censorship was on the way out; social movements and social groups were organizing, demanding, and protesting. The conference itself was also a small part of this process, as the first public meeting in which both Kuomintang (KMT) and DPP officials took part.

The changes taking place in Taiwan in 1989 were, of course, part of the vast third wave of democratization that had begun 15 years earlier in Southern Europe, and then moved on to Latin America and Asia. By 1989 this wave was in full flood, reaching its crest at the end of the year with the collapse of the communist regimes in Central and Eastern Europe, which was soon followed by the disintegration of the USSR.

These events generated a swelling tide of euphoria. Many believed that a global democratic revolution was under way, that liberal democracy was soon destined to triumph everywhere, that history was at an end, and that, as Francis Fukuyama put it, we might be approaching "the end point of man's ideological evolution and the universalization of Western liberal democracy as the final form of human government."[1] Similar euphoric expectations had appeared at the end of this century's other major conflicts. The First World War was thought to be the "war to end all wars" and the war to make the world safe for democracy. The Second World War, Franklin Roosevelt said, would lead to a new security system that would "end the system of unilateral action, the exclusive alliances, the balances of power, and all the other expedients that have been tried for centuries—and have always failed." Instead, we would have "a universal organization" of "peace-loving Nations" and the beginnings of a "permanent structure of peace."[2] The First World War, however, generated communism, fascism, and the reversal of the century-old first wave of democratization. The Second World War produced a Cold War that was truly global.

Now, eight years after the collapse of European communism, our euphoric moment has passed, and we too have become sadder but wiser. A single dominating ideological conflict has given way to a multiplicity of ethnic conflicts, the stability of a bipolar world to the confusion and instability of a multipolar and multicivilizational world, and the potential horror of global nuclear war to the daily horror of ethnic cleansing. The word "genocide" has been heard far more often in the past few years than it was in any half-decade during the Cold War.

In this sobering world, we need to have a sober view of the prospects for democracy and to recognize the possibility that this great third wave of democratization, having brought democracy to some 40 countries, may be losing its outward dynamic and moving from a phase of expansion to one of consolidation.

Among scholars of democratization, a major debate goes on concerning the issue of crafting versus preconditions. Some argue that movement toward democracy depends on the existence within society of particular social, economic, or cultural preconditions, although there is much disagreement over what those preconditions are. A different school of thought sees democratization as primarily the product of political leaders who have the will and the skill to bring it about. Clearly, however, both preconditions and crafting have roles to play, and certain preconditions can facilitate democratic crafting. These include a relatively high level of economic development and the prevalence of what can be termed Western culture and values, including Western Christianity. At present, virtually all of the non-oil-producing high-income or upper-middle-income countries, with the exception of Singapore, are democratic. Similarly, all of the countries that are Western or that have been influenced substantially by the West, with the exception of Cuba and perhaps one or two others, have become democratic. The countries that have not democratized are those in which the conditions favoring democratization are weak. This is not to say that these conditions are required for democratization. They are not: non-Christian, nonwealthy India is an obvious case in point. Almost all the remaining non-democracies in the world, however, are either poor, non-Western, or both. Their democratization is not impossible, but it is likely to be more difficult. In addition, many non-Western societies are going through pervasive processes of cultural indigenization. They increasingly resist Western attempts to export Western values and institutions and are searching for identity and meaning in their own cultural traditions.

Economic development can alter a country's culture and make it more supportive of democracy. If it occurs, economic development will presumably have this effect on Islamic, Buddhist, Eastern Orthodox, and Confucian societies. But apart from East Asia, economic development lags in much of the world, and in East Asia cultural change is likely to be a lengthy process. Recent transitions to democracy have served the historically important function of extending democracy throughout almost all the wealthier countries in the world and almost all countries that have largely Western cultures. Efforts to extend democracy further face much more significant economic and cultural obstacles than did the democratizations of the past two decades.

History unfolds in a dialectical fashion. Any substantial movement in one direction tends eventually to lose its momentum and to generate countervailing forces. Each of the first two waves of democratization was followed by a reverse wave in which some but not all of the new democracies reverted to authoritarianism. There are indications that a new reverse wave may be gathering which could lead to the erosion of some third wave gains. This again places a premium on the need to bolster and protect those gains. In some respects the democratic expansion since 1974 can be thought of as a military campaign, with country after country being liberated by the surging democratic forces. As any general knows, however, an offensive can advance too far too fast. Forces become overextended and vulnerable to counterattack. Even in the most dramatic of advances, such as that of the Allied armies across France in 1944, it becomes necessary to pause, regroup, and consolidate one's gains. It appears that the third wave of democratization may have reached that point.

Problems of Democratization

In the coming years, more countries will undoubtedly move toward democracy and some democratic transitions will occur. The established democracies should continue to promote democracy and human rights where they are absent and to support democratic opponents of authoritarian regimes. At this time, however, the primary emphasis needs to be placed on consolidation. The dominant theme should be not the creation of additional democracies but the consolidation of recently established democracies and the completion of the transitions to democracy already under way, especially in such key countries as Russia, Ukraine, South Africa, and Mexico.

The difficulties that new democracies face include problems inherited from their authoritarian predecessors, as well as others peculiar to democracy and democratizing societies. Democratization is the solution to the problem of tyranny, but the process of democratization itself can also create or exacerbate other problems with which new democracies must then grapple. I will mention three.

First, the initiation of elections forces political leaders to compete for votes. In many situations, the easiest way to win votes is to appeal to tribal, ethnic, and religious constituencies. Democratization thus promotes communalism and ethnic conflict, and relatively few new democracies have structured their institutions to minimize the incentives to make such appeals. In one notable case where this was done, South Africa, the leaders of the main parties representing the principal ethnic groups agreed before the election on what the outcome of the voting should be. The result was a peaceful transition from white to black rule but not exactly an exemplar of democracy. In the former Soviet Union and Yugoslavia, in contrast, the first elections brought nationalist parties to power, virtually ensuring the breakup of those countries. Similarly, in Bosnia voters conspicuously ignored the multireligious parties: Serbs voted for the Serb party, Croats for the Croat party, and Muslims for the Muslim party. People identify with family, faith, and blood, and unless the rules of electoral engagement are very carefully constructed, politicians competing for office have little choice but to appeal for votes in these terms. In non-Western societies, the introduction of democracy also creates what can only be described as "the democracy paradox." It facilitates the coming to power of groups that appeal to indigenous ethnic and religious loyalties and are very likely to be anti-Western and antidemocratic.

Second, democratization can make foreign war more likely. It is true that overwhelming evidence shows that democracies do not, except in rare, marginal circumstances, fight wars against other democracies. This has been particularly true in the years since World War II.[3] In a recent study, however, Edward Mansfield and Jack Snyder present impressive evidence, covering the same period of time, which shows that in the "transitional phase of democratization, countries become more aggressive and war-prone, not less. . . . democratizing states are more likely to fight wars than are mature democracies or autocracies. States like contemporary Russia that make the biggest leap in democratization—from total autocracy to extensive mass democracy—are about twice as likely to fight wars in the decade after democratization as are states that remain autocracies."[4] This proclivity of emerging democracies for interstate war stems in part, of course, from the same incentives to make communal appeals that also stimulate ethnic conflict within democratizing states.

Third, democratization involves the removal of state constraints on individual behavior, a loosening of social inhibitions, and uncertainty and confusion about standards of morality. By weakening state authority, as it must, democratization also brings into question authority in general and can promote an amoral, *laissez-faire*, or "anything goes" atmosphere. Hence, although the evidence is sketchy and unsystematic, democratization appears to involve an increase in socially undesirable behavior, including crime and drug use, and possibly to encourage disintegration of the family and other bastions of collective authority.

These problems of communal conflict, foreign war, and social decay, produced in some measure by the processes of democratization, join the many other problems that new democracies have inherited from the previous authoritarian regimes. While confronting these challenges, third wave democracies also face some distinctive new threats to the maintenance of the essential elements of liberal democracy.

During the 1960s and 1970s, second-wave democracies were threatened by forces from outside the political system. In many countries Marxist-Leninist insurgencies, usually but not always with a rural base, challenged both democratic and nondemocratic incumbent regimes. Military interventions overthrew democratic regimes in Greece, Turkey, South Korea, Pakistan, and many Latin American countries. These threats reflected the still relatively underdeveloped nature of the economies of these second-wave democracies. They still had substantial peasant populations that could provide a base for revolutionary movements, and their middle class and bourgeoisie, which were small and weak, often felt threatened by populist and lower-class movements, and hence acquiesced in military seizures of power.

Most third wave democracies are at much higher levels of economic development. In 1965, for instance, Latin America was 70 percent rural and 70 percent illiterate; it is now 70 percent urban and 70 percent literate. The threats to democracy in urban, literate, middle-class, industrial societies will not come from peasant revolutions, the last fading remnants of which can be seen in Chiapas, the Peruvian highlands, and central Luzon. Nor are military interventions likely to pose threats to such societies. Successful coups have occurred only in extremely poor third wave democracies, such as Sudan, Nigeria, Haiti, and more recently São Tomé and Príncipe and Niger. As I have suggested elsewhere, it is even possible to conceive of a "coup-attempt ceiling" at about $3,000 per-capita GNP and a "coup-success ceiling" at about $1,000.[5] In countries with per-capita incomes below $1,000, coups are often attempted and are usually successful; in countries with per-capita incomes between $1,000 and $3,000, coups are often attempted but are rarely successful; in countries with per-capita incomes above

$3,000, coups are rarely attempted and almost never succeed. In addition, the coups that have been attempted against third wave democracies have usually been led by field-grade officers, lieutenant colonels in particular, rather than by commanders in chief. Top military leaders have generally learned that military intervention is no solution to the problems of their countries and creates severe problems for the cohesion of their military establishments.

New Dangers

Threats to third wave democracies are likely to come not from generals and revolutionaries who have nothing but contempt for democracy, but rather from participants in the democratic process. These are political leaders and groups who win elections, take power, and then manipulate the mechanisms of democracy to curtail or destroy democracy. In the past, when democratic regimes fell as a result of coups or revolutions, no doubt existed as to what happened, and the transition to authoritarianism was brief, clear, and dramatic. With third wave democracies, the problem is not overthrow but erosion: the intermittent or gradual weakening of democracy by those elected to lead it.

These threats take various shapes. One, which I do not believe to be serious but which has received much attention, is the "red return"—that is, the restoration to power through elections of former communists and former communist parties in Central and Eastern Europe and the former Soviet Union. Indeed, apart from the Czech Republic, most of the leaders in all these countries are former communists. In some, old communist parties with new names have won majorities in parliament. In others, coalitions dominated by former communists have control of the government. In several, former communists reconfigured as nationalists have been elected to office. These developments have led observers to express deep concern about the future of democracy in these countries. So far, however, former communists and former communist parties have generally played by the democratic rules, and their economic policies have varied from stringent liberalization to softer social-democratic policies designed to lessen the burdens of shifting away from the command economy. It is conceivable that the red return may at some point undermine democracy, and to date Slovakia is, I believe, the only case where a government dominated by former communists has been voted out of office—and there it subsequently won reelection. But perhaps all that the red return signifies is that people who have the political talent to rise to the top in communist systems also have the political talent to rise to the top in democratic systems.

A second potential threat to new democracies comes from the electoral victory of parties or movements apparently committed to antidemocratic ideologies. This possibility arises most directly with

Islamic fundamentalist groups and has been rare only because meaning-ful elections in Muslim countries have been so rare. The issue did come up, however, in Algeria in 1992, when the military canceled the election that the Islamic Salvation Front (FIS) was certain to win. The issue could appear in Turkey, where the Welfare Party has been increasing its strength and won the most votes in the most recent parliamentary elections. Does the possible or actual victory of such parties justify the suspension of democratic procedures? In general, I believe the answer is no. With respect to Algeria, for instance, it is by no means clear that a fundamentalist movement that comes to power through the electoral process will necessarily act in the same way as one that achieves power through a revolution (as in Iran) or a coup (as in Sudan). In addition, there would have been powerful incentives for the FIS to act in a moderate and reasonable manner in order to secure the aid and investment it needed from the West. Finally, if a FIS government had moved in an extremist direction and begun to destroy democracy, the "Pinochet option" would still have been available. The Algerian army could have intervened in the same way that the Chilean army did when Allende's government moved sharply to the left. France, the United States, and the West in general did democracy a serious disservice in not preventing the preemptive action by the Algerian military and in not vigorously protesting that action when it did occur.

A third, more serious threat to democracy is executive arrogation, which occurs when an elected chief executive concentrates power in his own hands, subordinates or even suspends the legislature, and rules largely by decree. This has happened in some measure in Russia, in Belarus, and in some other former communist countries. It has also been prevalent in Latin America, where it has been variously referred to as "authoritarian democracy," "bounded strongmen," "caudillos by consent," and "delegative democracy." In Argentina and Venezuela, presidents have ruled largely by decree. In 1995, the president of Colombia, faced with charges of massive drug-related corruption, declared a state of emergency and announced that he would rule by decree for the next three months. In the most extreme case, President Fujimori carried out a full-scale executive coup in Peru, shutting down the legislative and judicial branches and political parties, imprisoning politicians and intellectuals, censoring the media, and drastically curtailing human rights. He then, however, used his authoritarian power to break the influence of the terrorist Sendero Luminoso (Shining Path), restore law and order, stabilize the currency, promote foreign investment, achieve the highest rate of economic growth in Latin America, and win overwhelming reelection in what was generally considered to be a fair vote. In a somewhat similar manner, President Menem of Argentina won reelection largely on the basis of results he achieved by the use of undemocratic means. Do these exercises of emergency powers and suspensions of democracy provide a means of strengthening democracy by enabling governments to achieve desirable goals that cannot be achieved by normal democratic procedures? Or is executive arrogation likely to feed on itself and become a political addiction from which the society will be unable to escape? Immediately after Fujimori's coup, Secretary of State James Baker publicly attacked it, saying, "You can't save democracy by destroying it." But perhaps Fujimori did precisely that.

Finally, many governments in new democracies have not hesitated to abridge political rights and civil liberties. Freedom of the press is limited, television and radio are strictly controlled by the government, editors are fired, editorial guidelines are imposed. Opposition politicians are harassed in subtle and not-so-subtle ways. Legitimate claims by ethnic minorities are rebuffed. Such minorities have been subjected to brutal suppression in democracies like India and Turkey just as they have been in nondemocracies like Indonesia and China.

A general tendency seems to exist for third wave democracies to become something other than fully democratic. In its Comparative Survey of Freedom for 1995, for instance, Freedom House identified 114 countries as democracies—more than at any other time in history. Yet it also classified 37 (or one-third) of these democracies as only "partly free," because of their abridgements of basic political liberties and human rights. Similarly, Larry Diamond, in a masterful 1993 analysis of Latin American democracy, identifies 4 clearly democratic countries, 3 authoritarian or totalitarian countries, and 15 countries that fall into one of four intermediate categories: "partially illiberal democracy," "competitive semidemocracy," "restrictive semidemocracy," and "semicompetitive partially pluralist authoritarian."[6] Between 1987 and 1993, moreover, the overall movement of Latin American countries was toward these intermediate categories, with 11 of the 22 countries becoming less democratic, 5 becoming more democratic, and 6 not changing their position. On the democratic–nondemocratic continuum, in short, we seem to be moving toward a classic bell-shaped curve, with a growing number of countries somewhere in the middle between Denmark and China. More generally, perhaps, one could say that as formal democratic institutions are adopted by more and more diverse societies, democracy itself is becoming more differentiated. Significant differences exist among Anglo-American, German, and Japanese capitalism; comparable differences may be emerging among Western, Latin American, East Asian, Eastern Orthodox, and African versions of democracy.

Surveying the Alternatives

Democracy, as Winston Churchill famously observed, is the worst form of government, except for all the others. What happens, however, if there are no others? That, in effect, is the situation in the wealthy industrialized democracies of the world. In these countries, however, people have become pervasively alienated from politics and public discourse, deeply cynical about their political leaders, decreasingly involved in political and other social organizations, and less and less trusting of other people. These attitudes perhaps reflect the absence of an alternative political system or ideology competing with democracy. If the choice is the "worst system" of government or no system of government, people may well prefer the latter.

Is this the situation, however, with respect to the new democracies of the third wave? Do they have alternatives to democracy? At one level, none exists because throughout most of the world it is necessary to pay deference to the ideas and procedures of democracy; the legitimacy of a government depends on the extent to which it can make a plausible claim to represent the will of the people. Yet this is not universally the case, and at least two alternatives to democracy have been advanced in the postcommunist world. One is the Islamist alternative, a political system based on the Koran and the *shari'a*, merging politics and religion in the *ummah*, or community of the faithful. The political institutions of an Islamist system, however, remain unclear and varied, and range from the absolute monarchy of Saudi Arabia to the circumscribed, religiously defined semidemocracy of Iran. Moreover, no society explicitly organized in terms of Islam has achieved the economic success or the political order that would give it a more general appeal, and the Islamist alternative has so far had relatively little appeal even to Muslims.

A second, much more significant, potential alternative to democracy is "Asian authoritarianism." The appeal here, of course, lies in the remarkable economic success of South Korea, Taiwan, Hong Kong, and Singapore under nondemocratic systems of government, a record of economic growth now being duplicated in some measure by Malaysia, Thailand, Indonesia, and, most importantly, mainland China. Except for another East Asian society, Japan, no democratic country has sustained for as long a period of time the 8 percent or higher growth rates that these countries have achieved under authoritarian rule. This achievement has tremendous appeal elsewhere, especially among the former Soviet republics. The case for the East Asian model is also bolstered by theoretical arguments first articulated in the concept of the "new authoritarianism" developed in mainland China in the late 1980s. This doctrine provided a theoretical substitute for Marxism-Leninism that would justify abandonment of totalitarianism, movement toward a market economy, and the maintenance of an authoritarian political system. More recently, similar arguments have been expounded by Prime Minister Mahathir of Malaysia and, most notably, by Senior Minister Lee Kuan Yew and other scholars and officials from Singapore. The last few years, indeed, have seen what might be termed a "Singaporean cultural offensive." The Singaporeans argue that fundamental differences exist between Asian values of community, order, discipline, and respect for authority and Western values of liberty, license, individualism, and disrespect for authority. The latter, Lee and his associates say, have led to the social decay and moral disintegration of Western societies; in order to prevent similar developments in their own societies, they must resist Western pressures for human rights and democracy. What people want and need, they argue, is not democratic government but good government—that is, government that will provide economic well-being, political stability, social order, communal harmony, and efficient and honest administration.

The contrast between this model and the democratic model is often set forth in terms of the contrast between Singapore and Taiwan, a contrast that is real if often exaggerated—as in the recent *New York Times* headline that summed it up as the difference between "clean and mean," on the one hand, and "filthy and free," on the other. As that article also pointed out, Taiwan and Singapore are the two most successful Chinese societies in the 5,000-year history of Chinese civilization, and one or the other is likely to be the model for the future of mainland China.[7]

Some authoritarian governments, Singapore's among them, have been remarkably successful in producing economic prosperity, social order, and general well-being. Other authoritarian governments, however, have been total disasters, producing economic catastrophe, domestic violence, pervasive corruption, and severe social inequalities. Authoritarian governments suffer from two profound and inherent weaknesses. First, they lack feedback mechanisms and hence they tend to ignore emerging disasters. As Amartya Sen has pointed out, a democratic country like India may not achieve the same high growth rates that a nondemocratic country like China does, but it also does not suffer from famines as China has.[8] Politicians concerned about reelection will not let their people starve. Second, the argument that authoritarian rule produces good government assumes that authoritarian rulers are good people. It is, however, far from certain that this is the case, and even rulers who initially aspire to be good and to do good can be corrupted by the temptations of power. The case for authoritarianism, in short, rests on unrealistic assumptions about human nature.

Singaporeans speak with justified pride about the lack of corruption in their political system, an achievement made possible by the example and discipline of Lee Kuan Yew. Yet while authoritarian rule may provide good government for a decade, or even a generation, it cannot provide—and throughout history never has provided—good government over a sustained period of time. It lacks the institutions for self-reform: public debate, a free press, protest movements, opposition political parties, and competitive elections. Democracy, in contrast, is based on a much more realistic and complex view of human nature and on the recognition that (as James Madison put it) "ambition must be made to counteract ambition." The basis for democracy was perhaps best expressed in the famous comment by Reinhold Niebuhr: "Man's capacity for justice makes democracy possible; but man's inclination to injustice makes democracy necessary."[9] The freedom and creativity that President Lee has introduced in Taiwan will survive him. The honesty and efficiency that Senior Minister Lee has brought to Singapore are likely to follow him to his grave. In some circumstances, authoritarianism may do well in the short term, but experience clearly shows that only democracy produces good government over the long haul.

NOTES

1. Francis Fukuyama, "The End of History," *The National Interest* 16 (Summer 1989): 4.

2. "Address to the Congress Reporting on the Yalta Conference," 1 March 1945, in Samuel I. Rosenman, ed., *Public Papers and Addresses of Franklin D. Roosevelt* (New York: Russell and Russell, 1969), 13:586.

3. Henry S. Farber and Joanne Gowa, "Politics and Peace," *International Security* 20 (Fall 1995): 123–46. There is a rich literature hotly debating the "democratic peace" thesis. For recent exchanges, see Christopher Layne, "Kant or Cant: The Myth of Democratic Peace," *International Security* 19 (Fall 1994): 5–49; David Spiro, "The Insignificance of the Liberal Peace," *International Security* 19 (Fall 1994): 50–86, and "Correspondence: The Democratic Peace," *International Security* 19 (Spring 1995): 164–84; Bruce M. Russett, *Grasping the Democratic Peace: Principles for a Post–Cold War World* (Princeton: Princeton University Press, 1993).

4. Edward Mansfield and Jack Snyder, "Democratization and the Danger of War," *International Security* 20 (Summer 1995): 5–6.

5. Samuel P. Huntington, "Reforming Civil-Military Relations," *Journal of Democracy* 6 (October 1995): 14–16.

6. Larry Diamond, "Democracy in Latin America: Degrees, Illusions, and Directions for Consolidation," in Tom Farer, ed., *Beyond Sovereignty: Collectively Defending Democracy in a World of Sovereign States* (Baltimore: Johns Hopkins University Press, 1996).

7. *New York Times*, 5 February 1995, E1, E4. It might be noted that a synthesis of seven surveys of corruption in 41 countries rated Singapore the third-least corrupt (after New Zealand and Denmark), while Hong Kong ranked seventeenth, Taiwan twenty-fifth, and China next to last, exceeded in corruption only by Indonesia. *New York Times*, 20 August 1995, E3.

8. Jean Drèze and Amartya Sen, *Hunger and Public Action* (Oxford: Clarendon Press, 1989), 210–15.

9. Reinhold Niebuhr, *Children of Light and Children of Darkness: A Vindication of Democracy and a Critique of Its Traditional Defense* (New York: Charles Scribner's Sons, 1950), xi.

2

TOWARD CONSOLIDATED DEMOCRACIES

Juan J. Linz & Alfred Stepan

Juan J. Linz is Sterling Professor of Political and Social Science at Yale University. Alfred Stepan, formerly rector and president of the Central European University in Budapest, is Gladstone Professor of Government and Fellow at All Souls College, University of Oxford. This essay is drawn from their book Problems of Democratic Transition and Consolidation: Southern Europe, South America, and Post-Communist Europe *(1996).*

It is necessary to begin by saying a few words about three minimal conditions that must obtain before there can be any possibility of speaking of democratic consolidation. First, in a modern polity, free and authoritative elections cannot be held, winners cannot exercise the monopoly of legitimate force, and citizens cannot effectively have their rights protected by a rule of law unless a state exists. In some parts of the world, conflicts about the authority and domain of the *polis* and the identities and loyalties of the *demos* are so intense that no state exists. No state, no democracy.

Second, democracy cannot be thought of as consolidated until a democratic transition has been brought to completion. A necessary but by no means sufficient condition for the completion of a democratic transition is the holding of free and contested elections (on the basis of broadly inclusive voter eligibility) that meet the seven institutional requirements for elections in a polyarchy that Robert A. Dahl has set forth.[1] Such elections are not sufficient, however, to complete a democratic transition. In many cases (e.g., Chile as of 1996) in which free and contested elections have been held, the government resulting from elections like these lacks the de jure as well as de facto power to determine policy in many significant areas because the executive, legislative, and judicial powers are still decisively constrained by an interlocking set of "reserve domains," military "prerogatives," or "authoritarian enclaves."[2]

Third, no regime should be called a democracy unless its rulers govern democratically. If freely elected executives (no matter what the magnitude of their majority) infringe the constitution, violate the rights of individuals and minorities, impinge upon the legitimate functions of the legislature, and thus fail to rule within the bounds of a state of law, their regimes are not democracies.

In sum, when we talk about the consolidation of democracy, we are not dealing with liberalized nondemocratic regimes, or with pseudo-democracies, or with hybrid democracies where some democratic institutions coexist with nondemocratic institutions outside the control of the democratic state. Only democracies can become consolidated democracies.

Let us now turn to examining how, and when, new political systems that meet the three minimal conditions of "stateness," a completed democratic transition, and a government that rules democratically can be considered consolidated democracies.[3]

In most cases after a democratic transition is completed, there are still many tasks that need to be accomplished, conditions that must be established, and attitudes and habits that must be cultivated before democracy can be regarded as consolidated. What, then, are the characteristics of a consolidated democracy? Many scholars, in advancing definitions of consolidated democracy, enumerate all the regime characteristics that would improve the overall quality of democracy. We favor, instead, a narrower definition of democratic consolidation, but one that nonetheless combines behavioral, attitudinal, and constitutional dimensions. Essentially, by a "consolidated democracy" we mean a political regime in which democracy as a complex system of institutions, rules, and patterned incentives and disincentives has become, in a phrase, "the only game in town."[4]

Behaviorally, democracy becomes the only game in town when no significant political group seriously attempts to overthrow the democratic regime or to promote domestic or international violence in order to secede from the state. When this situation obtains, the behavior of the newly elected government that has emerged from the democratic transition is no longer dominated by the problem of how to avoid democratic breakdown. (Exceptionally, the democratic process can be used to achieve secession, creating separate states that can be democracies.) Attitudinally, democracy becomes the only game in town when, even in the face of severe political and economic crises, the overwhelming majority of the people believe that any further political change must emerge from within the parameters of democratic procedures. Constitutionally, democracy becomes the only game in town when all of the actors in the polity become habituated to the fact that political conflict within the state will be resolved according to established norms, and that violations of these norms are likely to be both ineffective and costly. In short, with consolidation, democracy becomes routinized and deeply internalized in social, institutional, and even psychological life, as well as in political calculations for achieving success.

Our working definition of a consolidated democracy is then as follows: *Behaviorally,* a democratic regime in a territory is consolidated when no significant national, social, economic, political, or institutional actors spend significant resources attempting to achieve their objectives by creating a nondemocratic regime or by seceding from the state. *Attitudinally,* a democratic regime is consolidated when a strong majority of public opinion, even in the midst of major economic problems and deep dissatisfaction with incumbents, holds the belief that democratic procedures and institutions are the most appropriate way to govern collective life, and when support for antisystem alternatives is quite small or is more-or-less isolated from prodemocratic forces. *Constitutionally,* a democratic regime is consolidated when governmental and nongovernmental forces alike become subject to, as well as habituated to, the resolution of conflict within the bounds of the specific laws, procedures, and institutions that are sanctioned by the new democratic process.

We must add two important caveats. First, when we say a regime is a consolidated democracy, we do not preclude the possibility that at some future time it could break down. Such a breakdown, however, would be related not to weaknesses or problems specific to the historic process of democratic consolidation, but to a new dynamic in which the democratic regime cannot solve a set of problems, a nondemocratic alternative gains significant supporters, and former democratic regime loyalists begin to behave in a constitutionally disloyal or semiloyal manner.[5]

Our second caveat is that we do not want to imply that there is only one type of consolidated democracy. An exciting new area of research is concerned with precisely this issue—the varieties of consolidated democracies. We also do not want to imply that consolidated democracies could not continue to improve their quality by raising the minimal economic plateau upon which all citizens stand, and by deepening popular participation in the political and social life of the country. Within the category of consolidated democracies, there is a continuum from low-quality to high-quality democracies. Improving the quality of consolidated democracies is an urgent political and intellectual task, but our goal in this essay, though related, is a different one. As we are living in a period in which an unprecedented number of countries have completed democratic transitions and are attempting to consolidate democracies, it is both politically and conceptually important that we understand the specific tasks in "crafting" democratic consolidation. Unfortunately, too much of the discussion of the current "wave" of democratization focuses almost solely on elections or on the presumed democratizing potential of market mechanisms. Democratic consolidation, however, requires much more than elections and markets.

Crafting and Conditions

In addition to a functioning state, five other interconnected and mutually reinforcing conditions must be present, or be crafted, in order for a democracy to be consolidated. First, the conditions must exist for the development of a free and lively *civil society.* Second, there must be a relatively autonomous *political society.* Third, throughout the territory of the state all major political actors, especially the government and the state apparatus, must be effectively subjected to a *rule of law* that protects individual freedoms and associational life. Fourth, there must be a *state bureaucracy* that is usable by the new democratic government. Fifth, there must be an institutionalized *economic society.* Let us explain what is involved in crafting this interrelated set of conditions.

By "civil society," we refer to that arena of the polity where self-organizing and relatively autonomous groups, movements, and individuals attempt to articulate values, to create associations and solidarities, and to advance their interests. Civil society can include manifold social movements (e.g., women's groups, neighborhood associations, religious groupings, and intellectual organizations), as well as associations from all social strata (such as trade unions, entrepreneurial groups, and professional associations).

By "political society," we mean that arena in which political actors compete for the legitimate right to exercise control over public power and the state apparatus. Civil society by itself can destroy a nondemocratic regime, but democratic consolidation (or even a full democratic transition) must involve political society. Democratic consolidation requires that citizens develop an appreciation for the core institutions of a democratic political society—political parties, legislatures, elections, electoral rules, political leadership, and interparty alliances.

It is important to stress not only the difference between civil society and political society, but also their complementarity, which is not always recognized. One of these two arenas is frequently neglected in favor of the other. Worse, within the democratic community, champions of either civil society or political society all too often adopt a discourse and a set of practices that are implicitly inimical to the normal development of the other.

In the recent struggles against the nondemocratic regimes of Eastern Europe and Latin America, a discourse was constructed that emphasized "civil society versus the state"—a dichotomy that has a long philosophical genealogy. More importantly for our purposes, it was also politically useful to those democratic movements emerging in states where explicitly political organizations were forbidden or extremely weak. In many countries, civil society was rightly considered to be the hero of democratic resistance and transition.

The problem arises at the moment of democratic transition. Democratic leaders of political society quite often argue that civil society, having played its historic role, should be demobilized so as to allow for the development of normal democratic politics. Such an argument is not only bad democratic theory, it is also bad democratic politics. A robust civil society, with the capacity to generate political alternatives and to monitor government and state, can help start transitions, help resist reversals, help push transitions to their completion, and help consolidate and deepen democracy. At all stages of the democratization process, therefore, a lively and independent civil society is invaluable.

But we should also consider how to recognize (and thus help overcome) the false opposition sometimes drawn between civil society and political society. The danger posed for the development of political society by civil society is that normative preferences and styles of organization perfectly appropriate to civil society might be taken to be the desirable—or indeed the only legitimate—style of organization for political society. For example, many civil society leaders view "internal conflict" and "division" within the democratic forces with moral antipathy. "Institutional routinization," "intermediaries," and "compromise" within politics are often spoken of pejoratively. But each of the above terms refers to an indispensable practice of political society in a consolidated democracy. Democratic consolidation requires political parties, one of whose primary tasks is precisely to aggregate and represent differences between democrats. Consolidation requires that habituation to the norms and procedures of democratic conflict-regulation be developed. A high degree of institutional routinization is a key part of such a process. Intermediation between the state and civil society, and the structuring of compromise, are likewise legitimate and necessary tasks of political society. In short, political society—informed, pressured, and periodically renewed by civil society—must somehow achieve a workable agreement on the myriad ways in which democratic power will be crafted and exercised.

The Need for a *Rechtsstaat*

To achieve a consolidated democracy, the necessary degree of autonomy of civil and political society must be embedded in, and supported by, our third arena, the rule of law. All significant actors—especially the democratic government and the state apparatus—must be held accountable to, and become habituated to, the rule of law. For the types of civil society and political society we have just described, a rule of law animated by a spirit of constitutionalism is an indispensable condition. Constitutionalism, which should not be confused with majoritarianism, entails a relatively strong consensus regarding the constitution, and especially a commitment to "self-binding" procedures of governance that can be altered only by exceptional majorities. It also requires a clear hierarchy of laws, interpreted by an independent judicial system and supported by a strong legal culture in civil society.[6]

The emergence of a *Rechtsstaat*—a state of law, or perhaps more accurately a state subject to law—was one of the major accomplishments of nineteenth-century liberalism (long before full democratization) in continental Europe and to some extent in Japan. A *Rechtsstaat* meant that the government and the state apparatus would be subject to the law, that areas of discretionary power would be defined and increasingly limited, and that citizens could turn to courts to defend themselves against the state and its officials. The modern *Rechtsstaat* is fundamental in making democratization possible, since without it citizens would not be able to exercise their political rights with full freedom and independence.

A state of law is particularly crucial for the consolidation of democracy. It is the most important continuous and routine way in which the elected government and the state administration are subjected to a network of laws, courts, semiautonomous review and control agencies, and civil-society norms that not only check the state's illegal tendencies but also embed it in an interconnecting web of mechanisms requiring transparency and accountability. Freely elected governments can, but do not necessarily, create such a state of law. The consolidation of democracy, however, requires such a law-bound, constraint-embedded state. Indeed, the more that all the institutions of the state function according to the principle of the state of law, the higher the quality of democracy and the better the society.

Constitutionalism and the rule of law must determine the offices to be filled by election, the procedures to elect those officeholders, and the definition of and limits to their power in order for people to be willing to participate in, and to accept the outcomes of, the democratic game. This may pose a problem if the rules, even if enacted by a majority, are so unfair or poorly crafted and so difficult to change democratically that they are unacceptable to a large number of citizens. For example, an electoral law that gives 80 percent of the seats in parliament to a party that wins less than 50 percent of the vote, or an ideologically loaded constitution that is extremely difficult to amend, is not likely to be conducive to democratic consolidation.

Finally, a democracy in which a single leader enjoys, or thinks he or she enjoys, a "democratic" legitimacy that allows him or her to ignore, dismiss, or alter other institutions—the legislature, the courts, the constitutional limits of power—does not fit our conception of rule of law in a democratic regime. The formal or informal institutionalization of such a system is not likely to result in a consolidated democracy unless such discretion is checked.

Some presidential democracies—with their tendency toward populist, plebiscitarian, "delegative" characteristics, together with a fixed term of office and a "no-reelection" rule that excludes accountability before the electorate—encourage nonconstitutional or anticonstitutional behavior that threatens the rule of law, often democracy itself, and certainly democratic consolidation. A prime minister who develops similar tendencies toward abuse of power is more likely than a president to be checked by other institutions: votes of no confidence by the opposition, or the loss of support by members of his own party. Early elections are a legal vehicle available in parliamentarianism—but unavailable in presidentialism—to help solve crises generated by such abusive leadership.

A Usable Bureaucracy

These three conditions—a lively and independent civil society, a political society with sufficient autonomy and a working consensus about procedures of governance, and constitutionalism and a rule of law—are virtually definitional prerequisites of a consolidated democracy. However, these conditions are much more likely to be satisfied where there are also found a bureaucracy usable by democratic leaders and an institutionalized economic society.

Democracy is a form of governance in which the rights of citizens are guaranteed and protected. To protect the rights of its citizens and to deliver other basic services that citizens demand, a democratic government needs to be able to exercise effectively its claim to a monopoly of the legitimate use of force in its territory. Even if the state had no other functions than these, it would have to tax compulsorily in order to pay for police officers, judges, and basic services. A modern democracy, therefore, needs the effective capacity to command, to regulate, and to extract tax revenues. For this, it needs a functioning state with a bureaucracy considered usable by the new democratic government.

In many territories of the world today—especially in parts of the former Soviet Union—no adequately functioning state exists. Insufficient taxing capacity on the part of the state or a weak normative and bureaucratic "presence" in much of its territory, such that citizens cannot effectively demand that their rights be respected or receive any basic entitlements, is also a great problem in many countries in Latin America, including Brazil. The question of the usability of the state bureaucracy by the new democratic regime also emerges in countries such as Chile, where the outgoing nondemocratic regime was able to give tenure to many key members of the state bureaucracy in politically sensitive areas such as justice and education. Important questions about the usability of the state bureaucracy by new democrats inevitably emerge in cases where the distinction between the communist party and the state had been virtually obliterated (as in much of postcommunist Europe), and the party is now out of power.

Economic Society

The final supportive condition for a consolidated democracy concerns the economy, an arena that we believe should be called "economic society." We use this phrase to call attention to two claims that we believe are theoretically and empirically sound. First, there has never been, and there cannot be, a consolidated democracy that has a command economy (except perhaps in wartime). Second, there has never been, and almost certainly will never be, a modern consolidated democracy with a pure market economy. Modern consolidated democracies require a set of sociopolitically crafted and accepted norms, institutions, and regulations—what we call "economic society"—that mediate between the state and the market.

No empirical evidence has ever been adduced to indicate that a polity meeting our definition of a consolidated democracy has ever existed with a command economy. Is there a theoretical reason to explain such a universal empirical outcome? We think so. On theoretical grounds, our assumption is that at least a nontrivial degree of market autonomy and of ownership diversity in the economy is necessary to produce the independence and liveliness of civil society that allow it to make its contribution to a democracy. Similarly, if all property is in the hands of the state, along with all decisions about pricing, labor, supply, and distribution, the relative autonomy of political society required for a consolidated democracy could not exist.[7]

But why are completely free markets unable to coexist with modern consolidated democracies? Empirically, serious studies of modern polities repeatedly verify the existence of significant degrees of market intervention and state ownership in all consolidated democracies.[8] Theoretically, there are at least three reasons why this should be so. First, notwithstanding certain ideologically extreme but surprisingly prevalent neoliberal claims about the self-sufficiency of the market, pure market economies could neither come into being nor be maintained without a degree of state regulation. Markets require legally enforced contracts, the issuance of money, regulated standards for weights and measures, and the protection of property, both public and private. These requirements dictate a role for the state in the economy. Second, even the best of markets experience "market failures" that must be corrected if the market is to function well.[9] No less an advocate of the "invisible hand" of the market than Adam Smith acknowledged that the state is necessary to perform certain functions. In a crucial but neglected passage

in the *Wealth of Nations,* Adam Smith identified three important tasks
of the state:

> First, the duty of protecting the society from the violence and invasion
> of other independent societies; secondly, the duty of protecting, as far as
> possible, every member of the society from the injustice or oppression of
> every other member of it, or the duty of establishing an exact administra-
> tion of justice; and, thirdly, the duty of erecting and maintaining certain
> public works and certain public institutions which it can never be for the
> interest of any individual, or small number of individuals, to erect and
> maintain; because the profit could never repay the expense to any
> individual or small number of individuals, though it may frequently do
> much more than repay it to a great society.[10]

Finally, and most importantly, democracy entails free public contestation
concerning governmental priorities and policies. If a democracy never
produced policies that generated government-mandated public goods in
the areas of education, health, and transportation, and never provided
some economic safety net for its citizens and some alleviation of gross
economic inequality, democracy would not be sustainable. Theoretically,
of course, it would be antidemocratic to take such public policies off the
agenda of legitimate public contestation. Thus, even in the extreme
hypothetical case of a democracy that began with a pure market
economy, the very working of a modern democracy (and a modern
advanced capitalist economy) would lead to the transformation of that
pure market economy into a mixed economy, or that set of norms,
regulations, policies, and institutions which we call "economic society."[11]

Any way we analyze the problem, democratic consolidation requires
the institutionalization of a politically regulated market. This requires an
economic society, which in turn requires an effective state. Even a goal
such as narrowing the scope of public ownership (i.e., privatization) in
an orderly and legal way is almost certainly carried out more effectively
by a stronger state than by a weaker one. Economic deterioration due
to the state's inability to carry out needed regulatory functions greatly
compounds the problems of economic reform and democratization.[12]

In summary, a modern consolidated democracy can be conceived of
as comprising five major interrelated arenas, each of which, to function
properly, must have its own primary organizing principle. Rightly
understood, democracy is more than a regime; it is an interacting
system. No single arena in such a system can function properly without
some support from another arena, or often from all of the remaining
arenas. For example, civil society in a democracy needs the support of
a rule of law that guarantees to people their right of association, and
needs the support of a state apparatus that will effectively impose legal
sanctions on those who would illegally attempt to deny others that right.
Furthermore, each arena in the democratic system has an impact on

other arenas. For example, political society manages the governmental bureaucracy and produces the overall regulatory framework that guides and contains economic society. In a consolidated democracy, therefore, there are constant mediations among the five principal arenas, each of which is influenced by the others.

Two Surmountable Obstacles

Two of the most widely cited obstacles to democratic consolidation are the dangers posed by ethnic conflict in multinational states and by disappointed popular hopes for economic improvement in states undergoing simultaneous political and economic reform. These are real problems. Democratic theorists and crafters alike must recognize that there is often more than one "awakened nation" present in the state, and that there can be prolonged economic reversals after democratic transition begins. Nonetheless, we are convinced, on both theoretical and empirical grounds, that democracy can still make significant strides toward consolidation under such conditions. We are furthermore convinced that if democratic theorists conceptualize what such obstacles mean and do not mean, this may lessen the dangers of democratic disenchantment and help to identify obstacle-reducing paths. That is our task in the rest of this essay.

Under what empirical conditions do "nation-states" and "democratization" form complementary logics? Under what conditions do they form conflicting logics? If they form conflicting logics, what types of practices and institutions will make democratic consolidation most, or least, likely?

Many political thinkers and activists assume that Weberian states, nation-states, and democracy cohere as part of the very grammar of modern polities. In a world where France, Germany, Portugal, Greece, and Japan are all Weberian states, nation-states, and democracies, such an assumption may seem justified. Yet in many countries that are not yet consolidated democracies, a nation-state policy often has a different logic than a democratic policy. By a nation-state policy we mean one in which the leaders of the state pursue what Rogers Brubaker calls "nationalizing state policies" aimed at increasing cultural homogeneity. Consciously or unconsciously, the leaders send messages that the state should be "of and for" the nation.[13] In the constitutions they write and in the politics they practice, the dominant nation's language becomes the only official language and occasionally the only acceptable language for state business and for education; the religion of the nation is privileged (even if it is not necessarily made the official religion); and the culture of the dominant nation is privileged in state symbols (such as the flag, national anthem, and even eligibility for some types of military service) and in state-controlled means of socialization (such as radio, television, and textbooks). By contrast, democratic policies in the state-making process are those that emphasize a broad and inclusive citizenship that accords equal individual rights to all.

Under what empirical conditions are the logics of state policies aimed at nation-building congruent with those aimed at crafting democracy? Empirically, conflicts between these different policies are reduced when almost all of the residents of a state identify with one subjective idea of the nation, and when that nation is virtually coextensive with the state. These conditions are met only if there is no significant irredenta outside the state's boundaries, if there is only one nation existing (or awakened) in the state, and if there is little cultural diversity within the state. In these circumstances (and, we will argue, virtually *only* in these circumstances) leaders of the government can simultaneously pursue democratization policies and nation-state policies. This congruence between the *polis* and the *demos* facilitates the creation of a democratic nation-state; it also virtually eliminates all problems of "stateness" and should thus be considered a supportive condition for democratic consolidation. Under modern circumstances, however, very few states will begin a possible democratic transition with a high degree of national homogeneity. This lack of homogeneity tends to exacerbate problems of "stateness."

Democracy is characterized not by subjects but by citizens; thus a democratic transition often puts the question of the relation between *polis* and *demos* at the center of politics. From all that has been said thus far, three assertions can be made. First, the greater the extent to which the population of a state is composed of a plurality of national, linguistic, religious, or cultural societies, the more complex politics becomes, since an agreement on the fundamentals of a democracy will be more difficult. Second, while this does not mean that consolidating democracy in multinational or multicultural states is impossible, it does mean that especially careful political crafting of democratic norms, practices, and institutions is required. Third, some methods of dealing with the problems of "stateness" are inherently incompatible with democracy.

Clear thinking on this subject demands that we call into question some facile assumptions. One of the most dangerous ideas for democracy is that "every state should strive to become a nation-state and every nation should become a state." In fact, it is probably impossible for half of the territories in the world that are not now democratic ever to become both "nation-states" and "consolidated democracies," as we have defined these terms. One of the reasons for this is that many existing nondemocratic states are multinational, multilingual, and multicultural. To make them "nation-states" by democratic means would be extremely difficult. In structurally embedded multicultural settings, virtually the only democratic way to create a homogeneous nation-state is through voluntary cultural assimilation, voluntary exit, or peaceful creation and voluntary acceptance of new territorial boundaries. These are empirically and democratically difficult measures, and hence are exceedingly rare.

The other possibilities for creating a homogeneous nation-state in such settings involve subtle (or not-so-subtle) sanctions against those not speaking the language, wearing the attire, or practicing the religion of the titular nation. Under modern circumstances—where all significant groups have writers and intellectuals who disseminate national cultures, where communication systems have greatly increased the possibility for migrants to remain continuously connected to their home cultures, and where modern democratic norms accept a degree of multicultural-ism—such sanctions, even if not formally antidemocratic, would probably not be conducive to democratic crafting.[14] If the titular nation actually wants a truly homogeneous nation-state, a variant of "ethnic cleansing" is too often a temptation.

Another difficulty in the way of building nation-states that are also democracies derives from the manner in which humanity is spatially distributed across the globe. One building block for nations is language. But as Ernest Gellner observed, there are possibly as many as eight thousand languages (not counting important dialects) currently spoken in the world.[15] Even if we assume that only one out of every ten languages is a base for a "reasonably effective" nationalism, there could be as many as eight hundred viable national communities.[16] But cultural, linguistic, and religious groups are not neatly segmented into eight thousand or eight hundred nationalities, each occupying reasonably well defined territories. On the contrary, these groups are profoundly intermixed and overlapping.

We are not arguing against democratically crafted "velvet divorces." We should note, however, that relatively clear cultural boundaries facilitate such territorial separations. Latvia would like to be a nation-state, but in none of its seven most populous cities is Latvian spoken by a majority of the residents. In Tallinn, the capital of Estonia, barely half the people of this aspiring nation-state speak Estonian. For these and many other countries, no simple territorial division or "velvet divorce" is available.[17]

Democracy and Multinational States

Some analysts were happy when the separate nationalities of the USSR became 15 republics, all based on "titular nationalities," on the assumption that democratic nation-states might emerge. In fact, many political leaders in these republics sounded extreme nationalist (rather than democratic) themes in the first elections. One possible formula for diminishing conflict between titular nationalities and "migrants" is what David Laitin calls the "competitive-assimilation game." That is, it becomes in the best interests of some working-class migrants to assimilate in order to enhance the life chances of their children in the new environment. This may happen to Spanish working-class migrants in culturally and economically vibrant Catalonia, but is it likely to occur among Russians in Central Asia? In 1989 in Almaty, the capital of Kazakhstan, Russians constituted 59 percent of the population, and the Kazakhs, the titular nationality, only 22.5 percent. Less than 1 percent of the Russians spoke the titular language. In Bishkek, the capital of Kyrgyzstan, the comparable percentages were virtually identical. In such contexts, shaped by settler colonialism, it is utterly implausible that a nation-state would emerge voluntarily through a process of competitive assimilation.[18]

So how can democracy possibly be achieved in multinational states? We have a strong hypothesis about how *not* to consolidate democracy in multinational settings. The greater the percentage of people in a given state who either were born there or arrived without perceiving themselves as foreign citizens, and who are subsequently denied citizenship in the state (when their life chances would be hurt by such denial), the more unlikely it is that this state will consolidate democracy. Phrased more positively, our hypothesis is that in a multinational, multicultural setting, the chances of consolidating democracy are increased by state policies that grant inclusive and equal citizenship and give all citizens a common "roof" of state-mandated and state-enforced individual rights.

Such multinational states also have an even greater need than other polities to explore a variety of nonmajoritarian, nonplebiscitarian formulas. For example, if there are strong geographic concentrations of different groups within the state, federalism might be an option worth exploring. The state and the society might also allow a variety of publicly supported communal institutions—such as media and schools in different languages, symbolic recognition of cultural diversity, a variety of legally accepted marriage codes, legal and political tolerance for parties representing different communities, and a whole array of political procedures and devices that Arend Lijphart has described as "consociational democracy."[19] Typically, proportional representation, rather than large single-member districts with first-past-the-post elections, can facilitate representation of geographically dispersed minorities. Some strict adherents to the tradition of political liberalism, with its focus on universalism and individual rights, oppose any form of collective rights. But we believe that in a multinational, multicultural society and state, combining collective rights for nationalities or minorities with individual rights fully protected by the state is the least conflictual solution.[20]

Where transitions occur in the context of a nondemocratic, multinational federal system, the crafting of democratic federalism should probably begin with elections at the federal level, so as to generate a legitimate framework for later deliberations on how to decentralize the polity democratically. If the first competitive elections are regional, the elections will tend to favor regional nationalists, and ethnocracies rather than democracies may well emerge.[21] However, the specific ways of structuring political life in multinational settings need to be contextualized in each country. Along these lines, we believe that it is time to reevaluate some past experiments with nonterritorial autonomy such as the kinds of partially self-governing ethnic or religious communities exemplified by the Jewish Kabal of the Polish-Lithuanian Commonwealth, the millets of the Ottoman Empire, or the "national curias" of the late Hapsburg Empire. These mechanisms will not eliminate conflict in multinational states, but they may moderate conflict and help make both the state and democracy more viable.

We also believe that some conceptual, political, and normative attention should be given to the possibility of "state-nations." We call "state-nations" those multicultural or even multinational states that nonetheless still manage to engender strong identification and loyalty from their diverse citizens. The United States is such a multicultural and increasingly multilingual country; Switzerland is another. Neither is strictly speaking a "nation-state," but we believe both could now be called "state-nations." Under Jawaharlal Nehru, India made significant gains in managing multinational tensions by the skillful and consensual use of numerous consociational practices. Through this process India became, in the 1950s and early 1960s, a democratic "state-nation"; but if Hindu nationalists win power in the 1990s and attempt to turn India (with its 115 million Muslims) into a Hindu nation-state, communal violence would almost certainly increase and Indian democracy would be gravely threatened.

Multiple Identities

Let us conclude with a word about "political identities." Many writings on nationalism have focused on "primordial" identities and the need for people to choose between mutually exclusive identities. Our research into political identities, however, has shown two things. First, political identities are not fixed or "primordial" in the *Oxford English Dictionary*'s sense of "existing at (or from) the very beginning." Rather, they are highly changeable and socially constructed. Second, if nationalist politicians (or social scientists and census-takers with crude dichotomous categories) do not force polarization, many people may prefer to define themselves as having multiple and complementary identities.[22] In fact, along with a common political "roof" of state-protected rights for inclusive and equal citizenship, the human capacity for multiple and complementary identities is one of the key factors that makes democracy in multinational states possible. Because political identities are not fixed and permanent, the quality of democratic leadership is particularly important. Multiple and complementary political identities can be nurtured by political leadership, as can polarized and conflictual political identities. Before the conscious use of "ethnic cleansing" as a strategy to construct nation-states in the former Yugoslavia, Sarajevo was a multinational city whose citizens had multiple identities and one of the world's highest interfaith-marriage rates.

Our central proposition is that, if successful democratic consolidation is the goal, would-be crafters of democracy must take into careful consideration the particular mix of nations, cultures, and awakened political identities present in the territory. Some kinds of democracy are possible with one type of *polis*, but virtually impossible if political elites attempt to build another type of *polis*. Political elites in a multinational territory could initiate "nationalizing policies" that might not violate human rights or the Council of Europe's norms for democracy, but would have the effect, in each of the five arenas of the polity, of greatly diminishing the chances of democratic consolidation.

An example of such "nationalizing policies" in each of five arenas would be the following: In the arena of civil society, schooling and mass media could be restricted to the official language. In the arena of political society, nationalizing citizenship laws could lead to a significant overrepresentation of the dominant nationality in elected offices. In the arena of the rule of law, the legal system could subtly privilege a whole range of nationalizing customs, practices, and institutions. In the arena of the state bureaucracy, a rapid changeover to one official language could decrease other nationalities' participation in, and access to, state services. Finally, in the arena of economic society, the titular nationality, as the presumed "owners" of the nation-state, could be given special or even exclusive rights to land redistribution (or voucher distribution, if there was privatization). In contrast, if the real goal is democratic consolidation, a democratizing strategy would require less majoritarian and more consensual policies in each of the above arenas.

A final point to stress concerns timing. Potentially difficult democratic outcomes may be achievable only if some preemptive policies and decisions are argued for, negotiated, and implemented by political leaders. If the opportunity for such ameliorative policies is lost, the range of available space for maneuver will be narrowed, and a dynamic of societal conflict will likely intensify until democratic consolidation becomes increasingly difficult, and eventually impossible.

Problems of Simultaneous Reform

The widely held view that market reform and privatization can legitimate new democracies is based on the dubious assumption that economic improvement can be achieved simultaneously with the installation and legitimation of democratic institutions. We believe that, in countries with imploded command economies, democratic polities can and must be installed and legitimized by a variety of other appeals before the possible benefits of a market economy fully materialize. Many analysts and political advisors dismiss the case for giving priority to state restructuring because they assume that, due to people's demands for material improvements, economic and political gains must not only be pursued but occur simultaneously. Some even argue that simultaneous economic and political reforms are necessary, but that such simultaneity is impossible.[23]

We can call the two opposing perspectives about the relationship between economics and democratization the "tightly coupled" hypothesis and the "loosely coupled" hypothesis. By "loosely coupled," we do not mean that there is no relationship between economic and political perceptions, only that the relationship is not necessarily one-to-one. For at least a medium-range time horizon, people can make independent, and even opposite, assessments about political and economic trends. We further believe that when people's assessments about politics are positive, they can provide a valuable cushion for painful economic restructuring.[24] Let us look at the evidence concerning the relationship between economic growth and democratization in the first five years of postcommunist Europe. Certainly, if we look only at relatively hard economic data, none of the 27 countries in postcommunist Europe except Poland experienced positive growth in 1992. Indeed, in 1993 all postcommunist countries were still well below their 1989 industrial-output levels.[25]

If we look at subjective impressions of economic well-being in six East Central European countries, the mean positive rating (on a +100 to a −100 scale) among those polled between November 1993 and March 1994 was 60.2 for the communist economic system, but was only 37.3 for the postcommunist economic system—a drop of almost 23 points. The tightly coupled hypothesis would predict that attitudes toward the political system would also drop steeply, even if not by the full 23 points. What does the evidence show? The mean positive ranking of the communist political system was 45.7. Thus a one-to-one correlation between the political and economic evaluations would have yielded a positive evaluation of the political system of 22.6. Yet the mean positive ranking for the postcommunist political system, far from falling, rose to 61.5—or 38.9 points higher than a "perfectly coupled" hypothesis would have predicted.[26]

How can we explain such incongruence? First of all, human beings are capable of making separate and correct judgments about a basket of economic goods (which may be deteriorating) and a basket of political goods (which may be improving). In fact, in the same survey the respondents judged that, in important areas directly affected by the democratic political system, their life experiences and chances had overwhelmingly improved, even though they also asserted that their own personal household economic situations had worsened.[27]

We do not believe such incongruence can last forever; it does indicate, however, that in a radical transformation like that occurring in East Central Europe, the deterioration of the economy does not necessarily translate into rapid erosion of support for the political system. The perceived legitimacy of the political system has given democratic institutions in East Central Europe an important degree of insulation from the perceived inefficacy of the new economic system. Indeed, most people in East Central Europe in 1994 had a fairly long time horizon and expressed optimism that by 1999 the performance of both the new democracy and the new economic system would improve significantly.[28]

Thus the evidence in East Central Europe is strongly in favor of the argument that deferred gratification and confidence in the future are possible even when there is an acknowledged lag in economic improvement. Simultaneity of rapid political and economic results is indeed extremely difficult, but fortunately the citizens of East Central Europe did not perceive it as necessary.

Democracy and the Quality of Life

While we believe that it is a good thing for democracies to be consolidated, we should make it clear that consolidation does not necessarily entail either a high-quality democracy or a high-quality society. Democratic institutions—however important—are only one set of public institutions affecting citizens' lives. The courts, the central bank, the police, the armed forces, certain independent regulatory agencies, public-service agencies, and public hospitals are not governed democratically, and their officials are not elected by the citizens. Even in established democracies, not all of these institutions are controlled by elected officials, although many are overseen by them. These institutions operate, however, in a legal framework created by elected bodies and thereby derive their authority from them.

In view of all this, the quality of public life is in great measure a reflection not simply of the democratic or nondemocratic character of the regime, but of the quality of those other institutions.

Policy decisions by democratic governments and legislators certainly affect the quality of life, particularly in the long run, but no democracy can assure the presence of reputable bankers, entrepreneurs with initiative, physicians devoted to their patients, competent professors, creative scholars and artists, or even honest judges. The overall quality of a society is only in small part a function of democracy (or, for that matter, a function of nondemocratic regimes). Yet all of those dimensions of society affect the satisfaction of its citizens, including their satisfaction with the government and even with democracy itself. The feeling that democracy is to blame for all sorts of other problems is likely to be particularly acute in societies in which the distinctive contributions of democracy to the quality of life are not well understood and perhaps not highly valued. The more that democrats suggest that the achievement of democratic politics will bring the attainment of all those other goods, the greater will be the eventual disenchantment.

There are problems specific to the functioning of the state, and particularly to democratic institutions and political processes, that allow us to speak of the quality of democracy separately from the quality of society. Our assumption is that the quality of democracy can contribute positively or negatively to the quality of society, but that the two should not be confused. We as scholars should, in our research, explore both dimensions of the overall quality of life.

NOTES

This essay is largely drawn from our book *Problems of Democratic Transition and Consolidation: Southern Europe, South America, and Post-Communist Europe* (Baltimore: Johns Hopkins University Press, 1996). Interested readers can find more detailed documentation, analysis, and references there. We thank the Ford Foundation and the Carnegie Corporation of New York for help in our research.

1. See Robert A. Dahl, *Polyarchy: Participation and Opposition* (New Haven: Yale University Press, 1971), 3.

2. We document the incomplete status of the Chilean democratic transition in chapter 13 of our book. For military prerogatives, see Alfred Stepan, *Rethinking Military Politics: Brazil and the Southern Cone* (Princeton: Princeton University Press, 1988), 68–127. For the electoralist fallacy in Central America, see Terry Lynn Karl, "The Hybrid Regimes of Central America," *Journal of Democracy* 6 (July 1995): 72–86. Dahl in his *Polyarchy* has an eighth institutional guarantee, which does not address elections as such, but rather the requirement that "[Institutions] for making government policies [should] depend on votes and other expressions of preference" (p. 3). This addresses our concern about reserve domains.

3. Some readers have accused our work—and other studies of democratic transition and consolidation—of being teleological. If this means advocating a single end-state democracy, we decidedly do not share such a view. If, however, teleological means (as the *Oxford English Dictionary* says) "a view that developments are due to the purpose or design that is served by them," our analysis is in part teleological, for we do not believe that structural factors per se lead to democracy and its consolidation. Social actors (and in some measure particular leaders) must also act purposefully to achieve a change of regime leading to some form of governing that can be considered democratic. The design of democracy that these actors pursue may be different from the one resulting from their actions, but without action whose intent is to create "a" democracy (rather than the particular institutionalized form that results), a transition to and consolidation of democracy are difficult to conceive. The processes that we are studying do, therefore, involve a "teleological" element that does not exclude important structural factors (or many unpredictable events). In addition, there is not a single motive but a variety of motives for pursuing democracy (as we define it) as a goal.

4. For other discussions about the concept of democratic consolidation, see Scott Mainwaring, Guillermo O'Donnell, and J. Samuel Valenzuela, eds., *Issues in Democratic Consolidation: The New South American Democracies in Comparative Perspective* (Notre Dame, Ind.: University of Notre Dame Press, 1992).

5. In essence, this means that the literature on democratic breakdown, such as that found in Juan J. Linz and Alfred Stepan, eds., *The Breakdown of Democratic Regimes* (Baltimore: Johns Hopkins University Press, 1978), would be much more directly relevant to analyzing such a phenomenon than this essay or related books on democratic transition and consolidation. This is not a criticism of the transition literature; rather, our point is that the democratic-transition and democratic-breakdown literatures need to be integrated into the overall literature on modern democratic theory. From the perspective of such an integrated theory, the "breakdown of a consolidated democracy" is not an oxymoron.

6. On the relationships between constitutionalism, democracy, legal culture, and "self-bindingness," see Jon Elster and Rune Slagstad, eds., *Constitutionalism and Democracy* (Cambridge: Cambridge University Press, 1988), 1–18.

7. Robert A. Dahl, in a similar argument, talks about two arrows of causation that produce this result; see his "Why All Democratic Countries Have Mixed Economies," in John Chapman and Ian Shapiro, eds., *Democratic Community, Nomos XXXV* (New York: New York University Press, 1993), 259–82.

8. See, for example, John R. Freeman, *Democracies and Market: The Politics of Mixed Economies* (Ithaca, N.Y.: Cornell University Press, 1989).

9. For an excellent analysis of inevitable market failures, see Peter Murrell, "Can Neoclassical Economics Underpin the Reform of Centrally Planned Economies?" *Journal of Economic Perspectives* 5 (1991): 59–76.

10. Adam Smith, *The Wealth of Nations*, 2 vols. (London: J.M. Dent and Sons, Everyman's Library, 1910), 2:180–81.

11. Robert A. Dahl's line of reasoning follows a similar development. See his "Why All Democratic Countries Have Mixed Economies," 259–82.

12. In postcommunist Europe, the Czech Republic and Hungary are well on the way to becoming institutionalized economic societies. In sharp contrast, in Ukraine and Russia the writ of the state does not extend far enough for us to speak of an economic society. The consequences of the lack of an economic society are manifest everywhere. For example, Russia, with a population 15 times larger than Hungary's and with vastly more raw materials, received only 3.6 billion dollars of direct foreign investment in 1992–93, whereas Hungary received 9 billion dollars of direct foreign investment in the same two years.

13. See Rogers Brubaker's "National Minorities, Nationalizing States, and External National Homelands in the New Europe," *Daedalus* 124 (Spring 1995): 107–32.

14. See, for example, the outstanding monograph by Eugen Weber, *Peasants into Frenchmen: The Modernization of Rural France, 1870–1914* (Stanford: Stanford University Press, 1976), which analyzes in extensive detail the wide repertoire of nation-state mandated policies in the schools, the civil service, and the military that were systematically designed to repress and eliminate multilingualism and multiculturalism and to create a nation-state. From today's perspective, similar endeavors of modern states appear far from admirable and represent a cost that many of us would not like to pay. However, it is not just a question of how we evaluate such efforts of state-based nation-building, but of how feasible these efforts are in the contemporary context.

15. See Ernest Gellner, *Nations and Nationalism* (Ithaca, N.Y.: Cornell University Press, 1983), 44.

16. This conjecture is developed by Gellner in *Nations,* 44–45.

17. See the excellent, and sobering, book by Anatol Lieven *The Baltic Revolution: Estonia, Latvia, Lithuania and the Path to Independence* (New Haven: Yale University Press, 1993), 434.

18. For David Laitin's analysis of what he calls a "migrant competitive-assimilation game" in Catalonia, and his analysis of a possible "colonial-settler game" in the Central

Asian republics of the former Soviet Union, see his "The Four Nationality Games and Soviet Politics," *Journal of Soviet Nationalities* 2 (Spring 1991): 1–37.

19. See Arend Lijphart's seminal article "Consociational Democracy," *World Politics* 21 (January 1969): 207–25.

20. For interesting arguments that some notion of group rights is, in fact, necessary to the very definition of some types of individual rights and necessary to the advancement of universal norms in rights, see the work by the Oxford philosopher Joseph Raz *The Morality of Freedom* (Oxford: Oxford University Press, 1986), 165–217. Also see Will Kymlicka, *Multicultural Citizenship: A Liberal Theory of Minority Rights* (Oxford: Oxford University Press, 1995), 107–30.

21. We develop this point in greater detail in our "Political Identities and Electoral Sequences: Spain, the Soviet Union and Yugoslavia," *Daedalus* 121 (Spring 1992): 123–39; and in our *Problems of Democratic Transition and Consolidation* in the chapters on Spain, on "stateness" in the USSR, and on Russian speakers' changing identities in Estonia and Latvia.

22. In our *Problems of Democratic Transition and Consolidation,* we show how in Catalonia in 1982, when respondents were given the opportunity to self-locate their identities on a questionnaire offering the following five possibilities—"Spanish," "more Spanish than Catalan," "equally Spanish and Catalan," "more Catalan than Spanish," or "Catalan"—the most-chosen category, among respondents with both parents born in Catalonia, as well as among respondents with neither parent born in Catalonia, was the multiple and complementary category "equally Spanish and Catalan." We also show how identities in Catalonia were becoming more polarized and conflict-ridden before democratic devolution.

23. The title of a widely disseminated article by Jon Elster captures this perspective; see "The Necessity and Impossibility of Simultaneous Economic and Political Reform," in Douglas Greenberg, Stanley N. Katz, Melanie Beth Oliviero, and Steven C. Wheatley, eds., *Constitutionalism and Democracy: Transitions in the Contemporary World* (Oxford: Oxford University Press, 1993), 267–74.

24. The voters might, owing to negative economic performance, vote incumbents out of office, but the overall economic policies of their successors might well continue to be roughly the same. Poland in 1993–95 and Hungary in 1994–95 come to mind.

25. See our *Problems of Democratic Transition and Consolidation.*

26. See Richard Rose and Christian Haerfer, "New Democracies Barometer III: Learning from What Is Happening," *Studies in Public Policy* No. 230 (1994), questions 22–23, 32–33. Percentages have been rounded off.

27. Rose and Haerfer, "New Democracies," questions 26, 35, 36, 39, 40, and 42.

28. Rose and Haerfer, "New Democracies," questions 24, 26, 34, 35, 36, 39, 40, and 42.

3

DEVELOPMENT AND DEMOCRATIC CULTURE

Robert A. Dahl

Robert A. Dahl *is Sterling Professor of Political Science Emeritus at Yale University. He has served on the council of the American Academy of Arts and Sciences and as president of the American Political Science Association. His publications include* The New American Political (Dis)-Order *(1994),* Democracy and Its Critics *(1989), and* Polyarchy: Participation and Opposition *(1970).*

Juan Linz and Alfred Stepan define a consolidated democracy as a political system in which, among other things, "attitudinally, democracy becomes the only game in town when, even in the face of severe political and economic crises, the overwhelming majority of the people believe that any further political change must emerge from within the parameters of democratic procedures."[1] To put the same point in other terms, the consolidation of democracy requires a strong democratic culture that provides adequate emotional and cognitive support for adhering to democratic procedures.[2]

My focus on a democratic culture reflects two assumptions. First, all political systems, including democratic systems, sooner or later confront severe crises. Second, a robust democratic culture will help to carry a democratic country through its crises. Throughout a crisis, leaders supported by the public continue to adhere to democratic procedures even when the going gets tough. Surviving a crisis may even deepen confidence in democratic procedures.[3]

How, if at all, can a robust democratic culture be created in a country where it has been largely absent or weak, as it is in much of today's nondemocratic world and even in some newer democracies? Important as this question is, we do not seem to have altogether satisfactory answers. Rather than attempt to provide an answer, I will simply comment on one familiar answer that, though highly plausible, seems to me to be misleading.

One interpretation of a great mass of evidence is that an advanced market economy is both a necessary and a sufficient condition for a robust democratic culture. The close empirical link between twentieth-century democracy and the presence of an advanced market economy is beyond dispute. Despite the unquestionable validity of the empirical linkage, however, the exact nature of the relationship among socioeconomic modernization, democratization, and the creation of a democratic culture is almost as puzzling today as it was a quarter-century ago.

It is true that many systemic features of an advanced market economy and society are generally favorable to the development of a democratic culture. These include a stable legal system; considerable decentralization of economic decisions; wide use of information, persuasion, inducements, and rewards rather than open coercion to influence the behavior of economic actors; the creation of a middle class; access to fairly reliable information; and so on. Nonetheless, to assume that an advanced market economy is either strictly necessary or sufficient to create a robust democratic culture would be, I believe, a mistake.

The history of democratization in the United States, Canada, New Zealand, Australia, Switzerland, the Scandinavian countries, and no doubt others surely demonstrates that, well before an advanced market society had arrived, conditions were present for democratization and the development of a robust democratic culture. The systemic features associated with advanced market economies mentioned above were all significantly present in these countries, even when they were preindustrial, predominantly agrarian societies. Well before industrialization, structures already existed that facilitated a transition to democracy and its consolidation through the broad acceptance of democratic ideas and the development of a democratic culture.[4]

It is easy to dismiss this earlier democratic history as irrelevant in today's world. For many countries, perhaps it is. But reflecting on these earlier historical experiences can help us to discern more clearly the kinds of structures that may help to create a democratic culture in a country where it has hitherto been lacking.

Just as an advanced market society is not strictly necessary for the existence of a robust democratic culture, neither is it sufficient. For one thing, the belief systems integral to the structural features of market economies can also generate support for hierarchy and inequality, as they certainly have done in the past and continue to do, for example, in the internal governments of economic enterprises. Even more important, there is no reason to suppose that, as a byproduct of socioeconomic modernization, a democratic political culture will somehow emerge automatically as a kind of political *deus ex machina*.

Two culturally based practices are crucial to the survival of democracy through periods of crisis. First, the main public forces of organized coercion—the military and the police—must be firmly under the control

of democratically elected leaders. A democratic country is unlikely to
make a safe passage through its times of crisis unless this norm is so
deeply implanted that to civilian and military leaders alike the idea of
a military coup is almost literally unthinkable.

A second culturally based practice of crucial importance, and surely
one of the most difficult to sustain in any country, is a tolerance of and,
even more, firm legal protection for conflicting views and beliefs.
Mutual tolerance, however, has its limits. Agreement on the rules of
political life cannot be created or maintained in the face of fundamental
disagreements over the substance of policy or national identity. Ignoring
the complex moral issues, I do not believe we can specify the empirical
limits of mutual toleration with any degree of precision. Yet we surely
know something about the kind of terrain on which the outer limits will
be found. As the periods leading to democratic breakdowns and civil
wars amply demonstrate, political competition over mutually exclusive
ways of life is unlikely to stay within the bounds of mutual toleration.

Three Possible Paths

From the observation that a modern market economy is neither a
necessary nor a sufficient condition for the existence of democracy, it
is only a slight leap to the observation that no unique path links
socioeconomic development, political regime, and democratic culture.

The historical evidence so far seems to be consistent with a number
of possible paths. I want to emphasize three, though I have little doubt
that these greatly oversimplify the historical complexities.

*1) A common Western sequence: Democratization and a democratic
culture precede and ultimately favor socioeconomic development.* As I
suggested earlier, this path was followed by the United States, the
Scandinavian countries, and a good many others. It is so familiar to us
that perhaps I need say nothing more about it.

*2) An authoritarian-modernization sequence: Socioeconomic develop-
ment precedes and favors democratization and a democratic culture.* A
schematic account of an authoritarian-modernization process leading to
democratization would go as follows. By bringing about an advanced
market economy with the key features described earlier, the authoritarian
regimes create conditions that, in turn, stimulate demands for democratization among elites and the broader public. Previous forms of coercion
become more and more difficult, dangerous, and costly for the leaders
to impose on an increasingly mobilized, informed, and self-confident
public. The leadership itself is split between hard-liners and soft-liners.
That is, having instigated, witnessed, and even participated in the
benefits of the new social and economic order in which they now live,
some of the top leaders of the authoritarian regime, perhaps forming a
decisive soft-line faction, are no longer willing to take hard-line actions

that could seriously risk the previous achievements of the regime, particularly in economic expansion.

Political discussion—which has already become widespread, if circumspect—now becomes even more widely tolerated. The press, already somewhat unconstrained, is unshackled. Opposition leaders are allowed to participate in political life. Clandestine political movements become political parties. A constitution is adopted. Then, in the most critical move of all, relatively free and fair elections are held. Elected officials drawn from the older regime or from the democratic opposition now govern more or less in conformity with democratic practices and institutions. In sum, the authoritarian regime has given way to a substantially democratic government.

3) Democratization occurs incrementally as economic, social, and political developments mutually reinforce one another. To take a hypothetical example: The leaders deliberately seek to create elements of a market economy, foster exports, and stimulate rapid economic growth. Taking advantage of the new opportunities, entrepreneurs, businessmen, and financiers spring up. These groups then put pressure on the leaders for further expansion of the market sectors. Because of the benefits conferred by growth, the leaders respond. As a result, urbanization increases, the agricultural sector shrinks, and the middle and working classes expand. Demands arise for more education, specialized skills, and access to information and means of communication. The leaders respond. A new and now large urban middle class demands greater freedom of speech, press, and access to information. Opportunities for communication and expression, whether legal, quasi-legal, or technically illegal, expand further. Demands begin to surface for the rule of law, fair elections, a responsive legislature, constitutional reform, and so on. Thus the country reaches a threshold at which the leadership must either yield to the demand for democratization or face the prospect of reinstalling a repressive regime that, lacking legitimacy and the capacity to ensure further economic growth, would suffer from disorder, violent opposition, or perhaps revolution. The leaders yield; thus a democratic transition is completed in a country that now has a large, literate, educated population ready to support democratic ideas and practices.

Although this description is schematic and hypothetical, it seems to be a 'somewhat more accurate summary of the authoritarian-modernization sequence than the one described above and is consistent, I think, with descriptions of the process in Asia. My previous schematic account of the authoritarian-modernization sequence could easily be recast to reflect the incremental, mutually reinforcing course of development.

I find it interesting, too, that an incremental formulation seems closer to the experience of many of the Western democratic countries than the rigid sequence suggested in the first scenario above. For example, it fits better with the expansion of the suffrage, the development of political parties, and the growth of a democratic political culture as well.

I offer several tentative conclusions that we may reasonably draw about the relationship between political culture and socioeconomic development. First, even though an advanced market society brings with it many structures and beliefs that are helpful to democratization, such a market society is neither strictly necessary nor sufficient for creating a political culture that will be robust enough to preserve democracy through its inevitable times of crisis and conflict.

Second, there is, in fact, no single path leading from a nondemocratic regime to the inauguration of democratic political institutions. Although different from the common Western sequence, the authoritarian-modernization sequence has led to significant democratization in several countries, notably South Korea and Taiwan.

Third, because the institutional requirements for modern democracy are by now well known and do not need to be reinvented, the process of democratic transition and consolidation need not require as much time as it took to achieve these ends in most Western countries. Even with a faster rate of modernization, in a country with little or no previous democratic experience, the process is not brief. In South Korea and in Taiwan, for example, democratization has taken almost 40 years.[5]

Fourth, although introducing democratic institutions to a country without significant prior experience with democracy marks an extraordinary change, it does not ensure that those institutions will be grounded in a robust democratic culture. Introducing democratic political institutions is an important step along the path toward the consolidation of a stable democratic system, but it is not sufficient to create a political culture that will be strongly supportive of democracy.[6]

Fifth, because no two countries have identical historical experiences, it is unreasonable to suppose that all democratic countries will possess identical political cultures. Political cultures appear to vary considerably among democratic countries in Europe and America,[7] and they are likely to differ even more elsewhere.

Sixth, if the political institutions of a country are not supported by a strong democratic political culture, they may give way to authoritarianism when the country faces a severe crisis. And sooner or later, virtually all countries face severe crises.

NOTES

This essay draws heavily from my "Political Culture and Economic Development," in Ragnvald Kalleberg and Frederik Engelstad, eds., *Social Time and Social Change: Historical Aspects in the Social Sciences* (forthcoming).

1. See Juan J. Linz and Alfred Stepan's chapter in this collection, 15.

2. By "culture," I mean a body of norms that guide behavior, values that influence

judgments, and cognitive maps that are widespread and tend to persist from generation to generation. This loose definition is roughly consistent with that provided by A.L. Kroeber and Clyde Kluckhohn in 1952 after they reviewed several hundred definitions of "culture" in an effort to arrive at a concept that would be generally acceptable. See Milton Singer, "Culture: The Concept of Culture," in David Sills, ed., *International Encyclopedia of the Social Sciences* (New York: Macmillan, 1968), 527–43.

3. My second assumption is just that—an assumption. The methodological problems of verifying the assumption are acute, as the empirical proposition easily becomes circular. How do we know that the political culture, or system of political beliefs, in a democratic country is robust enough to provide adequate support for democratic procedures even during a severe crisis? We know this because democracy survived the crisis. Why did democracy survive? It survived because of the strength of democratic beliefs. Although the proposition is not inherently circular, the relative strength of beliefs is hard to determine. If a democratic country has weathered many crises in the past, it is reasonable to infer that democratic beliefs and culture are strong enough to support democratic procedures through yet another crisis. If the democratic transition is recent, however, how can we determine the depth and strength of democratic beliefs? Perhaps, then, we can judge that democratic consolidation has occurred in a country only after it has gone through a severe crisis that its democratic institutions have survived intact.

4. Gordon S. Wood concludes from recent historical studies that an agricultural market economy did not emerge in New England until the 1780s. He argues further that it was the change in political institutions and ideas that resulted in the region's "explosion of entrepreneurial power" in agriculture. See "Inventing American Capitalism," *New York Review of Books,* 6 June 1994, 44, 49.

5. I have not discussed the costs of authoritarian modernization, or of modernization generally. It is important to keep in mind, however, that these are heavy. Amartya Sen points out that, although life expectancy is higher in China than in India, since India achieved independence there have been no substantial famines there, a fact he attributes to the existence of a multiparty democratic system. By contrast, the Chinese famines of 1958–61 killed close to 30 million people, as cited in "Freedoms and Needs," *New Republic,* 10 and 17 January 1994, 31–38.

6. The extent to which post-Confucian culture may impede the development and deepening of a democratic culture is the subject of considerable discussion. Sung Chul Yang describes "persisting undemocratic values and behaviors" in South Korea in *The North and South Korean Political Systems: A Comparative Analysis* (Boulder, Colo.: Westview, 1994). See also Chaibong Hahm, "Democracy and Authority in the Post-Confucian Context," in Sung Chul Yang, ed., *Democracy and Communism: Theory, Reality and the Future* (Seoul: Korean Association of International Studies, 1995), 343–58; and Daniel A. Bell, "Democracy in Confucian Societies: The Challenge of Justification," in Bell et al., eds., *Towards Illiberal Democracy in Pacific Asia* (New York: St. Martin's, 1995), 17–40. A more positive assessment is by Lee Teng-hui, president of the Republic of China, in his contribution to this collection.

7. For variations in attitudes toward the scope of government among European countries, see Ole Borre and Elinor Scarbrough, eds., *The Scope of Government* (Oxford: Oxford University Press, 1995); for comparisons that include the United States, see Russell J. Dalton, *Citizen Politics, Public Opinion and Political Parties in Western Democracies,* 2nd ed. (Chatham, N.J.: Chatham House, 1996).

4

ILLUSIONS ABOUT CONSOLIDATION

Guillermo O'Donnell

Guillermo O'Donnell *is Helen Kellogg Professor of Government and International Studies at the University of Notre Dame. His books include* Modernization and Bureaucratic-Authoritarianism *(1979);* Bureaucratic Authoritarianism: Argentina, 1966–1973, in Comparative Perspective *(1988); and, with Philippe Schmitter and Laurence Whitehead,* Transitions from Authoritarian Rule *(1986).*

Democracies used to be few in number, and most were located in the northwestern quarter of the world. Over the last two decades, however, many countries have rid themselves of authoritarian regimes. There are many variations among these countries. Some of them have reverted to new brands of authoritarianism (even if from time to time they hold elections), while others have clearly embraced democracy. Still others seem to inhabit a gray area; they bear a family resemblance to the old established democracies, but either lack or only precariously possess some of their key attributes. The bulk of the contemporary scholarly literature tells us that these "incomplete" democracies are failing to become consolidated, or institutionalized.

This poses two tasks. One is to establish a cutoff point that separates all democracies from all nondemocracies. This point's location depends on the questions we ask, and so is always arbitrary. Many different definitions of democracy have been offered.[1] The one that I find particularly useful is Robert Dahl's concept of "polyarchy." Once a reasonably well delimited set of democracies is obtained, the second task is to examine the criteria that a given stream of the literature uses for comparing cases within this set. If the criteria are found wanting, the next step is to propose alternative concepts for these comparisons. This is what I attempt in this essay, albeit in preliminary and schematic fashion.

Contemporary Latin America is my empirical referent, although my discussion probably also applies to various newly democratized countries in other parts of the world. The main argument is that, contrary to what most current scholarship holds, the problem with many new polyarchies is not that they lack institutionalization. Rather, the way in which political scientists usually conceptualize some institutions prevents us from recognizing that these polyarchies actually have two extremely important institutions. One is highly formalized, but intermittent: elections. The other is informal, permanent, and pervasive: particularism (or clientelism, broadly defined). An important fact is that, in contrast to previous periods of authoritarian rule, particularism now exists in uneasy tension with the formal rules and institutions of what I call the "full institutional package" of polyarchy. These arguments open up a series of issues that in future publications I will analyze with the detail and nuance they deserve. My purpose at present is to furnish some elements of what I believe are needed revisions in the conceptual and comparative agenda for the study of all existing polyarchies, especially those that are *informally institutionalized*.[2]

Polyarchy, as defined by Dahl, has seven attributes: 1) elected officials; 2) free and fair elections; 3) inclusive suffrage; 4) the right to run for office; 5) freedom of expression; 6) alternative information; and 7) associational autonomy.[3] Attributes 1 to 4 tell us that a basic aspect of polyarchy is that elections are inclusive, fair, and competitive. Attributes 5 to 7 refer to political and social freedoms that are minimally necessary not only during but also between elections as a condition for elections to be fair and competitive. According to these criteria, some countries of Latin America currently are not polyarchies: the Dominican Republic, Haiti, and Mexico have recently held elections, but these were marred by serious irregularities before, during, and after the voting.

Other attributes need to be added to Dahl's list. One is that elected (and some appointed) officials should not be arbitrarily terminated before the end of their constitutionally mandated terms (Peru's Alberto Fujimori and Russia's Boris Yeltsin may have been elected in fair elections, but they abolished polyarchy when they forcefully closed their countries' congresses and fired their supreme courts). A second addition is that the elected authorities should not be subject to severe constraints, vetoes, or exclusion from certain policy domains by other, nonelected actors, especially the armed forces.[4] In this sense, Guatemala and Paraguay, as well as probably El Salvador and Honduras, do not qualify as polyarchies.[5] Chile is an odd case, where restrictions of this sort are part of a constitution inherited from the authoritarian regime. But Chile clearly meets Dahl's seven criteria of polyarchy. Peru is another doubtful case, since the 1995 presidential elections were not untarnished, and the armed forces retain tutelary powers over various policy areas. Third, there should be an uncontested national territory that clearly defines the voting population.[6] Finally, an appropriate definition of polyarchy should also include an intertemporal dimension: the generalized expectation that a fair electoral process and its surrounding freedoms will continue into an indefinite future.

These criteria leave us with the three polyarchies—Colombia, Costa Rica, and Venezuela—whose origins date from before the wave of democratization that began in the mid-1970s, and with nine others that resulted from this wave: Argentina, Bolivia, Brazil, Ecuador, Nicaragua, Panama, Uruguay and, with the caveats noted, Chile and Peru. Only in the oldest Latin American polyarchy (Costa Rica) and in two cases of redemocratization (Chile and Uruguay) do the executive branch, congress, parties, and the judiciary function in a manner that is reasonably close to their formal institutional rules, making them effective institutional knots in the flow of political power and policy. Colombia and Venezuela used to function like this, but do so no longer. These two countries, jointly with Argentina, Bolivia, Brazil, Ecuador, Nicaragua, Panama, and Peru—a set that includes a large majority of the Latin American population and GNP—function in ways that current democratic theory has ill prepared us to understand.

We must go back to the definition of polyarchy. This definition, precise in regard to elections (attributes 1 to 4) and rather generic about contextual freedoms (attributes 5 to 7), is mute with respect to institutional features such as parliamentarism or presidentialism, centralism or federalism, majoritarianism or consensualism, and the presence or absence of a written constitution and judicial review. Also, the definition of polyarchy is silent about important but elusive themes such as if, how, and to what degree governments are responsive or accountable to citizens between elections, and the degree to which the rule of law extends over the country's geographic and social terrain.[7] These silences are appropriate: the definition of polyarchy, let us recall, establishes a crucial cutoff point—one that separates cases where there exist inclusive, fair, and competitive elections and basic accompanying freedoms from all others, including not only unabashed authoritarian regimes but also countries that hold elections but lack some of the characteristics that jointly define polyarchy.

Among polyarchies, however, there are many variations. These differences are empirical, but they can also be normatively evaluated, and their likely effect on the survival prospects of each polyarchy may eventually be assessed. These are important issues that merit some conceptual clarification.

By definition, all the Latin American cases that I have labeled poly-archies are such because of a simple but crucial fact: elections are institutionalized. By an institution I mean a regularized pattern of interaction that is known, practiced, and accepted (if not necessarily approved) by actors who expect to continue interacting under the rules sanctioned and backed by that pattern.[8] Institutions are typically taken for granted, in their existence and continuity, by the actors who interact with and through them. Institutions are "there," usually unquestioned regulators of expectations and behavior. Sometimes, institutions become complex organizations: they are supposed to operate under highly formalized and explicit rules, and materialize in buildings, rituals, and officials. These are the institutions on which both "prebehavioral" and most of contemporary neo-institutionalist political science focus. An unusual characteristic of elections *qua* institutions is that they are highly formalized by detailed and explicit rules, but function intermittently and do not always have a permanent organizational embodiment.

In all polyarchies, old and new, elections are institutionalized, both in themselves and in the reasonable[9] effectiveness of the surrounding conditions of freedom of expression, access to alternative information, and associational autonomy. Leaders and voters take for granted that in the future inclusive, fair, and competitive elections will take place as legally scheduled, voters will be properly registered and free from physical coercion, and their votes will be counted fairly. It is also taken for granted that the winners will take office, and will not have their terms arbitrarily terminated. Furthermore, for this electoral process to exist, freedom of opinion and of association (including the freedom to form political parties) and an uncensored media must also exist. Countries where elections do not have these characteristics do not qualify as polyarchies.[10]

Most students of democratization agree that many of the new polyarchies are at best poorly institutionalized. Few seem to have institutionalized anything but elections, at least in terms of what one would expect from looking at older polyarchies. But appearances can be misleading, since other institutions may exist, even though they may not be the ones that most of us would prefer or easily recognize.

Theories of "Consolidation"

When elections and their surrounding freedoms are institutionalized, it might be said that polyarchy (or political democracy) is "consolidated," that is, likely to endure. This, jointly with the proviso of absence of veto powers over elected authorities, is the influential definition of "democratic consolidation" offered by Juan J. Linz, who calls it a state of affairs "in which none of the major political actors, parties, or organized interests, forces, or institutions consider that there is any alternative to democratic processes to gain power, and . . . no political institution or group has a claim to veto the action of democratically elected decision makers. . . . To put it simply, democracy must be seen as the 'only game in town.'"[11] This minimalist definition has important advantages. Still, I see little analytical gain in attaching the term "consolidated" to something that will probably though not certainly endure—"democracy" and "consolidation" are terms too polysemic to make a good pair.

Other authors offer more expanded definitions of democratic consolidation, many of them centered on the achievement of a high degree of "institutionalization."[12] Usually these definitions do not see elections as an institution.[13] They focus on complex organizations, basically the executive, parties, congress, and sometimes the judiciary. Many valuable studies have been conducted from this point of view. By the very logic of their assessment of many new polyarchies as noninstitutionalized, however, these studies presuppose, as their comparative yardstick, a generic and somewhat idealized view of the old polyarchies. The meaning of such a yardstick perplexes me: often it is unclear whether it is something like an average of characteristics observed within the set of old polyarchies, or an ideal type generated from some of these characteristics, or a generalization to the whole set of the characteristics of some of its members, or a normative statement of preferred traits. Furthermore, this mode of reasoning carries a strong teleological flavor. Cases that have not "arrived" at full institutionalization, or that do not seem to be moving in this direction, are seen as stunted, frozen, protractedly unconsolidated, and the like. Such a view presupposes that there are, or should be, factors working in favor of increased consolidation or institutionalization, but that countervailing "obstacles" stymie a process of change that otherwise would operate unfettered.[14] That some of these polyarchies have been in a state of "protracted unconsolidation"[15] for some 20 years suggests that there is something extremely odd about this kind of thinking.

A recently published book on democratic consolidation in Southern Europe is a case in point.[16] This is the first in a series of five volumes, resulting from an eight-year project that involved, as coauthors and discussants, many of the most active and distinguished students of democratization. The introduction (pp. 1–32) and the conclusions (pp. 389–413) by the coeditors and codirectors of the project offer an impressively learned distillation of these extensive scholarly exchanges. These texts are also paradigmatic of the views that I am criticizing. The editors use the concept of "*trajectories* of democratic transitions and consolidations," with which, even though they warn that it "should in no way be understood as implying a deterministic conceptual bias," they intend to "capture and highlight the particular combination and interplay of freedom and constraint *at each successive stage of the democratization process*" (p. xvi, emphasis added). Further on, they state, "We regard *continued movement towards the ideal type of democratic consolidation* as very significant" (p. 9, emphasis added). Consistent with this view, most of Latin America—in contrast to Southern European countries that the authors say became consolidated democracies in part because they "leap-frogged" democratization and developmental *stages*—

is seen as "*still* struggling with transitional problems of varying, and often major, magnitude and intensity" (pp. xiv–xvi, emphasis added). An exception is Chile, where the transition is "*moving towards consolidation*" (p. 19, emphasis added), and "seems to be *well on its way to successful completion*" (p. 389, emphasis added). The Southern European countries, after achieving consolidation, are said to be entering yet another stage of "democratic persistence," which is the "end product of a long democratization process" (p. xiii).

One way or the other, polyarchies that are seen as unconsolidated, noninstitutionalized, or poorly institutionalized are defined negatively, for what they lack: the type and degree of institutionalization presumably achieved by old polyarchies. Yet negative definitions shift attention away from building typologies of polyarchies on the basis of the specific, positively described traits of each type.[17] Such typologies are needed, among other purposes, for assessing each type's likelihood of endurance, for exploring its patterns of change, and for clarifying the various dimensions on which issues of quality and performance of polyarchy may be discussed and researched.

There is no theory that would tell us why and how the new polyarchies that have institutionalized elections will "complete" their institutional set, or otherwise become "consolidated." All we can say at present is that, as long as elections are institutionalized, polyarchies are likely to endure. We can add the hypothesis that this likelihood is greater for polyarchies that are formally institutionalized. But this proposition is not terribly interesting unless we take into account other factors that most likely have strong independent effects on the survival chances of polyarchies.[18] Consequently, calling some polyarchies "consolidated" or "highly institutionalized" may be no more than saying that they are institutionalized in ways that one expects and of which one approves. Without a theory of how and why this may happen, it is at best premature to expect that newer polyarchies will or should become "consolidated" or "highly institutionalized." In any event, such a theory· can only be elaborated on the basis of a positive description of the main traits of the pertinent cases.

The Importance of Informal Rules

Polyarchy is the happy result of centuries-long processes, mostly in countries in the global Northwest. In spite of many variations among these countries, polyarchy is embodied in an institutional package: a set of rules and institutions (many of them complex organizations) that is explicitly formalized in constitutions and auxiliary legislation. Rules are supposed to guide how individuals in institutions, and individuals interacting with institutions, behave. The extent to which behavior and expectations hew to or deviate from formal rules is difficult to gauge empirically. But when the fit is reasonably close, formal rules simplify our task; they are good predictors of behavior and expectations. In this case, one may conclude that all or most of the formal rules and institutions of polyarchy are fully, or close to fully, institutionalized.[19] When the fit is loose or practically nonexistent, we are confronted with the double task of describing actual behavior and discovering the (usually informal) rules that behavior and expectations do follow. Actors are as rational in these settings as in highly formalized ones, but the contours of their rationality cannot be traced without knowing the actual rules, and the common knowledge of these rules, that they follow. One may define this situation negatively, emphasizing the lack of fit between formal rules and observed behavior. As anthropologists have long known, however, this is no substitute for studying the actual rules that are being followed; nor does it authorize the assumption that somehow there is a tendency toward increasing compliance with formal rules. This is especially true when informal rules are widely shared and deeply rooted; in this case, it may be said that these rules (rather than the formal ones) are highly institutionalized.[20]

To some extent this also happens in the old polyarchies. The various laments, from all parts of the ideological spectrum, about the decay of democracy in these countries are largely a consequence of the visible and apparently increasing gap between formal rules and the behavior of all sorts of political actors. But the gap is even larger in many new polyarchies, where the formal rules about how political institutions are supposed to work are often poor guides to what actually happens.

Many new polyarchies do not lack institutionalization, but a fixation on highly formalized and complex organizations prevents us from seeing an extremely influential, informal, and sometimes concealed institution: clientelism and, more generally, particularism. For brevity's sake, I will put details and nuances aside[21] and use these terms to refer broadly to various sorts of nonuniversalistic relationships, ranging from hierarchical particularistic exchanges, patronage, nepotism, and favors to actions that, under the formal rules of the institutional package of polyarchy, would be considered corrupt.[22]

Particularism—like its counterparts, neopatrimonial[23] and delegative conceptions and practices of rule—is antagonistic to one of the main aspects of the full institutional package of polyarchy: the behavioral, legal, and normative distinction between a public and a private sphere. This distinction is an important aspect of the formal institutionalization of polyarchy. Individuals performing roles in political and state institutions are supposed to be guided not by particularistic motives but by universalistic orientations to some version of the public good. The boundaries between the public and the private are often blurred in the old polyarchies, but the very notion of the boundary is broadly accepted and, often, vigorously asserted when it seems breached by public officials acting from particularistic motives. Where particularism is pervasive, this notion is weaker, less widely held, and seldom enforced.

But polyarchy matters, even in the institutional spheres that, against their formal rules, are dominated by particularism. In congress, the judiciary, and some actions of the executive, rituals and discourses are performed as if the formal rules were the main guides of behavior. The consequences are twofold. On one side, by paying tribute to the formal rules, these rituals and discourses encourage demands that these rules be truly followed and that public-oriented governmental behavior prevail. On the other side, the blatant hypocrisy of many of these rituals and discourses breeds cynicism about the institutions of polyarchy, their incumbents, and "politicians" in general. As long as this second consequence is highly visible, particularism is taken for granted, and practiced as the main way of gaining and wielding political power. In such polyarchies, particularism is an important part of the regime.[24] Polyarchies are regimes, but not all polyarchies are the same kind of regime.

Here we see the ambiguity of the assertion made by Juan J. Linz, Adam Przeworski,[25] and others who argue that consolidation occurs when democracy becomes "the only game in town." It is clear that these authors are referring to the formal rules of polyarchy. More generally, even though they may not refer to "institutionalization," authors who limit themselves to the term "consolidation" also assert, more or less implicitly, the same close fit between formal rules and actual behavior.[26] For example, Przeworski argues that democratic consolidation occurs "when no one can imagine acting outside the democratic institutions." But this does not preclude the possibility that the games played "inside" the democratic institutions are different from the ones dictated by their formal rules. Przeworski also states: "To put it somewhat more technically, democracy is consolidated when compliance—acting within the institutional framework—constitutes the equilibrium of the decentralized strategies of all the relevant forces."[27] Clearly, Przeworski is assuming that there is only one equilibrium, the one generated by a close fit between formal rules and behavior. Yet however inferior they may be in terms of performances and outcomes that we value, the situations that I am describing may constitute an equilibrium, too.[28]

A Theoretical Limbo

If the main criterion for democratic consolidation or institutionalization is more or less explicitly a reasonably close fit between formal rules and actual behavior, then what of countries such as Italy, Japan, and India? These are long-enduring polyarchies where, by all indications, various forms of particularism are rampant. Yet these cases do not appear problematic in the literature I am discussing. That they are listed as "consolidated" (or, at least, not listed as "unconsolidated") suggests the strength—and the inconsistency—of this view. It attaches the label "consolidated" to cases that clearly do not fit its arguments but that have endured for a significantly longer period than the new polyarchies have so far. This is a typical paradigmatic anomaly. It deals with these cases by relegating them to a theoretical limbo,[29] as if, because they are somehow considered to be "consolidated," the big gaps between their formal rules and behavior were irrelevant. This is a pity, because variations that are theoretically and empirically important for the study of the whole set of existing polyarchies are thereby obscured.

Another confusing issue is raised by the requirement of "legitimacy" that some definitions of consolidation add. Who must accept formal democratic rules, and how deep must this acceptance run? Here, the literature oscillates between holding that only certain leaders need adhere to democratic principles and arguing that most of the country's people should be democrats, and between requiring normative acceptance of these principles and resting content with a mere perception that there is no feasible alternative to democracy. The scope of this adherence is also problematic: Is it enough that it refers to the formal institutions of the regime, or should it extend to other areas, such as a broadly shared democratic political culture?

Given these conceptual quandaries, it is not surprising that it is impossible clearly to specify when a democracy has become "consolidated." To illustrate this point, consider the "tests" of democratic consolidation that Gunther, Diamandouros, and Puhle propose. These tests supposedly help them to differentiate the consolidated Southern European cases from the unconsolidated Latin American, as well as East European and Asian, ones. The indicators that "may constitute evidence that a regime is consolidated" are: 1) "alternation in power between former rivals";[30] 2) "continued widespread support and stability during times of extreme economic hardship"; 3) "successful defeat and punishment of a handful of strategically placed rebels"; 4) "regime stability in the face of a radical restructuring of the party system"; and 5) "the absence of a politically significant antisystem party or social movement" (pp. 12–13).

With respect to Latin America, it bears commenting in relation to each of these points that: 1) alternations in government through peaceful electoral processes have occurred in Latin America as frequently as in Southern Europe; 2) in the former, support for regime stability has persisted—in Argentina, Brazil, and Bolivia, among other countries—even in the face of far more acute recessions than Southern Europe has seen, and in the midst of quadruple-digit inflation; 3) the record of punishment is poor, albeit with important exceptions in both regions; 4) even when thinking about Italy today, it is hard to imagine party-system restructurings more radical than the ones that occurred in

Bolivia, Brazil, and Ecuador; and 5) "antisystem" political parties are as absent from the Latin American as from the Southern European polyarchies. The indicators of democratic consolidation invoked by these authors (and shared by many others) suffer from extreme ambiguity.[31] Finally, one might note that their argument points toward a *reductio ad absurdum*, for one could in following its logic argue that Latin America's polyarchies are actually "more consolidated" because they have endured more "severe tests" (p. 12) than their Southern European counterparts.

Polyarchies, Particularism, and Accountability

It almost goes without saying that all actual cases exhibit various combinations of universalism and particularism across various relevant dimensions. This observation, however, should not lead to the Procrustean solution of lumping all cases together; differences in the degree to which each case approximates either pole may justify their separate classification and analysis. Of course, one may for various reasons prefer a political process that adheres quite closely to the formal rules of the full institutional package of polyarchy. Yet there exist polyarchies—some of them as old as Italy, India, and Japan, or in Latin America, Colombia, and Venezuela—that endure even though they do not function as their formal rules dictate. To understand these cases we need to know what games are really being played, and under what rules.

In many countries of the global East and South, there is an old and deep split between the *pays réel* and the *pays légal*. Today, with many of these countries claiming to be democracies and adopting a constitutional framework, the persistence and high visibility of this split may not threaten the survival of their polyarchies—but neither does it facilitate overcoming the split. Institutions are resilient, especially when they have deep historical roots; particularism is no exception. Particularism is a permanent feature of human society; only recently, and only in some places and institutional sites, has it been tempered by universalistic norms and rules. In many new polyarchies, particularism vigorously inhabits most formal political institutions, yet the incumbency of top government posts is decided by the universalistic process of fairly counting each vote as one. This may sound paradoxical but it is not; it means that these are polyarchies, but they are neither the ones that the theory of democracy had in mind as it grew out of reflection on the political regimes of the global Northwest, nor what many studies of democratization assume that a democracy should be or become.

That some polyarchies are informally institutionalized has important consequences. Here I want to stress one that is closely related to the blurring of the boundary between the private and the public spheres: accountability, a crucial aspect of formally institutionalized polyarchy, is seriously hindered. To be sure, the institutionalization of elections means that retrospective electoral accountability exists, and a reasonably free press and various active segments of society see to it that some egregiously unlawful acts of government are exposed (if seldom punished). Polyarchy, even if not formally institutionalized, marks a huge improvement over authoritarian regimes of all kinds. What is largely lacking, however, is another dimension of accountability, which I call "horizontal." By this I mean the controls that state agencies are supposed to exercise over other state agencies. All formally institutionalized polyarchies include various agencies endowed with legally defined authority to sanction unlawful or otherwise inappropriate actions by other state agents. This is an often-overlooked expression of the rule of law in one of the areas where it is hardest to implant, that is, over state agents, especially high-ranking officials. The basic idea is that formal institutions have well-defined, legally established boundaries that delimit the proper exercise of their authority, and that there are state agencies empowered to control and redress trespasses of these boundaries by any official or agency. These boundaries are closely related to the private-public boundary, in that those who perform public roles are supposed to follow universalistic and public-oriented rules, rather than their own particular interests. Even though its actual functioning is far from perfect, this network of boundaries and accountabilities is an important part of the formal institutionalization of the full package of polyarchy.[32]

By contrast, little horizontal accountability exists in most new polyarchies. Furthermore, in many of them the executive makes strenuous, and often successful, efforts to erode whatever horizontal accountability does exist. The combination of institutionalized elections, particularism as a dominant political institution, and a big gap between the formal rules and the way most political institutions actually work makes for a strong affinity with delegative, not representative, notions of political authority. By this I mean a caesaristic, plebiscitarian executive that once elected sees itself as empowered to govern the country as it deems fit. Reinforced by the urgencies of severe socio-economic crises and consonant with old *volkisch*, nonindividualistic conceptions of politics, delegative practices strive headlong against formal political institutionalization; congress, the judiciary, and various state agencies of control are seen as hindrances placed in the way of the proper discharge of the tasks that the voters have delegated to the executive. The executive's efforts to weaken these institutions, invade their legal authority, and lower their prestige are a logical corollary of this view.[33] On the other hand, as Max Weber warned, institutions deprived of real power and responsibility tend to act in ways that seem to confirm the reasons adduced for this deprivation. In the cases that concern us here, particularism becomes even more rampant in congress and parties, courts ostensibly fail to administer justice, and agencies of control are eliminated or reduced to passivity. This context encourages the further erosion of legally established authority, renders the boundary between public and private even more tenuous, and creates enormous temptations for corruption.

In this sea of particularism and blurred boundaries, why does the universalistic process of fair and competitive elections survive? Governments willing to tamper with laws are hardly solid guarantors of the integrity of electoral processes. Part of the answer, at least with respect to elections to top national positions, is close international attention and wide reporting abroad of electoral irregularities. Fair elections are the main, if not the only, characteristic that certifies countries as democratic before other governments and international opinion. Nowadays this certification has important advantages for countries and for those who govern them. Within the country, elections are a moment when something similar to horizontal accountability operates: parties other than the one in government are present at the polling places, sharing an interest in preventing fraud. Elections create a sharp focus on political matters and on the symbols and rituals that surround the act of voting. At this moment, the citizens' sense of basic fairness manifests itself with special intensity. Violations are likely to be immediately reported. Faced with the protests that might ensue and their repercussions in the international media, and considering the further damage that would come from trying to impose obviously tainted results, most governments are willing to run the risks inherent in fair and competitive elections.

Pervasive particularism, delegative rule, and weak horizontal accountability have at least two serious drawbacks. The first is that the generalized lack of control enables old authoritarian practices to reassert themselves.[34] The second is that, in countries that inaugurated polyarchy under conditions of sharp and increasing inequality, the making and implementation of policy becomes further biased in favor of highly organized and economically powerful interests.

In the countries that occupy us here, the more properly political, *democratic* freedoms are effective: uncoerced voting; freedom of opinion, movement, and association; and others already listed. But for large sections of the population, basic *liberal* freedoms are denied or recurrently trampled. The rights of battered women to sue their husbands and of peasants to obtain a fair trial against their landlords, the inviolability of domiciles in poor neighborhoods, and in general the right of the poor and various minorities to decent treatment and fair access to public agencies and courts are often denied. The effectiveness of the whole ensemble of rights, democratic and liberal, makes for full civil and political citizenship. In many of the new polyarchies, individuals are citizens only in relation to the one institution that functions in a manner close to what its formal rules prescribe—elections. As for full citizenship, only the members of a privileged minority enjoy it.[35] Formally institutionalized polyarchies exhibit various mixes of democracy, liberalism, and republicanism (understood as a view that concurs with liberalism in tracing a clear public-private distinction, but that adds an ennobling and personally demanding conception of participation in the public sphere). Informally institutionalized polyarchies are democratic, in the sense just defined; when they add, as they often do, the plebiscitarian component of delegative rule, they are also strongly majoritarian. But their liberal and republican components are extremely weak.

Freeing Ourselves from Some Illusions

I have rapidly covered complicated terrain.[36] Lest there be any misunderstanding, let me insist that I, too, prefer situations that get close to real observance of the formal rules of polyarchy, a citizenry that firmly approves democratic procedures and values, fair application of the law in all social and geographical locations, and low inequality. Precisely because of this preference, I have argued for the need to improve our conceptual tools in the complex task of studying and comparing the whole set of existing polyarchies. It is through a nonteleological and, indeed, nonethnocentric, positive analysis of the main traits of these polyarchies that we scholars can contribute to their much-needed improvement. This is especially true of the polyarchies that are institutionalized in ways we dislike and often overlook, even if they do not—and some of them may never—closely resemble the "consolidated democracies" of the Northwest.

For this purpose, we must begin by freeing ourselves from some illusions. As an author who has committed most of the mistakes I criticize here, I suspect that we students of democratization are still swayed by the mood of the times that many countries have more or less recently passed through. We believe that democracy, even in the rather modest guise of polyarchy, is vastly preferable to the assortment of authoritarian regimes that it has replaced. We shared in the joy when those regimes gave way, and some of us participated in these historic events. These were moments of huge enthusiasm and hope. Multitudes demanded democracy, and international opinion supported them. The demand for democracy had many meanings, but in all cases it had a powerful common denominator: "Never Again!"[37] Whatever confused, utopian, or limited ideas anyone held concerning democracy, it was clear that it meant getting rid of the despots once and for all. Democracy, even if—or perhaps precisely because—it had so many different meanings attached to it, was the central mobilizing demand that had to be achieved and preserved forever. Somehow, it was felt, this democracy would soon come to resemble the sort of democracy found in admired countries of the Northwest—admired for their long-enduring regimes and for their wealth, and because both things seemed to go together. As in these countries, after the transition democracy was to be stabilized, or consolidated; the Northwest was seen as the endpoint of a trajectory that would be largely traversed by getting rid of the authoritarian rulers. This illusion was extremely useful during the hard and uncertain times of the transition. Its residue is still strong enough to make democracy and consolidation powerful, and consequently pragmatically valid, terms of political discourse.[38] Their analytical cogency is another matter.

On the other hand, because the values that inspired the demands for democracy are as important as ever, the present text is an effort toward opening more disciplined avenues for the study of a topic—and a concern—I share with most of the authors that I have discussed: the quality, in some cases rather dismal, of the social life that is interwoven with the workings of various types of polyarchy. How this quality might be improved depends in part on how realistically we understand the past and present situation of each case.

NOTES

For their comments on an earlier version of this text, I am grateful to Michael Coppedge, Gabriela Ippolito-O'Donnell, Scott Mainwaring, Sebastián Mazzuca, Peter Moody, Gerardo Munck, and Adam Przeworski.

1. Reflecting the lack of clearly established criteria in the literature, David Collier and Steven Levitsky have inventoried and interestingly discussed the more than one hundred qualifiers that have been attached to the term "democracy." Many such qualifiers are intended to indicate that the respective cases are in some sense lacking the full attributes of democracy as defined by each author. See Collier and Levitsky, "Democracy 'With Adjectives': Finding Conceptual Order in Recent Comparative Research" (unpubl. ms., University of California–Berkeley, Political Science Department, 1995).

2. I have tried unsuccessfully to find terms appropriate to what the literature refers to as highly institutionalized versus noninstitutionalized (or poorly institutionalized), or as consolidated versus unconsolidated democracies, with most of the old polyarchies belonging to the first terms of these pairs, and most of the new ones to the second. For reasons that will be clear below, I have opted for labeling the first group "formally institutionalized" and the second "informally institutionalized," but not without misgivings: in the first set of countries, many things happen outside formally prescribed institutional rules, while the second set includes one highly formalized institution, elections.

3. This list is from Robert Dahl, *Democracy and Its Critics* (New Haven: Yale University Press, 1989), 221; the reader may want to examine further details of these attributes, discussed by Dahl in this book.

4. See especially J. Samuel Valenzuela, "Democratic Consolidation in Post-Transitional Settings: Notion, Process, and Facilitating Conditions," in Scott Mainwaring, Guillermo O'Donnell, and J. Samuel Valenzuela, eds., *Issues in Democratic Consolidation: The New South American Democracies in Comparative Perspective* (Notre Dame, Ind.: University of Notre Dame Press, 1992), 57–104; and Philippe C. Schmitter and Terry Lynn Karl, "What Democracy Is . . . and Is Not," *Journal of Democracy* 2 (Summer 1991): 75–88.

5. See Terry Lynn Karl, "The Hybrid Regimes of Central America," *Journal of Democracy* 6 (July 1995): 73–86; and "Imposing Consent? Electoralism vs. Democratization in El Salvador," in Paul Drake and Eduardo Silva, eds., *Elections and Democratization in Latin America, 1980–85* (San Diego: Center for Iberian and Latin American Studies, 1986), 9–36.

6. See especially Juan J. Linz and Alfred Stepan, *Problems of Democratic Transition and Consolidation: Southern Europe, South America, and Post-Communist Europe* (Baltimore: Johns Hopkins University Press, 1996); and Philippe Schmitter, "Dangers and Dilemmas of Democracy," *Journal of Democracy* 5 (April 1994): 57–74.

7. For a useful listing of these institutional variations, see Schmitter and Karl, "What Democracy Is . . . and Is Not."

8. For a more detailed discussion of institutions, see my "Delegative Democracy," *Journal of Democracy* 5 (January 1994): 56–69.

9. The term "reasonable" is admittedly ambiguous. Nowhere are these freedoms completely uncurtailed, if by nothing else than the political consequences of social inequality. By "reasonable" I mean that there are neither de jure prohibitions on these freedoms nor systematic and usually successful efforts by the government or private actors to annul them.

10. On the other hand, elections can be made more authentically competitive by, say, measures that diminish the advantages of incumbents or of economically powerful parties. These are, of course, important issues. But the point I want to make at the moment is that these differences obtain among countries that already qualify as polyarchies.

11. Juan J. Linz, "Transitions to Democracy," *Washington Quarterly* 13 (1990): 156. The assertion about "the only game in town" entails some ambiguities that I discuss below.

12. Even though most definitions of democratic consolidation are centered around "institutionalization" (whether explicitly or implicitly, by asserting acceptance or approval of democratic institutions and their formal rules), they offer a wide variety of additional criteria. My own count in a recent review of the literature is twelve; see Doh Chull Shin, "On the Third Wave of Democratization: A Synthesis and Evaluation of Recent Theory and Research," *World Politics* 47 (October 1994): 135–70.

13. Even though he does not use this language, an exception is the definition of democratic consolidation offered by J. Samuel Valenzuela, which is centered in what I call here the institutionalization of elections and the absence of veto powers; see his "Democratic Consolidation in Post-Transitional Settings," 69.

14. It is high time for self-criticism. The term "stunted" I used jointly with Scott Mainwaring and J. Samuel Valenzuela in the introduction to our *Issues in Democratic Consolidation*, 11. Furthermore, in my chapter in the same volume (pp. 17–56), I offer a nonminimalist definition of democratic consolidation, and propose the concept of a "second transition," from a democratically elected government to a consolidated democratic regime. These concepts partake of the teleology I criticize here. This teleological view is homologous to the one used by many modernization studies in the 1950s and 1960s; it was abundantly, but evidently not decisively, criticized at the time. For a critique of the concept of "democratic consolidation" that is convergent with mine, see Ben Ross Schneider, "Democratic Consolidations: Some Broad Comparisons and Sweeping Arguments," *Latin American Research Review* 30 (1995): 215–34; Schneider concludes by warning against "the fallacy of excessive universalism" (p. 231).

15. Philippe C. Schmitter with Terry Lynn Karl, "The Conceptual Travels of Transitologists and Consolidologists: How Far to the East Should They Attempt to Go?" *Slavic Review* 63 (Spring 1994): 173–85.

16. Richard Gunther, P. Nikiforos Diamandouros, and Hans-Jürgen Puhle, eds., *The Politics of Democratic Consolidation: Southern Europe in Comparative Perspective* (Baltimore: Johns Hopkins University Press, 1995).

17. We should remember that several typologies have been proposed for formally institutionalized polyarchies; see especially Arend Lijphart, *Democracies: Patterns of Majoritarian and Consensus Government in Twenty-one Countries* (New Haven: Yale University Press, 1984). This work has been extremely useful in advancing knowledge

about these polyarchies, which underscores the need for similar efforts on the now greatly expanded whole set of polyarchies. For an attempt in this direction see Carlos Acuña and William Smith, "Future Politico-Economic Scenarios for Latin America," in William Smith, Carlos Acuña, and Eduardo Gamarra, eds., *Democracy, Markets, and Structural Reform in Latin America* (New Brunswick, N.J.: Transaction, 1993), 1–28.

18. Adam Przeworski and his collaborators found that higher economic development and a parliamentary regime increase the average survival rate of polyarchies. These are important findings, but the authors have not tested the impacts of socioeconomic inequality and of the kind of informal institutionalization that I discuss below. Pending further research, it is impossible to assess the causal direction and weight of all these variables. I suspect that high socioeconomic inequality has a close relationship with informal institutionalization. But we do not know if either or both, directly or indirectly, affect the chances of survival of polyarchy, or if they might cancel the effect of economic development that Przeworski et al. found. See Adam Przeworski and Fernando Limongi, "Modernization: Theories and Facts" (Working Paper No. 4, Chicago Center for Democracy, University of Chicago, November 1994); and the chapter by Adam Przeworski et al. in this collection.

19. A topic that does not concern me here is the extent to which formal rules are institutionalized across various old polyarchies and, within them, across various issue areas, though the variations seem quite important on both counts.

20. The lore of many countries is filled with jokes about the naive foreigner or the native "sucker" who gets into trouble by following the formal rules of a given situation. I have explored some of these issues with reference to Brazil and Argentina in "Democracia en la Argentina: Micro y macro" (Working Paper No. 2, Helen Kellogg Institute for International Studies, Notre Dame, Ind., 1983); "Y a mí qué me importa? Notas sobre sociabilidad y política en Argentina y Brasil" (Working Paper No. 9, Helen Kellogg Institute for International Studies, Notre Dame, Ind., 1984); and "Micro-escenas de la privatización de lo público en Brasil" (Working Paper No. 21, with commentaries by Roberto DaMatta and J. Samuel Valenzuela, Helen Kellogg Institute for International Studies, Notre Dame, Ind., 1989).

21. For the purposes of the generic argument presented in this essay, and not without hesitation because of its vagueness, from now on I will use the term "particularism" to refer to these phenomena. On the contemporary relevance of clientelism, see Luis Roniger and Ayse Gunes-Ayata, eds., *Democracy, Clientelism, and Civil Society* (Boulder, Colo.: Lynne Rienner, 1994). For studies focused on Latin America that are germane to my argument, see especially Roberto DaMatta, *A Case e a rua: Espaco, cidadania, mulher e morte no Brasil* (São Paulo: Editora Brasiliense, 1985); Jonathan Fox, "The Difficult Transition from Clientelism to Citizenship," *World Politics* 46 (January 1994): 151–84; Francis Hagopian, "The Compromised Transition: The Political Class in the Brazilian Transition," in Mainwaring et al., *Issues in Democratic Consolidation*, 243–93; and Scott Mainwaring, "Brazilian Party Underdevelopment in Comparative Perspective," *Political Science Quarterly* 107 (Winter 1992–93): 677–707. These and other studies show that particularism and its concomitants are not ignored by good field researchers. But, attesting to the paradigmatic force of the prevalent views on democratization, in this literature the rich data and findings emerging from such case studies are not conceptually processed as an intrinsic part of the *problématique* of democratization, or are seen as just "obstacles" interposed in the way of its presumed direction of change.

22. Particularistic relationships can be found in formally institutionalized polyarchies, of course. I am pointing here to differences of degree that seem large enough to require conceptual recognition. One important indication of these differences is the extraordinary leniency with which, in informally institutionalized polyarchies, political leaders, most of public opinion, and even courts treat situations that in the other polyarchies would be considered as entailing very severe conflicts of interest.

23. For a discussion of neopatrimonialism, see my "Transitions, Continuities, and Paradoxes," in Mainwaring et al., *Issues in Democratic Consolidation*, 17–56. An interesting recent discussion of neopatrimonialism is Jonathan Hartlyn's "Crisis-Ridden

Elections (Again) in the Dominican Republic: Neopatrimonialism, Presidentialism, and Weak Electoral Oversight," *Journal of Interamerican and World Affairs* 34 (Winter 1994): 91–144.

24. By "regime" I mean "the set of effectively prevailing patterns (not necessarily legally formalized) that establish the modalities of recruitment and access to governmental roles, and the permissible resources that form the basis for expectations of access to such roles," as defined in my *Bureaucratic Authoritarianism: Argentina, 1966–1973, in Comparative Perspective* (Berkeley: University of California Press, 1988), 6.

25. Adam Przeworski, *Democracy and the Market: Political and Economic Reforms in Eastern Europe and Latin America* (Cambridge: Cambridge University Press, 1991).

26. See, among many others that could be cited (some transcribed in Shin, "On the Third Wave of Democratization"), the definition of democratic consolidation proposed by Gunther, Diamandouros, and Puhle in *Politics of Democratic Consolidation*, 3: "the achievement of substantial attitudinal support for and behavioral compliance with the new democratic institutions and the rules which they establish." A broader but equivalent definition is offered four pages later.

27. Przeworski, *Democracy and the Market*, 26.

28. In another influential discussion, Philippe C. Schmitter, although he does not use this language, expresses a similar view of democratic consolidation; see his "Dangers and Dilemmas of Democracy," *Journal of Democracy* 5 (April 1994): 56–74. Schmitter begins by asserting, "In South America, Eastern Europe, and Asia the specter haunting the transition is . . . nonconsolidation. . . . These countries are 'doomed' to remain democratic almost by default." He acknowledges that the attributes of polyarchy may hold in these countries—but these "patterns never quite crystallize" (pp. 60–61). To say that democracy exists "almost by default" (i.e., is negatively defined) and is not "crystallized" (i.e., not formally institutionalized) is another way of stating the generalized view that I am discussing.

29. An exception is Gunther et al., *Politics of Democratic Consolidation*, where Italy is one of the four cases studied. But the way they deal with recent events in Italy is exemplary of the conceptual problems I am discussing. They assert that in Italy "several important partial regimes . . . were challenged, became deconsolidated, and entered into a significant process of restructuring beginning in 1991" (p. 19). On the same page, the reader learns that these partial regimes include nothing less than "the electoral system, the party system, and the structure of the state itself." (Added to this list later on is "the basic nature of executive-legislative relations" [p. 394].) Yet the "Italian democracy remains strong and resilient"—after practically every important aspect of its regime, and even of the state, became "deconsolidated" (p. 412). If the authors mean that, in spite of a severe crisis, the Italian polyarchy is likely to endure, I agree.

30. Actually, the authors are ambiguous about this first "test." Just before articulating their list of tests with this one at its head, they assert that they "reject [peaceful alternation in government between parties that were once bitterly opposed] as a *prerequisite* for regarding a regime as consolidated" (emphasis added). See Gunther et al., *Politics of Democratic Consolidation*, 12.

31. In the text on which I am commenting, the problem is further compounded by the use of categories such as "partial consolidation" and "sufficient consolidation" (which the authors say preceded "full consolidation" in some Southern European cases). They even speak of a stage of "democratic persistence" that is supposed to follow the achievement of "full [democratic] consolidation."

32. I may have sounded naive in my earlier comments about how individuals performing public roles are supposed to be guided by universalistic orientations to some version of the public good. Now I can add that, as the authors of the *Federalist Papers* knew, this is not only, or even mostly, a matter of the subjective intentions of these individuals. It is to a large extent contingent on institutional arrangements of control and accountability, and on expectations built around these arrangements, that furnish incentives

(including the threats of severe sanctions and public discredit) for that kind of behavior. That these incentives are often insufficient should not be allowed to blur the difference with cases where the institutional arrangements are nonexistent or ineffective; these situations freely invite the enormous temptations that always come with holding political power. I wish to thank Adam Przeworski and Michael Coppedge for raising this point in private communications.

33. The reader has surely noticed that I am referring to countries that have presidentialist regimes and that, consequently, I am glossing over the arguments, initiated by Juan J. Linz and followed up by a number of other scholars, about the advantages of parliamentarism over the presidentialist regimes that characterize Latin America. Although these arguments convince me in the abstract, because of the very characteristics I am depicting I am skeptical about the practical consequences of attempting to implant parliamentarism in these countries.

34. For analyses of some of these situations, see Paulo Sérgio Pinheiro, "The Legacy of Authoritarianism in Democratic Brazil," in Stuart S. Nagel, ed., *Latin American Development and Public Policy* (New York: St. Martin's, 1995), 237–53; and Martha K. Huggins, ed., *Vigilantism and the State in Modern Latin America: Essays on Extralegal Violence* (New York: Praeger, 1991). See also the worrisome analysis, based on Freedom House data, that Larry Diamond presents in his "Democracy in Latin America: Degrees, Illusions, and Directions for Consolidation," in Tom Farer, ed., *Beyond Sovereignty: Collectively Defending Democracy in the Americas* (Baltimore: Johns Hopkins University Press, 1996). In recent years, the Freedom House indices reveal, more Latin American countries have regressed rather than advanced. For a discussion of various aspects of the resulting obliteration of the rule of law and weakening of citizenship, see Guillermo O'Donnell, "On the State, Democratization, and Some Conceptual Problems: A Latin American View with Glances at Some Post-Communist Countries," *World Development* 21 (1993): 1355–69.

35. There is a huge adjacent theme that I will not discuss here: the linkage of these problems with widespread poverty and, even more, with deep inequalities of various sorts.

36. Obviously, we need analyses that are more nuanced, comprehensive, and dynamic than the one that I have undertaken here. My own list of topics meriting much further study includes: the opportunities that may be entailed by demands for more universalistic and public-oriented governmental behavior; the odd coexistence of pervasive particularism with highly technocratic modes of decision making in economic policy; the effects of international demands (especially regarding corruption and uncertainty in legislation and adjudication) that the behavior of public officials should conform more closely to the formal rules; and the disaggregation of various kinds and institutional sites of clientelism and particularism. Another major issue that I overlook here, raised by Larry Diamond in a personal communication, is locating the point at which violations of liberal rights should be construed as canceling, or making ineffective, the political freedoms surrounding elections. Finally, Philippe C. Schmitter makes an argument worth exploring when he urges that polyarchies be disaggregated into various "partial regimes"; most of these would surely look quite different when comparing formally versus informally institutionalized cases. See Schmitter, "The Consolidation of Democracy and Representation of Social Groups," *American Behavioral Scientist* 35 (March–June 1992): 422–49.

37. This is the title of the reports of the commissions that investigated human rights violations in Argentina and Brazil. For further discussion of what I call a dominant antiauthoritarian mood in the transitions, see my "Transitions, Continuities, and Paradoxes" and Nancy Bermeo, "Democracy and the Lessons of Dictatorship," *Comparative Politics* 24 (April 1992): 273–91.

38. Symptomatically illustrating the residues of the language and the hopes of the transition as well as the mutual influences between political and academic discourses, on several occasions the governments of the countries that I know more closely (Argentina, Brazil, Chile, and Uruguay) triumphantly proclaimed that their democracies had become "consolidated."

5

BATTLING THE UNDERTOW IN LATIN AMERICA

Abraham F. Lowenthal

Abraham F. Lowenthal *is president of the Pacific Council on International Policy, professor of international relations, and director of the Center for International Studies at the University of Southern California in Los Angeles. Among his publications are* Partners in Conflict: The United States and Latin America in the 1990s *(1991),* The California-Mexico Connection *(1993), and* Latin America in a New World *(1994).*

The "third wave" of democratization identified by Samuel P. Huntington has been especially visible in Latin America and the Caribbean. It is in the Americas, consequently, that discussion of "consolidating" democracy has been most insistent. The current effort to "consolidate third wave democracies" is premature in much of Latin America and the Caribbean, however. As a result, the attention of policy makers is often misdirected, and available instruments for nurturing democratic governance are often ineffectively employed.

It is true that transitions from various forms of authoritarian rule toward popularly elected governments have been particularly striking and nearly universal in Latin America and the Caribbean. In 1975, only two South American countries (Colombia and Venezuela) had elected leaders, while Central America was ruled by praetorian dictators in every nation but Costa Rica. Today, democratically elected governments rule in every country in Latin America except Cuba. Many countries have held regular elections for years, and smooth transitions of power from a ruling party to an opposition party occur with increasing frequency.

With few exceptions, elected presidents have served their constitutionally stipulated terms of office. In those countries where reversals have taken place, elected governments have soon been restored. In Peru, where an elected president himself closed down democratic institutions for a short time, international pressure helped produce a reasonably prompt, if gradual, return to electoral politics. Effective international pressure reversed a similar *autogolpe* (self-coup) in Guatemala even more quickly. The same was true in Haiti, which has virtually no history of democracy. There, the elected regime of Jean Bertrand Aristide, overthrown by a military coup, was restored with the help of strong multilateral pressure and U.S. intervention sanctioned by the Organization of American States.

All important actors in Latin America have recognized that legitimate authority can derive only from free, fair, and broadly participatory elections. Individuals from varying ideological and social backgrounds—military officers and former guerrillas, peasants and industrial workers, intellectuals and industrialists—now embrace elections and relevant political freedoms. It was not always thus; just 25 years ago, "vanguards" on the left and "guardians" on the right—each with considerable support—openly expressed their disdain for democratic politics.

This trend from authoritarianism toward electoral democracy is encouraging, to be sure, for it is a prerequisite of effective democratic governance. It alone is not sufficient to bring about democracy, however. Effective democratic governance—the daily practice of constitutional rule with stable institutions—involves much more than the electoral legitimation of governmental authority. It implies the broadly shared expectation that political institutions will be subject to periodic popular review. It also requires that executive power be restrained in practice by law, by an independent judiciary, and by what Guillermo O'Donnell calls "horizontal accountability"—that is, intergovernmental checks and balances.[1] Finally, it calls for the clear and consistent subordination of the military and police to civilian control.

Effective democratic governance implies the existence of political parties that effectively aggregate and express social interests. It also requires that government officials have the authority and capacity to implement policies that privilege national interests over those of economic or social sectors, regions, or private individuals.

In many Latin American countries, unfortunately, effective democratic governance is not gaining appreciable ground; it is weak, uneven, contradicted, and in some cases deteriorating. Venezuela's once robust two-party democracy has been "anesthetized" in recent years, with parties and other democratic institutions thoroughly discredited.[2] Colombia's democratic institutions struggle with widespread corruption and violence.[3] Brazil is still recovering from political and economic crises exacerbated by poor leadership, a condition Bolívar Lamounier has aptly termed the "hyper-active paralysis syndrome."[4] Parallel conditions impair democratic governance in Peru, Argentina, and other countries.[5]

Elections have become commonplace in Latin America and the Caribbean, but their meaning and validity vary greatly. Eighty years after fighting a revolution on the slogans of "effective suffrage, no reelection," Mexico has firmly institutionalized a one-term limit on the presidency, but "effective suffrage" is still far from a reality; national and local elections are routinely manipulated and subject to fraud. Elections in the Dominican Republic, Paraguay, and other countries are often marred by gross irregularities.[6]

Delegative Democracy

Even where elections have been generally free and fair, they have sometimes led to what O'Donnell calls "delegative democracy."[7] As O'Donnell has noted, many Latin American executives behave as if their election represented an unquestionable mandate to govern the country as they see fit. Accordingly, they have treated the legislature, judiciary, and other agencies—whose existence and proper operation are imperative for effective democratic governance—as obstacles to their political goals.

The clearest example of delegative democracy was Peruvian president Alberto Fujimori's *autogolpe*, which involved the closing of Congress, the courts, and other political institutions.[8] Other instances of extraordinary executive authority include the prolonged rule of former president Joaquín Balaguer in the Dominican Republic, characterized by extreme presidentialism and the subordination of weak political and civil institutions; and Argentine president Carlos Menem's frequent practice of ruling by decree to bypass opposition to his policies in the legislature.[9]

Despite constitutional reforms in Mexico, Brazil, Argentina, and elsewhere, presidentialism is not significantly checked by countervailing powers. In many countries throughout the region (notably Argentina, Peru, Bolivia, Paraguay, Honduras, El Salvador, Guatemala, and Mexico) the judiciary has been politicized and intimidated. The Argentine Supreme Court has been reconstituted three times since 1983, including one instance of outright court packing by President Menem. Similar interference has occurred in Peru.[10] Judges who have opposed the regime have been demoted, removed, or, as in the case of Guatemala, subjected to threats to their physical security. As a result, the courts are often unable to apply the constitution or the laws with impartiality or to challenge the legality of presidential acts.[11]

The region's military and police forces continue to enjoy significant influence and independence. In some cases, military autonomy is limited to issues concerning internal promotions and the like, but sometimes the military has engaged in open insubordination. Coups have been attempted in Venezuela, Ecuador, and Argentina. In Paraguay, General Lino Oviedo periodically placed his troops on high alert in order to discourage the government of President Juan Carlos Wasmosy from exercising its constitutional authority over the armed forces.[12] The Honduran military has likewise resisted efforts to cut its forces and redefine its role.[13]

In battling terrorism and guerrilla violence in Peru, Guatemala, and elsewhere, armed forces have trampled on various constitutional protections. Similar patterns have emerged in Colombia and Bolivia, where the fight against the narcotics traffickers and drug cartels has been used to justify the military's growing involvement in politics.

Democratic governance in Latin America has also been marred by corruption, clientelism, and what O'Donnell calls "particularist" politics.[14] The infusion of drug money into all levels of Colombian politics (reportedly all the way up to President Ernesto Samper) is notorious, as is narcotics-related corruption in Panama, Bolivia, and elsewhere. Rampant corruption prevails in Mexico, where reports of very large, irregular payments to cabinet and subcabinet officers circulate and are widely regarded as credible. In Argentina, President Menem's administration has been blemished by scandals of graft in the privatization of state-owned properties, a problem that exists in many other countries as well. Presidents have been removed for corruption in Venezuela and Brazil—certainly an unprecedented and essentially positive development, but one that weakens political institutions nonetheless.

Talk of consolidating democracy is premature and misleading, therefore, because it implies that democratic institutions exist and need only to be reinforced. This is not the case in most of Latin America, where democratic governance is far from assured. The region has experienced at least as much "undertow" as "wave" in the 1990s.

Only in the third wave democracies of Chile and Uruguay can effective democratic governance be said to exist. But these countries had well-established democracies 40 years ago, which were interrupted by military rule. They have been able to successfully *re*construct democratic governance because aspects of their political culture persisted even though democratic institutions were suspended during the years of authoritarian rule.

Consolidation cannot take place before democratic governance is solidly constructed. Political institutions that are conducive to democracy—including the legislature, political parties, courts, and civil society—need to be reformed and strengthened.[15] Practices that are inconsistent with representative and responsive politics, that defy horizontal accountability, and that subordinate legislatures and courts need to be discredited and replaced. Moreover, the rule of law must be uniformly extended to all citizens.[16]

Democracy should not be conceived of as an "on/off" condition; it is not a state that is simply arrived at when certain electoral criteria are met. Threshold events or actions—including the institution of competitive elections, smooth transfers of power, the signing of pacts, and so on—do not by themselves signal the consolidation of democratic governance. Identifying the obstacles to democratic governance and determining how these obstacles can be overcome will do more to promote democracy than focusing on how or when consolidation is achieved.

The emphasis on consolidation has led policy makers to invest a great deal of energy in holding and monitoring elections and in preventing or reversing coups. But "democracy for the long haul," as Huntington phrases it, may depend less on these easily identifiable moments of decision than on the painstaking construction and quotidian care of democratic political institutions, practices, and culture. Only deliberate and sustained support will equip democratizing countries with the tools to make democracy thrive. This is hard work, work that is not soon (if ever) completed, but it is a challenge that must first be acknowledged and understood if it is to be met.

NOTES

I have drawn here on ideas expressed in Abraham F. Lowenthal and Jorge I. Domínguez, "Constructing Democratic Governance," in Domínguez and Lowenthal, eds., *Constructing Democratic Governance: Latin America and the Caribbean in the 1990s* (Baltimore: Johns Hopkins University Press, 1996), pt. 1, 3–8, and in other essays contained in that volume. I gratefully acknowledge the assistance of Christopher M. Larkins in the preparation of this essay.

1. See Guillermo O'Donnell's chapter in this collection, 50–51.

2. See Anibal Romero, "La democracia anestesiada: Venezuela bajo Rafael Caldera" (paper presented at a conference on "Constructing Democracy and Markets: East Asia and Latin America," sponsored by the International Forum for Democratic Studies and the Pacific Council on International Policy, Los Angeles, January 1996).

3. See Harvey Kline, "Colombia: Building Democracy in the Midst of Violence and Drugs," in Domínguez and Lowenthal, eds., *Constructing Democratic Governance*, pt. 3, 20–41.

4. See Bolívar Lamounier, "Brazil: The Hyperactive Paralysis Syndrome," in Domínguez and Lowenthal, eds., *Constructing Democratic Governance*, pt. 3, 166–88.

5. See Susan Stokes, "Peru: The Rupture of Democratic Rule," and Liliana De Riz, "Argentina: Democracy in Turmoil," in Domínguez and Lowenthal, eds., *Constructing Democratic Governance*, pt. 3, 58–71 and 147–65. See also Carlos Monge, "Fault Lines of Democratic Governance in the Americas" (conference report of the North-South Center, University of Miami, January 1996).

6. See Diego Abente Brun, "Paraguay: Transition from *Caudillo* Rule," in Domínguez and Lowenthal, eds., *Constructing Democratic Governance*, pt. 3, 118–32; and Rosario Espinal, "The Dominican Republic: An Ambiguous Democracy," in Domínguez and Lowenthal, eds., *Constructing Democratic Governance*, pt. 4, 118–34.

7. See O'Donnell's chapter in this collection, 50–51.

8. See Stokes, "Peru: The Rupture of Democratic Rule."

9. In his first four years of office, Menem issued more than three hundred such decrees, as compared with only 29 in the six-year administration of his predecessor, Raúl Alfonsín. See De Riz, "Argentina: Democracy in Turmoil." See also Alejandro M. Garro, "Nine Years Transition to Democracy in Argentina: Partial Failure or Qualified Success?" *Columbia Journal of Transnational Law* 31 (1993): 1–102.

10. See Garro, "Nine Years Transition to Democracy in Argentina," 74–78; and Stokes, "Peru: The Rupture of Democratic Rule."

11. Monge, "Fault Lines of Democratic Governance," 8–9. See also Irwin Stotzky, ed., *Transition to Democracy in Latin America: The Role of the Judiciary* (Boulder, Colo.: Westview, 1993); and Christopher M. Larkins, "Judicial Independence and Democratization: A Theoretical and Conceptual Analysis," *American Journal of Comparative Law* 44 (Fall 1996): 605–26.

12. See Abente Brun, "Paraguay: Transition from *Caudillo* Rule."

13. See Mark B. Rosenberg and J. Mark Ruhl, "Honduras: Democratization and the Role of the Armed Forces," in Domínguez and Lowenthal, eds., *Constructing Democrat ι Governance,* pt. 4, 64–77.

14. See O'Donnell's chapter in this collection, 46–47.

15. See Edgardo Boeninger's chapter in this collection.

16. See Monge, "Fault Lines of Democratic Governance," 8–9.

II

Institutional Design

II

Institutional Design

6

INSTITUTIONAL DESIGN
AND PARTY SYSTEMS

John M. Carey

John M. Carey *is assistant professor of political science at Washington University in St. Louis.* He has taught at the University of Rochester and the Instituto de Ciencias Políticas, Universidad Católica de Chile, and has served as a consultant to Chile's Presidential Commission on Public Ethics. Among his publications are Presidents and Assemblies: Constitutional Design and Electoral Dynamics *(1992) and* Term Limits and Legislative Representation *(1996).*

Students of comparative politics have long debated the impact that formal rules of political contestation have on party systems.[1] Research has focused overwhelmingly on parties as they are represented in legislative assemblies, especially on aggregate-level data about parties—for example, the number of parties represented, the disproportionality of seats won to votes cast, and the likelihood of single-party majorities. Implicit in this work are two assumptions: first, that majorities are of critical importance because most representative institutions operate by majority rule; and second, that party label is the most important predictor of how individual politicians will behave and what sorts of coalitions they will enter. I do not reject either of these assumptions here. I suggest, however, that institutional analysis can—indeed should—tell us more about political parties than we learn from the aggregate data alone. In particular, I suggest that basic elements of institutional design tell us quite a bit about the sorts of policies and coalitions legislators will value, and about the capacity of legislators to act collectively on those values.

Most institutional analyses of party systems approach these subjects in the same way. Values are evaluated in terms of the diversity of parties that win representation in the assembly and the extent to which the distribution of seats among parties accurately reflects the distribution of votes cast. It is frequently argued that the broader the range of winning parties, the greater the ability of the party system to represent diversity of values in the electorate.[2] Similarly, it is argued that the more proportional the translation of votes to seats, the less the electoral mechanism violates the electorate's expressed preferences.

On the other hand, a party system that maximizes the capacity of the legislature to act is generally considered a trade-off against the accurate representation of values. Because parties are assumed to be the building blocks of coalitions, the greater fragmentation of the party system that is associated with proportionality and multipartism is potentially problematic for legislative capacity. A party system that is too representative can contribute to policy deadlock. Finally, apart from the questions of the number and diversity of the parties that win representation is the question of parties' *internal* cohesion and discipline. The formal rules of political competition can generate incentives or disincentives for cohesiveness, which in turn imply trade-offs between responsiveness to citizens and the capacity to act decisively to break deadlock.

Below, I briefly discuss how the effects of institutional design on party systems affect two issues critical to the consolidation of new democracies: regime support and governability. I then review some of the main results of institutional analyses of party systems. Here, I identify and measure the formal rules that contribute to party-system fragmentation, disproportionality, and the majority or minority partisan status of governments.[3] The formal institutions regarded as most critical in shaping these characteristics of party systems are the electoral system and constitutional provisions regarding the origin and survival of the executive and legislative branches. I supplement this review by introducing additional institutional factors that shape party systems and representation at this aggregate level. Then my focus shifts to elements of institutional design whose influence is felt at the level of individual politicians within parties. I argue that these elements affect individual legislators' choice of policies and their ability to act collectively with copartisans to pursue policy goals. Finally, I review the effects of institutional design on party systems at both the aggregate level and the level of individual politicians, and evaluate the current research agenda.

Regime Support and Governability

Why is institutional analysis of particular importance to the consolidation of new democracies? Because formal rules, through their impact on party systems, can affect both the acceptance of new regimes and the governability of the system. If, for example, large numbers of voters feel that their preferences are unaccounted for because the electoral system distributes legislative seats disproportionately[4] or because the legislature is relatively powerless in setting policy vis-à-vis the executive, then popular support for representative institutions is undermined. Governability, moreover, can be undermined even where the rules of competition produce parties with widespread popular support if the parties prove unable to form stable coalitions that can act decisively to make policy.

As the majority of "third wave" countries have passed their first decades while maintaining support for democratic institutions, the issue of governability is becoming increasingly salient. This essay focuses largely on governability's roots in institutional design. Consider some common phenomena. Executives who consistently lack majority support in the legislature contribute to chronic conflict between the branches of government, which can in turn generate constitutional crises. The conflicts between Peruvian president Alberto Fujimori and his congress in 1992 and between Russian president Boris Yeltsin and the Supreme Soviet in 1993, both of which ended with tanks in the streets, are perhaps the most dramatic examples of this. But the 1994–95 struggle over reforms between Nicaraguan president Violeta Chamorro and a highly fragmented congress that could agree only on its opposition to the executive nearly ended in constitutional collapse as well. Throughout 1995 and 1996, Belarusian president Alexander Lukashenka's two-year standoff with a fragmented parliament produced policy deadlock broken only by sporadic bursts of presidential decrees, which in turn were regularly challenged by legislators before the Constitutional Court.

In addition to affecting relations between legislatures and executives by shaping the party system, institutional design affects the internal cohesiveness of parties themselves. At one extreme, parties so internally divided that they cannot act collectively are unable to respond quickly to policy crises and to present voters with coherent choices in elections. The Brazilian electoral system, for example, creates strong incentives for legislators to cultivate personalistic loyalties among voters, even when doing so means ignoring their parties' broader agenda.[5] One result is that presidents cannot count on stable legislative coalitions to negotiate policy; presidents frequently resort to using provisional decree authority.[6] Another is that legislators' relentless pursuit of government patronage and pork-barrel spending contributes to rampant political corruption.[7]

Conversely, where central party leaders have the power to impose discipline on elected politicians, responsiveness to minority groups and local interests is necessarily compromised. This was the case in Venezuela prior to the electoral reforms of the early 1990s, by which time popular support for the two main political parties had eroded considerably.[8] This situation also contributes to the excruciatingly slow process of opening Mexican elections to greater competition.[9]

In short, institutional design shapes both the broad nature of political-party systems and the behavior of individual politicians within parties. Formal rules determine which interests in society are represented in the policy-making process and what the balance of power among those interests will be. For young democracies that struggle to establish popular support for new political procedures—and to strike a balance between government decisiveness on one hand and deliberation on the other—the design of institutions is a critical issue that engenders a great deal of political wrangling.

The Impact of Electoral Systems

The most prominent school of research on institutional design focuses on the impact of electoral systems on party systems. Building on seminal work by Anthony Downs and Maurice Duverger, scholars have generated well-developed literatures both on the formal spatial theory of party competition under various electoral systems and on the empirical impact of electoral rules on party competition.[10] What have come to be known as Duverger's Law (that single-member-district plurality elections encourage a two-party system) and Duverger's Hypothesis (that proportional representation [PR] allows for multipartism) are among the most widely recognized results of this work. The specific mechanisms of these phenomena have been identified and estimated with increasing precision.

Recent scholarship has shown that although the electoral formulas by which votes are translated into seats are significant in affecting proportionality and the distribution of seats at the margin, the critical element of electoral systems driving these results is the number of legislative seats allocated in a given electoral district, or district magnitude (M).[11] The potential for disproportionality exists under any electoral system, provided that there are fewer seats to distribute than votes cast. Moreover, the lower the ratio of seats to votes, the greater the potential for disproportionality.[12] This is the basis of the insight that M is the critical factor driving the aggregate effects of electoral systems on party systems. A related insight is that the distinction between majoritarian and PR systems is not dichotomous, as Duverger had implied, but rather that there is a continuum from $M = 1$ (single-member districts, or SMDs) through $M = S$ (where S is the total number of seats in the legislature), and that the number of parties winning seats, as well as the proportionality of electoral systems, generally rises along that continuum.

In addition to M, of course, other elements of electoral systems affect the aggregate shape of party systems. Although less decisive than once thought, the differences among formulas are significant.[13] Generally, among divisor systems the smaller the increment among successive divisors, the less proportional the results, the fewer the expected number of parties, and the greater the likelihood of partisan majorities.[14] Among quota/remainder systems, small quotas have a similar effect of favoring large parties and generating partisan majorities.[15] A more blunt mechanism among electoral systems for affecting aggregate results is the minimum threshold. Even in relatively large districts, many systems require parties to secure a fixed minimum percentage of the vote, or threshold, in order to be awarded their proportional share of seats. The effects of such legal thresholds are straightforward: higher thresholds mean that fewer parties win seats and the likelihood of partisan majorities increases.

District magnitude, formula, and threshold have been the principal elements of institutional analyses of party systems, and the effects of each are reasonably well understood. In practice, of course, we find variations on these characteristics even within electoral systems. The most significant of these is the phenomenon of mixed, or multitiered, electoral systems, in which geographic districts overlap. Multitiered systems provide for a legislature in which some members represent specific local constituencies, but in which some number of seats is distributed in larger districts, mitigating the disproportionality inherent in small districts.

An increasingly popular variant of mixed systems combines SMD elections for part of the legislature with party-list elections by a highly proportional electoral formula for the remaining seats in the upper tier. The impact on the party system at the aggregate level depends on the sizes of the respective districts, the formula used to allocate seats, legal threshold requirements, and the distribution method used for the seats of the upper tier.

Upper-tier seats may be distributed *independently of* the results in the smaller districts (e.g., Russia, Ecuador, Hungary, Japan), or *as compensation for* disproportionalities in the partisan distribution of votes and seats among small districts (e.g., Germany and Sweden). Although mixed systems introduce certain complexities into institutional analysis, their effects on party systems at the aggregate level can be accommodated relatively easily by existing theories. In estimating mixed systems' effects on proportionality, fragmentation, and partisan majorities, for example, the relevant properties of compensatory systems are those of the upper tier, where the partisan distribution of seats is ultimately decided. Where the multiple tiers operate independently, they can be evaluated independently, and their effects averaged according to the ratio of seats allocated in each.

In short, at the aggregate level, theories about the impact of electoral institutions on party systems are reasonably well developed and supported by empirical evidence. The analytical focus on assembly electoral systems, however, has distracted research from a critical point: in systems where executives are chosen by popular election, as opposed to parliamentary selection, the effects of executive and legislative elections interact.[16] To understand how institutional design affects party systems outside of pure parliamentary regimes, then, it is critical to examine electoral systems for executives and their relationship with assembly elections. Matthew Shugart and I have directed attention to two primary determinants of this relationship: executive electoral formula and the electoral cycle.[17]

Executive Electoral Formulas

Two types of formula account for almost all presidential elections: 1) plurality, and 2) majority runoff (MRO).[18] Under a plurality system, the candidate with the most votes is elected, period. Under an MRO system, a majority of votes is required for election in the first round. If no candidate secures a majority, then the top two candidates compete in a runoff election. The most important difference between these systems is that the MRO format encourages a greater number of presidential candidates to compete than does plurality. Under plurality, where the threshold for success is high, the best strategy for a presidential aspirant who cannot reasonably expect to win the most votes is to enter into a preelectoral coalition with a viable candidate. Under MRO, on the other hand, the threshold is much lower. One need only finish second in the first round to survive. Moreover, given that electoral coalitions can be renegotiated after the first round in anticipation of the runoff election, even nonviable candidates must compete in the first round to establish formally their electoral strength and the value of their second-round endorsement.

The initial result is that the MRO format encourages greater fragmentation of the first-round vote among presidential candidates than does plurality. Data from 54 elections across 13 countries show that the mean effective number of presidential candidates winning votes was 3.8 under MRO, as opposed to 2.8 under plurality (see Table 1).[19] This has important implications for the *legislative* party system as well, for two reasons. First, where executives and legislatures are both popularly elected, executive elections tend to be more salient to voters than legislative elections.[20] As a result, the effects of institutional rules governing executive elections tend to spill over into legislative party systems. Second, where presidential and legislative elections are held at the same time, legislative elections are almost always held concurrently with the *first round* of MRO presidential elections, rather than with the second round.[21] The result is that legislative party systems tend to mirror the fragmentation of presidential contests: Where plurality elections encourage broad coalitions at the presidential level, legislative party systems are less fragmented. Where MRO encourages more fragmentation in presidential campaigns, on the other hand, legislative party systems reflect this pattern as well.

The irony here is that one of the principal arguments in favor of MRO has been that it would ensure the election of a president with a mandate from a majority of voters.[22] To the extent that MRO contributes to fragmentation of the legislative party system, however, it makes

Table 1 — Electoral Formula, Electoral Cycle, and Party-System Fragmentation

Presidential-Election Formula	Electoral Cycle	
	Concurrent Elections	*Nonconcurrent Elections*
Plurality	$N_P = 2.7$ $N_S = 2.8$	$N_P = 2.9$ $N_S = 4.2$
MRO	$N_P = 3.7$ $N_S = 5.0$	$N_P = 3.8$ $N_S = 5.0$

Source: Data from Dieter Nohlen, *Enciclopedia electoral latinoamericana y del Caribe* (San José, Costa Rica: Instituto Interamericano de Derechos Humanos, 1993).

Note: Figures are based on data from 54 presidential elections and 65 assembly elections in the following countries: Brazil, Chile, Colombia, Dominican Republic, Ecuador, El Salvador, France, Guatemala, Nicaragua, Peru, Poland, Portugal, Venezuela. Data from countries using SMD plurality elections for the legislative assembly are not included because SMD systems tend to depress the number of parties in assembly elections, independent of the effects of the electoral formula for president and the electoral cycle.

MRO, majority runoff; N_P, effective number of candidates in presidential election (first round, if MRO); N_S, effective number of seat-winning parties in lower chamber of legislative assembly. The number of seat-winning parties is used rather than the number of vote-winning parties because vote-distribution data were not available for all elections in all countries. These results, however, are consistent with those from a previous, smaller data set, in which the distribution of votes was used.

legislative coalition building more difficult and thus undermines the ability of presidents to act.

Finally, it is worth noting that the distinction between plurality and MRO presidential elections need not be a strict dichotomy. Plurality elections are widely distrusted on the grounds that, while they usually encourage broad coalitions, they also allow the election of a candidate supported by only a minority of voters (and opposed by a clear majority) if the field of candidates is divided. Salvador Allende's victory with 36.6 percent of the vote in Chile in 1973 is often cited in this regard. But even though the goal of a two-round system is to avoid such an outcome, it does not follow that the requisite vote share for a first-round victory must be 50 percent. In 1949, for example, Costa Rican presidential elections began to require a first-round share of 40 percent. This hurdle has been low enough to encourage broad first-round coalitions, as in plurality systems, and to discourage the fragmentation of MRO elections; Costa Rica has had a first-round winner in all 11 presidential elections since. In 1995, Argentina replaced its electoral college for the presidency with a system similar to Costa Rica's, but with a 45 percent first-round requirement.[23]

Lowering the first-round hurdle suggests a compromise between plurality and MRO formats. Such systems do not, however, preclude the possibility of narrow victories by minority candidates. Moreover, the height of the hurdle is essentially arbitrary. For example, a 40 percent to 39 percent to 21 percent distribution of votes would produce a first-round winner in Costa Rica, but not in Argentina.

One solution is to weight the extent to which the leading candidate falls short of a majority against the extent to which she defeats the other candidates. A simple formula to achieve this is known as the Double Complement Rule, under which the leading candidate (v_1) wins in the first round if the extent by which she falls short of a majority is less than half the extent by which the second-place candidate (v_2) falls short.[24] Arithmetically, the first-place candidate wins if: 50 percent − v_2 > 2 (50 percent − v_1). Under this rule, a minority candidate wins in the first round only if she is significantly stronger than her competitors. The hypothetical 40 percent to 39 percent to 21 percent distribution above would require a runoff election, whereas a 40 percent to 25 percent to 20 percent to 15 percent distribution would not. Yet, in the latter case, if the first candidate were highly objectionable to her opponents, there would be strong incentives for the opponents to coalesce prior to the first round, unlike under MRO. Thus the Double Complement Rule could sustain the coalition-building incentives of plurality rule without allowing weak minority candidates a victory over a divided field and without establishing arbitrary hurdles for victory in the first round.

The Electoral Cycle

Where executives are popularly elected, another critical feature of institutional design affecting party systems is the relative timing of presidential and assembly elections, or the electoral cycle. As suggested above, the fragmenting effect of MRO presidential elections on the legislative party system is relevant when elections for the two branches are held at the same time. Across political systems, however, there is enormous variance in electoral cycles. In many cases, presidential and assembly elections are always concurrent and members of both branches serve simultaneous terms (e.g., Costa Rica, Venezuela, Uruguay, Nicaragua). In others, concurrent elections alternate with assembly mid-term elections (e.g., the United States, the Philippines, Argentina). In still others, presidential and assembly terms are asynchronous; assembly elections occur sometimes early in presidential terms and sometimes later (e.g., France, Korea since 1987, Chile since 1993).

Two related effects of the electoral cycle are important to the shape of party systems: first is the effect, in conjunction with the presidential-election formula, on party-system fragmentation; second is the effect on partisan support in the legislature for the president. The combined effects of the presidential-election formula and the electoral cycle are illustrated in Table 1. The same data are broken down by electoral format and by country in Tables 2 and 3.

Table 2 — Concurrent Elections, Plurality and MRO Formulas

Country	Number of Elections	Mean N_P	Mean N_S
	Plurality Formula		
Brazil (1945–50)	2	2.8	3.4
Dominican Republic (1978–90)	4	2.7	2.4
Nicaragua (1990)	1	2.1	2.1
Venezuela (1958–88)	7	3.0	3.2
Total	14	2.7	2.8
	MRO Formula		
Brazil (1994)	1	2.7	8.1
Chile (1989–93)	2	2.5	4.9
Ecuador (1979–88)	3	5.3	4.8
Guatemala (1985–90)	2	4.8	3.8
Peru (1980–90)	3	3.4	3.6
Total	11	3.7	5.0

Table 3 — Nonconcurrent Elections, Plurality and MRO Formulas

Country	Number of Presidential Elections	Mean N_P	Number of Assembly Elections	Mean N_S
	Plurality Formula			
Brazil (1954–62)	2	3.5	3	4.6
Chile (1932–73)[a]	8	2.7	11	5.8
Colombia (1974–90)	5	2.4	5	2.2
Total	15	2.9	19	4.2
	MRO Formula			
Brazil (1989–90)	1	4.8	1	8.7
El Salvador (1985–91)	2	3.8	3	2.5
France (1965–95)	6	4.2	8	3.3
Poland (1990–93)	1	3.9	2	7.1
Portugal (1976–91)	4	2.4	7	3.5
Total	14	3.8	21	5.0

[a]Technically, Chile's presidential-election law required a majority for victory in the popular election; otherwise the president was chosen from among the two top candidates by Congress. In all four elections that failed to produce popular majorities, Congress picked the plurality winner. This was the case even in the selection of Salvador Allende, the Socialist candidate whose plurality in 1973 was fewer than 2 percentage points above the second-place candidate. Moreover, in the absence of a runoff election, presidential aspirants frequently dispensed with campaigns and formed preelection coalitions. Thus Chile is included among the cases of plurality systems.

Table 1 illustrates a number of points. First, as discussed above, the effective number of presidential candidates is substantially higher under MRO than under plurality elections. Second, the distinct effects of plurality and MRO presidential-election formulas are more relevant to the legislative party system when elections are concurrent than when they are nonconcurrent. In plurality systems, broader coalitions behind presidential candidates translate into less fragmentation of the vote among legislative parties. Voters are most likely to cast legislative votes for the slate of candidates associated with their presidential choice.[25] Thus fragmentation of the legislative party system is lowest under the plurality/concurrent format, even with PR assembly elections. Conversely, highly fragmented presidential contests under MRO generate highly fragmented legislative party systems as well. Where elections are not concurrent, and legislative campaigns are conducted on their own terms, the effects are mitigated somewhat, but the tendency of plurality presidential elections to reduce party-system fragmentation remains impressive and the contagion to the legislative party system remains substantial.

The other important effect of the electoral cycle is on partisan support for the president. This is clearly related to party-system fragmentation: The more fragmented the party system, the lower the expected share of legislative seats held by the president's party. But the effects of the electoral cycle are even more precise. One reason is voters' tendency to cast straight partisan ballots for both president and legislature when elections are concurrent; as a result, parties running strong presidential candidates are rewarded in the legislature. The other reason has to do with cycles of presidential popularity. Presidents tend to enjoy their greatest popularity in the honeymoon phase early in their terms; levels of popular support decrease thereafter. Shugart shows that this effect is manifest in the electoral fortunes of presidents' parties across the whole range of electoral cycles.[26]

Figure 1 shows the percent change in partisan support for presidents in lower legislative chambers, plotted against the proportion of a president's term that has passed when legislative elections take place. Time = 0 indicates concurrent elections. The pattern is strikingly clear. In concurrent elections, the parties of winning presidential candidates almost always gain seats in the legislature as well. The same is true for elections that take place during the president's honeymoon period. As time progresses, however, presidential fortunes decline. By the halfway point in a presidential term, legislative elections more often than not bring losses for the president's party. This effect is even more pro-nounced in late-term elections.

The general decline in presidential support is particularly important with regard to asynchronous electoral cycles, where presidential and legislative terms are of different lengths. In France, for example, the

Figure 1
Electoral Cycle and Change in Partisan Support for the President

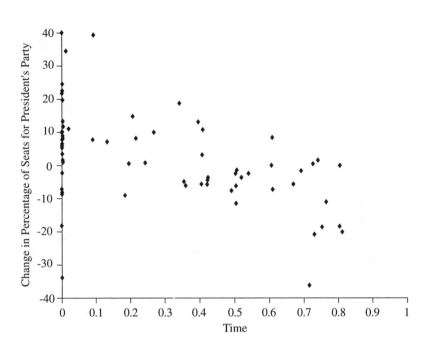

Source: Reprinted, by permission, from Matthew S. Shugart, "The Electoral Cycle and Institutional Sources of Divided Government," *American Political Science Review* 89 (June 1995): 332.
Note: Data are from 76 elections in Argentina, Brazil, Chile, Colombia, Costa Rica, Ecuador, El Salvador, France, Philippines, Portugal, the United States, and Venezuela.

seven-year presidential term and five-year parliamentary term have been critical in determining the nature of relations between the president and parliament. French president François Mitterand used his authority to dissolve parliament and call elections during both of his honeymoon periods, securing large gains for the Socialists in each case. But five years into each of his terms, the Socialists endured significant losses in parliament, ushering in two-year periods of *cohabitation,* marked by strained relations between the president and the cabinet and parliament.

Where cabinets are responsible exclusively to presidents, rather than to assemblies, the implications of asynchronous electoral cycles may be even more dramatic. In Chile, a 1994 amendment to the constitution established a six-year presidential term, but left assembly terms at four and eight years for the lower and upper chambers, respectively. As a result, some presidents will benefit from concurrent elections, but will face another round of assembly elections four years into their terms, when their parties' prospects are much worse. Other presidents will be elected nonconcurrently, but will subsequently face assembly elections two years into their terms. The nature of the electoral cycle suggests that the prospects for support in congress are quite different for alternate presidents. But the difference is completely arbitrary—the result of an asynchronous electoral cycle.

Three sets of institutional factors are most important in shaping party systems at the aggregate level: assembly electoral rules, executive electoral rules, and the electoral cycle. Assembly electoral rules are the subject of an extensive literature, a few of whose main results are reviewed above. The impact of executive electoral rules and the electoral cycle on legislative party systems has received far less attention. I have argued here that the effects of executive elections spill over into the assembly party system. Plurality presidential elections decrease party-system fragmentation and increase the chances of presidential majorities. The effect is most pronounced when elections are concurrent. Moreover, across all formats, cycles of presidential popularity affect assembly elections; presidents' parties fare well during concurrent and honeymoon elections but do much worse thereafter.

The importance of these effects is underscored by the fact that so many new democracies have popularly elected presidents. The Latin American states that democratized and redemocratized in the 1980s all elect their chief executives. The same is true for some of the most notable cases of recent democratization in Asia—the Philippines, South Korea, Taiwan—as well as many of the emerging democracies in Africa. Amost all the post-Soviet states have elected presidents, as do Poland and Romania. In short, no theory of institutional design and party systems is complete that does not account for the important interaction between legislative and executive elections.

Politicians and Parties

The first part of this essay reviewed a host of institutional factors that affect the aggregate representation of parties in legislatures. As important as this is, however, it tells us relatively little about the kind of representation legislators are likely to provide, or the ability of parties to act collectively to implement policy.

For example, aggregate indicators of fragmentation and partisan majorities suggest that the Colombian and Venezuelan party systems were strikingly similar throughout the 1970s and 1980s: both systems were marked by low levels of fragmentation and frequent partisan majorities behind presidents. Yet legislators provided strikingly different brands of representation in the two countries. Colombian legislators focused on personalized representation of distinct clienteles, usually with specific geographic bases. The principal resources mobilized to garner electoral support were those that could be attributed to individual legislators: patronage jobs, local public-works projects, subsidies and regulatory protection for specific businesses and industries.[27] Venezuelan legislators, on the other hand, virtually ignored the geographic districts from which they were elected; they provided almost no constituency service, but observed near-airtight party voting discipline on policy initiatives handed down by national party leaders.[28] Institutional factors are enormously important in explaining this difference and, more generally, in explaining the motivations of legislators and the ability of legislative parties to act collectively. As above, my analysis focuses on regime type and on electoral systems.

The critical distinction here is between institutional arrangements that encourage legislators to cultivate personal reputations among voters and those that put the collective reputation of the party first. This distinction has long been a staple of the literature on the U.S. Congress,[29] but only recently have scholars of comparative party systems devoted much attention to it.[30] The behavior associated with each type of reputation—personal and partisan—is not always antithetical. For example, party leaders may encourage rank-and-file legislators to cultivate personal reputations if leaders expect that attention to constituency service will pay electoral dividends to the party as a whole.[31] Widespread cultivation of personalized support by individual legislators, however, undermines parties' ability to develop and maintain collective reputations for consistent public policy. Where legislators focus on personal representation, party cohesion on major public policies is apt to suffer because legislators are more likely to craft cross-party coalitions on an issue-by-issue basis.

There are a number of reasons for the tension between personal and partisan reputation. First, the kinds of goods and services for which legislators can claim personal credit are usually costly; their provision by all legislators can make fiscal discipline—a collective good for which parties might claim credit—unfeasible. This is the familiar logic used by critics of pork-barrel politics.[32] It is worth noting that the pork barrel is not unique to SMD systems, but is also evident in multimember districts where individual politicians carve out distinct geographic constituencies, or bailiwicks.[33] Second, the time and effort they devote to cultivating personal reputations prevents legislators from developing broader public policy and shepherding it through the legislative process. If legislators are devoted mainly to serving a constituency, then they are less willing to bear the significant costs of acquiring expertise on complex policy questions. As a result, the quality of public policy—another collective good for which parties might claim credit—suffers.[34] Third, electoral rules that require competition *among members of the same party* as well as competition among parties motivate legislators to cultivate a personal reputation. Where this is the case, a legislator's political survival depends on distinguishing herself politically from her copartisans. Under these circumstances, party leaders' ability to impose voting discipline and generate collective action by legislative parties is weakened.

Because variations in institutional design directly shape the trade-off between personal and partisan representation, they help explain the types of policies and coalitions legislators will value and predict the ability of legislative parties to act collectively. Two important aspects of institutional design are regime type and electoral rules.

Regime Type and Electoral Rules

Those who study comparative politics and formal theories of coalitions generally agree that parliamentary government produces more cohesive parties than does presidential government. Recently, the case has been presented most forcefully as part of widespread criticisms of presidentialism in general.[35] The logic of the argument, however, can be traced back to Walter Bagehot's 1867 book *The English Constitution*, in which the author observes that the mutual dependence of cabinet and parliament for survival creates a strong incentive for legislators to form stable coalitions behind broad policy platforms. As Bagehot puts it, "The legislature chosen, in name, to make laws, in fact finds its principal business in making and in keeping an executive."[36] Expecting to be judged at the polls according to the executive's success in implementing broad policies, members of the British Parliament began in the nineteenth century to subordinate local demands to national party objectives. Bagehot calls the result the "efficient secret" of cabinet government. Subsequent studies of English politics support the claim: the willingness of parliamentarians to submit themselves to the strict discipline of party leaders was tied directly to changes in voting patterns by which the electorate began to use their ballots as a way to influence the partisan composition of the executive.[37]

The traditional distinction between presidential and parliamentary government on these grounds, however, is of only limited value, for two reasons. First, across regimes with elected presidents, constitutional powers allocated to presidents and legislatures, both over legislation and over the composition of the executive itself, vary tremendously. As a result, even in regimes conventionally referred to as "presidential," the extent to which legislatures are responsible for "making and keeping an executive" and for crafting broad public policies varies enormously.[38] Second, among new democracies, the tendency to establish presidencies but to endow assemblies with some level of control over cabinet survival has increased markedly. Thus, rather than rely on the familiar dichotomy between "presidential" and "parliamentary" regimes, it is necessary to examine the formal rules that govern cabinet responsibility.

The common property shared by those regimes—with presidents or without—whose parties exhibit the "efficient secret" of cohesive support for executives is that once selected, cabinets are responsible exclusively to the assembly. Even where presidents play some role in the initial selection of ministers (as in France, Finland, and Portugal), the cabinet's survival, once invested, is dependent on parliamentary support. Where cabinet responsibility is clearly the assembly's prerogative, legislators can expect voters to evaluate their performance largely on the basis of the executive's performance, so they are more willing to submit to the discipline of party leaders.

A slight variant on this arrangement is dual responsibility of cabinet ministers to both the president and the legislature. This format has been used in a number of Latin American countries, including Ecuador, Peru prior to 1992, Colombia beginning in 1991, and Chile before 1925. It also describes cabinet responsibility during the Weimar Republic in Germany. Although systematic data on cabinet stability are not yet available, these dual-responsibility regimes appear to be marked by far greater cabinet instability and conflict between presidents and assemblies than systems with exclusive responsibility to either the assembly or the president. Of particular importance here is that the motivation for party discipline in the legislature is absent when legislators do not expect to bear full responsibility for executive performance. It is troubling, then, to note that dual responsibility over cabinets is common among the new post-Soviet states, and that control over cabinet composition and responsibility has been an ongoing point of contention between presidents and assemblies in Russia, Ukraine, and Poland.

The cohesiveness of parties and the efforts by legislators to develop personal reputations vary significantly even across systems with similar constitutional rules governing the origin and survival of executives. I argue here that much of that variance can be explained by the incentives generated by the rules of electoral competition. Moreover, I suggest that the emphasis electoral studies have placed on the distinction between SMD and PR systems and their respective effects on aggregate party representation neglects important variations in the way voter preferences are aggregated *within* these categories of systems. I suggest that four critical variables determine the relative incentives for legislators to cultivate personal versus partisan reputations: 1) the degree of control that party leaders exercise over use of the party label; 2) the number and type of votes citizens cast in any given election; 3) the degree to which votes cast for a given candidate from a party contribute to the party's electoral fortunes more generally; and 4) district magnitude (M).[39] District magnitude is discussed separately, for reasons elaborated below.

In most systems, party labels convey information to voters that would be extremely expensive for candidates to communicate on their own. Thus the ability of party leaders to control access to the party label is a critical resource in organizing and motivating rank-and-file politicians.

There are two elements to control over the label: control over party endorsements of candidates, and control over the rank of candidates on the ballot in electoral-list systems. When party leaders can prevent legislative candidates from running under the party label, or when they can establish list positions that effectively determine the likelihood of any given candidate's election (as in closed-list systems such as Argentina, and Venezuela before 1993), legislators have strong incentives to abide by the directives of the central party leadership. Alternatively, in systems where leaders control access to the ballot under the party's label but candidates win election in order of personal votes received (Poland, Finland), there remains a strong incentive for copartisans to distinguish themselves by developing distinct personal reputations.

In still other systems, individual candidates gain access to the party label by collecting a requisite number of signatures and paying a registration fee (Colombia), by winning primary elections (United States), or through a guaranteed "right" among incumbent legislators (Brazil); party leaders cannot deny use of the label. In these cases, incentives against party cohesiveness and for personalism are greatest.

The manner in which citizens cast votes and the manner in which votes are aggregated across candidates and parties also influence party cohesion. Consider the number and types of votes. Citizens might cast a single vote for a specific candidate; they might be allowed to cast multiple votes for different candidates; or they might be required to cast a single vote at the level of party, without being able to distinguish among candidates at all. The first situation describes the open-list PR system (Brazil), the single nontransferable vote (SNTV) system (Taiwan, Japan prior to 1994), or the double-simultaneous vote system (DSV) (Uruguayan presidency). In all these systems, voters are forced to state a single, indivisible personal preference, and candidates must compete simultaneously against both copartisans and other parties for that vote. Personal reputations are critical; party cohesiveness suffers.

In other systems, voters cast multiple votes for different candidates; elections may be conducted over two rounds (U.S. primary and general elections), multiple preference votes may be allowed (Italy prior to 1993), or rank ordering of candidates may be allowed (Ireland's single transferable vote [STV]). Here, intrapartisan competition remains important to candidates, but the urgency of the one-time, all-against-all competition for personal votes is mitigated. Under limited-vote or STV systems, candidates from the same party can run as a bloc and appeal to voters to distribute their preference votes among copartisans only.

Finally, where voters cast only a single vote at the level of party (Argentina, Israel, Spain) and cannot distinguish among candidates, the incentive to cultivate personal reputations is weakest, and the value of the party label is correspondingly most important.

An issue related to but distinct from the number and type of votes is the degree to which citizens' preference votes benefit only the preferred candidates or are pooled across the entire party. Consider the difference between an open-list PR system (Brazil) and an SNTV system (Taiwan). In both, voters specify a single candidate within a party list. In the open-list PR system, votes are aggregated first at the party level to determine how many seats the party wins; then those seats are distributed among the most preferred candidates within each party. Thus extremely popular candidates have "coattails" that can carry less popular copartisans into office. Despite personal-preference voting, the popularity of the party list as a whole is valuable to its members.

In the SNTV system, votes won by a candidate count only for that candidate; from the party's perspective, surplus votes for an individual candidate are wasted. Moreover, no candidate stands to benefit from the popularity of copartisans from her district. Indeed, one candidate's gains are likely her copartisan's losses. Thus incentives for personalism are greatest and for party cohesion weakest when votes are not pooled across candidates.

Intrapartisan Competition

It is critical to underscore that the variables discussed above—control over party labels, types of votes, and pooling of votes—are unrelated to the distinction between SMD and $M > 1$ electoral systems. That is, all three variables fluctuate in electoral systems on both sides of the conventional dichotomy between PR and SMD systems. In some SMD systems, party leaders exert strong ballot control (Canada); in others, they cannot control access to party labels (United States, the Philippines). Likewise, $M > 1$ systems have both strong (Argentina) and weak (Colombia) leadership control over ballots. SMD systems vary as to whether they require a single, partisan vote (Britain), or allow multiple votes (Australia's alternative-vote system) and intrapartisan preference voting (U.S. primaries). $M > 1$ systems likewise vary on partisan voting (Spain), multiple votes (Italy pre-1993), and individual-preference votes (Brazil). Some SMD systems allow pooling across multiple candidates from the same party (Honduras's experiment with DSV in 1985); some do not (the Philippines). And some $M > 1$ systems allow pooling (Nicaragua) and some do not (Taiwan). In short, there is enormous empirical differentiation across all these variables, regardless of political regime type. Table 4 summarizes the scope of variation and illustrates the different formats with empirical examples.

In other work, I systematically evaluate all the feasible combinations of these variables and their empirical occurrence.[40] For now, the critical point is that control over party labels, types of votes, and pooling of votes determine the degree to which candidates from the same party must compete against one another to win election. These three variables

Table 4 — Electoral Systems and Incentives for Party Cohesion

Leadership Control	Type of Vote	Vote Pooling	Examples ($M = 1$)	Examples ($M > 1$)
High	Partisan	Yes	Britain, Canada	Israel, Spain, Argentina
High	Multiple	Yes	France	Mali
Low	Multiple	Yes	Australia	Pre-1994 Italy, Ireland
Low	Multiple	No	United States	Philippines (Senate)
Low	Personal	Yes	Uruguay (presidency)	Brazil, Poland, Finland
Low	Personal	No	Philippines (House)	Pre-1994 Japan, Taiwan, Colombia

have straightforward effects on the trade-off between personal and partisan representation in legislatures. Stronger leadership control over party labels generates more partisan and less personal representation. The requirement of partisan votes, rather than personal-preference votes, likewise favors partisan representation. The same is true with respect to pooling preference votes across party lists. The converse of these statements hold as well.

In the discussion of aggregate-level effects on party systems, I noted that M is the primary determinant of proportionality among electoral systems. It is also critical in determining the electoral value of personal reputations among candidates, and so in shaping the trade-off between personal and partisan representation. The basic proposition here is that M's effect on this trade-off depends on whether there is *intrapartisan competition* for votes.

First consider the case in which there is no intrapartisan competition. Here, party leaders control party labels and the structure of party lists, so candidates have incentives to abide by leadership directives. If M = 1, though, and a party nominates one candidate in each district, the party and the candidate are effectively identical to voters; there remains a strong incentive for candidates to cultivate personal support among voters—and for parties to tolerate this behavior in moderation. As M increases under such closed-party-list systems, however, the number of candidates on each party list grows. The individual impact of each candidate's personal reputation on the party's electoral fortunes necessarily declines and the importance of the collective party reputation rises. As M increases under closed-list systems, then, partisan representation increases in importance relative to personal representation.

Next consider the case in which there is intrapartisan competition for votes. At any M, it is reasonable to expect personal reputation to matter more than it would under closed lists. But as M rises, the number of copartisans from which each candidate must distinguish herself rises as well. In high-M systems with intrapartisan competition, then, the imperative to carve out a personal reputation distinct from that of one's party is strongest. In fact, this is consistent with empirical accounts of legislative behavior in systems like Brazil, Colombia, and pre-1994 Japan, where catering to particularistic interests superseded legislators' adherence to party discipline.[41]

In addition to weakening party discipline, and so destabilizing legislative coalitions, the quest for legislative particularism is expensive. Pork-barrel projects may build electoral support, but they also drain the treasury of funds that might be used more efficiently on global public goods.[42] This particularly troubling scenario faces many new democracies that confront simultaneous demands for economic and political reform.

The bottom line here is that M is an important determinant of the trade-off between personal and partisan representation, but its effect depends on the values of the other electoral-system variables—party-label control, types of votes, and pooling of votes. Where these other factors allow for intraparty competition among candidates, increasing M favors personal representation at the expense of partisan representation. Where electoral rules prevent intrapartisan competition, the effect is reversed—increasing M favors partisan representation over personal representation. This somewhat complex relationship is illustrated graphically, again with empirical examples, in Figure 2.

Mixed Electoral Systems

Given these general propositions about the effects of electoral rules on representation, it is worthwhile to note that mixed electoral systems can provide separate sets of incentives for distinct sets of legislators in the same assembly. Indeed, a commonly stated goal of mixed systems is to represent legislators with strong personal links to constituents in one tier of the electoral system, and parties with policy interests that transcend narrow geographical constituencies in the other. Toward this end, the most popular format among countries that have recently adopted mixed systems combines SMD elections for some proportion of seats with closed-list PR election in large districts in the rest. This describes electoral reforms adopted in Italy and Japan as of 1994, Russia and Venezuela as of 1993, Bulgaria in 1990, and Hungary as of 1989.

Two points are important with regard to the mixed SMD-PR format. First, there appears to be genuine popular support for electoral rules that encourage strong personal ties and personal accountability between legislators and constituents. Scholars have frequently noted the importance of strong parties to democratic development, and almost as

Figure 2
Effects of District Magnitude (M) on Party Cohesiveness

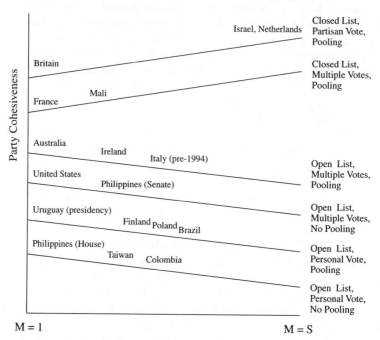

frequently criticized personalistic representation and its association with the pork barrel. Yet in Venezuela, for example, public dissatisfaction with the old closed-list PR system was largely targeted at "partyocracy," in which legislators' electoral dependence on national party leaders precluded flexibility in responding to demands from their districts.[43] One advocate of the SMD system summed up the case as follows: "Elected representatives ought to act in the interests of those who elected them, ought to attend to their complaints and demands, ought to respond to their correspondence. . . . The SMD system does not guarantee the proportional representation of parties, but in exchange it is the best at allowing the representation of the interests that really stir society."[44] In Japan and in Italy as well, the adoption of mixed systems was fueled by massive public dissatisfaction with the perceived excessive control by factional leaders over legislative parties and elections.[45] In all these cases, SMD elections were popular precisely because they were expected to foster direct links between representatives and constituents without the intermediation of political parties. In short, some prominent cases of electoral reform suggest that very strong political parties may stand as low in popular opinion as very weak parties do in academic opinion.

The questions remain whether the SMD-PR format does in fact create two different "types" of legislators, and what the implications of this might be for party systems. The analysis above suggests that those legislators elected under SMD systems should be significantly less inclined toward party cohesiveness than their counterparts chosen by closed-list PR election. This difference will be even more pronounced if party leaders do not control access to party labels in SMD elections.

Where leaders do not control access to party labels, two completely distinct, parallel party systems may develop within the same legislative chamber. This may be the most apt description for the party system of the Russian Duma as a result of both the 1993 and 1995 elections. The results of the 1993 nationwide closed-list PR elections, won by Vladimir Zhirinovsky's Liberal Democratic Party, were strikingly different from those of the SMD elections, where a majority of all candidates actually ran as independents.[46] The disjuncture between members elected under the PR system versus those elected under the SMD system persisted as a primary point of contention in negotiations between the Duma and the Federation Council over a new electoral law in early 1995. The Council held out—ultimately unsuccessfully—for an increase in the ratio of SMD to PR seats in the Duma on the grounds that representatives of regional interests produced by SMD elections were preferable to the representatives from Moscow-based parties produced by PR lists.

Although signs in the summer of 1995 indicated that the major Duma blocs were adapting to the mixed system by establishing regional-level branches to organize campaigns for the SMD seats, these adaptations proved only moderately successful. The large plurality (77) of SMD seats were won once again by independent candidates.[47] Ultimately, the construction of a unified party system within the Duma will hinge on the ability of national-level organizations to integrate candidates for regional SMD seats into platforms focused on broad national issues.

To sum up, the nature of parties under mixed electoral systems depends on the extent to which party organizations and leaders command the resources necessary to win election in the SMDs, versus the extent to which SMD candidates act as individual political entrepreneurs. In the newer mixed systems, it is not yet clear how the balance between party control and candidate independence will be struck, but this promises to be an intriguing area for research.

The Current Research Agenda

This essay reviews current institutional theories of party systems and adds to two specific areas. First, I suggest that theories of the aggregate effects of institutional design on party systems owe more attention to the effects of executive elections on assembly party systems, and that two characteristics of executive elections are particularly important here: the electoral formula, and the relative timing of executive and assembly elections. Plurality elections encourage broader coalitions in presidential competition than do MRO elections, along with a less fragmented assembly party system, especially where elections to the two branches are concurrent. Across all electoral cycles, moreover, the general tendency of presidential popularity to decline over time directly affects the level of partisan support for presidents in assemblies.

The second point is that the aggregate effects of institutions on party systems do not tell us enough about how individual politicians behave and parties perform. Data on party-system fragmentation, proportionality, and majorities do not shed much light on the motivations of politicians, the types of public policies they value, and the ability of parties to act collectively in pursuit of partisan goals. I suggest that policy preferences and partisan capacity are products of a fundamental tension between personal and partisan representation, and that elements of constitutional and electoral-system design affect the level of this tension in predictable ways. Specifically, partisan representation is encouraged by exclusive cabinet responsibility to the assembly, by centralized control over party labels in elections, by the lack of personal-preference voting among copartisans, by the pooling of votes across copartisans, and by M.

Implicit in much of the research agenda discussed in this essay is the premise that party systems are largely the products of institutional rules. The most fundamental challenge to this agenda is the straightforward observation that institutional design is not simply imposed on political systems exogenously. The rules of political contestation are themselves the products of political processes, and are subject to ongoing dispute and negotiation.[48] For example, this essay focuses on constitutional design and on the rules of electoral competition and their effects on party systems. Yet constitutions are amended and electoral systems are reformed, for the most part, by partisan politicians. Therefore, the extent to which it is useful to think of institutional design as an independent variable in shaping party systems warrants serious attention.

The question of what factors drive the choice and stability of political institutions is simultaneously one of the most challenging and most promising agendas for future research in comparative politics. Two results of this early research suggest that treating formal rules as independent variables, and examining them as products of political contestation, are not necessarily antithetical approaches. Treating formal rules as independent variables derives from game models of institutional choice; even where the fundamental rules of contestation are not enforced by an outside actor, patterns of behavior, once established, quickly come to shape the expectations and strategies of political actors.[49] Even if institutions are defined minimally as shared sets of expectations about the behavior of other political actors, there is a theoretical basis for believing that institutions shape the alternatives that are viable in political competition and coalition building.

Examining formal rules as products of political contestation essentially provides empirical support for the theoretical claim. Recent studies of institutional choices in postcommunist countries demonstrate that not only do formal rules quickly establish mutual expectations about future behavior, they also quickly establish sets of political winners who have control over subsequent institutional changes and who generally have an interest in maintaining stability in institutional formats.[50] Thus, although formal institutions are very much the product of political contestation, institutional design has important independent effects on the strategies and behavior of political actors.

Future research on institutions as independent factors in shaping party systems might well proceed along two paths—one technical and the other normative. The former would aim at estimating more precisely institutional variables of the sort discussed in this essay. For example, although we can describe abstract models of the institutional factors contributing to intrapartisan competition, the specific effects of such competition on public policy have not been estimated in a way that is broadly comparable across systems.[51] Neither does current research illuminate the effects of institutional design on party systems at the aggregate level and at the individual level. For example, do increased incentives for intrapartisan competition produce the same results in highly fragmented party systems as they do in less fragmented systems?

A second path of research would evaluate institutional arrangements by the degree to which the policy they produce accords with various concepts of collective social preferences. Linking citizen preferences with public policies, after all, is one of the fundamental normative claims of democracy. Yet the connection between collective preferences and the institutions that translate them into policies remains a point of serious debate.[52] With regard to political-party systems, this essay has tried to make some claims about the comparative statics of institutional design— for example, that specific changes in formal rules contribute to specific changes in party-system fragmentation or levels of intraparty competition. The more difficult question of whether general normative implications for democracy are associated with such changes remains to be addressed.

NOTES

1. Maurice Duverger, *Political Parties: Their Organization and Activity in the Modern State* (New York: Wiley, 1954); Anthony Downs, *An Economic Theory of Democracy* (New York: Harper and Row, 1957); Rein Taagepera and Matthew S. Shugart, *Seats and Votes* (New Haven: Yale University Press, 1989); Bernard Grofman and Arend Lijphart, eds., *Electoral Laws and Their Political Consequences* (New York: Agathon, 1986); Douglas Rae, *The Political Consequences of Electoral Laws* (New Haven: Yale University Press, 1971); William Riker, *Liberalism Against Populism* (Prospect Heights, Ill.: Waveland Press, 1982).

2. Implicit here is the assumption that there exists a broad diversity of politically relevant values in the electorate that warrant representation.

3. See also Arend Lijphart, *Electoral Systems and Party Systems* (New York: Oxford

University Press, 1994); and Kaare Strom, *Minority Government and Majority Rule* (New York: Cambridge University Press, 1990).

4. Disproportional distribution of legislative seats is a widely—and rightly—criticized product of plurality elections, yet plurality is by no means the only institutional source of disproportionality. Consider the Russian Duma elections of December 1995, in which 37 percent of the vote for the 225 nationwide seats was won by lists that failed to clear the threshold of 5 percent, and so won no representation. See Laura Belin and Robert Orttung, "On the Political Front: Slow Progress Toward Democracy," in J.F. Brown, ed., *Building Democracy: The OMRI Annual Survey of Eastern Europe and the Former Soviet Union* (New York: M.E. Sharpe, 1996), 210–23.

5. Scott Mainwaring and Anibal Perez Linan, "Party Discipline in Multiparty Systems: A Methodological Note and an Analysis of the Brazilian Constitutional Congress" (paper presented at the Ninety-second Annual Meeting of the American Political Science Association, San Francisco, 29 August–1 September 1996); Barry Ames, "Electoral Strategy Under Open List Proportional Representation," *American Journal of Political Science* 39 (May 1995): 406–33.

6. Timothy Power, "The Pen Is Mightier Than the Congress: Decree Authority in Brazil," in John M. Carey and Matthew S. Shugart, eds., *Executive Decree Authority: Calling Out the Tanks or Just Filling Out the Forms?* (New York: Cambridge University Press, forthcoming).

7. Barbara Geddes and Arturo Ribeiro Neto, "Institutional Sources of Corruption in Brazil," *Third World Quarterly* 13 (1992): 641–61.

8. Michael Coppedge, *Strong Parties and Lame Ducks: Presidential Partyarchy and Factionalism in Venezuela* (Stanford: Stanford University Press, 1994); John M. Carey, *Term Limits and Legislative Representation* (New York: Cambridge University Press, 1996), ch. 2.

9. Ann L. Craig and Wayne A. Cornelius, "Houses Divided: Parties and Political Reform in Mexico," in Scott Mainwaring and Timothy R. Scully, eds., *Building Democratic Institutions: Party Systems in Latin America* (Stanford: Stanford University Press, 1995), 249–97.

10. For a summary of the literature on spatial modeling, see Kenneth Shepsle, *Models of Multiparty Electoral Competition* (New York: Harwood Academic, 1991); on the empirical effect of electoral rules, see Taagepera and Shugart, *Seats and Votes*.

11. Taagepera and Shugart, *Seats and Votes*, 112–25.

12. Although the effect is not as strong as with M, it is also the case that disproportionality tends to be greater in assemblies with fewer total seats.

13. If electoral formulas empirically have less impact than once thought, it is likely because only a relatively small number of possible electoral-formula variants are regularly used. The range of divisors and quota that could be employed is theoretically unbounded, but only a handful of formulas are actually used across polities.

14. Divisor systems are those in which seats are distributed among parties by establishing a matrix of quotients, calculated by dividing each party's vote total by series of divisors (e.g., 1, 2, 3, 4 . . . or 1, 3, 5, 7 . . .). As many seats as are available are then awarded in sequence to the parties with the largest quotients.

15. Quota/remainder systems simply establish a vote quota (e.g., Total Votes/M, or Total Votes/[M + 1]) that is sufficient for the "purchase" of a seat. Each party then is awarded as many seats as it has won quotas. If any seats remain unfilled, they are distributed to parties in order of the size of their remaining votes—those not used toward the accumulation of quotas. For a more thorough discussion of the mechanics of various PR formulas, see Taagepera and Shugart, *Seats and Votes*, 19–37.

16. The distinction between popular election and parliamentary selection of the executive is not perfectly clean. Systems with elected presidents but with cabinets selected by, and responsible to, assemblies are increasingly common. For the purposes of this

analysis, it suffices to note that the more politically important the popularly elected executive, the greater the impact of the executive election on the assembly party system.

17. Matthew S. Shugart and John M. Carey, *Presidents and Assemblies: Constitutional Design and Electoral Dynamics* (New York: Cambridge University Press, 1992), 206–72.

18. The U.S. president, of course, is still elected indirectly, through an electoral college, although the electoral college has failed to select the popular-vote plurality winner only three times—in 1824, 1876, and 1888. In Bolivia, if no candidate wins a majority of the popular vote, the president is selected by a joint session of Congress.

19. Effective number of parties (N) is the standard index of party-system fragmentation developed by Markku Laakso and Rein Taagepera, "'Effective' Number of Parties: A Measure with Application to West Europe," *Comparative Political Studies* 12 (1979): 3–27. It is calculated as: $N = 1/\sum v_i^2$, where v_i is the proportion of the vote (or seats) won by the ith party.

20. There are a number of plausible reasons for this: voters perceive the executive branch as the more important one; more money is spent on executive campaigns; and there are economies of scale in transmitting information about executive candidates.

21. The single exception to this of which I am aware is the Ecuadorian election of 1979, in which congressional elections were held concurrently with the second round of presidential balloting.

22. Mark P. Jones, *Electoral Rules and the Survival of Presidential Democracy* (Notre Dame, Ind.: University of Notre Dame Press, 1995), 88–102.

23. Under the new Argentine rule, the first-place candidate wins in the first round if she has more than 45 percent of the vote, or if she has at least 40 percent of the vote and has beaten the second-place candidate by more than 10 percent.

24. Shugart and Carey, *Presidents and Assemblies*, 217–19.

25. In Bolivia, Honduras, and Uruguay, and intermittently in the Dominican Republic, ballots have been "fused," meaning that voters cast a single vote for president and congress. Even where ticket splitting is possible, however, the parties of presidential winners tend to win inordinate vote shares in concurrent elections.

26. Matthew S. Shugart, "The Electoral Cycle and Institutional Sources of Divided Government," *American Political Science Review* 89 (June 1995): 327–43.

27. Francisco Leal Buitrago and Andres Dávila Ladrón de Guevara, *Clientelismo: El sistema político y su expresión regional* (Bogotá: Tercer Mundo Editores, 1990), 74–77.

28. Coppedge, *Strong Parties and Lame Ducks*, 23–26; Arnoldo José Gabaldón and Luis Enrique Oberto, *La reforma parlamentaria: Necesidad y alternativas de modernización de la acción legislativa* (Caracas: Congreso de la Republica, 1985), 46.

29. David Mayhew, *Congress: The Electoral Connection* (New Haven: Yale University Press, 1974); Gary W. Cox and Mathew D. McCubbins, *Legislative Leviathan* (Berkeley: University of California Press, 1993).

30. Bruce Cain, John Ferejohn, and Morris Fiorina, *The Personal Vote: Constituency Service and Electoral Independence* (Cambridge: Harvard University Press, 1987); Mathew D. McCubbins and Frances M. Rosenbluth, "Party Provision of Personal Politics: Dividing the Vote in Japan," in Peter F. Cowhey and McCubbins, eds., *Structure and Policy in Japan and the United States* (New York: Cambridge University Press, 1995), 35–55.

31. Carey, *Term Limits and Legislative Representation*, 117–35.

32. Morris Fiorina, *Congress: Keystone of the Washington Establishment* (New Haven: Yale University Press, 1989).

33. Barry Ames, "Electoral Strategy Under Open-List Proportional Representation," *American Journal of Political Science* 39 (May 1995): 406–33.

34. Keith Krehbiel, *Information and Legislative Organization* (Ann Arbor: University of Michigan Press, 1991), 61–104.

35. Juan J. Linz, "Presidential or Parliamentary Democracy: Does It Make a Difference?" and Arturo Valenzuela, "Party Politics and the Crisis of Presidentialism in Chile," both in Juan J. Linz and Arturo Valenzuela, eds., *The Failure of Presidential Democracy* (Baltimore: Johns Hopkins University Press, 1995), 2:34–36 and 2:116–29.

36. Walter Bagehot, *The English Constitution* (Ithaca, N.Y.: Cornell University Press, 1981), 66.

37. Gary W. Cox, *The Efficient Secret* (New York: Cambridge University Press, 1987).

38. Shugart and Carey, *Presidents and Assemblies*, 131–66.

39. The importance of these variables is discussed briefly in this essay. A model to estimate the value of personal reputation based on these variables is developed more fully in John M. Carey and Matthew S. Shugart, "Incentives to Cultivate a Personal Vote: A Rank Ordering of Electoral Systems," *Electoral Studies* 14 (1994): 417–39.

40. Carey and Shugart, "Incentives to Cultivate a Personal Vote."

41. Ames, *Political Survival*; Buitrago and Dávila, *Clientelismo*; Raymond V. Christensen, "Electoral Reform in Japan: How It Was Enacted and Changes It May Bring," *Asian Survey* 34 (July 1994): 589–605.

42. Gary W. Cox and Mathew D. McCubbins, "Institutional Determinants of Policy Outcomes," in Mathew D. McCubbins and Stephan Haggard, eds., *Structure and Outcomes: Comparative Regulatory and Budget Policy* (Washington, D.C.: World Bank, forthcoming).

43. Gabaldón and Oberto, *La reforma parlamentaria*, 46.

44. Manuel Rachadell, "El sistema electoral y la reforma de los partidos," in Comisión Presidencial para la Reforma del Estado, ed., *Venezuela, democracia y futuro: Los partidos políticos en la decada de los 90* (Caracas: Grafisistem, 1991), 208.

45. Christensen, "Electoral Reform in Japan," 589–91; Richard S. Katz, "The 1993 Parliamentary Electoral Reform," in Carol Mershon and Gianfranco Pasquino, eds., *Italian Politics: Ending the First Republic* (Boulder, Colo.: Westview, 1995), 93–95.

46. Thomas Remington, "Representative Power and the Russian State," in Stephen White, Alex Pravda, and Zvi Gitelman, eds., *Developments in Russian and Post-Soviet Politics* (Durham, N.C.: Duke University Press, 1994), 81–84.

47. Belin and Orttung, "On the Political Front," 217.

48. Guillermo O'Donnell and Philippe C. Schmitter, *Transitions from Authoritarian Rule: Tentative Conclusions About Uncertain Democracies* (Baltimore: Johns Hopkins University Press, 1986).

49. Randall Calvert, "The Rational Choice Theory of Social Institutions: Cooperation, Coordination, and Communication," in Jeffrey Banks and Eric Hanushek, eds., *Modern Political Economy: Old Topics, New Directions* (New York: Cambridge University Press, 1995), 216–68.

50. Arend Lijphart, "Democratization and Constitutional Choices in Czecho-Slovakia, Hungary and Poland, 1989–91," *Journal of Theoretical Politics* 4 (1992): 207–23; Barbara Geddes, "Institutional Choice in Post-Communist East Europe" (paper presented at the Eighty-ninth Annual Meeting of the American Political Science Association, Washington, D.C., September 1993).

51. Comparison across two and three countries is attempted by Cain, Ferejohn, and Fiorina, *The Personal Vote*; Cowhey and McCubbins, eds., *Structure and Policy in Japan and the United States*; and Carey, *Term Limits and Legislative Representation*.

52. Riker, *Liberalism Against Populism*.

7

POLITICAL PARTIES
IN EAST CENTRAL EUROPE

Gábor Tóka

Gábor Tóka *is a lecturer in political science at the Central European University in Budapest and the principal investigator of the university's project on "The Development of Party Systems and Electoral Alignments in East Central Europe." He was formerly a research fellow at the Social Research Information Centre (TÁRKI) in Budapest.*

Recent scholarship on democracy presumes a causal link between institutionalized party systems and democratic consolidation. Yet, as will be shown below, survey and electoral data indicate that in the first half of the 1990s, the party systems of East Central Europe remained unstable by any measure, even though most of the countries in the region could be considered consolidated democracies as of 1995.[1] Indeed, there is no evidence in these countries of the mechanisms that supposedly create the causal link between party-system institutionalization and democratic consolidation. Thus the presence of reasonably institutionalized political parties is not, in fact, a prerequisite of democratic consolidation.

The present assessment of the development and performance of political parties in the Czech Republic, Hungary, Poland, and Slovakia begins with an examination of electoral volatility.[2] Electoral volatility is often argued to be the primary independent variable that motivates party elites to act either in accordance with or in disregard of democratic values. At the same time, volatility is the most important indicator of the degree of a system's stability.

Other indicators of party-system institutionalization will also be examined here: age and organizational style of parties, party fragmentation, stability of electoral institutions, links between social groups and political parties, and programmatic structuring—that is, the degree to which electoral competition is structured by clear differences in party programs.[3] These indicators also serve as independent variables and influence the all-important factor of electoral volatility.[4] An examination of these variables in East Central Europe reveals a comparatively weak institutionalization of party systems.

These findings must be reconciled with those of other studies on the impact of parties and party systems on democratic consolidation. This essay offers an explanation for the frequent correlation between party-system institutionalization and the consolidation of democracy, and argues for the importance of the development of political parties even if democratic consolidation does not presume stable party structures.

Two caveats are in order. First, although the analysis here focuses on relatively stable systemic characteristics of party-voter linkages in the region, it must be recognized at the outset that "the very notion of a newly-emerging party *system* may well be a contradiction in terms, . . . in that to speak of a system of parties appears to ascribe some degree of stability and predictability to the interactions (i.e. the mechanics) of the parties concerned."[5]

Second, party institutionalization may be thought of as one of many factors that contribute to democratic consolidation. Given the large number of relevant variables and the lack of comparable data for a sufficient number of countries, however, this way of modeling the relationship between party system and democratic consolidation cannot be evaluated empirically here. Therefore, a more restrictive model, which posits that a degree of party institutionalization is a necessary but insufficient condition for a certain degree of democratic consolidation, will be examined here.[6]

East European Political Organizations

Historically, political parties have played little or no role in transitions to democracy, and the case of Eastern Europe has been no different. After the long suppression of multiparty politics, the only parties that had something to contribute to the East European transitions to democracy from 1989 to 1991 were the incumbent communist parties and their former satellites—various peasant, artisan, and Christian Democratic parties—which were licensed to build socialism in East Germany, Poland, and Czechoslovakia. As for the unambiguously prodemocratic forces, only in Hungary were the major participants in negotiations of the terms of the transition organized along lines that were probably meant to become persistent party identities. Elsewhere, broad umbrella organizations, such as Solidarity (NSZZ "S") in Poland or Public Against Violence (VPN) in Slovakia, proved more suitable forms to mobilize the populace.[7]

Most of these organizations eventually entered the electoral arena; the Lithuanian Reform Movement (Sajūdis) and the Union of Democratic Forces (SDS) in Bulgaria survived as major parties. But initially, these organizations consciously avoided anything resembling party discipline, office-seeking behavior, elaborate bureaucracy, and any but the vaguest liberal democratic ideology. Before the June 1990 elections, the campaign slogan of the most popular of these organizations, the Czech Civic Forum (OF), was "Parties for party members—Civic Forum for everybody." The Confederation for an Independent Poland (KPN), the only party-like organization of the East European prodemocratic forces established well before the transition (it was founded in 1979), found practically no role to play in the transition until the first completely free (presidential) election was set for November 1990.

Yet, in Maurice Duverger's words, "the development of parties seems bound up with that of democracy, that is to say with the extension of popular suffrage and parliamentary prerogatives."[8] There are at least two fundamentally different ways of interpreting this relationship. One view is that reasonably stable political parties are the inevitable by-products of a viable mass democracy. Since only the electoral arena gives formally equal influence to all citizens, political parties are the central agents of democratic representation. Thus the influence of parties and party systems on the quality of democracy can hardly be overstated.[9]

Another way of interpreting Duverger's observation is that parties come first. Scott Mainwaring and Timothy Scully state, "In modern mass societies, building a party system appears to be a necessary though insufficient condition for consolidating democracy and governing effectively."[10] The very notion of consolidation separates the political system's potential to survive from its actual endurance, which can result from factors other than sufficient consolidation and can be observed only *ex post facto*. While this conceptual distinction is easily made, the operational definition of consolidation is a matter of considerable controversy. Juan Linz and Alfred Stepan propose that democratic consolidation implies at least three conditions. First, all political actors are "subject to, as well as habituated to, the resolution of conflict within the bounds of the specific laws, procedures, and institutions that are sanctioned by the new democratic process"—which also implies that a full-fledged democracy is in place. Second, "no significant . . . actors spend significant resources attempting to achieve their objectives by creating a nondemocratic regime or by seceding from the state." Finally, "a strong majority of public opinion, even in the midst of major economic problems and deep dissatisfaction with incumbents, holds the belief that democratic procedures and institutions are the most appropriate way to govern collective life, and . . . support for antisystem alternatives is quite small or is more-or-less isolated from prodemocratic forces."[11]

By 1995, of the four countries considered here, only in Slovakia was democratic consolidation possibly in doubt according to these three criteria. After the October 1991 legislative elections in Poland, all four countries were full-fledged democracies according to the widely accepted minimalist definitions: public officials were democratically elected or subordinated to control by elected representatives, free and fair elections occurred, governments emerged and fell, and constitutional reform was negotiated according to a due democratic process. Political conduct was regulated by the legal system, vigilant parliamentary oppositions guarded the separation of powers and attacked the abuse of power, political rights were comprehensive and uncurtailed, and political violence was nearly unknown.

An overwhelming majority of the public, and certainly all politicians, expressly endorsed the democratic order while in the depths of a recession greater than that from 1928 to 1932. Certainly no significant—or even insignificant—actors spent "resources attempting to achieve their objectives by creating a nondemocratic regime or by seceding from the state." The majority of the public probably disapproved of the "velvet divorce" of the Czech and Slovak republics on 1 January 1993, but that dissolution in no way violated existing laws or the ideals of representative democracy. There is no indication that political actors would have considered any route to power other than the democratic process; although some observers might call the Czech Republican Party (SPR-RSČ) and the Communist Party of Bohemia and Moravia (KSČM) antisystem parties, they are thoroughly isolated politically and formally endorse democracy.

The only truly worrisome breach of democratic procedure occurred in Slovakia, where in late 1994 the government and the parliamentary majority prevented opposition representatives from supervising the privatization agency, public television, and secret police, in violation of some written procedures. Later, the government and parliament failed to denounce, and effectively blocked any investigation of, a politically motivated abuse of power by the secret police.

Yet democratic consolidation in East Central Europe could hardly have been the result of strongly institutionalized party systems; as will be argued below, party systems of all four countries remained relatively unstable throughout the period, and Slovakia's was the most or second most institutionalized of the four.

Why would party systems influence democratic consolidation at all? According to the recent literature, although the degree of party fragmentation and ideological polarization are not irrelevant, the critical party-system factor in consolidation is the institutionalization of a party system.[12] "Party-system institutionalization" entails the stabilization and social embeddedness of the major party alternatives and their relative policy positions, hence a regularity in the patterns of interparty competition. Party institutionalization may also mean that "party organizations are not subordinated to the interests of ambitious leaders; they acquire an independent status and value of their own. The party becomes autonomous vis-à-vis movements or organizations that initially may have created it for instrumental purposes."[13]

The link between party-system institutionalization and democratic consolidation may be approached in several ways. If party institutionalization entails that the "major political actors accord legitimacy to the electoral process and to parties,"[14] and the consolidation of the democratic regime includes the same element in its description, these are by definition simultaneous processes. Another theoretically unsatisfactory argument says that, "given the many crucial functions performed by political parties, their relevance to the consolidation of democracy is obvious."[15] This reasoning fails to specify why the institutionalization (or any other particular trait) of parties matters specifically to consolidation. What prohibits unstable parties from performing "crucial functions" for consolidation?

Leonardo Morlino has suggested that firm control of civil society by party elites who have a direct stake in the continuation of the democratic process may be necessary for democratic consolidation. Alternatively, legitimacy of the democratic process must be widespread among relevant political actors shortly after the transition to democracy. Since this latter condition arguably obtained in East Central Europe, Morlino's argument will not be examined here.[16]

Electoral Volatility

If establishing a party system primarily means developing a stable pattern of interactions among the competing party elites on the one hand, and among these elites and the voters on the other, then the greatest obstacle to establishing party systems is instability of party support and party identities. In the absence of reasonably strong party attachments in the electorate, electoral support for a party can change drastically—particularly in times of economic trouble. Highly volatile party support should suggest to elite actors that there is no payoff in sticking with an unpopular party label. Easy access to the media by parliamentarians and other notables, the skills of a well-paid campaign staff, the personal appeal of new faces, or carefully chosen positions on topical issues may all prove more important electoral assets than an established trademark. Voters are not fools; they do not necessarily presume that a four-year-old party label guarantees more reliable quality and ideology than do these other factors.

Peter Mair has persuasively argued that the typical condition of consolidated democracies—low volatility of the mass electorate—promotes a willingness to compromise by making party leaders believe that they cannot achieve either total or long-lasting victory over their rivals. Thus the relatively high electoral volatility characteristic of new democracies is not conducive to political moderation. This may have grave consequences in postcommunist democracies, where extremely competitive elite behavior is likely to prevail. The reason for this is threefold. First, the most important determinants of electoral volatility are 1) the extent and frequency of any changes in the electoral system, in the number of parties, in the identity of parties, and in voting rights; and 2) the mobilization of social cleavages, which is likely to be weak given the oft-noticed weakness of civil society in former communist countries. Second, since they originated in legislatures in the era of electronic mass media, East European parties are unlikely to establish the elaborate and comprehensive mass organization and social-group identification that are credited with stabilizing West European electorates.[17] Third, the stakes are unusually high in postcommunist politics because of the depth of institutional and socioeconomic transformations under way.[18]

Tables 1 through 4 show our first piece of evidence on the weakness of party loyalties in East Central Europe. The most readily available tool of cross-national research on this issue is computation of aggregate volatility—that is, the percentage of the vote that changes hands between two consecutive elections. This is most easily done by summing the percentage gains of the entirely new parties and those established parties that increased their support relative to the previous election. In comparing the four countries, it helps to distinguish between two different components of total volatility. Vote transfers between parties that retain their identity stem directly from the volatility of voters' decisions, whereas the volatility that results from some parties' disappearing or splitting and others' emerging anew reflects at least as much the volatility of elite behavior as of mass behavior.

Table 1 shows that in Poland between 1991 and 1993, voters' shifting party alignments proved to be the dominant source of total volatility.[19] Altogether, 34.5 percent of the vote "changed hands"; only about a third of this change (12.2 percent) could be attributed to parties' disbanding by the time of the second election. Even allowing for this component leaves Poland with a total volatility of 22.3 percent, almost three times as high as the West European average (below 8.5 percent) from 1945 to 1989, and well above the standard of the first 15 years of new party systems in Western Europe (varying rather predictably around 13 to 14 percent across Germany, Italy, Spain, Portugal, and Greece after 1974, exceeded only by Greece's 19 percent between 1946 and 1964).[20] For international comparison, we can use only the 34.5 percent figure for total volatility, which shows the Polish party system to be more unstable than that of Uruguay, Colombia, Costa Rica, Chile, Venezuela, or Argentina (all of which had an average volatility below 20 percent during the last two decades), and in the same class as Bolivia and Ecuador.[21]

In the early 1990s, Hungary had somewhat more loyal voters than did Poland; Hungary's total volatility over a four-year period was 28.3 percent (see Table 2). If we add the 1994 votes of four new splinter

Table 1 — Polish Party-List Vote, October 1991 and September 1993

	1991 (%)	1993 (%)
KLD	7.49	3.99
KPN	8.88	5.77
MN	1.49	0.70
NSZZ "S"	5.05	4.90
Partia "X"	0.47	2.74
PL (PL-SLCh coalition in 1991)	5.47	2.37
POC (PC-ZP in 1993)	8.71	4.42
PPPP	2.97	0.10
PSL	9.22	15.40
SLD	11.99	20.41
UD	12.32	10.59
UP (SP in 1991)	2.06	7.28
UPR	2.25	3.18
WAK (KKWO in 1993)	8.98	6.37
Others	12.62	11.78

Source: Stanislaw Gebethner, "System wyborczy: Deformacja czy reprezentacja?" (The electoral system: Distortion or representation?), in Stanislaw Gebethner, ed., *Wybory parlamentarne 1991 i 1993* (The parliamentary elections of 1991 and 1993) (Warsaw: Wydawnictwo Sejmowe, 1995), 10.

Notes: Lower-house elections. Parties collapsed into "Others" contested only one of the two elections, or won less than 1 percent of the vote in both elections. Of them, the ChD won five seats and five others won one seat each in 1991. The BBWR received 5.41 percent of the vote, winning 16 seats, or 3.5 percent of the total, in 1993.

Table 2 — Hungarian Party-List Vote, March 1990 and May 1994

	1990 (%)	1994 (%)
ASZ	3.13	2.10
FIDESZ	8.95	7.02
FKGP	11.73	8.82
KDNP	6.46	7.03
MDF	24.73	11.74
MP (ex-MSZMP)	3.68	3.19
MSZDP	3.55	0.95
MSZP	10.89	32.99
SZDSZ	21.39	19.74
VP	1.89	0.62
Others	3.60	5.80

Sources: "Az Országos Választási Bizottság jelentése" (Report of the National Election Committee), *Magyar Közlöny* (Hungarian official gazette), 13 May 1990, 1083; and 24 June 1994, 2611.

Notes: Parliamentary elections. Parties collapsed into "Others" contested only one of the two elections; none won seats.

Table 3 — Czech Party-List Vote, June 1990, June 1992, May–June 1996

	1990 (%)	1992 (%)	1996 (%)
ČMUS (former HSD-SMS)	—	—	0.5
ČSS (part of LSU in 1992)	2.8	—	—
ČSSD	3.8	7.7	26.4
HDŽJ (part of SZV in 1990, DZJ in 1996)	—	3.3	3.1
HSD-SMS	7.9	4.2	—
KAN (part of OF in 1990)	—	2.0	—
KDU	8.7	—	—
KDU-ČSL (KDU in 1990)	—	6.0	8.1
KSČM (KSČS in 1990, LB in 1992)	13.5	14.3	10.3
LB (splinter from KSČM)	—	—	1.4
LSU (joint list of ČSS, SZ, and ZS)	—	5.8	—
ODA (part of OF in 1990)	—	5.0	6.4
ODS (ODS-KDS in 1992)	—	—	29.6
ODS-KDS (successor to OF)	—	33.9	—
OF	53.2	—	—
OH (successor to OF)	—	4.4	—
SD-LSNS (successor to OH)	—	—	2.1
SDL (splinter from KSČM)	—	—	0.1
SPP	0.1	1.1	—
SPR-RSČ (part of VDSPR in 1990)	—	6.5	8.0
SZ (part of LSU in 1992)	3.1	—	—
Others	7.0	5.5	4.1

Sources: For 1990 results: Czechoslovak Statistical Office, *Volbý do Federalního shromazdení Česke a Slovenske Federativni Republiký v roče 1990* (Elections to the Federal Assembly of the Czecho-Slovak Federal Republic in 1990) (Prague: Federal Statistical Office, 1991), 26. For 1992: *Lidové noviny* (People's daily), 8 and 12 June 1992 (for some corrections, see Lubomír Brokl, "The Results and Consequences of the 1992 Elections," *Czechoslovak Sociological Review* 28 [Special Issue, 1992]: 119–23). For 1996: Czech Statistical Office World-Wide Web site, located at http://www.volby.cz.

Notes: Data refer to the June 1990 and June 1992 elections to the Chamber of People (the lower house of the Czechoslovak Federal Assembly) and the May–June 1996 elections to the lower house of the Czech Parliament.

In calculating the volatility data reported in the main text, parties subsumed under "Others" are assumed to have contested only one of the three elections. This assumption is contestable in the case of the 1990 VDSPR and SZV electoral coalitions; though these coalitions dissolved after the 1990 election, three of their component parts participated in later elections. The three-party VDSPR, which won 0.9 percent of the votes and no seats, included the SPR-RSČ; the nine-party SZV, which won 3.8 percent of the vote but no seats, included the HDŽJ and the ZS.

parties to the votes of their mother organizations, the Hungarian Democratic Forum (MDF) and the Independent Smallholders' Party (FKGP), volatility declines to 25.8 percent, which resembles that of partially free or nonfree legislative elections in Mexico and Paraguay reported by Mainwaring and Scully.

In the 1990 and 1992 Czechoslovak elections, voters cast three different ballots for party lists competing for seats in the National

Councils of the two subnational (Czech and Slovak) legislatures, and for the two houses of the Federal Assembly (see Table 3). On 1 January 1993, the country split, the Federal Assembly was dissolved, and the Czech and Slovak National Councils elected in the 1992 Czechoslovak elections became the unicameral legislatures of the two new states. The volatility estimates for the Czechoslovak elections of 1990–92, the Czech elections of 1992–96, and the Slovak elections of 1992–94 vary slightly depending on which of the 1990 and 1992 votes are considered, but the differences have no major consequence for our conclusions.[22]

At first, Table 3 seems to show astronomical volatility in the Czech electorate. The 1990 figures for the Czech Socialist Party (ČSS), the Green Party (SZ), and the Agricultural Party (ZS) should be combined and treated as if the Liberal Social Union (LSU) (their later joint electoral list) had reached those results in 1990.

A bigger question is whether to combine results of the Civic Democratic Alliance (ODA), the Civic Democratic Party (ODS), the Civic Movement (OH), and the Club of Committed Non-Party Members (KAN), all of which originated from the OF. Without this grouping, Czech volatility for 1990–92 is 67.3, beating Peru's average volatility of roughly 50 percent from 1978 to 1990. Alternatively, collapsing all four products of the OF yields a total volatility of 22 percent, appreciably below the 1990–94 Hungarian levels discussed above.

Comparing the 1992 and 1996 lower-house election results in the Czech Republic, a total volatility of 31.4 percent obtains, but it should be remembered that the 1996 Free Democrats–Liberal Social National Party (SD-LSNS) is, for all practical purposes, the heir to the OH of 1992. Thus 29.3 is a better approximation of Czech volatility for 1992–96—nearly the same as Hungary's for 1990–94. Only a fraction of this volatility resulted from party splits; the Left Bloc (LB) and the Democratic Left Party (SDL)—the two splinters from the orthodox KSČM—won less than 2 percent of the 1996 vote.

Slovakia from 1990 to 1992 appears to have been similar to the Czech part of the federation in both degree and source of volatility (see Table 4). VPN, the broad-based movement that led the November 1989 "velvet revolution" in Slovakia, split in March–April 1991. Treating the Movement for a Democratic Slovakia (HZDS) as the organizational and ideological heir to VPN, a total volatility of 23.1 percent obtains. Otherwise, volatility measures 55.7 percent. In the third round of free parliamentary elections in Slovakia, total volatility was 23.8 percent.[23] Given the uncertainty of the "true" volatility in Slovakia in 1990–92, it is hard to tell if this figure signals a massive decrease from or a maintenance of the previous level of electoral instability.

In the other three countries, too, aggregate electoral data are of little help in determining whether party loyalties had strengthened over the first six years of democracy in East Central Europe. Further, the aggregate-

Table 4 — Slovak Party-List Vote, June 1990, June 1992, September 1994

	1990 (%)	1992 (%)	1994 (%)
DS (DS-ODS in 1992)	4.40	3.31	3.42
DU (splinter from HZDS)	—	—	8.57
HZDS (splinter from VPN)	—	37.26	34.96
KDH	18.98	8.88	10.08
KSS (KSČS in 1990)	—	0.76	2.72
MK (joint list of MKM, ESWS, and MOS)	—	—	10.18
MKM-ESWS (joint list of MKM and ESWS)	8.58	7.42	—
MOS (part of VPN in 1990)	—	2.29	—
ODU (successor to VPN; renamed SKD in 1993; merged with DS in 1994)	—	4.04	—
ROI (part of VPN in 1990)	—	0.60	0.67
SDL (KSČS in 1990; part of SV in 1994)	13.81	14.70	—
SDSS (SD in 1990)	1.89	4.00	—
SKDH (splinter from KDH, renamed KSU before the 1994 election)	—	3.05	2.05
SNS	10.96	7.93	5.40
SV (joint list of SDL, SDSS, and SZS)	—	—	10.41
SZ	3.20	1.08	—
SZS	—	2.14	—
VPN	32.54	—	—
ZRS (splinter from SDL)	—	—	7.34
Others	5.63	2.53	4.09

Sources: Czechoslovak Statistical Office, Volbý do Federalního shromazdení České a Slovenske Federativni Republiký v roče 1990, 27; Slovak Statistical Office, Statistická rocenka Slovenskej republiky 1993 (The statistical yearbook of the Slovak Republic) (Bratislava: Slovak Statistical Office, 1994), 485–88.

Notes: Data refer to the June 1990 elections to the Chamber of People (the lower house of the Czechoslovak Federal Assembly) and the June 1992 and September 1994 elections to the Slovak National Council (the sole chamber of the Slovak national parliament).

Parties subsumed under "Others" contested only one of the three elections.

level data hide the number of voters who move in opposite directions (e.g., from ex-communist to conservative and vice versa). We must turn to individual-level data for more evidence on volatility.

Table 5 shows survey data on the temporal stability of electoral preferences. The first notable detail is that volatility is higher than that found in Western democracies.[24] Second, as time since the last election increases, volatility increases. Third, as the number of elections since the transition increases, volatility decreases. For example, 44 months after the first Hungarian election, Hungary's electoral volatility was significantly higher than that of the Czech Republic 43 months after the second Czech election. But 13 months after the second Hungarian election, Hungary's electoral volatility was close to that of the Czech Republic 16 months after the second Czech election.

Table 5 also suggests a relatively clear ranking of the four countries.

Table 5 — Stability of Electoral Preferences

	% of Standpatters Among Former Voters	Number of Months Passed Since Last Election
Slovakia, November 1994	88	2
Slovakia, September 1992	76	3
Czech Republic, September 1992	78	3
Poland, April 1994	76	8
Slovakia, July 1995	79	10
Czech Republic, April 1993	67	10
Slovakia, April 1993	65	10
Poland, October 1992	51	12
Hungary, June 1995	69	13
Poland, January 1993	60	15
Poland, December 1994	73	16
Czech Republic, November 1993	65	17
Slovakia, November 1993	61	17
Poland, June 1995	59	21
Czech Republic, April 1994	61	22
Slovakia, April 1994	60	22
Poland, August 1993	43	23
Poland, December 1995	49	27
Czech Republic, November 1994	60	29
Hungary, September 1992	50	29
Hungary, January 1993	51	33
Czech Republic, June 1995	61	36
Czech Republic, January 1996	66	43
Hungary, December 1993	47	44
Hungary, April 1994	44	49

Source: CEU surveys.

Note: Figures in the left-hand column show the proportion of respondents who voted in the last parliamentary election who said—"if there were an election next weekend"—they would vote for the same party again. Respondents who preferred not to vote or did not know which party to support were excluded from this analysis, as were respondents who did not reveal or did not know which party they voted for in the last election.

The data on participation and vote in the last election are based on the respondents' memory, and are thus likely to overstate the percentage of "standpatters." Respondents who said they would vote for a new party that absorbed the party (e.g., KLD, UD) they had supported in the last election were counted as standpatters. Similarly, the Czech respondents who recalled voting for the LSU in 1992 and said they would vote for the ZS or ČSS, or recalled voting for the LB in 1992 and said they would vote for the KSČM, were counted as standpatters.

Aggregate electoral data suggest that party loyalty was strongest in Slovakia and weakest in Poland and that loyalties in the Czech Republic and Hungary were between these two extremes and about equal to each other. Individual-level data, however, indicate that Czechs and Slovaks showed much more stable party loyalty in 1992–95 than did Hungarians, and that Hungarians were more loyal than Poles.

To sum up, West European and North American voters show greater party loyalty than their East Central European counterparts. Likewise, most Latin American countries show a lower aggregate volatility for the previous two decades than do these four countries for the 1990s. If it is correct to describe the Czech Republic, Hungary, and Poland as "consolidated" democracies, then the expected correlation between party-system institutionalization (as measured by volatility) and democratic consolidation does not obtain. As suggested below, considering four other criteria of party institutionalization does not change this picture. These other criteria do, however, help explain the different degrees of electoral volatility observed.

Party Age, Organization, and Fragmentation

One reason for the weakness of party loyalties in East Central Europe may be the youth of most parties there. Mainwaring and Scully note that in the early 1990s, parties established before 1950 held 56 to 98 percent of lower-chamber seats in all of the better-institutionalized party systems in Latin America, whereas in the "inchoate" party systems of Brazil, Bolivia, Peru, and Ecuador such parties controlled 0.6 to 4.0 percent of the seats. Again, the East Central European countries appear to resemble this latter group. East Central European countries had too little democratic experience to develop well-entrenched parties before the communist takeover. Authoritarianism lasted an unusually long time, suppressed civil society, and transformed the economy and culture to an exceptional degree. It is not surprising that attempts to revive once-significant parties often led nowhere.[25]

By the conservative criteria of Mainwaring and Scully, few of East Central Europe's parties qualify as historic: the Polish Peasant Party (PSL), the Communist Party of Bohemia and Moravia (KSČM), and the Christian and Democratic Union–Czech People's Party (KDU-ČSL). The Czech Socialist Party (ČSS) and the Polish Democratic Party (SD) used to belong to this group but had a minimal electorate and disbanded soon after the transition to democracy. Despite minor changes in label, these parties have clearly maintained organizational continuity since the late 1940s. Other parties were established long before the communist takeover, but their historical continuity is limited to label, symbol, ideology, and—where property restitution took place after the transition—real estate. Significant players in this league of quasi-historic parties are the Czech Social Democratic Party (ČSSD), the Slovak Democratic Party (DS), the Slovak National Party (SNS), and Hungary's FKGP.

An analysis of the data by party shows that the constituencies of the PSL, KSČM, and KDU-ČSL displayed stronger than average party loyalty, whereas among the quasi-historic parties only the ČSSD could make the same claim.[26] Since the three historic parties are also the only mass parties in the region, it is difficult to tell which is more effective in stabilizing a party's basis—historical continuity or organizational encapsulation of voters. It is clear that the communist regimes deprived virtually all parties of both. Equally clearly, given the greater incidence of historic mass parties in Poland and the Czech Republic than in Hungary and Slovakia, these criteria account neither for Poland's relatively high volatility nor for the similarity between the Czech and Slovak volatility figures.

Party fragmentation may explain Poland's particularly high volatility. Clearly, the greater the number of parties, the more likely voters are to find an alternative party for which to abandon their previous partisanship.[27] Fractionalization of the vote in the 1991 and 1993 Polish elections was excessive by any measure. Hungarian, Czech, and Slovak elections produced less fragmentation than did the two Polish elections, but appreciably more than those of any West European democracy in the postwar period.

Following Douglas W. Rae, the fractionalization of the electoral vote can be calculated as one minus the sum of the squares of the proportion of the vote won by each party.[28] For instance, if two parties share the vote equally, the Rae index of fractionalization (F) is 0.50 (i.e., 1 − 2[.50 × .50]). If ten parties each win 10 percent of the vote, then F = 0.90 (i.e., 1 − 10[.10 × .10]). In West European elections between 1945 and 1985, the average fractionalization of the national vote ranged from 0.585 in Austria and 0.610 in the United Kingdom to 0.814 in Switzerland and 0.815 in Finland.[29] Using the electoral data summarized in Tables 1 through 4, the fractionalization of the vote in successive elections was 0.92 and 0.90 in Poland; 0.85 and 0.82 in Hungary; 0.68,[30] 0.81, and 0.84 in the Czech Republic; and 0.82, 0.81, and 0.83 in the three Slovak elections.

Thus a look at the age, organizational style, and fragmentation of parties also confirms that East Central European party systems of the early 1990s displayed a low level of institutionalization and explains much of the high volatility observed in this region. These factors still do not explain, however, why Slovak voters had more party loyalty than did Hungarian voters in 1992–95.

Unstable Electoral Institutions

Another possible explanation of cross-national differences in electoral volatility is the varying stability of electoral institutions: changes in election laws, splits and mergers among established parties, and the emergence of new parties. Changes in election laws or party systems can split the vote of previously unitary political actors and alter party behavior, thus generating massive movement of voters.

Indeed, the most significant change of election law occurred in

Poland, the most volatile of the four countries in the period examined. This change, however, had little detectable impact on the behavior of voters or politicians. Overall fragmentation decreased slightly, but only because the combined vote of the two front-runners leapt from 24.3 percent in 1991 to 35.8 percent in 1993.[31] Contrary to expectations,[32] the total vote share gathered by parties and coalitions that each won less than 5 percent of the national vote individually actually increased from 22 to 29 percent. A new 5 percent threshold for entry into parliament meant that none of these parties and coalitions won representation. This was the most important reason why the PSL and the ex-communist Democratic Left Alliance (SLD) won a 66 percent majority in the lower house with returns that would have earned them just 37 percent of the seats under the previous election law.[33] Thus, although the 1993 electoral reform was bound to affect behavior later—the period from 1994 to 1995 saw at least one important party merger (the Democratic Union [UD] and the Liberal Democratic Congress [KLD]) and the establishment of "Solidarity" Electoral Action (AW "S," a broad coalition of the anticommunist right) that involved a number of right-wing parties left unrepresented after the 1993 Sejm (lower-house) election—the electoral volatility between 1991 and 1993 appeared to have little to do with the reform. Since the other three countries had only marginal changes in their electoral laws, this factor cannot explain their differences in electoral volatility either.

The emergence of new parties and the disappearance of others generated more voter movement in Slovakia and the Czech Republic than in Hungary (cf. Tables 2 through 4). Similarly, general flux of established party identities had a stronger influence in the former two than in Hungary. Almost all the significant Slovak parties that were founded or reborn between 1990 and 1991 eventually split between radical nationalists and moderates.[34]

In the four years between the elections of June 1992 and May–June 1996, 4 of the 11 parties initially represented in the Czech National Council disappeared.[35] While financial scandal seemed to drive the ODA into electoral oblivion, a new right-wing formation—the Democratic Union (DEU)—and two splinters from the KSČM—the SDL and the Left Bloc Party (SLB)—made inroads into the electoral territories of the older parties. While the ODS and the KDU-ČSL, major players in the right-wing governing coalition, retained their electoral support from 1992, their competitive edge changed drastically. Having faced a deeply divided and fragmented opposition for four years, they might have ended up on the opposition benches in 1996. The Czech Social Democrats, who in Czech National Council elections won less than 4 percent in 1990 and less than 7 percent in 1992, might have found themselves able to form a left-wing majority government in 1996.[36]

But the story is not just about volatile voters. In the Czech case, a wholesale alternation of government and opposition would require the Czech Social Democrats to offer a coalition to the KSČM, by far the most stubborn communist party in the entire region. Much of the ČSSD's success, however, was attributed to its credible dissociation from the KSČM. Only one thing was more unlikely than a ČSSD-KSČM coalition: a coalition of the Social Democrats, the Communists, and the xenophobic-anticommunist Republicans. Yet these three opposition parties gained an absolute majority of seats in the 1996 elections, creating uncomfortable choices for the Czech political elite.

Both the Social Democrats and the center right favored an implicit (and presumably even an explicit) grand coalition to compromising themselves by cooperating with either the far right or the ex-communists. In 1996, the appearance of an outright grand coalition of center left and center right was avoided by a tacit agreement on legislative cooperation. That there were no Social Democrat ministers for the center-right cabinet did not alter the fact that, among the opposition parties, only the Social Democrats could be called upon to let the government pass any legislation. The monopoly of "true" opposition thus had to be conceded to the far right and the orthodox Communists, although these parties' anti–European Union and anti-German stances make their inclusion in any government unlikely.

This Czech National Assembly illustrates the configuration that Giovanni Sartori has labeled "polarized pluralism." He described its persistence as an irresistible incentive to engage in centrifugal instead of centripetal party competition—increasing ideological polarization, ideological "patterning" of society, irresponsible opposition behavior, and the "politics of outbidding."[37] Although either the electoral decay or the "domestication" of the two extremist parties, which were so readily stigmatized by both the center left and the center right, has the potential to restore a predominantly centripetal competition, the emergence of the "grand coalition" ironically served to maintain the extremist parties. Barring major realignment of parties, the alternation of government and opposition has become for all practical purposes impossible in the Czech Republic.[38]

If institutional changes do not explain why volatility was higher in Poland in 1992–93 than in the former Czechoslovakia, neither do they add to our understanding of the second most volatile country of the period. From 1990 to 1994 in Hungary, either institutional changes were absent or their significance was minimal.[39]

Social Groups and Political Parties

One of the most frequently heard assertions about electoral politics in East Central Europe is: "[The Czech party system] is anchored neither in a social nor in an interest structure, and that is why the parties do not have regular voters. . . . This unanchored system of parties will for a long time not be a support, but rather a danger for democracy."[40] Logical as these remarks are, they do not help empirical researchers specify what embeddedness in the social structure means. One approach is to look at the sociodemographic composition of the constituencies of individual parties. Such an enterprise produces the unappealing conclusion, however, that in the four East Central European countries, the typical supporters of agrarian parties are farmers, those of Christian parties are frequent churchgoers, those of market liberals are better-educated and younger urban dwellers, and those of ex-communist parties are former communist party members. More disturbing is that the party's age is unrelated to the social distinctiveness of the party's electorate. Whichever social-background variable we consider, its correlation with party choice shows as much variation among Western countries as in the four East Central European countries, with the average correlation being similar in the two regions.[41]

No theory justifies judging the social anchoring of new party systems by standards other than those applied to older democracies. By concentrating on the most widely discussed social cleavage, class, we see that the coefficient for class voting is much higher in Britain than in Poland, the Czech Republic, Slovakia, or Hungary, but the rest of contemporary continental Western Europe hardly differs from Poland, the Czech Republic, and Slovakia. (Hungary looks rather like the United States and Ireland on this count.) East Central Europe's similarity to the continental pattern is also underlined by the common effect of church attendance on party choice in West Germany, Italy, the Czech Republic, Slovakia, and Hungary. Though the peculiarities of individual countries are readily visible—for example, agricultural employment and place of residence had a uniquely strong effect on party preferences in Poland—there are no signs of systematic differences between those Eastern and Western democracies that we could compare quantitatively. Therefore, East-West differences in electoral volatility are not easy to explain with the "catchall" appeal of the East Central European parties. Furthermore, as the sociodemographic embeddedness of the vote seems to have been stronger in Poland than in the other three East Central European countries as early as 1992, it is again unlikely that this line of reasoning is useful in explaining the weakness of party loyalties.

Party Competition

Yet another way of explaining the weakness of party loyalty refers to political cognitions and looks for evidence that voters in less-developed party systems see smaller programmatic differences among the parties. Educating voters about party ideologies may take time; strong ideological differences may not exist in the postcommunist countries, or may exist but are not easily comprehended because of their multidimensional nature. The larger the number of ideological dimensions (and thus of parties), the more precisely sophisticated voters can express their policy preferences. Beyond a very small number of dimensions (i.e., two or three), however, these gains are likely to be lost in the trade-off between the number of dimensions on the one hand, and the predictability and stability of the resulting government coalitions on the other. Even voters of the most "sectional" parties—that is, parties characterized by intense and noncentrist preferences in a narrow issue domain and relative indifference on all other issues—would like to know, when they vote for their first choice, which other parties may be helped to office. If the ideological structuring of the party system is weak (i.e., variations in parties' positions on individual issues are only weakly constrained by the parties' location on one or two ideological "superdimensions," such as left vs. right or nationalist vs. cosmopolitan), voters are likely to remain ignorant of the consequences of their vote.

The distribution of "issue advantages" among the various parties can also determine the meaningfulness of electoral choice. The accumulation of a disproportionate number of advantages by any single party is likely to result in the emergence of a dominant party. This may have a number of advantages, but does nothing to promote meaningful elections.

To clarify the factors that are postulated here as conducive to the emergence of a dominant party, let me summarize an argument from Ian Budge and Dennis Farlie's analysis of electoral competition.[42] Left-wing parties owe much of their appeal to the perception that they are more credible and effective than their competitors on issues of socioeconomic redistribution. The normally high saliency of these issues thus favors the Left. Balanced party competition depends on competitors' ability to establish electoral advantages on a large number of other issues (e.g., general competence, foreign policy, religion, law and order). Following this reasoning, the prolonged electoral hegemony of the U.S. Democrats, the Canadian Liberals, the Irish Fianna Fail, and the Indian Congress party can be convincingly explained by their ability to combine a left-of-center image with long-term advantages over their competitors on a number of issues that, in the more balanced party systems of continental Europe, normally benefit the right-wing parties.

Lack of data prevents us from comparing in terms of programmatic structuring the East Central European party systems with those of Latin America and Western Europe. But we can examine whether the cross-national differences in electoral volatility across East Central Europe might be explained by cross-national differences in the programmatic structuring of the party systems. The twin problems of ideological structuring and conceivable electoral dominance are assessed here on the basis of mass survey data.

Respondents to the CEU surveys were asked which parties were most and least likely to pursue various political goals, and to rank the importance of these goals. Results from the Fall 1992 survey show that, just as Budge and Farlie postulated, a good number of the "left-wing" socioeconomic goals—reducing unemployment, inequality, and the people's burden during transformation of the economy—were ranked important or very important by nearly everyone. A pro-market party would not necessarily fail to deliver on these issues: normally increases in state pensions are less a function of commitment to the welfare state than a by-product of economic growth. But most left-wing parties would trade off social gains for increased corporate taxes and other measures that go against pro-market positions.

A few natural "right-wing" goals (e.g., fighting crime) are almost as popular with voters as left-wing goals, but most (e.g., increasing the influence of religion and the churches; strengthening patriotism; "decommunization," or the removal of former communists from positions of influence) are salient only for a small part of the public. Thus a party that establishes high credibility on left-wing economic goals can be matched in electoral strength only by competitors who achieve credibility—and several smaller net gains—on a wide range of issues in addition to economic competence.

This "natural advantage" of the Left is much smaller in the Czech Republic than in the other three countries; Czechs tend to attach slightly lower priority to the typical left-wing socioeconomic goals, and slightly higher priority to the typical right-wing economic goals than do Poles, Slovaks, or Hungarians. This alone may explain why the secular right-wing parties have much greater electoral strength in the Czech than in the Slovak and Polish lands.[43]

Aggregated answers concerning which parties were likely to pursue these goals in Poland and the Czech Republic—the two countries that show the biggest differences from each other—are shown in Tables 6 and 7. Two points should be emphasized from the outset. Respondents were to judge parties' commitment or lack of commitment to certain goals, not to place parties on a continuum. Therefore, the data describe the popularly perceived *direction* of party positions, not their *intensity*. High absolute values mean that many respondents agreed that a party "owned" a particular issue, not that the party held an extreme position on that issue. This is an important point for both methodological and normative reasons: normative evaluation of the development of party systems must consider the *distinctiveness* of party positions a positive trait.

The CEU surveys showed that many more Czechs and Slovaks than Hungarians, and more Hungarians than Poles, can point to one or another party as the "owner" of an issue. Furthermore, there tends to be a good deal of consensus in these Czech and Slovak answers. Here we at last seem to encounter a finding that may help explain why party

Table 6 — Party Positions on Various Issues, Poland, Fall 1992

	PSL	ZChN	UD	SLD	PC	KLD	KPN	PL
Reduce inequality	10	2	18	18	−1	−3	8	1
Develop free market	2	4	27	−13	10	29	2	1
Manage economy	7	−2	24	7	4	13	6	1
Defend democracy	5	1	24	7	1	5	10	1
Lessen economic burden	7	2	10	18	−1	−7	6	1
Protect environment	9	1	10	2	1	0	2	3
Improve social services	8	1	18	17	2	0	4	1
Renew morality	3	38	9	−2	1	1	3	1
Allow abortion	3	−41	20	35	2	6	4	1
Protect companies	3	0	4	18	0	−11	4	0
Strengthen patriotism	4	11	11	3	2	1	24	0
Increase social benefits	6	0	15	20	−1	−7	7	0
Increase church influence	1	54	−2	−32	2	0	0	0
Speed privatization	1	5	24	−15	13	30	1	0
Reduce unemployment	7	1	14	22	0	−6	7	1
Fight crime	4	4	16	6	4	5	11	1
Speed decommunization	1	27	1	−37	18	2	34	0
Promote interests abroad	5	3	21	4	3	11	7	0
Protect food market	30	0	4	4	1	−8	3	12

Source: Fall 1992 CEU surveys.

Note: Figures were obtained by subtracting the percentage of responses naming the party least likely to pursue the goal in question from the percentage of responses naming the party most likely to pursue the goal. Thus a rating of −6 indicates that 6 percent more respondents thought the party was unlikely to pursue that goal than thought the party was likely to pursue it.

Table 7 — Party Positions on Various Issues, Czech Republic, Fall 1992

	ČSSD	HSD-SMS	KDU-ČSL	KSČM	LSU	ODA	ODS	SPR-RSČ
Reduce inequality	29	2	13	10	12	8	−10	0
Develop free market	1	0	11	−58	2	39	70	−3
Manage economy	8	1	10	−29	5	36	56	−3
Defend democracy	11	2	17	−17	6	22	29	−6
Lessen economic burden	39	0	9	9	16	11	−17	−1
Protect environment	2	0	6	−13	41	4	0	−4
Improve social services	16	0	15	0	5	14	17	−4
Renew morality	9	0	35	−17	5	13	16	−4
Allow abortion	10	0	−44	10	2	13	21	2
Protect companies	26	1	0	36	9	4	−34	0
Strengthen patriotism	7	21	10	−11	3	14	9	8
Increase social benefits	33	0	5	20	7	3	−14	−3
Increase church influence	1	1	75	−60	3	2	5	−2
Speed privatization	−1	0	10	−59	1	45	77	−1
Reduce unemployment	32	1	6	28	10	7	−13	1
Fight crime	7	1	9	−6	3	18	33	1
Speed decommunization	1	1	9	−70	0	24	42	26
Promote interests abroad	3	0	7	−20	1	34	55	−8
Preserve Czech-Slovak relations	23	6	11	20	12	4	5	−2
Speed separation of Czech and Slovak republics	−17	0	10	−40	−5	41	73	−1

Source: See Table 6.
Note: See Table 6.

attachments in 1992–93 tended to be stronger in the Czech and Slovak republics than in Hungary, and why they were stronger in Hungary than in Poland: because voters in the former had a clearer image of what the major parties stood for in programmatic terms.[44] This ranking of the countries was consistently repeated elsewhere on several other indicators of what I call "the meaningfulness of electoral choice," such as the strength and dispersion of partisan attachments in the voting population; voters' ability to identify government and opposition parties correctly; richness and sophistication of voters' reasoning about preference for or dislike of significant parties; or the probability that a voter's party choice was predictable from his or her issue positions.[45]

Second, whereas the data about the popular perception of party positions on moral and social issues, such as strengthening patriotism and increasing church influence, faithfully reflect the parties' pledges, the same is not necessarily true in the socioeconomic domain. Apparently no party, regardless of its stated policies, is able to establish greater credibility on either left- or right-wing socioeconomic issues than it scores on general economic competence. It seems that, unless a party is credited with at least some managerial competence, it is not believed to be capable of delivering on either left- or right-wing socioeconomic goals.

The East Central European publics see little difference among the four ex-communist parties' commitment to such goals as reducing inequality, lessening the people's burden during the transformation of the economy, and providing better health care and education. The four parties are also viewed similarly with regard to patriotism. There are, however, large differences between the Czech KSČM, at one extreme, and the Slovak Party of the Democratic Left (SDL) and the Hungarian Socialist Party (MSZP), at the other, regarding general competence and these parties' perceived attitudes toward clerical, anticommunist, and pro-market policies. Many more Czechs than Slovaks and Hungarians attribute lack of competence and opposition to typically right-wing goals to the ex-communist parties. Whereas the image of the Polish SLD is usually closer to that of the KSČM on this count, by 1992 the SDL and the MSZP had established a very positive reputation on competence issues.

The cross-national variation in the image of the Christian parties is even smaller. Relatively few people attribute to them policy priorities other than those directly related to religious appeal. Those who associated socioeconomic goals with Christian parties thought the parties were committed to developing a market economy, to providing better health care and education, or to both. Cross-national variations reflect a correct popular understanding of these parties. On socioeconomic issues, the image of the Slovak Christian Democratic Movement (KDH) is a bit more right-wing and that of the Hungarian Christian Democratic

People's Party (KDNP) more left-wing than that of the Polish Christian National Union (ZChN) and the Czech KDU-ČSL. Among the agrarian parties, the Polish PSL and the Hungarian FKGP achieved greater visibility and a more elaborate ideological profile than did the post-Solidarność Peasant Alliance (PL). Whereas the FKGP has a rather clerical, patriotic, and pro-market profile, the Polish PSL is thought to be left of center and rather secular.

Thus the integration of Christian and agrarian party images into what appears to be the main ideological dimensions of party competition in East Central Europe was already advanced by the fall of 1992. The coalition preferences of these parties also became known; they are generally consistent with their ideological positions. These facts suggest that the electoral bases of these parties may become less sectional in the near future than they were at the time of the survey. These prospects, however, are likely to be closed for the regionalist Movement for Self-Governing Democracy–Association for Moravia and Silesia (HSD-SMS) in the Czech Republic, for the Polish PL, and for the Hungarian Christian Democratic Movement–Coexistence (MKM-ESWS) coalition that speaks for the interests of ethnic Hungarians in Slovakia. These three parties have a single-issue image.

The remaining significant East Central European parties fall into three categories; the individual parties are often too idiosyncratic to be unambiguously classified as secular-liberal or secular-conservative (as with the Czech ODA and ODS), or secular-conservative or nationalist-anticommunist (as with the Center Alliance [PC] in Poland and the MDF in Hungary). The Polish KPN is certainly perceived as secular, anticommunist, nationalist, and—on the questions of economic policy —distinctively left-wing. The Republicans are seen by Czechs as anticommunist and nationalist—in fact, presumably xenophobic and anti-Gypsy—with rather left-wing views on economics. The third clear case in this class is the Slovak National Party.

The group of liberal and secular-conservative parties also shows a good deal of cross-national variation. The Czech ODA and ODS, the rather insignificant DS and Conservative Democratic Party (SKD) in Slovakia, and the Alliance of Free Democrats (SZDSZ) and Federation of Young Democrats (FIDESZ) in Hungary were often believed to be strongly anticommunist, while in Poland the KLD and the UD were not. Apparently, the legacy of Poland's liberal-dominated government of Prime Minister Tadeusz Mazowiecki (1989–90), which aimed to draw a "thick line" between past and present, remained visible in this case. These parties are invariably associated with pro-market policies, economic competence, pro-choice views on abortion, and little enthusiasm for protecting unprofitable companies. Where they most differ from each other is their perceived commitment to left-wing economic goals. The Czech ODA and ODS, the Slovak SKD and DS, and the Polish

KLD have virtually no credibility at all on this issue, but the Polish UD and the two Hungarian liberal parties do.

Finally, Slovakia's natural party of government, the HZDS, is in a class by itself. With extraordinarily high ratings on every issue except the most right-wing ones (decommunization, increasing church influence, and maintaining good relations between Czechs and Slovaks), by the fall of 1992 the HZDS came close to establishing a profile promising long-term electoral hegemony. The only East Central European parties with such a broad appeal at that time were the Hungarian liberals, the SZDSZ and FIDESZ. More information about these parties' promises would be necessary to understand the origin of such intense popularity. The Hungarian examples suggest that relatively popular opposition parties can afford to promise pro-market policies. As long as parties are perceived as more competent than their competitors and do not pledge to freeze state pensions once they take office, they can trust the wishful thinking of desperate voters to do the rest.

The example of the HZDS, however, also suggests that injudiciously designed election pledges may also raise popular expectations that are hard to meet. In April 1993, the CEU survey registered a huge fall in the HZDS's credibility from September 1992 on virtually every issue, although less so on pro-market policies than on left-wing socioeconomic goals. Similar losses were also registered in voting support for the HZDS. This suggests that the depth of socioeconomic problems guarantees that, in the short term, no party in the region is likely to maintain the promise of hegemony that the HZDS displayed in 1992.

Ideological structuring involves the degree to which there are coherent dimensions of ideological cleavage that distinguish the parties. To determine the degree of ideological structuring, the raw data from the CEU surveys were subjected to a factor analysis.[46] The proportion of variance explained by the first one or two factors can be taken as a measure of ideological structuring. The higher these figures are, the more easily the complexity of party images can be reduced to variation in party positions on one or two ideological dimensions.

The first factor is a general left-right dimension: increasing church influence, decommunization, free-market economy, and other right-wing goals at one extreme, and reducing inequality and other left-wing goals at the other. The second factor pits the secular liberal and conservative parties, which emphasize pro-market goals, against the Christian parties, which stress religious and social-service issues. The third dimension (which does not occur in Hungary) pits the anticommunist nationalist parties against the rest.

The first two dimensions explain 74 percent of the total variance in party images in Poland, 68 percent in the Czech Republic, 75 percent in Slovakia, and 83 percent in Hungary. This suggests that the ideological structuring of party images is stronger in Hungary than in the other three countries. Party positions on nationalist and anticommunist issues are not as closely related to party positions on clerical-secular issues in the other three countries as they are in Hungary.

The fact that Czech and Slovak voters around 1992 faced a three-dimensional party system while Hungary's system had two dimensions did not prevent Czechs and Slovaks from developing clearer party images than did Hungarians. The higher absolute values in Table 7 than in Table 6, and corresponding data for Slovakia and Hungary (not shown here), clearly suggest that Czechs and Slovaks knew more than Poles and Hungarians about parties' programmatic profiles.

Can the greater clarity of party images be the factor that makes gross electoral volatility (shown in Table 5) lower in the Czech Republic and Slovakia than in Hungary and Poland? To test this proposition, we examined empirically which groups of voters were most likely to remain loyal to their preferred party over time: those whose party preferences were consistent with their political attitudes (Type 1); those whose party preferences were rooted in sociodemographic traits such as class, residence, age, or denomination (Type 2); or those whose party preferences were tied to either of these factors weakly or not at all (Type 3). The results suggested that Type 1 voters were least likely to change their party choice over time.[47]

Furthermore, the degree to which the voters' choices between opposition and government parties were influenced by their issue positions in Slovakia and the Czech Republic in 1992 is probably less than in Britain in 1987 (the only Western country with which such a comparison was made), but more than in Poland and Hungary in 1992. Thus the extent to which programmatic differentiation between the parties influences electoral behavior may explain East-West and East-East differences in the degree of electoral volatility.[48]

Intervening Variables

None of the four East Central European party systems analyzed in this essay meet Mainwaring and Scully's liberal criteria for an institutionalized party system. Rather, some of them would fall among what Mainwaring and Scully call "inchoate party systems" (e.g., those of contemporary Brazil, Ecuador, Peru, and Bolivia). Yet as I argued above, at least three of these four postcommunist systems are "consolidated" democracies. This is not to say that a lack of party-system institutionalization does not undermine accountability, or that it does not pave the way for "populist" appeals, as Mainwaring and Scully argue. But it does not prevent democratic consolidation. How is this possible?

Contrary to Mainwaring and Scully's expectations of how inchoate party systems hamper democratic consolidation, in East Central Europe social actors do not confront one another without the mediation of political representatives, nor do they "question the legitimacy of the electoral process and engage in actions that imply rejecting government legitimacy."[49] Second, though extremely high electoral volatility prevails in East Central Europe, making election outcomes unpredictable, this uncertainty fails to undermine politicians' commitment to the democratic rules of the game.

Neither does the increasing institutionalization of political parties boost the popular legitimacy of the new regimes. Here, the problematic aspect is not so much the level of popular support for the abstract idea or principles of democracy. This is relatively high anyway.[50] My point here is twofold. First, normative support for the abstract ideal of democracy among the masses, which was often claimed to be largely unrelated to economic evaluations in postcommunist Eastern Europe,[51] was shown to have behavioral consequences for regime stability only under the most unusual circumstances.[52] In contrast, there is convincing evidence that widespread dissatisfaction with democracy can affect regime stability in a wide variety of democratic regimes.[53] Second, satisfaction with democracy corresponds with the popular evaluation of economic conditions, but not with the evaluation of democratic institutions such as parties.

Elsewhere it was shown that Poles, Czechs, Slovaks, and Hungarians who think that "their views and interests are well represented" by at least one of the major parties do *not* tend to be more satisfied with the functioning of democracy and do *not* feel politically more effective than those who do not think they are represented by any of the major parties.[54] Table 8 also shows that—even though political parties have surely become more institutionalized in most of the four countries between 1992 and 1996—satisfaction with political parties has *not* increased over time. Moreover, while in three of the four countries temporal fluctuations in the evaluation of political parties are positively correlated with changes in the level of satisfaction with democracy— which fits the hypothesis that satisfaction with political intermediaries generates satisfaction with democracy—the opposite is true in the Czech Republic. That is, the greater the number of Czechs who evaluated political parties favorably at a certain point in time, the smaller the number who were satisfied with democracy.

In contrast, satisfaction with personal economic conditions correlates positively with satisfaction with democracy in each of the four countries. As explained elsewhere,[55] the critical evidence to look at is the aggregate-level correlations within each country between the *percentage* of people satisfied with democracy at a given place and time and the *percentage* of people happy with economic conditions.

Across the five to seven observations available in each country, this aggregate-level correlation is 0.77 in Poland, 0.89 in the Czech Republic, an insignificant but still positive 0.31 in Slovakia, and 0.83 in Hungary.

Table 8 — Satisfaction with Democracy, Parties, and the Economy

	"Very" or "rather" satisfied with the functioning of democracy (%)	Disagree that parties are only interested in votes (%)	Disagree that economic conditions are very unfavorable (%)
Poland			
October 1992	19	10	18
January 1993	19	7	13
August 1993	22	9	18
April 1994	26	8	15
December 1994	24	9	23
June 1995	20	10	25
December 1995	35	15	38
Czech Republic			
September 1992	39	29	44
April 1993	47	26	46
November 1993	53	25	52
April 1994	44	21	46
November 1994	48	19	49
June 1995	47	19	46
January 1996	52	21	54
Slovakia			
September 1992	28	24	26
April 1993	25	11	20
November 1993	28	11	27
April 1994	21	10	24
November 1994	21	14	27
June 1995	28	17	29
Hungary			
September 1992	22	14	19
January 1993	22	14	16
December 1993	28	15	16
April 1994	39	23	25
July 1995	21	13	17

Source: CEU surveys.

The comparable aggregate-level correlations between the percentage of respondents satisfied with democracy and the percentage positively evaluating the political parties are 0.77, −0.40, 0.50, and 0.97, respectively.

Given the small number of cases in the four national time series, most of these correlations are, statistically speaking, too weak to allow us to infer interrelationships among the three factors. Yet the data give the impression that a positive assessment of personal economic conditions is more universally important for satisfaction with democracy than is the assessment of political parties.

It has been shown elsewhere that differences in the popular evaluation of economic conditions indeed give a potent explanation both for the observed differences among the four East Central European countries and for the temporal trends in levels of satisfaction with democracy.[56] This holds true across a larger sample of postcommunist countries as well. Comparative data also confirm that nations showing lower levels of political satisfaction tend to be more pessimistic regarding economic prospects.[57]

This finding may also explain the robust East-West difference concerning satisfaction with democracy.[58] Cross-national comparisons of generalized trust in elected officials, in contrast, reveal little difference between East Central Europe and Western democracies. This again suggests that the institutionalization of political parties per se has little to do with the popular legitimacy of the democratic regime. Cross-national survey data from the last decade suggest that the percentage of people who agree with statements such as "Most people with power try to take advantage of people like myself," and "Most elected officials care what people like me think," or "Generally speaking, elected officials lose touch with the people pretty quickly," averages about the same in Western democracies as in the four East Central European democracies.[59]

Policy Success

Mainwaring and Scully argue that party institutionalization helps democratic consolidation through the former's beneficial impact on "whether effective policy making will result."[60] This effect is hard to trace in East Central Europe. Ranking the four countries in terms of governmental stability does not match their likely ranking in terms of policy successes in the 1990–95 period.

From 1990 to 1993, Poland had little coherent legislative majority to back an "effective" executive.[61] From 1990 to 1992, delays and stalemates in passing many important economic bills were reportedly caused by considerable ideological divisions and paralyzing splits in the OF and VPN, the winners of the 1990 Czechoslovak elections.[62] Following the June 1992 elections, an ideologically compact national government was formed in the Czech Republic with the ODS, ODA, KDU-ČSL, and Christian Democratic Party (KDS) providing a steady 52.5 percent legislative support for the government in the following years. In June 1992, Slovakia started off with a near-majority single-party (HZDS) government. A majority emerged when the HZDS formed a coalition with the SNS, but—after splits in both government parties—the government was replaced by a minority government of the former opposition from March 1994 until the early elections in September 1994.

In contrast, Hungary had much the same coalition government from May 1990 to May 1994, with a relatively disciplined and ideologically compact legislative majority providing solid support for an entire legislative term despite the death of the original prime minister and numerous splits in the government parties.[63] After Hungary's second free election in May 1994, two former opposition parties formed another apparently stable majority government.

Thus if the only determinant of policy success were a political system's capacity to generate lasting legislative majorities that back stable governments, Hungary would be the most, the Czech Republic the second-most, and pre-1993 Poland the least successful. Macroeconomic data (such as 1995 levels of economic growth and unemployment and change in inflation between the beginning of transition and 1995) suggest the following "success ranking" instead: Poland or the Czech Republic in first place, Slovakia in second, and Hungary the least successful.

Explaining the Findings

Why, then, is there no apparent indication in East Central Europe that higher levels of party institutionalization would promote democratic consolidation and policy effectiveness? First, as Morlino and Mainwaring and Scully stress, democratic consolidation may not require "hyperinstitutionalized" parties. Second, when and where conditions are even more favorable for democratic consolidation than they were in Latin America in the 1970s and 1980s or postwar Italy, even Bolivia's or Ecuador's level of party institutionalization may suffice to make electoral success the only "currency of power."

Reasons to suspect that the four East Central European countries in the 1990s are just such a place abound: they are geographically close to the European Union and all the policy constraints that this implies; they have traditions of firm civilian control of the military;[64] and last but not least, in the words of Samuel Huntington, "After democratization a former monopolistic party is in no better position than any other political group to reinstate an authoritarian system."[65]

Even if political parties were not necessary for democratic transition and their development was not crucial to democratic consolidation, the fact that the remnants of the *ancien régime* were organized along party lines might have been highly conducive to democratic consolidation. It is far-fetched to think that this was the only factor that made the development of other parties less relevant for consolidation. Suffice it to refer to the troublesome cases of Russia and Belarus. Their cases might, in the long run, support Morlino's observation that wherever the "acknowledgment of democratic institutions and practices is not initially widespread [i.e., among the organized political actors], a dominant partisan control of society may be the only route to [democratic] consolidation."[66]

Second, one could try to argue that the East Central European party systems are, on the whole, no less institutionalized than some of the party systems in the more consolidated Latin American democracies. Although in organizational terms Colombia, Costa Rica, Chile, or Venezuela may have better-developed parties than can be found in Eastern Europe, the programmatic structuring of East Central European party systems may still be stronger. But if that is so, and a stronger ideological structuring of the political field can compensate for weaker institutionalization to make democratic politics relatively predictable and credible, then East Central European party systems probably should not be grouped with the "inchoate" party systems of some fragile democracies.

Finally, it may be that Mainwaring and Scully's observation about the impact of party institutionalization on effectiveness in policy making and on democratic consolidation has less validity in parliamentary than in presidential systems. In parliamentary systems the legislature cannot continue opposing the policies of the executive and implicitly letting the bureaucracy or the presidency implement necessary but unpopular policies. Those legislators who support the government in a no-confidence motion are easy to identify and certain to take blame or credit for it.

Alternatively, it may be the case that a stricter definition of democratic consolidation should be used. In the four East Central European countries political actors seem to calculate that only electoral success can lead to political power, but many do not believe that their rivals would not try other routes to power. True, these party elites have not shown an appetite for preemptive strikes against imagined threats to democracy so far. But it is reasonable to define a consolidated democracy in somewhat stricter terms regarding the expectations of politicians. Suppose that politicians believe in the law-abiding behavior of their competitors only if past behavior in a similar situation warrants it. The probability of trust that the winner of the next election will not use illegitimate means to stay in power is greatly increased if 1) all potential contenders are collective actors (parties) with established reputations, and 2) the past actions of these collective actors are believed to be a reliable predictor of the behavior of individual politicians. What these conditions together describe is, of course, the institutionalization of a party system. Thus incorporating expectations about other actors' likely behavior in the definition of consolidation may eliminate the difficulty of some postcommunist countries' qualifying as consolidated democracies even though their party systems are extremely volatile.

Quality of Democracy

Obviously, political actors without long track records are less constrained in their election pledges than strongly institutionalized parties. It is not obvious, however, that this consequence of party weakness would endanger either democratic consolidation or prudent policy choices. When parties won elections in East Central Europe on ambitious platforms of a less painful, softer course of economic reform, they usually hastened to announce that the fiscal problems revealed to them when they first took office were much deeper than expected, and that they were therefore forced to follow a somewhat different course of action than previously planned. This was the case with the Christian-national government of Jan Olszewski in Poland in 1991, with the government of József Antall in Hungary in 1990, with the first HZDS government formed after the June 1992 elections in Slovakia, and with most leaders of the ex-communist MSZP after their victory in the 1994 Hungarian elections.[67] Though the eventual economic policies of these governments were more in line with the wisdom of finance-ministry bureaucrats than with election pledges, in retrospect the parties were electorally accountable for their actions—and the gap between their words and deeds. Clearly, electoral control of public officials suffers when every second or third government in the region acts this way, but that is a matter of the quality, not the very survival, of newborn democracies.

But the *quality* of democracy is important enough to justify the development of a strong party system, even if the latter does not contribute to the *consolidation* of democracy. Stressing "democracy" over "consolidation" suggests somewhat different priorities. For instance, clear-cut programmatic competition between somewhat ideological parties may be favored over the moderation, convergence, consensus, and low volatility that are typically stressed in scholarly discussions of democratic consolidation. As the dilemmas of the emerging polarized pluralism in the Czech Republic indicate, ideological polarization beyond a certain point hurts the quality of democracy. Yet vigorous partisan clashes over ideological differences can enable voters to make sense of the choices they face.[68] Once party profiles are clearly drawn and initial electoral alignments forged, more moderate stimuli may suffice to make voters believe that elections offer real choices—but not when a new party system is built from scratch.

Attributing to political parties more of a contribution to the quality than to the mere consolidation of democracy also prompts another explanation of why parties and democracy tend to develop together. Vote trading inevitably emerges in any decision-making body that has real powers and adopts the principle of majority rule for important collective decisions.[69] The coordinated strategic behavior of any one group, by increasing voting support for a set of otherwise nonwinning proposals, is sure to hurt the aspirations of other assembly members. The latter can counteract only by forming another voting bloc. If freedom and majority rule prevail, no reasonable assembly member can avoid vote trading.

Furthermore, if the assembly faces a large number of decisions that have little to do with one another (as modern legislatures do), the voting record of most individual assembly members follows the predictable lines of the coalition to which they have pledged support.[70] Thus voters have strong incentives to abandon independent (and thus incalculable) candidates for representatives aligned with the desirable legislative coalitions (party labels).

By this line of reasoning, institutionalized parties are more the by-products of democracy than its creators. Parties are necessary to make representative democracy work since the decisions of legislative assemblies composed of isolated individuals would be incalculable.[71] The important point is that the *quality* of democracy would suffer in the absence of relatively cohesive and persistent parties. In the words of Richard Katz,

> Once the scale of society makes direct popular rule impossible and the complexity of political life renders selection by lot unacceptable, representation based on popular elections appears to be the only way to preserve elements of popular participation, direction, and control implicit in democracy. . . . Without parties to structure the campaign, to provide continuity from one election to the next, and to provide links among candidates in different localities and for different offices, the resulting elections are unlikely to be meaningful, even if they are technically free.[72]

Appendix

Following is a brief guide to abbreviations and party names appearing in this essay.

Czech Republic

ČMSS: Českomoravská strana středu—Czech-Moravian Party of the Center. In 1993 the parliamentary club of HSD-SMS split. The more moderately regionalist wing formed the HSDMS, which in 1994 was transformed into a political party called ČMSS. In December 1994 the ČMSS fused with the LSU to form the ČMUS. For a while the LSU and ČMSS retained their separate legal identities to remain eligible for public funding, but in fact they merged (cf. ČMUS, HSD-SMS).

ČMUS: Českomoravská unie středu—Czech-Moravian Union of the Center. A center-left party formed on 17 December 1994 by the remainder of the LSU and the ČMSS (former HSDMS, previously HSD-SMS) (cf. HSD-SMS, LSU).

ČSL: Česk(oslovensk)á strana lidová—Czech (previously Czechoslovak) People's

Party. A historic Christian party that used to be one of the satellites of the KSČS. One of the Czech government parties since July 1992 (cf. KDU-ČSL).

ČSS: Česká strana socialistická—Czech Socialist Party. A slightly left-of-center historic party that was one of the satellite parties during the communist period. In 1992 it became part of the LSU. In November 1992 some ČSS deputies and three former SPR-RSČ deputies formed a separate parliamentary club called the LSNS, and the June 1993 ČSS conference renamed the Socialist Party LSNS and broke ties with the LSU. Some former ČSS members and deputies decided to remain in the LSU as individual members (cf. SD-LSNS).

ČSSD: Československá sociální demokracie—Czechoslovak Social Democracy, later Czech Social Democratic Party. A historic party that "merged" with the KSČS after the February 1948 coup and was reorganized only after the November 1989 revolution.

DEU: Democratická unie—Democratic Union. An extreme anticommunist and otherwise libertarian-leaning party established in late 1993, registered in March 1994, and regularly polling 1 to 2 percent in surveys of electoral preference since then.

DŽJ or **HDŽJ:** (Hnutí) důchodců za životní jistoty—Pensioners for Life Securities. A slightly left-of-center single-issue party using the HDŽJ label in 1992 and the DŽJ label in the 1996 elections.

HDŽJ: See DŽJ.

HSDMS: See ČMSS.

HSD-SMS: Hnutí za samosprávnou demokracii–Společnost pro Moravu a Slezsko—Movement for Self-Governing Democracy–Association for Moravia and Silesia. A center-left, very moderately regionalist organization that contested the 1990 and 1992 elections (cf. ČMUS).

KAN: Klub angažovaných nestraníků—Club of Committed Non-Party Members. An association dating back to 1968, and revived after November 1989. It was a part of the OF in 1990 (cf. OF).

KDS: Křest'anskodemokratická strana—Christian Democratic Party. A part of the KDU in 1990; later appeared as part of the ODS-KDS coalition in 1992. The KDS was a somewhat more conservative Christian party than the KDU-ČSL, and participated in each Czech cabinet between July 1990 and June 1996. Formally merged with the ODS before the 1996 election.

KDU: Křest'anská a demokratická unie—Christian and Democratic Union. The ČSL and some smaller Christian groupings contested the 1990 Czechoslovak election under this label (cf. KDU-ČSL, ČSL).

KDU-ČSL: Křest'anská a demokratická unie–Česká strana lidov—Christian and Democratic Union–Czech People's Party. Little more than just another name for the ČSL (cf. KDU, ČSL).

KSČM: Komunistická strana Čech a Moravy—Communist Party of Bohemia and Moravia. The major component of the LB, formerly the KSČS (cf. KSČS, LB).

KSČS: Komunistická strana Československenska—Communist Party of Czechoslovakia. The historic communist party in Czechoslovakia, which split between the Slovak SDL and the Czech-Moravian KSČM in the second half of 1990 (cf. KSČM).

LB: Levý blok—Left Bloc. The 1992 electoral list and 1992–94 parliamentary club of the KSČM and some smaller left-wing groups. In 1994 the parliamentary club split; the majority of deputies retained the LB label but joined the SLB. The deputies who remained loyal to the KSČM established a separate Communist Club in the parliament. In the 1996 election, the LB label was used by the SLB (cf. KSČM, KSČS, SLB).

LSNS: Liberální strana národní sociální—Liberal Social National Party. Not long after the 1992 election, the ČSS (a part of the LSU coalition) adopted LSNS as its new name. Later, some LSU and SPR-RSČ deputies also established the parliamentary club of LSNS. In 1995 the LSNS merged with the SD (ex-OH) (cf. ČSS, LSU, SD-LSNS).

LSU: Liberální sociální unie—Liberal Social Union. The 1992 joint electoral list of three left-of-center parties—the ČSS, the SZ, and the ZS—which was formally registered as a separate political party. After the defection of the SZ and LSNS, its remainder (composed of the ZS and some former ČSS members) continued to exist as a parliamentary club and also had a grassroots organization, but was absorbed by the ČMUS in December 1994 (cf. ČSS, SZ, ZS, SD-LSNS, ČMUS).

ODA: Občanská demokratická aliance—Civic Democratic Alliance. A libertarian-leaning party of notables, a part of the OF in 1990, represented in every Czech government since the 1989 revolution (cf. OF).

ODS: Občanská demokratická strana—Civic Democratic Party. The main market-liberal party in the Czech Republic. A successor to the OF initiated and led by the 1990–92 federal finance minister—and, from July 1992 to present, Czech premier Václav Klaus (cf. OF). A participant in every Czech government since the party was established—that is, since before the inception of the Czech Republic as a sovereign state on 1 January 1993. (Between 1990 and 1992, the Czech and Slovak republics had their own legislatures and republican governments, apart from the Federal Assembly and the federal government.)

ODS-KDS: Občanská demokratická strana–Křest'anskodemokratická strana—Civic Democratic Party–Christian Democratic Party. The 1992 electoral coalition of the ODS and the tiny KDS (cf. ODS, KDS).

OF: Občanské Fórum—Civic Forum. The Czech umbrella organization that was the leading force of the November 1989 revolution, and the main noncommunist political organization in the 1990 Czechoslovak elections and the 1990–91 governments (cf. ODA, ODS, OH, KAN).

OH, SD: Občanské hnutí—Civic Movement, later renamed SD (Svobodní Demokraté—Free Democrats). A centrist, pro-market successor to the OF, led by former foreign minister Jiří Dienstbier and joined by a plurality of the 1990–92 Czech cabinet members (cf. SD-LSNS).

SD: See OH.

SDL: Strana demokratické levice–Democratic Left Party. A splinter from the KSČM critical of the somewhat orthodox position of the KSČM (cf. KSČM, LB).

SD-LSNS: Svobodní Demokraté–Liberální strana národně sociální—Free Democrats–Liberal Social National Party. A centrist party created via the merger of the SD (ex-OH) and the LSNS (ex-ČSS).

SLB: Strana levého bloku—Left Bloc Party. In the 1992 election the KSČM and some insignificant groups ran under the LB (Left Bloc) label, and until January 1994 all of their elected deputies sat in the LB parliamentary club. Founded in December 1993, the SLB is a small splinter from the KSČM that claims to be more pragmatic than the KSČM. After the party split, the LB parliamentary club split into two parts as well; the larger retained the LB label and sided with the SLB. A minority of deputies remained in the KSČM and founded the Communist Club in the parliament. The SLB decided to contest the 1996 election under the LB label (cf. KSČM, LB).

SPP: Strana přátel piva—Beerlovers' Party. A small electoral organization with a limited anti-establishment appeal.

SPR-RSČ: Sdružení pro republiku–Republikánská strana Československá—Association for the Republic–Czech Republican Party. A xenophobic, anticommunist, anti-Gypsy party with somewhat social-protectionist economic policies, led by Miroslav Sládek. It contested the 1990 election under the VDSPR label.

SZ: Strana zelených—Green Party. A left-of-center environmentalist party, part of the LSU in 1992. The SZ set up its own lists for the 1990 election and 1996 elections, but could not contest the latter for failing to make the deposits required by the election list (cf. LSU).

SZV: Spojenectví zemědělců a venkova—Alliance of Peasants and Countryside. The 1990 joint electoral list of nine different interest groups and small parties that also included the ZS and DŽJ.

VDSPR: Koalíce vselídové demokratické strany—Coalition of All-Nation Democratic Party. The 1990 joint electoral list of the SPR-RSČ and the All-Nation Democratic Party.

ZS: Zemedelska strana—Agricultural Party. Not to be confused with the right-wing Agrarian Party of the interbellum period (1918–38), the ZS used to be the left-of-center political arm of Czech and Moravian collective farms. Its candidates appeared on the 1990 SZV and the 1992 LSU electoral lists. Through a number of organizational changes the remainder of the ZS was eventually absorbed by the ČMUS (cf. LSU, ČMUS).

Hungary

ASZ: Agrárszövetség—Agrarian Alliance. A moderate agrarian party that also contested elections and saw two candidates in 1990 and one candidate in 1994 elected in single-member districts in the parliamentary elections. Two ASZ deputies joined the SZDSZ parliamentary club; one remained independent.

FIDESZ: Fiatal Demokraták Szövetsége—Federation of Young Democrats. A secular and pro-market (in Hungarian parlance, liberal) youth organization that, alongside the MDF and SZDSZ, was among the most prominent opposition forces in the 1988–90 democratic transition. It was eventually transformed into an ordinary political party and became a middle-of-the-road ally first of the SZDSZ and then (after 1994) of the MDF and KDNP.

FKGP: Független Kisgazda Párt—Independent Smallholders' Party. An agrarian party of long historical pedigree, after 1990 it became the most nationalist, anticommunist, and populist of the six main parties in Hungary. Until early 1992 the FKGP was a junior partner in the post-1990 governments, but then the party went into opposition and expelled most of its parliamentary deputies for their refusal to leave the government benches. Between 1990 and 1994 a large number of smaller groups defected from the FKGP and fielded candidates under various "smallholder" labels without success.

KDNP: Kereszténydemokrata Néppárt—Christian Democratic People's Party. A strongly social-protectionist Christian party and a junior partner in the 1990–94 coalition government.

KP: Köztársaság Párt—Party of the Republic. A small SZDSZ-leaning party founded by a popular defector from the MDF caucus in 1993.

MDF: Magyar Demokrata Fórum—Hungarian Democratic Forum. A Christian-conservative party basing its identity on a strongly patriotic appeal and advocating a social market economy. The main government party between the 1990 and 1994 elections.

MP (formerly MSZMP): Munkáspárt—Workers' Party. A small antimarket subcultural (*Weltanschauung*) party with a considerable membership but limited electoral success, founded by orthodox communists in late 1989.

MSZDP: Magyarországi Szociáldemokrata Párt—Hungarian Social Democratic Party. Dating back to 1890, the image of the MSZDP in postcommunist Hungary was shaped primarily by its controversial historical record and personalistic infighting between 1989 and 1993.

MSZMP: Magyar Szocialista Munkáspárt—Hungarian Socialist Workers' Party. The name of Hungary's ruling communist party from the time of the 1956 revolution until October 1989. The MSZMP officially disbanded in 1989. Its sole legal heir became the newly founded MSZP. In November 1989 some less prominent elements of the former MSZMP "reorganized" the MSZMP as a relatively orthodox communist party that nevertheless accepted the democratic rules of the game. This new MSZMP was later renamed the MP (cf. MSZP, MP).

MSZP: Magyar Szocialista Párt—Hungarian Socialist Party. The predominantly reformist successor of the former communist party called MSZMP, which was officially disbanded in October 1989. The single government party before the 1990 election, and the main government party after the 1994 election.

SZDSZ: Szabad Demokraták Szövetsége—Alliance of Free Democrats. A secular, pro-market, cosmopolitan (in Hungarian parlance, liberal) party, the junior partner in the post-1994 government.

VP: Vállalkozók Pártja—Party of Entrepreneurs. An insignificant pro-business party that won one single-member seat in 1994 with support from the FIDESZ, SZDSZ, and ASZ.

Poland

AW "S": Akcja Wyborcza "Solidarność"—"Solidarity" Electoral Action. A broad electoral alliance created after the 1995 presidential election with the participation of parts of the BBWR, KPN, the former NSZZ "S," PC, PK, PL, SLCh, ZChN, and other small groupings. The programmatic profile of the coalition was rather obscure; the unifying goal of the participants was to remove the ex-communists from power in the next parliamentary election.

BBWR: Bezpartyjny Blok Wspierania Reform—Nonparty Bloc in Support of Reform. A heterogeneous electoral organization created before the 1993 election on the apparent initiative of President Lech Wałęsa, which, however, was never joined or endorsed publicly by him. In 1996 a part of the BBWR joined AW "S" (cf. AW "S").

ChD: Chrzescijanska Demokracja—Christian Democrats. The 1991 electoral coalition of two small Christian parties.

KdR: See RdR.

KKWO: Katolicki Komitet Wyborczy "Ojczyzna"—"Unity" Catholic Electoral Committee. A 1993 electoral coalition of the ZChN, the PK (a splinter group from the UD), and two smaller Christian parties (cf. ZChN, WAK).

KLD: Kongres Liberalno-Demokratyczny—Liberal Democratic Congress. The most market-liberal offspring of the Solidarność camp led by former premier Jan Krzysztof Bieleczki. Supported three of the four (the market-liberal Mazowiecki, Bieleczki, and Suchocka) governments in 1989–93 (cf. UW).

KPN: Konfederacja Polski Niepodległej—Confederation for an Independent Poland. An anticommunist and nationalist party with distinctively left-of-center economic policies, led by the veteran dissenter Leszek Moczulski (cf. AW "S").

MN: Mniejszosc Niemiecka—German Minority. The electoral list of German minority organizations.

NSZZ "S": NSZZ "Solidarność"—"Solidarity" Independent Trade Union. The name of the 1991 and 1993 electoral lists, and the 1991–93 parliamentary club of the trade union that was founded in August 1980, was banned between December 1981 and late spring 1989, and served as a rallying point of opposition forces throughout the 1980s. While represented in the lower house, it first supported, then brought down, both governments of that period (the Olszewski and the Suchocka cabinets). After the 1995 presidential election, this political arm of the trade union was transformed into the more encompassing AW "S" coalition (cf. AW "S").

Partia "X": Partia "X"—Party X. An anticommunist, secular, nationalist, anti-establishment, and social-protectionist party associated with Stanisław Tymiński, the surprise runner-up in the 1990 presidential election.

PC, POC: Porozumienie Centrum—Center Alliance. A Christian-conservative offspring of the Solidarność camp led by Jarosław Kaczyński. In 1991 its electoral list was labeled POC (Porozumienie Obywatelskie Centrum). Supported the Olszewski government in 1991–92 (cf. AW "S").

PK: Partia Konserwatywna—Conservative Party. A conservative Christian Democrat splinter from the UD, led by Aleksandr Hall. It was a member of the KKWO electoral alliance in 1993.

PL, PL-PSL: Porozumienie Ludowe—Peasant Alliance. A Christian-oriented agrarian party, offspring of the Solidarność camp. In the 1991 election it appeared as Porozumienie Ludowe–Polskie Stronnictwo Ludowe. Formally supported each noncommunist government while represented in the lower house (cf. AW "S").

PPPP: Polska Partia Przyjaciol Piwa—Polish Party of the Friends of Beer. A strongly market-liberal party that originated from a 1991 protest party of the same name. It supported the Suchocka government in 1992–93.

PSL: Polskie Stronnictwo Ludowe—Polish Peasant Party. A "historic" peasant party with a vast grassroots organization, which existed in the communist period as the ZSL (United Peasant Party), a satellite of the PZPR. One of the two coalition partners in the post-1993 governments.

PZPR: Polska Zjednoczona Partia Robotnicza—Polish United Workers' Party. The ruling party in the communist period, voluntarily disbanded in January 1990 (cf. SLD).

RdR: Ruch dla Rzeczypospolitej—Movement for the Republic, later KdR (Coalition for the Republic). A strongly anticommunist Christian-nationalist party founded by former premier Jan Olszewski and other defectors from the ZChN and PC in 1992 (cf. ZChN, PC, ROP).

ROP: Ruch Odbudowy Polski—Movement for the Reconstruction of Poland. A strongly anticommunist electoral alliance formed by the RdR and two other small parties in 1995 (cf. RdR).

SD: Stronnictwo Demokratyczne—Democratic Party. As a satellite of the communist party, the SD had been in existence throughout the communist period. It was expected to "represent" artisans and other members of the remaining urban petite bourgeoisie. After its failure in the 1991 election, the SD quickly disappeared.

SdRP: Socjaldemokracja Rzeczpospolitej Polskiej—Social Democracy of the Polish Republic. The de facto political heir of the PZPR, the communist party of the *ancien régime* (cf. SLD).

SLCh: Stronnictwo Ludowo-Chrześcijańskie—Christian People's Party. A small Christian party in the post-Solidarność camp. It was a member of the KKWO electoral alliance in 1993.

SLD: Sojusz Lewicy Demokratycznej—Democratic Left Alliance. The joint electoral list and parliamentary club of SdRP and the postcommunist trade-union federation (cf. SdRP).

SP or **UP:** Solidarność Pracy—Labor Solidarity. A participant in the 1991 parliamentary elections, later renamed UP (Labor Union) (cf. UP).

UD: Unia Demokratyczna—Democratic Union. The main market-liberal offspring of the Solidarność camp led by a host of prominent politicians such as former premiers Mazowiecki and Suchocka, and 1995 presidential candidate Jacek Kurón. Supported the Mazowiecki, Bieleczki, and Suchocka governments in 1989–93 (cf. UW).

UP: Unia Pracy—Labor Union. A strongly secular social-democratic party led partly by some former prominent leaders of the Solidarność trade union (cf. SP).

UPR: Unia Polityki Realnej—Realpolitik Union. An extreme libertarian-conservative party with a somewhat anti-establishment appeal, led by Janusz Korwin-Mikke.

UW: Unia Wolnosci—Freedom Union. A party of notables led by former finance minister Leszek Balczerowicz, and created by the merger of the UD and KLD after the latter failed to gain seats in the 1993 parliamentary elections (cf. KLD, UD).

WAK: Wyborcza Akcja Katolicka—Catholic Electoral Action. A 1991 electoral list based mostly on the ZChN (cf. ZChN, KKWO).

ZChN: Zjednoczenie Chrześcijańsko-Narodowe—Christian National Union. The main Christian party in Poland, an offspring of the Solidarność camp. It supported each noncommunist government while represented in the lower house (cf. KKWO, WAK, AW "S").

ZSL: Zjednoczone Stronnictwo Ludowe—United Peasant Party. Under communist rule, the PSL continued to exist as a satellite party but changed its name to ZSL.

Slovakia

DS: Demokratická strana—Democratic Party. A right-of-center historic party in Slovakia traditionally favoring the Czechoslovak federation to Slovak independence. Since 1992 it has absorbed several other federalist-leaning pro-market parties, including the SKD. Participated in the 1990–92 Slovak national (i.e., republican) governments (cf. SKD).

DU: Demokratická Unia Slovenska—Democratic Union of Slovakia. A party of notables founded in 1994 by prominent defectors from the HZDS. Party leader Jozef Moravčík was prime minister of the March–September 1994 interim government given by a rainbow coalition of anti-Mečiar forces (cf. HZDS).

HP: Hnutie pol'nohospodárov—Farmers' Movement. A small agrarian party, part of the 1994 SV electoral coalition. The HP did not contest the 1990 and 1992 elections.

HZDS: Hnutie za demokratické Slovensko–Movement for a Democratic Slovakia. The HZDS was founded in March 1991 by then Slovak premier Vladimir Mečiar as a faction within VPN, and formally left VPN after the bulk of the federalist and pro-market tendency in the VPN leadership decided to oust the popular Mečiar from the premiership. The HZDS was joined by about half of the VPN deputies and members, and adopted a more nationalist, less pro-market platform than VPN. The HZDS was the major government party between July 1992 and March 1994, and after the September 1994 election. While governing the independent Slovakia, the economic policy preferences of the HZDS have become somewhat blurred, but the party established a clear identity through its combatant advocacy of a distinctly majoritarian form of democratic government, an increasingly nationalist position on domestic issues, and a cautious balancing of the Eastern (i.e., pro-Russian) and Western orientations in foreign policy (cf. VPN).

KDH: Krest'anskodemokratické hnutie—Christian Democratic Movement. A right-of-center Christian party, participated in the 1990–92 Slovak national governments and the 1994 Moravčík government (cf. SKDH).

KSČS: Kommunistická strana Československa—Czechoslovak Communist Party. The name of the predecessor of the Czech KSČM and the Slovak SDL and KSS before October 1990.

KSS: Kommunistická strana Slovenska—Communist Party of Slovakia. Originally, the name of the Slovak sister party of the Czechoslovak communist party; from 1991 the name of a small communist party dissatisfied with the reformist leadership of SDL.

KSU: See SKDH.

MK: Magyar Koalíció—Hungarian Coalition. An electoral coalition and parliamentary club of the MKM, ESWS, and MOS.

MKM-ESWS: Magyar Kereszténydemokrata Mozgalom–Együttélés-Spoluzití-Wspólnota—Hungarian Christian Democratic Movement–Coexistence. The 1992 coalition and 1992–94 parliamentary club of two Christian-nationalist parties speaking for ethnic Hungarians.

MOS: Mad'arská občianska strana—Hungarian Civic Party. A liberal party of ethnic Hungarians, a part of VPN in 1990, and of the MK in 1994. A supporter of the 1990–92 Slovak national governments.

ODU: Občianska demokratická únia—Civic Democratic Union. The secular, pro-market, federalist, and anti-Mečiar offspring of VPN. One of the two most important partners in the 1991–92 Slovak national government headed by Ján Čarnogurský (cf. VPN, SKD).

ROI: Rómska občianska iniciatíva—Civic Initiative of Gypsy Citizens. An ethnic organization that was part of the VPN/OF in 1990, but had its own list in the 1992 Czechoslovak elections.

SDL: Strana demokratickej l'avice—Party of the Democratic Left. The main ex-communist party in Slovakia, which is reputed for its moderation and reformist stance. Gave occasional but important legislative support for the July 1992–October 1993 Mečiar government, but participated in the March–September 1994 Moravčík government supported by a rainbow coalition of anti-Mečiar forces (cf. KSS, SV).

SDSS: Sociálnodemokratická strana na Slovensku—Social Democratic Party of Slovakia. The Slovak wing of the historic Czechoslovak Social Democratic Party, joined by Alexander Dubček in 1991 (cf. SV).

SKD: Strana konzervatívnych demokratov—Conservative Democratic Party. A secular, federalist, pro-market party formed mostly by former prominent politicians of the ODU. Merged with the DS before the 1994 election (cf. ODU, DS).

SKDH or **KSU:** Slovenské krest'anskodemokratické hnutie—Slovak Christian Democratic Movement; later renamed Christian Social Union. A small party founded by the more nationalist elements of the KDH in March 1992 (cf. KDH).

SNS: Slovenská národná strana—Slovak National Party. A nationalist party with a long prewar history, which began advocating the independence of Slovakia in 1990. Though the SNS signed a formal coalition agreement with the HZDS only in October 1993, the party already gave legislative support to, and its leader had a portfolio in, the Mečiar government between July 1992 and April 1993. From October 1993 the SNS was part of all HZDS-led governments and went into opposition when Mečiar was temporarily ousted by a vote of no confidence in March 1994. A pro-market splinter group, the NDS (Narodno-demokratická strana—National Democratic Party), left the party in winter 1993–94, supported the March–October 1994 Moravčík government, and won parliamentary seats on the 1994 DU list.

SV: Spoločná vol'ba—Common Choice. A 1994 electoral coalition comprising the SDL, SDSS, SZS, and HP (cf. SDL, SDSS, SZS).

SZ: Strana zelených—Green Party. A left-of-center environmentalist party that, after the 1993 split of Czechoslovakia, survived only in the Czech Republic. In the 1990 elections, the SZ had its own lists in both the Czech and Slovak republics. In 1992, the SZ had its own lists of candidates in the Slovak electoral districts, but was a part of the LSU electoral coalition in the Czech Republic.

SZS: Strana zelených na Slovensku—Green Party of Slovakia. A left-of-center party; part of the SV in 1994 (cf. SV).

VPN: Verejnost' Proti Násiliu—Public Against Violence. The umbrella organization that was the leading force in the November 1989 revolution in Slovakia, and the main noncommunist political organization in the 1990 elections and the 1990–91 governments in Slovakia (cf. HZDS, ODU, MOS).

ZRS: Združenie robotníkov Slovenska—Association of Workers of Slovakia. A social-protectionist association, harshly critical of the privatization process. In 1992 one ZRS representative was elected on the SDL list, but in 1994 it fielded its own lists of candidates (cf. SDL).

NOTES

Some relevant analysis and supporting tables have not been included here for reasons of space. They appear in the full version of this essay, available as a working paper from the Centre for the Study of Public Policy at the University of Strathclyde in Glasgow, Scotland.

1. Most of the quantitative evidence cited in this essay comes from a series of comparative mass surveys sponsored by the Central European University, which monitored the development of electoral alignments in the four Visegrad countries. For reasons of brevity, these will be referred to as CEU surveys. The surveys have been carried out since the fall of 1992 with the assistance of a commercial political polling institute in each country: CBOS in Poland, STEM in the Czech Republic and Slovakia, and Median in Hungary. The samples were representative for the adult population of each country. In Poland, clustered random sampling was used, with sample sizes of 1,149, 1,188, 1,468, 1,209, 1,162, 1,173, and again 1,173 in the successive waves. In the Czech Republic and Slovakia, surveys started with clustered random sampling but switched to quota sampling in 1993. The Czech sample sizes were 815, 939, 1,117, 1,562, 1,515, 1,291, and 1,569. Slovak sample sizes were 712, 920, 871, 845, 757, and 1,213. In the Hungarian studies the sample sizes have been 1,200 (1,196 in June 1995); clustered random route sampling was used. Dates of the surveys are shown in the tables.

2. Aggregate-level or net volatility is half the sum of the absolute value of the differences between the vote shares of each party in two consecutive elections. For example, three parties contest the first election; each receives 33.3 percent of the vote. One party disbands by the next election, and the remaining two receive 60 and 40 percent of the vote, respectively. The total volatility between the two elections is $(33 + |33 - 60| + |33 - 40|)/2 = (33 + 27 + 7)/2 = 33.5$ percent. In this essay, individual-level or gross volatility is the percentage of voters who change their voting preference from one point in time to another.

3. "Programmatic structuring" entails clarity of party positions on various issues, the degree of the difference ("spatial distance") between the party positions, and the extent to which party

positions on all the relevant (salient) issues can be predicted on the basis of the party positions on a few ideological superdimensions (e.g., clerical vs. secular, left vs. right, and so on).

4. See Scott Mainwaring and Timothy R. Scully, "Introduction: Party Systems in Latin America," in Mainwaring and Scully, eds., *Building Democratic Institutions: Party Systems in Latin America* (Stanford: Stanford University Press, 1994), 1–34; and Leonardo Morlino, "Political Parties and Democratic Consolidation in Southern Europe," in Richard Gunther, P. Nikiforos Diamandouros, and Hans-Jürgen Puhle, eds., *The Politics of Democratic Consolidation: Southern Europe in Comparative Perspective* (Baltimore: Johns Hopkins University Press, 1995), 315–88.

5. Peter Mair, "How, and Why, Newly-Emerging Party Systems May Differ from Established Party Systems" (paper presented at a conference on "The Emergence of New Party Systems and Transitions to Democracy," Centre of Mediterranean Studies, University of Bristol, 17–19 September 1993), 1.

6. The credit for trying to identify quantitative indicators of when the institutionalization of a party system has passed the critical threshold goes to Peter Mair, Scott Mainwaring, and Timothy Scully.

7. Throughout this essay, the abbreviations and short-form English names of Polish, Czech, Slovak, and Hungarian parties and organizations are used. The full names of the parties and a brief description of the most salient features of each are given in the Appendix.

8. Maurice Duverger, *Political Parties: Their Organization and Activity in the Modern State*, 2nd ed. (London: Methuen, 1964), xxiii. Leonardo Morlino also notes, "Earlier experiences with democratization suggest a strong relationship between regime consolidation and the stabilization and structuring of parties and party systems." Morlino, "Political Parties and Democratic Consolidation in Southern Europe," 316.

9. While this notion is not easy to define operationally, at its heart is the belief that those systems that are—judging from their procedural norms and practices—rightly recognized as democratic may still approximate democratic ideals to widely different degrees. Whatever else one would want to include, few would exclude accountability and responsiveness to popular preferences from among these ideals. It is in this narrow sense that "quality of democracy" is used below.

10. Mainwaring and Scully, "Introduction: Party Systems in Latin America," 27. Note that Mainwaring and Scully themselves have a more complex view of this relationship than is implied by this short quotation. They, in fact, posit the mutual dependence of the institutionalization of parties and democratic stabilization.

11. See Juan J. Linz and Alfred Stepan's chapter in this collection, 16.

12. See Mair, "How, and Why, Newly-Emerging Party Systems May Differ from Established Party Systems"; Morlino, "Political Parties and Democratic Consolidation in Southern Europe"; and especially Mainwaring and Scully, "Introduction: Party Systems in Latin America."

13. Mainwaring and Scully, "Introduction: Party Systems in Latin America," 5.

14. Ibid.

15. Morlino, "Political Parties and Democratic Consolidation in Southern Europe," 315. Note that Morlino himself does not subscribe to this view without further qualification.

16. There is a nonaccidental similarity between Arend Lijphart's theory of consociational democracy and Morlino's proposition. In the former, democratic stability is facilitated by the effective control of cohesive and deeply divided ethnoreligious groups by cooperating subcultural elites. Though minority rights are a salient issue in Slovakia, the four countries analyzed here have limited ethnoreligious fragmentation. Therefore, Lijphart's reasoning will not be considered below.

17. See Stefano Bartolini and Peter Mair, *Identity, Competition, and Electoral*

Availability: The Stabilisation of the European Electorates 1885–1985 (Cambridge: Cambridge University Press, 1990), 212–49 and 276–84. Note, however, that their empirical evidence only demonstrates an empirical link between the organizational encapsulation of the left-wing electorate and the ethnoreligious heterogeneity of the country on the one hand, and aggregate-level electoral volatility on the other.

18. Mair, "How, and Why, Newly-Emerging Party Systems May Differ from Established Party Systems."

19. Although they used different names in the two elections, the 1991 Catholic Electoral Action (WAK) list and the 1993 list of the "Unity" Catholic Electoral Committee (KKWO) coalition may be considered as the ticket of the same party, the Christian National Union (ZChN); likewise, it is reasonable to treat SP (Labor Solidarity) and UP (Labor Union) as the same formation.

20. See Mair, "How, and Why, Newly-Emerging Party Systems May Differ from Established Party Systems," 3, Table 1.

21. The source of the Latin America data is Mainwaring and Scully, "Introduction: Party Systems in Latin America," 8.

22. This analysis concentrates on the most salient elections of each year. It assumes that in 1990, elections to the lower house of the Federal Assembly were the most salient. In 1992, this continued to be the case in the Czech Republic; in Slovakia, however, the Slovak National Council elections were more important. Indeed, in 1992 most Slovak party leaders stood for election to the National Council, not the Federal Assembly.

23. This figure was computed from the electoral data in Table 4 by treating the sum of the 1992 votes for the Party of the Democratic Left (SDL), the Social Democratic Party of Slovakia (SDSS), and the Green Party of Slovakia (SZS) as the 1992 result for their later electoral coalition, Common Choice (SV). Also, the sum of the 1992 figures for the Hungarian Civic Party (MOS) and the Hungarian Christian Democratic Movement–Coexistence (MKM-ESWS) was treated as the 1992 result for their later coalition, the Hungarian Coalition (MK). Also, because the Conservative Democratic Party (SKD), the successor to the Civic Democratic Union (ODU), merged with the Democratic Party (DS) in early 1994, the 1992 votes for the ODU and DS might be combined and compared with the 1994 DS vote. Doing so reduces the 1992–94 total volatility from 23.8 to 23.7 percent.

Although the Association of Workers of Slovakia (ZRS) and the Democratic Union of Slovakia (DU) were founded by deputies defecting from the SDL and the HZDS, respectively, it would be inappropriate to treat them as successors to the SDL and the HZDS (they do not claim to be successors and in fact there is absolutely no organizational continuity). Even if these two incorrect assumptions were made, estimated volatility would go down to 14.1, indicating that—unlike in the other three countries—elite-level fissures remained an important cause of electoral volatility in Slovakia.

24. See Ivor Crewe and David Denver, eds., *Electoral Change in Western Democracies: Patterns and Sources of Electoral Volatility* (Beckenham–Surry Hills, England: Croom Helm, 1985).

25. See Maurizio Cotta, "Building Party Systems After Dictatorship: The East European Cases in Comparative Perspective," in Geoffrey Pridham and Tatu Vanhanen, eds., *Democratization in Eastern Europe: Domestic and International Perspectives* (London: Routledge, 1994), 99–127.

26. Data not shown for reasons of space.

27. For empirical evidence supporting this proposition, see Bartolini and Mair, *Identity, Competition, and Electoral Availability,* 135ff., 276–77.

28. See Douglas W. Rae's classic *The Political Consequences of Electoral Laws* (New Haven: Yale University Press, 1967).

29. See Jan-Erik Lane and Svante Ersson, *Politics and Society in Western Europe* (Beverly Hills, Calif.: Sage, 1987), 165.

30. The 1990 Czech figure was unusually low because the broad-based Civic Forum—which split very soon after the election—won more than 50 percent of the vote.

31. See data presented above on the fractionalization of the vote.

32. Since 1991, Poland has had proportional representation with party lists. The 1993 electoral reform introduced a threshold of 5 percent (7 percent for coalitions) of the national total to win seats in the primary electoral districts, and further reduced proportionality by altering the method of seat allocation for both tiers in the lower-house elections. Before this reform, an unusually large number of small parties could win seats in districts where their vote exceeded 5 to 10 percent of the regional total.

33. See Stanislaw Gebethner, "System wyborczy: Deformacja czy reprezentacja?" (The electoral system: Distortion or representation?) in Stanislaw Gebethner, ed., *Wybory parlamentarne 1991 i 1993* (The parliamentary elections of 1991 and 1993) (Warsaw: Wydawnictwo Sejmowe, 1995), 21.

34. This is an essentially accurate description of what happened to the nationalist-leaning HZDS in 1993 and 1994; to the radical nationalist SNS in 1994; to the SZ in 1990; and to the market-liberal VPN and Christian Democratic Movement (KDH) in 1991. A similar split in the SDL, while long awaited, was realized only inasmuch as many of the SDL's 1992 voters and some of its members defected to the ZRS in 1994. The ZRS had a few places on the SDL list in 1992, but decided to go it alone in the 1994 election.

35. The rather insignificant Christian Democratic Party (KDS) merged with its coalition partner, the ODS; the Movement for Self-Governing Democracy–Association for Moravia and Silesia (HSD-SMS) and the ČSS split and eventually merged with the ZS, leaving their successor party with just one-tenth of the votes required to pass the electoral threshold in the 1996 election.

36. This scenario presumed that the Social Democrats would receive 20 to 25 percent of the vote in the upcoming elections, and that scandal-stricken ODA would not pass the 5 percent threshold. Public-opinion polls in 1995 showed that both possibilities were quite likely; projected compositions of the next legislature were widely discussed in the Czech press from June 1995 on. See "Preference ODA klesly pod pět procent" (Support for ODA drops below five percent), *Lidové Noviny* (People's daily), 20 June 1995, 3; and STEM, "Volební preference" (Electoral preferences) (memorandum prepared for a June 1995 press conference on poll results).

37. See Giovanni Sartori, *Parties and Party Systems: A Framework for Analysis* (Cambridge: Cambridge University Press, 1976), vol. 1, ch. 9. An empirical test of Sartori's proposition refuted one of his key hypotheses, namely, that polarized pluralism would cause the center to continuously lose votes. See G. Bingham Powell, Jr., "The Competitive Consequences of Polarized Pluralism," in Manfred J. Holler, ed., *The Logic of Multiparty Systems* (Dordrecht, the Netherlands: Kluwer, 1987), 173–90.

38. The cohesion and strategic position of the right-wing protocoalition and the disproportionate distribution of electoral support among its three components make it extremely unlikely that a bare majority government of some but not all center-right parties with the Social Democrats could survive for any length of time.

39. The only noteworthy change in the election law was that the January 1994 amendment to the law raised the electoral threshold for party lists from 4 percent to 5 percent.

40. Lubomír Brokl, "Between November 1989 and Democracy—Antinomies of Our Politics," *Czechoslovak Sociological Review* 28 (Special Issue, 1992): 33.

41. See Gábor Tóka, "Political Parties and Electoral Choices in East Central Europe," in Paul Lewis and Geoffrey Pridham, eds., *Rooting Fragile Democracies* (London: Routledge, 1996), 116–17.

42. Ian Budge and Dennis J. Farlie, *Explaining and Predicting Elections: Issue Effects and Party Strategies in Twenty-three Democracies* (London: Allen & Unwin, 1983).

43. Forty percent of the total Czech sample preferred the ODS or the ODA, while only 19 percent of the Polish sample preferred the UD or the KLD, and 6 percent of the Slovak sample preferred the DS and the SKD.

44. See the full version of the present essay for complete data.

45. See Tóka, "Political Parties and Electoral Choices in East Central Europe," 102–8, 117–21.

46. Because of their single-issue identities, the PL, the HSD-SMS, and the MKM-ESWS were not considered.

47. The analysis was based on data from a total of seven panel studies carried out in the four East Central European countries. All respondents were interviewed at two different times. The analysis compared the statistical relationship between respondents' issue positions, sociodemographic traits, and party choice in the first interview with respondents' change in party preference by the second wave of interviews. See Gábor Tóka, "The Electoral Payoff on Various Modes of Party Appeals: Evidence from New Democracies" (unpubl. ms., Department of Political Science, Central European University, Budapest, 1996).

48. See Gábor Tóka, "Being Represented—Being Satisfied? Political Support in East Central Europe," in Hans-Dieter Klingemann and Dieter Fuchs, eds., *Citizens and the State* (Oxford: Oxford University Press, 1995), 323ff. and Table 12.6.

49. These are some of the likely consequences of an inchoate party system according to Mainwaring and Scully in "Introduction: Party Systems in Latin America," 23.

50. The most comprehensive piece of evidence on this comes from a ten-country survey, the main results of which are reported in László Bruszt and János Simon, *Political and Economic Orientations During the Transition to Democracy: Codebook* (Budapest: Institute of Social Science, 1992).

51. See Geoffrey Evans and Stephen Whitefield, "The Politics and Economics of Democratic Commitment: Support for Democracy in Transition Societies," *British Journal of Political Science* 25 (October 1995): 485–514; James L. Gibson, "A Mile Wide but an Inch Deep(?): The Structure of Democratic Commitments in the Former USSR," *American Journal of Political Science* 40 (May 1996): 396–420; and Raymond M. Duch, "Economic Chaos and the Fragility of Democratic Transition in Former Communist Regimes," *Journal of Politics* 57 (February 1995): 121–58.

52. See Gibson, "A Mile Wide but an Inch Deep(?)."

53. G. Bingham Powell, Jr., "Extremist Parties and Political Turmoil: Two Puzzles," *American Journal of Political Science* 30 (May 1986): 357–78.

54. See Tóka, "Being Represented—Being Satisfied?"

55. See the full version of the present essay.

56. Tóka, "Being Represented—Being Satisfied?"

57. Extensive evidence is presented in the full version of this essay.

58. On the East-West gap in satisfaction with democracy, see Tóka, "Being Represented—Being Satisfied?" On East-West differences in economic evaluations in 1991, see Times Mirror Center for the People and the Press, *East–West Attitude Survey: Codebook* (Washington, D.C.: Times Mirror Center, 1991). In May 1991 this Times Mirror survey found that about 50 percent of Spaniards and French, about 60 percent of Italians and Britons, and 70 percent of West Germans agreed with the statement, "I am pretty well satisfied with the way things are going for me financially." Agreement ran 34 percent in Czechoslovakia, 25 percent in Poland, and 21 percent in Hungary. With the exception of Italy, the differences between East and West nicely parallel the 1991 Eurobarometer and Eastern Eurobarometer findings about differences in satisfaction with democracy in these countries. Note that satisfaction with democracy is influenced by economic evaluations not just in new democracies, but also in Western Europe. See Brad Lockerbie, "Economic

Dissatisfaction and Political Alienation in Western Europe," *European Journal of Political Research* 23 (April 1993): 281–93.

59. See the full version of this essay for more detail.

60. Mainwaring and Scully, "Introduction: Party Systems in Latin America," 2.

61. In June 1989, the semifree elections to the lower chamber granted the Communist Party and its satellites a majority of almost two-thirds, but the free competition for the Senate seats returned a 99 percent Solidarity supermajority in the upper chamber. See Zbigniew Pelczynski and Sergiusz Kowalski, "Poland," *Electoral Studies* 9 (December 1990): 346–54. Though the Sejm formally had the right, it obviously lacked the political legitimacy to bring down the Solidarity-led governments, no matter how strong the policy disagreements between them. The predictable result was a stalemate, and when the Sejm declined to give decree powers to the government or to pass the financial bills deemed absolutely necessary by the government, early elections were called. The October 1991 election became notorious for awarding seats to 24 different electoral lists; the "winner" received only 12.3 percent of the vote and 13.8 percent of the seats, and the three biggest parties were excluded from the resulting minority government. After the freely elected Sejm brought down three different governments, a new election law was passed and another early election called for September 1993. The ex-communist SLD and the heir of its former satellite (the United Peasant Party, or ZSL), now called the PSL, won a 66 percent majority in the Sejm.

62. This well-known story is best related in Carlos Flores Juberias, "The Breakdown of the Czecho-Slovak Party System," in György Szoboszlai, ed., *Flying Blind* (Budapest: Hungarian Political Science Association, 1992), 147–76.

63. See András Körösényi, "Stable or Fragile Democracy? Party System in Hungary," *Government and Opposition* 28 (January 1993): 87–105.

64. Poland is a debatable case, but in Czechoslovakia and Hungary the military is not viewed as a potential political actor. See Pietro Grilli di Cortona, "From Communism to Democracy: Rethinking Regime Change in Hungary and Czechoslovakia," *International Social Science Journal* 43 (1991): 315–30.

65. Samuel P. Huntington, *The Third Wave: Democratization in the Late Twentieth Century* (Norman: University of Oklahoma Press, 1991), 120.

66. Morlino, "Political Parties and Democratic Consolidation in Southern Europe," 361–62.

67. The one remaining representative of this league, the 1993 SLD-PSL government in Poland, tried to reconcile the fiscal constraints with their election pledges. This also characterized the later years of the Antall government in Hungary.

68. This point was developed in some detail in Tóka, "Political Parties and Electoral Choices in East Central Europe."

69. Vote trading is the strategic coordination of votes among a small number of actors to make collective decisions reached by a larger group more beneficial to the smaller group than they otherwise would be.

70. See, for example, Michael Dummett, *Voting Procedures* (Oxford: Clarendon Press, 1984), ch. 2. Well before the postwar boom in the development of social-choice theory, Eric Elmer Schattschneider explained the inevitable emergence of political parties in democracies along these lines. See Schattschneider, *Party Government* (New York: Rinehart, 1942), 30–39.

71. See William H. Riker, *Liberalism Against Populism: A Confrontation Between the Theory of Democracy and the Theory of Social Choice* (Prospect Heights, Ill.: Waveland Press, 1982).

72. Richard S. Katz, *A Theory of Parties and Electoral Systems* (Baltimore: Johns Hopkins University Press, 1980), 1.

8

PARTY SYSTEMS IN TAIWAN AND SOUTH KOREA

Teh-fu Huang

Teh-fu Huang is professor of political science and director of the Election Study Center at National Chengchi University in Taipei. He is also president of the Chinese Association of Political Science. He has contributed to a number of publications, including Democracy and the New International Order in the 21st Century *(1993) and* Taiwan's Electoral Politics and Democratic Transition: Riding the Third Wave *(1996).*

In the last decade, the party systems of Taiwan and South Korea have undergone drastic changes as part of the transition from authoritarianism to democracy. Taiwan's Democratic Progressive Party (DPP), established in 1986, has proved to be a viable political challenger of the Nationalist Party, or Kuomintang (KMT)—Taiwan's ruling party since 1945. The KMT's dominance was further threatened when several of its members defected to form the New Party (NP) in 1993. In South Korea, a number of opposition parties banded together prior to the 1985 National Assembly elections and formed the New Korea Democratic Party (NKDP) to challenge the predominant Democratic Justice Party (DJP). The ruling DJP was defeated in the 1988 National Assembly election, and a minority government was formed. In the early 1990s, the ruling DJP and the main opposition parties, the New Democratic Republican Party (NDRP) and the Reunification Democratic Party (RDP), unexpectedly merged to form the Democratic Liberal Party (DLP), which held a majority in the National Assembly.

No type of regime, whether democratic or authoritarian, is immune to challenges from a political opposition. The existence of a political opposition alone, however, is not sufficient to ensure democratic governance. Whether a government is democratic or not depends on the extent to which political opposition or party competition is institutionalized. The scholar Robert Dahl has claimed that the political democratization of authoritarian regimes consists mainly of the institutionalization of the opposition's participation and competition in the political arena.[1] Why is the institutionalization of political opposition the key to democratic consolidation? And what has been the effect of constitutional and electoral engineering on the party systems of Taiwan and South Korea?

Political Institutions

Recent research has resulted in an abundance of literature on the effects of political institutions on the transition from authoritarianism to democratic rule. This in some ways has contributed to the rise of the theory of "new institutionalism" in comparative politics, which assumes that political democracy depends not only on economic and social conditions but also on the engineering of political institutions.[2] Most scholars agree that democratization occurs in two phases. The first phase is transition, in which power is transferred from a military or an authoritarian government to a popularly elected civilian government. The second phase is consolidation, in which the democratic government becomes an effective, functioning democratic regime, and democratic institutions are established and acquire legitimacy.[3] Despite differing focuses, most scholars try to answer the following questions: Why does the authoritarian regime break down? What are the historical conditions that contribute to regime change? In what way does democratic transition occur?

Most studies of democratic consolidation focus on such issues as establishing democratic institutions, building consensus among political elites, and cultivating public confidence in democracy. For example, J. Samuel Valenzuela indicates four potential obstacles to the establishment of democratic institutions: 1) continuing domination of the popularly elected government by nondemocratic authoritarian forces; 2) reserved domains of authority and policy making that popularly elected officials are unable to change; 3) biased electoral systems that discriminate against certain groups; and 4) lack of agreement that governments should be constituted only through free elections.[4]

Consolidation of a democratic regime has behavioral, attitudinal, and constitutional dimensions. Behaviorally, no significant national, racial, social, economic, political, or institutional actors should spend significant resources on attempts to overthrow the regime. Attitudinally, the majority of the people must believe that democratic procedures and institutions are the most appropriate way to govern collective life in a society. Constitutionally, both governmental and nongovernmental elites must become accustomed to solving conflicts through democratic procedures.[5]

Emerging intermediary social institutions and their relations with the state have attracted less scholarly attention; in fact, however, the development of civil society is the most important aspect of democrati-

zation. Several issues are crucial in this regard: How does the popularly
elected government govern? How are channels through which the people
can check government power established? What kind of intermediary
institutions are provided for political participation? Are these channels
designed by parties, by corporatism, or by populism?[6]

Clearly, political parties and their interplay with the people contribute
to the development of democracy. The beliefs and attitudes of the
people will influence the emergence of political parties; the characteristics of political parties will in turn shape the mode of people's
participation.[7] J. Ronald Pennock argues that party systems are the
common characteristic of democratic regimes.[8] H.B. Mayo[9] and Robert
Dahl[10] add that the existence of political parties in a system is a major
criterion of democracy. E.E. Schattschneider even declares that political
parties create democracy, and that the development of modern democracy is founded on the political party.[11]

Most scholars agree that the political party is an intermediary between
citizens and the government. It provides an alternative pool of political
leaders and public policies. By vying for power through regular
elections, the political party provides the dynamic of modern democracy.
Thus it is commonly believed that modern democracy is the politics of
political parties and that the existence of political parties is a prerequisite for modern democracy. Seymour Martin Lipset indicates that a
stable democracy depends on a permanent and significant base of
support for political parties that provide a variety of alternatives.[12] A
study conducted by Atul Kohli suggests a correlation between the
volatility and decay of the party system in India and the decline in the
quality and stability of democracy in that country.[13] Leonardo Morlino
indicates that in Italy, Greece, Spain, and Portugal, countries whose
democratic institutions lacked general legitimacy, strong party systems
were crucial for democratic consolidation.[14]

The evidence suggests, then, that political parties and party systems
play a decisive role in the consolidation of democracy in countries that
have recently undergone a transition from authoritarianism. Institutionalization of party competition is the most important indicator of modern
democracy. Thus the establishment of a stable and sound party system
is crucial in the process of democratization.

The choice of political institutions is very important during a
transition to democracy. To consolidate democracy, political actors have
to accommodate themselves to these institutions; actors choose their
political strategies accordingly. During the transition period, political
actors have increased opportunities to design or redesign political institutions.[15] Among all the choices that must be made regarding political
institutions, none is more determinant than the choice of the constitutional structure (i.e., the system of government) and of the electoral
system. Political scientists and constitutional engineers have only recently

begun to seriously debate the impact of constitutional structures and electoral systems on party systems in democratic regimes.

Constitutional Structures

Constitutional structures are institutional frameworks that provide the basic rules and incentives for government formation—the conditions under which governments continue to rule or are peacefully terminated in functioning democracies—and organizations within which a variety of political actors interact.[16] Generally speaking, there are two possible constitutional structures in democratic countries: parliamentarism and presidentialism.

The first crucial difference between the two systems is that the chief executive of a parliamentary government—the prime minister or premier—and his or her cabinet depend on the legislature's confidence and can be dismissed from office by a legislative vote of no confidence or censure. The chief executive of a presidential government—the president—is elected for a fixed term and in normal circumstances cannot be removed by the legislature. The second significant difference is that the chief executive of a presidential government is popularly elected, either directly or indirectly; the chief executive of a parliamentary government is selected by the legislature.

Constitutional structures have an impact on the operation of political parties. Political parties play a central role in a parliamentary system, while the personal leadership and charisma of a president exert a decisive influence in a presidential system. In a parliamentary system, the party chooses the cabinet and the prime minister and retains responsibility for supporting the government. Most parliamentary democracies have majority government most of the time, so the government has a secure base of legislative support. In parliamentary systems, majority governments are those in which the party or parties with cabinet portfolios have a majority in parliament. Even in a coalition parliamentary government, party support for the government tends to be secure because of the way executive power is formed and dissolved. Some arrangements help ensure that there will be either legislative support for the executive or a means of toppling the government.

In contrast, the very notion of majority government is problematic in presidential democracies without a majority party. Presidents put together their own cabinets, and the parties are less firmly committed to supporting the government. In fact, the majority of the party may oppose the government. Incentives for parties to break coalitions are generally stronger in presidential systems than in parliamentary systems. Whether a party is allocated a cabinet position is not always relevant, for the personal characteristics of the individual who fills a position may be more important than his or her party affiliation.[17]

The absence of relatively disciplined parties may thus be an unavoidable result of a presidential system. Since the president is responsible and accountable for government stability and policy, parties are likely to concentrate their efforts on criticizing the executive rather than responding to or assuming responsibility for policy initiatives. It is natural that parties would focus on the wishes of special interests, localized interests, and clientelistic networks in their constituencies: Parties reap no reward from supporting a president's unpopular policies and risk no great penalty for not doing so. In short, presidential systems incorporate no incentives for party responsibility and party discipline.[18]

Electoral Systems

The main goal of political parties and candidates in a democratic society is to win elections. By limiting the sites of electoral competition and campaign strategies, electoral systems characterize the formation of party politics and influence the choice of many contending parties and candidates in three dimensions: specific voters, specific behaviors of voters, and effective forms of influence.[19] In this regard, electoral systems exert a significant impact on party politics in democratic countries.

There is no question that electoral systems significantly influence the number of parties in a society. More than four decades ago, Maurice Duverger pioneered the investigation of the relationship between electoral systems and the number of parties. He found that "the simple-majority single-ballot system favors the two-party system."[20] The reason is that, under this kind of electoral system, only one candidate can be elected in a given district. The best strategy of contending parties and candidates is to group into two blocs; this contributes to the development of a two-party system. The electoral system also influences the behavior of voters. Since only one candidate can be elected in a district, voters will not support the candidates of small parties, but instead will favor the candidates of the two largest parties. In the long run, this too will lead to the development of a two-party system. Because so many studies have confirmed this argument,[21] it has come to be known as Duverger's Law.

Duverger also proposed that "the simple-majority rule with two ballots and proportional representation favor multipartyism."[22] But scholars do not agree that proportional-representation (PR) systems contribute to multipartism. In principle, PR systems distribute seats according to the proportion of votes gained by each party. Because they have more opportunities to win seats in this system, small parties have no incentive to form preelection coalitions with one another. At the same time, voters have no need to shift their support from small parties to the two largest parties. Douglas Rae has shown, however, that for the development of a successful new party, a PR system is neither a necessary nor a sufficient condition.[23] Arend Lijphart also indicates that the effect of the proportional formula on multipartism, though not negligible, is quite modest.[24]

The empirical evidence in favor of the two-ballot majority system is also problematic. It has been claimed that this electoral system sometimes permits new parties to get a share of political influence with relatively few votes; a candidate who initially has the second-largest number of votes can ultimately win the election if supporters of eliminated candidates vote for him or her in the second round. Thus if politicians believe they have a chance of coming in second or third in the first round, it is worth their while to form a new party. But this incentive is not strong enough to confirm that the two-ballot system favors multipartism. The incentive can work only when people want to form new parties for other reasons. Although there is a strong association between the two-ballot majority and PR systems on the one hand and multipartism on the other, the former does not invariably lead to the latter. This is why some scholars call this Duverger's Hypothesis rather than Duverger's Law.[25]

What effects does the single nontransferable vote (SNTV) system have on party systems?[26] The SNTV system presents two serious problems for large parties. First, a large party has to decide how many candidates it can safely nominate; a large party can suffer a severe loss if it nominates either too many or too few candidates in a district. Second, a large party must distribute its votes as equally as possible among its candidates.[27] While small parties can follow a simple strategy to win a seat in a district, either of these two problems can cost a large party seats. Since the SNTV system reduces the electoral advantages of large parties, some scholars have concluded that it produces more proportional results than PR systems if district magnitude is held constant.[28] One empirical study found, however, that the allocation of seats in the SNTV system tends to be more proportional than that in a majoritarian system but less proportional than that in a PR system. Indeed, SNTV systems may be said to behave like semiproportional systems.[29] From this perspective, it can be argued that the impact of SNTV on party systems lies somewhere between that of majoritarianism and PR.

While applying Duverger's argument, we should not neglect the impact of the process of executive formation on the number of parties in a given country. To do so would distort our understanding of the number of parties not only in presidential systems, but in parliamentary systems as well. When presidential and legislative elections are held at the same time, the presidential election imposes a single-member nationwide district over the legislative districts. If the president is elected by simple majority, the presidential election falls under Duverger's Law, which suggests two parties. The legislative election, if it is held in multimember districts using a PR system, suggests the possibility of multipartism in accordance with Duverger's Hypothesis. Therefore, the outcome may go either way and depends to a large degree on the timing of the two kinds of elections.[30]

Institutional Design in Taiwan

The Constitution of the Republic of China on Taiwan (ROC) came into force on 25 December 1947 during the civil war between the KMT and the Communists. Under this Constitution, the government resembles a parliamentary system, though certain features of the Constitution deviate from "pure" parliamentarism. For example, members of the Legislative Yuan cannot serve as government officials; the Executive Yuan cannot dissolve the Legislative Yuan; and the Legislative Yuan has no explicit power to enforce a vote of no confidence. Although all these features depart from the practice in many parliamentary systems, they do not alter the fact that government power resides in the hands of the Executive Yuan, which is supported by the Legislative Yuan.

According to the Constitution, the power of the president is quite limited; he or she has to obtain the signatures of the premier or of the premier and relevant ministers when promulgating laws and issuing mandates. This means that the president can act only with the consent of the cabinet (i.e., the Executive Yuan), which is led by the premier. The highest administrative organ is the Executive Yuan. It is responsible to the Legislative Yuan, which is the highest legislative organ in the country. The head of the Executive Yuan—the premier—is nominated by the president but approved by the Legislative Yuan. Although the premier cannot be a member of the Legislative Yuan, he or she must be acceptable to the majority party or parties in the Legislative Yuan. These specific arrangements make Taiwan's system of government a parliamentary one.

On 18 April 1948, Taiwan's National Assembly amended the Constitution by means of the "Temporary Provisions Effective During the Period of Communist Rebellion." This and the imposition of martial law in Taiwan on 19 May 1949 (two acts that were prompted by civil war with the Communists) restricted civil rights and political liberties and bestowed emergency powers on the president. Although the president had more influence in state affairs than the premier, the system of government specified in the Temporary Provisions and the Constitution still closely resembled a parliamentary system.

The third amendment of the Temporary Provisions, adopted by the National Assembly on 22 March 1966, changed the system of government in Taiwan from parliamentarism to semipresidentialism. The new articles gave the president the power to establish a variety of organizations to provide policy guidelines for the "Period of Mobilization for the Suppression of the Communist Rebellion" and to handle civil administration in a war zone. The president also acquired the power to restructure the administrative and personnel organs of the central government.

In the early 1980s, rising expectations of democratic reform within Taiwan persuaded the KMT government to accelerate political liberalization and democratization. Under the direction of then-President Chiang Ching-kuo, martial law was lifted on 15 July 1987. The National Assembly adopted ten additional articles to the Constitution in 1991. On this basis President Lee Teng-hui announced the termination of the "Period of Mobilization for the Suppression of the Communist Rebellion" and its associated Temporary Provisions as of 1 May 1991. Although certain features of the Temporary Provisions were retained, the president's power was reduced, and the system of government in the ROC reverted to parliamentarism.

The latest amendment of the additional articles to the Constitution in 1994 led to another change in the constitutional structure in Taiwan. Article 2 of the new amendment adopted by the National Assembly on 28 July 1994 dictated that the president of the ROC would for the first time be elected directly by simple plurality in 1996. The same article eliminated the need for the president to obtain the premier's signature on nominations requiring the consent of the National Assembly and the Legislative Yuan. All these measures seem to reduce the power of the premier and expand the power of the president within the system of government in Taiwan. Thus the constitutional structure of the ROC has undergone a shift away from parliamentarism toward semipresidentialism.

Since 1945, the National Assembly and the Legislative Yuan had been elected according to the SNTV system. In accordance with the additional articles adopted on 1 May 1991, the elections of the Second National Assembly in 1991 and the Second Legislative Yuan in 1992 used a combination of the SNTV system and party-list PR by single vote, with a 5 percent threshold for parties to allocate seats in proportion to their vote shares. Under this system, about two-thirds of National Assembly seats are elected by the SNTV system and one-third by the list-PR system; for the Legislative Yuan the proportion is three-fourths by SNTV and one-fourth by list PR. Seats per district under the SNTV system ranged from two to ten for the National Assembly elections and from one to 16 for the Legislative Yuan elections. The distribution of districts for the National Assembly and Legislative Yuan elections for the period 1991–96 is summarized in Table 1.

Impact on Party Politics

What impact do constitutional structure and electoral systems have on Taiwan's party politics? Soon after the Japanese surrender and Taiwan's

Table 1 — Distribution of Districts for Elections in Taiwan, 1991–96

	Number of Districts			
	National Assembly		Legislative Yuan	
District Magnitude	1991	1996	1992	1995
1	0	0	5	5
2	8	8	5	5
3	23	18	5	5
4	15	15	3	3
5	4	10	2	1
6	3	2	3	4
7	2	1	3	2
8	1	2	0	1
9	0	1	2	2
10	2	1	0	0
16	0	0	1	0
17	0	0	0	1
SNTV Seats	225	234	125	128
PR Seats	100	100	36	36
Total Seats	325	334	161	164

Source: Data from Central Election Commission of the Ministry of the Interior, Republic of China.

return to China in 1945, the KMT government permitted limited autonomy on the island and local elections were held. Continuous setbacks in the civil war resulted in the KMT's declaring martial law and retreating to Taiwan in 1949. Although the KMT government had an easy excuse for suspending elections, it chose to continue holding local elections. During the 1950s and 1960s, the KMT's strategy was to localize political participation and electoral competition and repress the development of highly organized opposition parties. It appears that the KMT allowed the opposition to contest local elections only to legitimize and consolidate its authoritarian rule on Taiwan.[31] In this regard, the constitutional structure and electoral systems did not have a significant effect on Taiwan's party system, which was basically a single-party system.

A legitimacy crisis originating from diplomatic setbacks in the early 1970s induced the democratic transformation of the authoritarian KMT regime on Taiwan. The regime came to rely more on the legitimizing function of electoral competition. In addition to holding local elections, the KMT allowed limited elections to national representative bodies in 1972.[32] Surprisingly, this strategy failed to ease the legitimacy crisis. The holding of local elections and the limited opening of national representative bodies to electoral competition expanded the opposition's ability to mobilize and gave it more political leverage. Increasing popular support for the opposition gradually eroded the KMT's dominance in electoral contests. With the founding of a formal opposition party—the DPP—in 1986, electoral support for the opposition rendered the transformation of the KMT regime irreversible. The lifting of martial law and other political restrictions signaled the end of authoritarian rule altogether. Above all, the termination of the "Period of Mobilization for the Suppression of the Communist Rebellion" and the resumption of full elections for the National Assembly and Legislative Yuan opened up the possibility of further democratization for Taiwan.[33]

Under the authoritarian rule of the KMT, the semipresidential structure of the Constitution and the method of electing the president by simple plurality did not have a great effect on Taiwan's party system. In theory, both the shift from parliamentarism toward presidentialism and the change in the presidential-election formula enacted in August 1994 could have led to the development of a two-party system. Contrary to the arguments of Matthew Shugart and John Carey, however, the new constitutional structure and electoral system seemed to contribute instead to the emergence of multipartism. Four groups were represented in the presidential election of 1996: the KMT, the DPP, the NP, and independents. Although the KMT candidates predominated, competing candidates played a significant role in the presidential election (see Table 2). The election may have resulted from the established ideological confrontation among three major parties consolidated through the operation of the SNTV system in the Legislative Yuan and National Assembly elections.

Legislative Elections

An analysis of National Assembly and Legislative Yuan elections since 1972 sheds some light on the evolution of Taiwan's party system. Although National Assembly elections have shown no significant change in terms of the KMT's shares of the vote and seats, support for the KMT gradually declined as the opposition exercised increasing influence in Legislative Yuan elections beginning in 1980. Above all, the formation of the DPP in 1986 accelerated the collapse of authoritarian KMT rule. Through the 1986 and 1989 legislative elections, the DPP consolidated its significant role in Taiwan (see Tables 3 and 4). The distribution of votes and seats in the elections of 1991 and 1992 seems to indicate a two-party model of political competition in Taiwan. The SNTV system did not result in a high degree of electoral disproportionality between the seats and votes won by political parties in these elections.

The emergence of the NP, founded in August 1993 by a group of dissident KMT legislators, accelerated the decline in the KMT's electoral performance. Although the NP won no seats and only 3.1 percent of the vote in the 1993 election for county magistrates and city mayors, it was

Table 2 — Vote Shares in the 1993, 1994, and 1996 Elections in Taiwan (%)

Election	KMT	DPP	NP	Others
1993 election of magistrates and mayors	47.3	41.2	3.1	8.5
1994 election of provincial assemblymen and municipal councilors[a]				
Taipei City	39.5	30.4	20.9	9.2
Kaohsiung City	46.2	24.9	4.8	24.1
Taiwan Province	50.6	32.9	3.8	12.7
Total	49.2	31.6	6.1	13.2
1994 election of governor and mayors				
Taipei City	25.9	43.7	30.2	0.3
Kaohsiung City	54.5	39.3	3.5	2.8
Taiwan Province	56.2	38.7	4.3	0.8
Total	52.1	39.4	7.7	0.8
1996 presidential election	54.0	21.1	14.9	10.0

Source: Data on party affiliation and electoral turnout for each candidate from Taiwan Provincial Election Commission of the Department of Civil Affairs; Central Election Commission of the Ministry of the Interior, Republic of China; and newspaper reports.

[a]Vote statistics for the 1994 election of provincial assemblymen and municipal councilors do not include those of ethnic groups.

a significant force in the 1994 elections. Under the SNTV system, it gained 7.7 percent of the vote in the gubernatorial and mayoral elections and 6.1 percent in the elections for the Taiwan Provincial Assembly and the city councils of Taipei and Kaohsiung. In the race for mayor of Taipei, the NP's share of the vote was 30.2 percent—higher than that of the KMT. The party also won 11 of 52 seats in the election for the Taipei Municipal Council, garnering 20.9 percent of the vote (see Table 2). As a result, none of the three main parties holds a majority of seats in the Taipei Municipal Council. This is the first time that the KMT has been deprived of a majority in any representative body at any level of government since 1945. Although it would be premature to say that the two-party model of political competition between the KMT and the DPP has changed, the results of the 1994 elections imply the possibility of a three-party system in Taiwan. Examination of the 1995 and 1996 election statistics seems to reveal that Taiwan's party system is evolving into a three-party model of political competition (see Tables 2, 3, and 4).

Undoubtedly, the SNTV system has contributed to party factionalism in Taiwan. On the one hand, by reducing the role of political parties in

Table 3 — Vote and Seat Shares in the National Assembly Elections in Taiwan, 1972–96

Year	Total Seats	KMT % of Vote	KMT % of Seats (N)	Tangwai/DPP % of Vote	Tangwai/DPP % of Seats (N)	NP % of Vote	NP % of Seats (N)	Others % of Vote	Others % of Seats (N)
1972[a]	53	64.0	81.1 (43)		—	—	—	36.0	18.9 (10)
1980[a]	76	66.3	81.6 (62)	8.6	3.9 (3)	—	—	25.1	14.5 (11)
1986[a]	84	64.2	81.0 (68)	19.9	13.1 (11)	—	—	15.9	6.0 (5)
1991	325	68.8	78.2 (254)	23.6	20.3 (66)	—	—	7.6	1.5 (5)
1996	334	49.7	54.8 (183)	29.9	29.6 (99)	13.7	13.8 (46)	6.8	1.8 (6)

Source: See Table 2.

[a]Vote statistics do not include those of ethnic groups and occupational groups. Statistics on seats do not include those of overseas Chinese groups.

Parties: KMT, Kuomintang; DPP, Democratic Progressive Party; NP, New Party.

Table 4 — Vote and Seat Shares in the Legislative Yuan Elections in Taiwan, 1972–95

Year	Total Seats	KMT % of Vote	KMT % of Seats (N)	Tangwai/DPP % of Vote	Tangwai/DPP % of Seats (N)	NP % of Vote	NP % of Seats (N)	Others % of Vote	Others % of Seats (N)
1972[a]	36	73.1	83.3 (30)	—	—	—	—	26.9	16.7 (6)
1975[a]	37	77.6	81.1 (30)	—	—	—	—	22.4	18.9 (7)
1980[a]	70	71.9	80.0 (56)	13.0	11.4 (8)	—	—	15.1	8.6 (6)
1983[a]	71	69.4	87.3 (62)	18.9	8.5 (6)	—	—	11.7	4.2 (3)
1986[a]	73	66.7	80.8 (59)	24.6	16.4 (12)	—	—	8.7	2.7 (2)
1989	101	59.2	71.3 (72)	29.9	20.8 (21)	—	—	10.9	7.9 (8)
1992	161	52.7	58.4 (94)	31.4	31.7 (51)	—	—	15.9	9.9 (16)
1995	164	46.1	51.8 (85)	33.2	32.9 (54)	13.0	12.8 (21)	7.8	2.4 (4)

Source: See Table 2.

[a]Vote statistics do not include those of ethnic groups and occupational groups. Statistics on seats do not include those of overseas Chinese groups.

Parties: KMT, Kuomintang; DPP, Democratic Progressive Party; NP, New Party.

elections, it overemphasizes candidates' personal charisma and qualifications regardless of party platforms and policies. On the other hand, the system encourages intraparty power struggles instead of interparty competition for candidacies in each constituency. In both cases, it is difficult to maintain discipline within political parties, especially larger parties.[34]

The development of KMT subgroups in the Legislative Yuan is an indication of party factionalism in Taiwan. The KMT had many powerful legislative factions during its period of rule on the mainland, but in Taiwan, factional politics in the Legislative Yuan were suppressed until recently. Subgroups consisting of newly elected legislators began to emerge after the 1986 Legislative Yuan election. Between 1987 and 1989 as many as 11 new subgroups were formed, mostly out of nonpartisan organizations (see Table 5). After the 1989 election, the activities of subgroups began to interfere with the KMT's ability to dominate the legislative process. Seven out of the eight subgroups in existence between the elections of 1989 and 1992 were formed by KMT members; during this period, confrontation between the mainstream and nonmainstream factions extended to the Legislative Yuan in the form of tension between the Collective Wisdom Club and the New KMT Alliance.

The general legislative election in 1992 marked a turning point in factional politics in the Legislative Yuan. Some key members of the Collective Wisdom Club lost their seats, and the faction disintegrated. Active members of the New KMT Alliance became increasingly alienated from the party leader; they broke away to establish the NP on the eve of the KMT's Fourteenth National Congress in 1993. By this stage, six of the seven subgroups consisted of KMT members only (see Table 5). Factionalism in the largest opposition party—the DPP—is no less significant than that in the ruling KMT. Political confrontation among different factions caused serious problems of organizational coherence and resource mobilization within the DPP.[35]

Thus the SNTV system used in Taiwan's National Assembly and Legislative Yuan elections has exerted a greater influence on the development of the party system than have Taiwan's constitutional structures and presidential-election system. Also, the SNTV system has not produced a high degree of disproportionality in favor of the ruling party. Above all, the system has contributed to Taiwan's moving toward a multiparty system as well as to factionalism within the KMT and DPP. Finally, the direct popular election of the president by simple plurality —reinforced by the SNTV system of Legislative Yuan and National Assembly elections—may also contribute to multipartism in Taiwan.

Electoral Systems in South Korea

The first republic in South Korea was established in 1948 after 35 years of Japanese colonial rule followed by a U.S. military-occupation

Table 5 — New Subgroups in the Legislative Yuan of Taiwan

Period	Name	Date of Formation	No. of Members	Partisanship
Before the 1989 election	Triplet Club	March 1987	9	Nonpartisan
	JCI Congressman Club	December 1987	12	Nonpartisan
	D.C. Club	February 1988	10	Nonpartisan
	Sea Dragon Club	February 1988	9	Nonpartisan
	Overseas Club	February 1988	5	Nonpartisan (overseas members)
	Collective Wisdom Club	22 April 1988	27	KMT (includes two independents)
	Sino-USA Congressman Club	17 June 1988	42	Nonpartisan
	Double Five Policy Club	July 1988	5	KMT
	Esprit Club	September 1988	13	KMT
	Universal Club	17 November 1988	24	KMT (overseas members)
	Construction Club	16 May 1989	21	KMT
Between the 1989 election and the 1992 election	Collective Wisdom Club	22 April 1988	13	KMT (includes one independent)
	Universal Club	17 November 1988	19	KMT (overseas members)
	Construction Club	16 May 1989	9	KMT
	Hairlock Club	19 December 1989	8	KMT (female members)
	New KMT Alliance	9 February 1990	10	KMT
	Heritage Club	22 February 1990	18	KMT
	Concord Club	1 March 1990	20	KMT
	Welfare Club	5 March 1990	9	Nonpartisan
After the 1992 election	Concord Club	1 March 1990	25	KMT
	Yu-san Club	1 February 1993	14	KMT
	Public Policy Roundtable	11 February 1993	7	Nonpartisan
	Breakfast Club	11 February 1993	16	KMT
	Public Opinion Club	18 February 1993	20	KMT
	New Era Club	9 September 1993	18	KMT
	Policy Study Bloc	18 September 1993	16	KMT

Source: Chieh-lin Hsu, *The Order and Ethics of Party Politics* (in Chinese) (Taipei: Institute for National Policy Research, 1989), 31; Jui-hsi Hsu, "The Study of the KMT's Factions in the Legislative Yuan After Its Retreat to Taiwan: The 5th to 83rd Sessions" (M.A. thesis, National Chengchi University, 1989), 59; *China Times Express,* 24 February 1990, 2; *China Times,* 2, 3, and 10 September 1993, 2.

government. The republic was the product of the determination and persistence of Syngman Rhee, a venerable leader of the independence movement, and his conservative nationalist supporters. They insisted on the immediate establishment of an independent government in the south even if this meant the permanent loss of the northern half of the peninsula to communist rule.[36] While there was an effort to limit the powers of Syngman Rhee by expanding the legislative function of the National Assembly and creating the position of prime minister, the system of government under this constitution was a presidential one based on the principle of the separation of powers.

Although the new government was born with a democratic constitution, the Rhee government became increasingly arbitrary and dictatorial. Rhee used a variety of strategies to ensure his continuation in office. To this end, Rhee's supporters pushed for constitutional amendments in 1952 and in 1954. Rhee also intensified governmental repression by mobilizing his bureaucratic organizations, the state police, and terrorist organizations; promulgating a National Security Act; and even resorting to the use of martial law.[37] His dictatorship was heading toward a confrontation with the public, which was increasingly alienated from his government, when large-scale election fraud in March 1960 resulted in massive student uprisings in April. The military refused to use violence to put down the popular demonstrations, leading to the ultimate fall of the Rhee regime.

Right after the Rhee regime fell, a plan got under way to revise the constitution and lay the groundwork for the Second Republic. The National Assembly passed a constitutional amendment on 15 June 1960 establishing a parliamentary system. The democratically elected government of Chang Myon was unable to deal effectively with serious ideological and social cleavages; Chang consequently lost much of his original support. This second democratic experiment ended when a military coup ousted Chang only nine months after his inauguration. With the fall of Chang came an end to parliamentarism in South Korea.

A presidential system was reintroduced when Park Chung Hee came to power in May 1961 after toppling the democratically established government of Chang Myon. For the remainder of the Second Republic (1961–67), and throughout the Third (1969–71), Fourth (1972–80), Fifth (1980–87), and Sixth (1987–present) Republics, South Korea has maintained a presidential system of government.

Since the establishment of the First Republic in 1948, South Korea's systems for electing the president and the National Assembly have changed often. According to the original articles of the Constitution, the president is elected by the National Assembly. As Rhee felt his power slipping in the National Assembly, he abandoned indirect election for direct election by simple plurality in 1952 and 1956. With the provision that the president be elected at a joint session of the upper and lower houses on 12 August 1960, the electoral system reverted to an indirect method in the first nine months of the Second Republic.

Shortly after the military regime seized power in May 1961, Park created a constitution that provided for direct election of the president by simple plurality. The presidential elections held during the Third Republic also used direct popular election. In the face of serious challenges within and outside the country, however, Park declared martial law and implemented the infamous Yushin ("Revitalizing") Constitution at the end of 1972; presidential elections during the Fourth Republic were held indirectly through the National Conference for Reunification (NCR). The constitution of the Fifth Republic proposed by Chun Doo Hwan kept an indirect system of presidential election.

Chun lacked legitimacy and was beset by opposition. He was confronted with ever-increasing challenges from dissidents, including students and opposition parties. Although he repeatedly stressed his determination to step down at the end of his seven-year term in early 1988, he could not mollify the anger of those who saw their hopes and struggles for democracy frustrated by a group of ambitious military officers. The tragedy of the Kwangju massacre, in which several hundred citizens involved in a mass demonstration were killed, brought an end to the Chun government. Following a series of negotiations between the government and opposition parties, the new constitution of the Sixth Republic adopted direct popular election of the president by simple plurality.

Like Taiwan, South Korea adopted the SNTV system for National Assembly elections during the First and Second Republics. Under Park Chung Hee's authoritarian rule, the rules for National Assembly elections differed considerably from those of the other republics. The Third Republic added the party-list PR system for the nationwide district to its previous system of National Assembly elections. On the one hand, regional districts constituted three-fourths of the total seats that employed the SNTV system. On the other hand, the nationwide district as a whole constituted one-fourth of the total seats that used the party-list PR system. In accordance with the election law, the leading party alone received half of the regional seats. In the Third Republic, this combination of SNTV and party-list PR by single vote was implemented in the National Assembly elections as well.

With the advent of the Yushin regime, the system for electing the National Assembly was changed radically. The most important feature was the creation of the NCR. The NCR chose one-third of the total membership of the National Assembly. These members chosen by the NCR had to be members of the Yushin Political Friendship Society, which was organized by Park Chung Hee. The remaining two-thirds of National Assembly seats employed the two-member-district SNTV system.

A few more significant changes were made in the laws governing National Assembly elections in the Fifth Republic. A combination of the two-member-district SNTV system and party-list PR by single vote was employed. The former accounted for two-thirds of the total seats, with the latter accounting for the remaining one-third. The system set a five-seat threshold for allocating seats in the nationwide district. The leading party in regional elections received two-thirds of the total seats in the National Assembly; the remaining third of the seats was divided among other parties according to the number of seats they won in the regional elections.

In the Sixth Republic, the electoral system shifted to a combination of single-member-district (SMD) plurality and party-list PR by single vote. Three-fourths of the total seats were allocated for the former, one-fourth of the seats for the latter. The five-seat threshold for allocating the seats of the nationwide district was maintained. The leading party in regional elections receives half of the total seats in the nationwide district; the remaining half is divided among other parties on the basis of seats won in regional elections. The electoral system used in 1992 was the same as that used in 1988 except that the SMD plurality system was employed for four-fifths of the nationwide members, with the remaining fifth filled by party-list PR.

Authoritarian Politics

With the exception of a nine-month interlude in 1960 and 1961, South Korea did not enjoy real democracy from its independence in 1948 to the establishment of the Sixth Republic in 1987. The country's governments during the 26 years between 1961 and 1987 can be characterized as authoritarian regimes. It is said that the structure and practice of South Korean authoritarian politics can be traced to the 18-year rule of Park Chung Hee from 1961 to 1979. In particular, Park's authoritarian rule obstructed the institutionalization of political parties and a party system within which a new generation of leaders could emerge and could bring a variety of social forces and interests into politics.

Yushin authoritarianism collapsed in 1979 with Park's assassination by his chief intelligence aide. Park's death was accompanied by the expectation that authoritarian rule would come to an end and full democracy would be restored. With the support of key military leaders, however, General Chun Doo Hwan declared martial law in 1980 and was then elected president without competition for a seven-year term in January 1981 under a new constitution. Upon assuming power, Chun disbanded all political parties of the previous regime, purged their leaders, and restricted political activities. In addition to his own DJP, Chun allowed the formation of several parties by political personalities and organizations that could not challenge the ruling group in any effective way.[38]

As mentioned above, Chun Doo Hwan lacked political legitimacy and popular support, and his rule was challenged by the antigovernment, democratic movement. As it became clear toward the end of the Chun regime that his idea of "peaceful transfer of power" was to be within the "power bloc," antigovernment activities intensified until Chun was forced to choose between total repression through coercive instruments of power, including the military, and conceding to opposition demands for democratic transition.

Facing massive, prolonged, often violent antigovernment demonstrations, Roh Tae Woo, the DJP's presidential candidate and Chun's handpicked successor, surprisingly accepted the opposition's demands, including speedy amendment of the Constitution, acceptance of direct presidential elections, and amnesty for Kim Dae Jung and the restoration of his civil rights.[39] The process of political democratization in South Korea was set in motion.

Weakened Parties

It is quite clear that the presidential system of government weakened the South Korean party system. First of all, privatization of political parties tends to hinder the emergence of strong party leadership. Personal ties constitute an extremely important political factor even when political activities are curtailed. A study conducted by Tamio Hattori indicated that interpersonal networks based on such connections as kinship, marriage, education, and geography exert an important impact on South Korean politics.[40] Privatization consequently became a major obstacle to the development of a stable and strong party system.

The personalization of political parties is another reason for the weakness of the South Korean party system. Most political leaders consolidated and strengthened their power by taking advantage of political parties. For example, both Park Chung Hee and Chun Doo Hwan disbanded all political parties upon assuming rule, establishing a new party to strengthen the authority of their governments. In preparation for his presidential candidacy, Kim Young Sam merged his RDP with the ruling DJP and another opposition party, the NDRP, forming the new DLP in 1990. Finally, nominated by the DLP, Kim Young Sam was elected president in December 1992.

The discontinuity of political parties also contributed to the weakness of political parties and the party system. The many dramatic changes of regime and constitution in South Korea were usually effected through extraordinary measures by governments that came to power by nondemocratic means. No party has survived long enough to claim the loyalty and support of the public. Instead, parties and their leaders have often been purged and discredited after uprisings, coups, or upheavals. All these measures reduce South Korea's chances for party continuity and stability.[41]

Another reason for the weakness of South Korea's political parties is their regionalism. Regional antagonisms, often expressed in violent disruption of campaign rallies by presidential candidates from rival provinces, are most conspicuous between the southeast and southwest. The strong regional identification that candidates foster ensure that campaigns are divisive and emotional. Ultimately, each candidate's level of electoral support closely coincides with his regional background. In both the 1987 and 1992 presidential elections, about 90 percent of the votes for Kim Dae Jung were from his home provinces—North Cholla and South Cholla—and less than 5 percent were from the southeastern provinces.[42]

The polarization of the party system could be the final reason for the weakness of South Korea's party system. A presidential system of government has led to a tendency for politicians to group into two major parties—one for and the other against the government. A brief examination of the evolution of South Korea's party system since the establishment of an independent government confirms this observation (see Figure 1). Accompanied by the regionalism and privatization of political parties, polarization intensifies political confrontation between the government and the opposition. It has thus retarded the development of a stable party system in South Korea.

The constitution in the Sixth Republic adopted direct popular vote by simple plurality for presidential elections. This method is politically convenient and expedient; contrary to the arguments of Shugart and Carey, however, it does not necessarily lead to the institutionalization of a two-party system. This is because the presidential-election system encourages more than two competitors who are nominated by two major parties. The personalization and regionalism of political parties also contributes to multipartisan competition. The results of the 1987 and 1992 presidential elections show that three major parties competed for both elections, and none won more than 50 percent of the total vote (see Table 6). This means that in 1987 and 1992, the presidents were elected by a minority.

The system used in the National Assembly elections did have a negative impact on the South Korean party system. In the Fifth Republic, a combination of the two-member-district SNTV system and party-list PR contributed to a high degree of proportionality between the seats and votes won by the parties, which favored the ruling party. On the one hand, the two-member-district SNTV system for regional districts put the opposition party at a disadvantage. On the other hand, the rule for allocating seats of the party-list PR system in the nationwide district strongly favored the ruling party. Although in the Sixth Republic

Figure 1
Evolution of the Party System in South Korea Through 1995

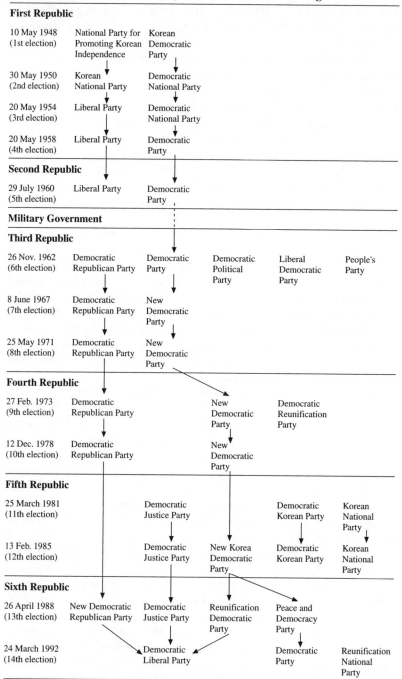

First Republic

10 May 1948 (1st election)	National Party for Promoting Korean Independence	Korean Democratic Party
30 May 1950 (2nd election)	Korean National Party	Democratic National Party
20 May 1954 (3rd election)	Liberal Party	Democratic National Party
20 May 1958 (4th election)	Liberal Party	Democratic Party

Second Republic

| 29 July 1960 (5th election) | Liberal Party | Democratic Party |

Military Government

Third Republic

26 Nov. 1962 (6th election)	Democratic Republican Party	Democratic Party	Democratic Political Party	Liberal Democratic Party	People's Party
8 June 1967 (7th election)	Democratic Republican Party	New Democratic Party			
25 May 1971 (8th election)	Democratic Republican Party	New Democratic Party			

Fourth Republic

| 27 Feb. 1973 (9th election) | Democratic Republican Party | | New Democratic Party | Democratic Reunification Party |
| 12 Dec. 1978 (10th election) | Democratic Republican Party | | New Democratic Party | |

Fifth Republic

| 25 March 1981 (11th election) | | Democratic Justice Party | | Democratic Korean Party | Korean National Party |
| 13 Feb. 1985 (12th election) | | Democratic Justice Party | New Korea Democratic Party | Democratic Korean Party | Korean National Party |

Sixth Republic

| 26 April 1988 (13th election) | New Democratic Republican Party | Democratic Justice Party | Reunification Democratic Party | Peace and Democracy Party |
| 24 March 1992 (14th election) | | Democratic Liberal Party | | Democratic Party | Reunification National Party |

Source: Ruoh-yuh Lin, "The Comparative Study of Political Markets and the Transitions of Authoritarianism in Singapore, Taiwan, and South Korea" (Ph.D. diss., National Taiwan University, 1995), 168, 171, 180, 182, 188; Byong-man Ahn, Soong-hoom Kil, and Kwang-woong Kim, *Elections in Korea* (Seoul: Seoul Computer Press, 1988), 3–41.

Note: All elections noted are National Assembly elections; only major parties are shown here.

Table 6 — Presidential Election Results in South Korea, 1987 and 1992

Candidate	Party	No. of Votes	% of Total
1987 Election			
Roh Tae Woo	DJP	8,282,738	36.7
Kim Young Sam	RDP	6,337,581	28.1
Kim Dae Jung	PDP	6,113,375	27.1
Kim Jong Pilm	NDRP	1,823,057	8.1
Total		22,556,751	100.0
1992 Election			
Kim Young Sam	DLP	9,943,510	42.0
Kim Dae Jung	DP	8,025,488	33.9
Chung Joo Young	RNP	3,846,787	16.2
Four others	Other/ independent	1,867,783	7.9
Total		23,683,568	100.0

Source: Man-woo Lee, *The Odyssey of Korean Democracy: Korean Politics, 1987–1992* (New York: Praeger, 1992), 84; *Central Daily,* 20 December 1992, 3.
    Parties: DJP, Democratic Justice Party; RDP, Reunification Democratic Party; PDP, Peace and Democracy Party; NDRP, New Democratic Republican Party; DLP, Democratic Liberal Party; DP, Democratic Party; RNP, Reunification National Party.

the SNTV system has been changed to an SMD plurality system, the electoral method still favors the ruling party. A minor change in the party-list PR system for the nationwide district, which reduced the percentage of seats allocated for the leading party from two-thirds to one-half of the total, did not make up for the disadvantages suffered by opposition parties (see Table 7).

The forces of privatization, personalization, discontinuity, and regionalism in political parties and overall polarization resulting from presidentialism have contributed to the weakness and instability of South Korea's party system. The direct election of the president by simple plurality may contribute to the emergence of multipartism instead of a two-party system. Finally, the electoral systems of the Fifth and Sixth Republics have greatly favored the ruling party in terms of dispropor-tionality between votes won and seats awarded.

Toward Institutionalized Parties

Constitutional structure and electoral systems have played different roles in the development of party systems in Taiwan and South Korea. Neither the constitutional structure nor the presidential-election system in Taiwan significantly influenced the institutionalization of the party system. The direct popular election of the president by simple plurality

Table 7 — National Assembly Election Results in South Korea, 1981–92

Party	% of Vote	Seats for Regional Districts (%)		Seats for Party-List PR (%)		Total Seats (%)	
1981 Election							
DJP	35.6	90	(48.9)	61	(66.3)	151	(54.7)
DKP	21.6	57	(31.0)	24	(26.1)	81	(29.3)
KNP	13.3	18	(9.8)	7	(7.6)	25	(9.1)
Other/ Independent	29.5	19	(10.3)	0	(0.0)	19	(6.9)
Total	100.0	184	(66.7)	92	(33.3)	276	(100.0)
1985 Election							
DJP	35.3	87	(47.2)	61	(66.3)	148	(53.6)
NKDP	29.3	50	(27.2)	17	(18.5)	67	(24.3)
DKP	19.7	26	(14.1)	9	(9.8)	35	(12.7)
KNP	9.2	15	(8.2)	5	(5.4)	20	(7.2)
Other/ Independent	6.5	6	(3.3)	0	(0.0)	6	(2.2)
Total	100.0	184	(66.7)	92	(33.3)	276	(100.0)
1988 Election							
DJP	34.0	87	(38.8)	38	(50.7)	125	(41.8)
PDP	19.3	54	(24.1)	16	(21.3)	70	(23.4)
RDP	23.8	46	(20.5)	13	(17.3)	59	(19.7)
NDRP	15.6	27	(12.1)	8	(10.7)	35	(11.7)
Other/ Independent	7.3	10	(4.5)	0	(0.0)	10	(3.3)
Total	100.0	224	(74.9)	75	(25.1)	299	(100.0)
1992 Election							
DLP	38.5	116	(48.9)	33	(53.2)	149	(49.8)
DP	29.2	75	(31.6)	22	(35.5)	97	(32.4)
RNP	17.4	24	(10.1)	7	(11.3)	31	(10.4)
Other/ Independent	14.9	22	(9.3)	0	(0.0)	22	(7.4)
Total	100.0	237	(79.3)	62	(20.7)	299	(100.0)

Source: Ruoh-yuh Lin, "The Comparative Study of Political Markets and the Transitions of Authoritarianism in Singapore, Taiwan, and South Korea" (Ph.D. diss., National Taiwan University, 1995), 185, 188; *United Daily,* 26 March 1992, 2.

Parties: DJP, Democratic Justice Party; DKP, Democratic Korean Party; KNP, Korean National Party; NKDP, New Korea Democratic Party; PDP, Peace and Democracy Party; RDP, Reunification Democratic Party; NDRP, New Democratic Republican Party; DLP, Democratic Liberal Party; DP, Democratic Party; RNP, Reunification National Party.

may eventually reinforce the trends toward multipartism. The SNTV system has also encouraged factionalism within the KMT and DPP, thereby increasing the possibility of multipartism in Taiwan.

In South Korea, on the other hand, the presidential system of government inhibited the stability and continuity of that country's party system. The election of the president by simple plurality also seems to undermine a stable two-party system. While the electoral system did not contribute to a high degree of electoral disproportionality in Taiwan, South Korea's ruling party took advantage of the SNTV system in particular and the electoral system in general to maintain its dominant role.

The institutionalization of party systems continues to challenge Taiwan and South Korea as they move toward the consolidation of democracy. Taiwan must reduce the influence of factional politics and strengthen party discipline. The country would do well to increase the number of seats elected through PR and introduce an SMD system into its parliamentary elections.

If South Korea is to consolidate democracy, it must break away from privatization, personalization, discontinuity, regionalism, and polarization of political parties. To accomplish this, the number of National Assembly members elected through PR should be increased, while the proportion of seats allocated to the leading party should be decreased.

NOTES

1. Robert A. Dahl, *Polyarchy: Participation and Opposition* (New Haven: Yale University Press, 1971), 4–14.

2. Alfred Stepan and Cindy Skach, "Presidentialism and Parliamentarism in Comparative Perspective," in Juan J. Linz and Arturo Valenzuela, eds., *The Failure of Presidential Democracy: Comparative Perspectives* (Baltimore: Johns Hopkins University Press, 1994), 119.

3. Frances Hagopian and Scott Mainwaring, "Democracy in Brazil: Prospects and Problems," *World Policy Journal* 4 (December 1987): 485–514; Guillermo O'Donnell, "Transitions, Continuities, and Paradoxes," and Adam Przeworski, "The Games of Transition," in Scott Mainwaring, Guillermo O'Donnell, and J. Samuel Valenzuela, eds., *Issues in Democratic Consolidation: The New South American Democracies in Comparative Perspective* (Notre Dame, Ind.: University of Notre Dame Press, 1992), 17–56 and 105–52.

4. J. Samuel Valenzuela, "Democratic Consolidation in Post-transitional Settings: Notion, Process, and Facilitating Conditions," in Mainwaring, O'Donnell, and Valenzuela, eds., *Issues in Democratic Consolidation*, 62–70.

5. Juan J. Linz and Alfred Stepan, *Problems of Democratic Transition and Consolidation: Southern Europe, South America, and Post-Communist Europe* (Baltimore: Johns Hopkins University Press, 1996), 8. See also their chapter in this collection.

6. According to Philippe C. Schmitter, "corporatism can be defined as a system of interest intermediation in which the constituent units are organized into a limited number of singular, compulsory, noncompetitive, hierarchically ordered, and functionally differentiated categories, recognized or licensed (if not created) by the state and granted a deliberate representational monopoly within their respective categories in exchange for observing certain controls on their selection of leaders and articulation of demands and

supports." Philippe C. Schmitter, "Modes of Interest Intermediation and Models of Societal Change in Western Europe," *Comparative Political Studies* 10 (April 1977): 9.

7. Scott Mainwaring, "Transitions to Democracy and Democratic Consolidation: Theoretical and Comparative Issues," in Mainwaring, O'Donnell, and Valenzuela, eds., *Issues in Democratic Consolidation*, 302–4.

8. J. Ronald Pennock, *Democratic Political Theory* (Princeton: Princeton University Press, 1979), 275.

9. H.B. Mayo, *An Introduction to Democratic Theory* (New York: Oxford University Press, 1960), 66.

10. Robert A. Dahl, *Pluralist Democracy in the United States* (Chicago: Rand McNally, 1967), 203.

11. E.E. Schattschneider, *Party Government* (New York: Cambridge University Press, 1942), 1.

12. Seymour Martin Lipset, "The Social Requisites of Democracy Revisited," *American Sociological Review* 59 (February 1994): 14.

13. Atul Kohli, "Indian Democracy: Stress and Resilience," *Journal of Democracy* 3 (January 1992): 52–64.

14. Leonardo Morlino, "Consolidation and Party Government in Southern Europe," *International Political Science Review* 16 (April 1995): 161–62.

15. Scott Mainwaring, "Presidentialism, Multipartism, and Democracy: The Difficult Combination," *Comparative Political Studies* 26 (July 1993): 199.

16. Stepan and Skach, "Presidentialism and Parliamentarism in Comparative Perspective," 119.

17. Mainwaring, "Presidentialism, Multipartism, and Democracy," 216, 220.

18. Juan J. Linz, "Presidential or Parliamentary Democracy: Does It Make a Difference?" in Linz and Valenzuela, eds., *The Failure of Presidential Democracy*, 63.

19. Richard S. Katz, *A Theory of Parties and Electoral Systems* (Baltimore: Johns Hopkins University Press, 1980), 17–18.

20. Maurice Duverger, *Political Parties: Their Organization and Activity in the Modern State*, trans. Barbara North and Robert North (London: Methuen, 1964; orig. publ. 1951), 217.

21. E.g., Douglas W. Rae, *The Political Consequences of Electoral Laws*, rev. ed. (New Haven: Yale University Press, 1971); William H. Riker, "The Two-Party System and Duverger's Law: An Essay on the History of Political Science," *American Political Science Review* 76 (September 1982): 753–66; Giovanni Sartori, "The Influence of Electoral Systems: Faulty Laws or Faulty Methods?" in Bernard Grofman and Arend Lijphart, eds., *Electoral Laws and Their Political Consequences* (New York: Agathon, 1986), 43–68.

22. Duverger, *Political Parties*, 239.

23. Rae, *The Political Consequences of Electoral Laws*.

24. Arend Lijphart, "The Political Consequences of Electoral Laws, 1945–85," *American Political Science Review* 84 (June 1990): 481–96.

25. Riker, "The Two-Party System and Duverger's Law," 754, 759–60.

26. The single nontransferable vote (SNTV) system is an electoral system under which each voter has only one vote in a multimember district, and the candidates who get more votes than others win the seats.

27. Arend Lijphart, Rafael Pintor, and Yasunori Sone, "The Limited Vote and the

Single Nontransferable Vote: Lessons from the Japanese and Spanish Examples," in Grofman and Lijphart, eds., *Electoral Laws and Their Political Consequences*, 159.

28. Rein Taagepera and Matthew S. Shugart, *Seats and Votes: The Effects and Determinants of Electoral Systems* (New Haven: Yale University Press, 1989), 170.

29. Lijphart, Pintor, and Sone, "The Limited Vote and the Single Nontransferable Vote," 163, 168.

30. Matthew S. Shugart and John M. Carey, *Presidents and Assemblies: Constitutional Design and Electoral Dynamics* (Cambridge: Cambridge University Press, 1992), 207. See also John M. Carey's chapter in this collection.

31. Teh-fu Huang, "Electoral Competition and Democratic Transition in the Republic of China," *Issues and Studies* 27 (October 1991): 101–7.

32. In the constitution enacted in 1947, the national representative bodies included the National Assembly, the Legislative Yuan, and the Control Yuan. In accordance with Article 15 of the additional articles, adopted in 1992, the Control Yuan was converted into a semijudicial organ and the indirect election of its members was abolished. As of February 1993, members of the Control Yuan are appointed by the president with the consent of the National Assembly.

33. Teh-fu Huang, "Electoral Competition and the Evolution of the Kuomintang," *Issues and Studies* 31 (May 1995): 97–99.

34. Teh-fu Huang, "Local Factions, Party Competition, and Political Democratization in Taiwan," *Journal of National Chengchi University* 61 (June 1990): 728.

35. Teh-fu Huang, *The Democratic Progressive Party and Political Democratization in Taiwan* (in Chinese) (Taipei: Taiwan Elite, 1992), 74–96.

36. Sung-joo Han, "South Korea: Politics in Transition," in Larry Diamond, Juan J. Linz, and Seymour M. Lipset, eds., *Democracy in Developing Countries*, vol. 3, *Asia* (Boulder, Colo.: Lynne Rienner, 1989), 268.

37. Byong-man Ahn, Soong-hoom Kil, and Kwang-woong Kim, *Elections in Korea* (Seoul: Seoul Computer Press, 1988), 6.

38. Han, "South Korea: Politics in Transition," 280.

39. Ibid., 282–88.

40. Tamio Hattori, *The State and Society in East Asia*, vol. 4, *South Korea*, trans. Ming-jung Lee (in Chinese) (Taipei: Yueh-dann, 1992).

41. Han, "South Korea: Politics in Transition," 296.

42. Yan-yuan Ni, "A Comparative Study of Authoritarian Transition in South Korea and Taiwan" (in Chinese) (Ph.D. diss., National Chengchi University, 1993), 330; Hong-yung Lee, "South Korea in 1992: A Turning Point in Democratization," *Asian Survey* 33 (January 1993): 38.

9

DESIGNING COHERENT GOVERNMENT

Emerson M.S. Niou & Peter C. Ordeshook

Emerson M.S. Niou *is associate professor of political science at Duke University and a member of the editorial board of* International Studies Quarterly. *He is the coauthor of* The Balance of Power: Stability in International Systems *(1989).* ***Peter C. Ordeshook*** *is professor of political science at the California Institute of Technology and has published widely in the areas of political theory, international relations, and Russian politics.*

Constitutional and political reform seems to be a perpetual issue in Taiwan. Yet, aside from negating the Temporary Provisions Effective During the Period of Communist Rebellion, adopted in 1948, the focus of that reform has been limited to the method of selecting the president, the powers of the presidency, and the authority of the Legislative Yuan and the National Assembly. Future reform should focus on different matters, especially the timing of elections and the number of public offices filled by direct election. These factors will determine the extent to which stability characterizes reform in Taiwan and the extent to which consensus is achieved on the most divisive issues—the rights of minorities and national identity.

Most public debates over constitutional reform are structured by the question whether a presidential or parliamentary system of government is more stable.[1] Considering the evident self-interest normally represented in such debates (recall, for instance, Boris Yeltsin's conflict with Russia's old parliament, the Congress of People's Deputies), it is not surprising that debates over Taiwan's political structure focus on the powers of the branches of the national government, the legislative authority of the president versus that of the prime minister, the role of the National Assembly, the meaning of a legislative vote of no confidence, and the appointment powers of the president and legislature.

A different classification of political systems should be considered. "Integrated" systems, wherein political elites of the legislature, executive branch, and national, provincial, and local governments reach accommodation out of a shared self-interest, should be distinguished from "bargaining" systems, wherein temporary coalitions form around specific issues and depend on personalities and personal relationships. The distinction here is not a mere reinterpretation of the presidential-parliamentary dichotomy. For example, both the United States and Russia have presidential systems. Of the two, however, only the United States corresponds to the definition of an integrated system used here. Similarly, although both Canada and Germany are parliamentary democracies, Canada's politics is distinctly more confrontational and dependent on intergovernmental and intragovernmental bargaining.

Admittedly, our dichotomy corresponds somewhat to the more common presidential-parliamentary one. Germany and Canada differ in their degrees of integration only because both are federations; the differences between them might not appear in a unitary state. Indeed, the integration seen in smaller nonfederal countries is ostensibly one of the primary benefits of parliamentary government. The separation of powers essential to a presidential system makes a degree of executive-legislative conflict one of the "rules of the game."

Circumstances are more confused in the case of the Republic of China (ROC). Having opted for a mixed system, Taiwan leaves unresolved the issue of how—or even if—it will achieve integration at the national level. An integrated system is more likely than a bargaining system to lead to societal consensus on foreign policy and can help defuse such issues as the rights of "native Taiwanese" versus "mainlanders." Yet bargaining among political elites appears to be emerging as the dominant mode of resolving conflict over Taiwan's domestic policy. Indeed, many of today's issues are precisely those that will ensure that such bargaining persists for the foreseeable future, reinforcing this trend.

Resolving such matters as the appointment powers of the president and the prime minister's legislative role are certainly important. But our classification method directs us to search for stable political structures in a different set of design variables: methods of electing the president and the Legislative Yuan; the timing of national, provincial, and local elections; and the structure of provincial and local elections. If Taiwan's democracy is to evolve in the direction of an integrated polity, it is these variables—and not those that directly affect the power of officeholders—that need to be reexamined.

Contemporary Disputes

Taiwan's history of constitutional reform illustrates that the island's government is not integrated and that contentious bargaining is the predominant mode of political discourse: The Constitution of the Republic of China on Taiwan came into force on 25 December 1947 and appeared to implement a governmental form similar to parliamentary democracy. The constitution deviated from strict parliamentarism, however; it disallowed Legislative Yuan members from serving in government, prohibited the executive branch from dissolving the legislature, and gave the Legislative Yuan no authority to enforce a vote of no confidence. Aside from the Temporary Provisions, few amendments were made until 1966, when the National Assembly implemented a semipresidential system of government whereby the president was empowered explicitly to restructure the administrative and personnel organs of the central government. Amendments added in 1987 arguably moved the political system a step in the direction of parliamentary government, but a shift back toward semipresidentialism occurred in 1994 when amendments were passed allowing the direct election of the president and permitting the president to submit nominations for government positions without the prime minister's signature.[2]

To this day, the most noteworthy changes in Taiwan's constitutional structure—in addition to general liberalization of political competition—have revolved around the powers of the presidency. Following the 1995 Legislative Yuan election, the cabinet of Lien Chan resigned in January 1996, as required by constitutional interpretation, and was renominated by President Lee Teng-hui and approved by the Legislative Yuan in February. Following the presidential election of 23 March 1996, Premier Lien submitted his resignation again in anticipation of Lee's inauguration on May 20 so that the "new" president could nominate a new government. Lee, however, argued that no resignation was required, and that therefore there was no need to secure legislative approval of Lien's new government. Both opposition parties in the Legislative Yuan resisted Lee's maneuver and refused to consider legislation submitted by that government.

This conflict and the history of constitutional amendment illustrate the general character of political maneuver and reform in Taiwan. Although the composition and authority of the National Assembly are not addressed above, it is evident that contention in Taiwan focuses on the relative powers of the separate branches of government. Issues are debated with specific personalities or balances of political power among the parties in mind, and resolutions are reached—if at all—through protracted bargaining.

The evolutionary and negotiated character of political reform in Taiwan is not unique; it is duplicated in the history of most democracies.[3] Unfortunately, blindly following an evolutionary path entails consequences, the most important of which is that political institutions develop without a plan. Choices of constitutional authority, election laws, and the like are made on a case-by-case basis and depend on the interests of the one who has the upper hand at the moment of decision. Sometimes such incrementalism achieves an optimal or near-optimal result, as appears to be the case with American constitutional development. But the history of failed democracies suggests that, more often than not, unplanned institutional development yields suboptimal results. Canada, for instance, appeared relatively stable as long as Britain's Privy Council could referee conflicts between Canada's provinces and central government. But since the decision to supplant the council with a strictly Canadian court, the other parts of Canada's institutional structure have appeared unable to accommodate Quebec's demands for autonomy. Similarly, there is no reason to suppose that a bargain between elites designed to satisfy some short-term objective will not yield undesirable long-term consequences.

In Taiwan, these dangers extend beyond conflicts among political elites at the national level and debates over presidential versus legislative authority. Originally designed to direct the governance of the mainland, the Republic of China's constitution has been adapted to oversee the governance of an island whose national and provincial governments oversee geographically identical territories and whose move toward full democracy has been largely incremental. Despite the island's small size, its governmental structure is relatively complex. In addition to a five-branch national government (consisting of Executive Yuan, Legislative Yuan, Judicial Yuan, Control Yuan, and Examination Yuan), Taiwan also has a provincial government and a provincial assembly, along with two special-status municipalities (Taipei and Kaohsiung), 16 counties, 5 provincial municipalities, and 309 townships with their own governmental organizations. The extent to which this structure can function efficiently, however, depends not on labeling and counting government entities, but on the nature of intergovernmental relations and the incentives for political elites in all parts of government to coordinate their actions.

Integration versus Bargaining

Elaborating the dangers that can beset a democratic society that explicitly or implicitly establishes bargaining as the primary mode of democratic governance first requires clear definitions of "integrated" and "bargaining" polities. Granted that no political system corresponds perfectly to an ideal, "ideal types" are nonetheless valuable because they allow us to classify the primary political processes that characterize a polity. Here there are essentially two types that tell us a great deal about the consequences of the institutional arrangements that are available for manipulation in Taiwan.

An *integrated system* is one in which: 1) politicians active within one level (national, regional, or local) or branch (legislative, executive, or judicial) of government generally find it in their self-interest to cooperate and coordinate with political elites from other levels or branches; and

2) jurisdictional disputes (definitions of the authority of different levels and branches) are resolved in a nonconfrontational way by the uncoordinated, self-interested actions of individual politicians.

Jurisdictional disputes in an integrated polity are resolved at the margin so that the roles of different levels or branches of government evolve largely to serve the interests of all political actors. In the United States, for example, the authority of the executive branch relative to that of the legislature has changed over time not on the basis of constitutional amendment or landmark legislation, but in slow evolution to serve the interests of politicians within both branches of government.

A *bargaining system*, in contrast, is one in which politicians' electoral appeal derives from their ability to succeed in conflicts with other levels or branches of government and their ability to negotiate an advantageous position for their constituents, regardless of the overall social cost of doing so. In a bargaining polity, politicians have an incentive 1) to articulate (perhaps even invent) disagreements with policies or demands emanating from other levels or branches of government; and 2) to compete directly with other levels or branches for jurisdiction over policy. Accommodation comes in a series of compromises, each of which remains in force only until the next opportunity to renegotiate appears.

To better distinguish between an integrated and a bargaining polity, we note that the concept of an integrated polity is especially important in a federal state, wherein major disputes are likely to arise over the jurisdictions of different levels of government.[4] One question dominates all others in the design of a federal state: given the inherent conflict between federal subjects (states, provinces, *Länder*) and the national government over the authority to make policy, how does a government craft public institutions that ensure the enforcement and stability of those constitutional provisions intended to protect the rights of federal subjects, the authority of the national government, and the viability of the federation itself?[5]

The United States and Canada

Different societies resolve this question in different ways. For example, although both Canada and the United States are longstanding democracies, they differ in at least one respect: Approximately half of those who held elective office before succeeding to the presidency of the United States served as governor of a state, but no prime minister of Canada has ever served as head of a provincial government. Thus while Joseph Schlesinger writes of U.S. politics that "within the states the most vigorous and ambitious men are drawn inexorably to the national arena, either to the Senate or to some place in the presidential office complex,"[6] Roger Gibbins notes that for Canada "there is very little movement from provincial to national office. Aspiring politicians appear to make an early choice between a provincial or a national career, and once launched on their path very few cross over. Provincial office is not a way station on the road to national office but rather an alternative."[7]

The United States is perhaps the purest example of an integrated polity, whereas Canada, in which provincial politicians are typically elected on a platform of opposition to the national government, illustrates a bargaining polity. Although Taiwan can concern itself less with the incessant intragovernmental conflict that characterizes a bargaining polity, it cannot wholly escape these issues. Chapter XI of the ROC constitution specifies that each province shall directly elect a provincial government and provincial assembly and shall write its own laws, but 40 percent of the Taiwan provincial government's budget comes from the national government. County and municipal departments of police, health, and taxation are subordinate to corresponding offices of the Taiwan provincial government. Such overlapping jurisdictions and finances set the stage for either considerable intergovernmental bargaining or simple top-down command and control.

Even if inefficient bargaining is avoided on day-to-day matters, there is the danger that politicians or political parties will "invent" issues with which to confront opponents or will otherwise exacerbate latent conflicts within society that threaten political stability. In a bargaining polity such issues are especially dangerous because they are in constant play. Because no coalition or cooperative arrangement is permanent, the losers from any temporary alliance must use all available tactics to upset the status quo. In an integrated polity, on the other hand, political elites have stronger incentives to cooperate and will therefore work together to remove divisive issues from competition.

The most dangerous issues in Canada concern regionalism in all its varied forms—from language and ethnicity in Quebec to control of natural resources. Similar issues exist in Taiwan—independence and the rights of "native" Taiwanese versus "mainlanders."[8] While we might want political candidates and parties to address only those issues that can be resolved in some "natural" way, a bargaining polity virtually ensures continued appeals to divisive issues.

Self-interest compels broader and more permanent coalitions in an integrated polity. Not only is competition in an integrated polity less personalized and more institutionalized, but established political elites and parties do not allow issues that are disruptive of cooperation and competition to become politically salient. For example, pure regional conflict is disallowed by both major parties in the United States, just as they in the past "took out of competition" such issues as foreign policy with respect to the Soviet Union, and today the parties eschew anything but political correctness with respect to the rights of minorities. Throwing these issues back into competition in order to unseat an incumbent in a particular constituency would disrupt the overall cohesion of the parties. Thus, although a racist like David Duke might be a viable candidate for governor of Louisiana, he is repudiated by the Republican Party in order to avoid jeopardizing the party's chances in elections elsewhere.

Even in integrated polities, political processes will not resolve all divisive issues smoothly. But to the extent that integration precludes divisive competition, institutions should be crafted so that major parties have little incentive to exploit divisive issues in competition for public office. Unfortunately, this is difficult to accomplish, even by those with the greatest skill at constitutional engineering. The proper balance is achieved only through continuous adjustment and requires a near-perfect compatibility of incentives. Although development of a self-enforcing and self-regulating state requires certain favorable preconditions, it also depends on extraconstitutional factors, such as political parties, to endure. The same is true with regard to the powers that separate different branches of government, even in nonfederal states such as Taiwan. Indeed, in every political system there are sometimes incentives for executive and legislative branches to invade each other's prerogatives, for different levels of government to compete for financial resources, for parties to campaign on divisive issues, and for political competitions to become personal.

Competition for power—even among members of the same party—is an inherent problem in a presidential or quasi-presidential system where the personnel of executive and legislative branches are wholly separate. Too often, political reformers try to achieve a constitutional balance between executive and legislative branches by manipulating the relative powers of the two or by using the judiciary as a referee. In unitary states, reformers try to integrate and balance the system by merely itemizing policy jurisdictions. But using direct constitutional means to balance and implement an integrated polity is at best problematic and at worst impossible. It is the structure of political parties that best determines the character of a state's politics, and the rules, laws, and institutions that direct the character of parties that should be manipulated to move a system toward an integrated or a bargaining polity.

Political Parties

Political motives in a democracy are conditioned by the ways in which politicians attain and maintain office, and parties are the primary vehicle by which politicians mobilize their electoral support. Thus political parties and the election laws under which they operate become the critical determinant of whether a state will be integrated. As Richard Hofstadter says in reference to the U.S. Constitution:

the balance of social interests, the separation and balance of powers, were meant to secure liberty, but it was still uncertain, after the instrument had been framed and ratified, whether the balance would not be too precarious to come to rest anywhere; and whether the arms of government, separated in parchment, could come together in reality to cooperate in the formation and execution of policy . . . a mechanism had to be found . . . [and] the national parties, for all their faults, were to become at an early hour primary and necessary parts of the machinery of government.[9]

Consider Samuel Lubell's account of a Democratic candidate for judge in New York City in a year when many local and state offices were up for election and Franklin Roosevelt was running for president. The candidate gave his campaign funds to the local Democratic Party, expecting professional assistance in return. Weeks went by, but he saw nothing on his behalf—no posters, buttons, or radio broadcasts. When he returned to party headquarters to complain, the head of the party took him to the southern tip of Manhattan where the ferry from Staten Island was docking. The party head pointed to the debris that swirled in the ferry's wake and said, "The name of your ferry is Franklin Delano Roosevelt."[10]

This story eloquently illustrates the relationship between local and national politicians, the means for implementing an integrated polity, and, most important, the way parties ensure that integration occurs as a part of "normal" politics. The critical characteristics of integration are demonstrated: 1) elections simultaneously fill a great many public offices; 2) a local organization facilitates the election of party candidates to local offices; and 3) local elections coincide with the election for a singularly visible national office, the presidency. In an election in which voters confront scores of candidates about whom they know little, a candidate's essential appeal is his or her party affiliation and the fact that this affiliation is shared by more visible candidates. Even when local and national issues do not coincide, the fates of a party's candidates cannot be wholly separated. The multitude of candidates for local office rely on the few national political figures to give meaning to the party labels that direct voters, who know little else about local candidates. At the same time, no presidential candidate—including Roosevelt—has had the resources to mobilize voters as effectively as existing local party structures. Thus, although the name Roosevelt and the label "Democrat" certainly helped the local candidate for judge, Roosevelt depended on the local party just as much.

This lesson is repeated in a second example, drawn from the U.S. Civil War. Historians have long noted that President Abraham Lincoln was far more successful in coordinating the Union effort than his Confederate counterpart, Jefferson Davis, was in organizing the South. Eric McKitrick, in his seminal comparison of the political strategies and fortunes of the opposing leaders, attributes this difference to the existence of a competitive party system in the North and an uncompetitive party system in the South.[11] Following secession, the South was left with essentially a single party, the Democrats, whereas the North retained not only the Republican Party but the northern wing of the Democratic Party. Although Republicans controlled all northern governorships immediately after secession, they lost some during the war, just as they failed to maintain control of all state legislatures. Throughout the war, Republican political candidates relied on Lincoln's national leadership for their political survival, just as Lincoln, uncertain of success in the presidential election of 1864, never lost sight of the need to maintain the support of state and local Republican Party organizations. The situation of Davis as well as the governors of the Confederate states was quite different. With a discredited Republican Party, governors in the South faced few immediate challenges to their political status and had little to gain from coordinating with Davis.

A Symbiotic Relationship

A symbiotic relationship exists among politicians up and down America's political system; we could easily substitute a candidate for the U.S. Congress for the candidate for judge without appreciably changing the story. The fates of candidates elected from local or regional constituencies are intimately connected to those of their parties' candidates elected nationally; at the same time, a presidential candidate's success depends on how effectively he or she mobilizes state and local party organizations. Notice, moreover, that this symbiotic relationship is accompanied by—indeed requires—considerable autonomy within the structure of a political party. No national organization dictates a party's nominees for local office or even for the national legislature. Those levels are controlled largely by local organizations, which together control the nomination for the presidency. National parties, then, are wholly decentralized, and this decentralization is critical. Without autonomy at local and regional levels, symbiosis is replaced by a contentious bargaining system in which national political elites struggle either with local elites or among themselves for control of the party.

Canada, which exemplifies a bargaining polity, contrasts significantly with the United States. Not only do the political histories of presidents and prime ministers differ, but Canada's two primary national parties, the Liberals and Conservatives, differ greatly from those in the United States. First, although the Conservatives and Liberals compete nationally in Canada, a variety of regional or purely provincial parties enter competitions for provincial office. Second, the performances of Liberals and Conservatives in the provincial and national elections do not correlate within a province. Third, selection of delegates to the Democratic and Republican national party conventions in the United

States are dominated by state party organizations, which are in turn largely creatures of local party organizations. In the national conventions of Canada, on the other hand, parties are dominated by national party organizations, which are generally distinct from provincial organizations bearing the same party label.

In general, then, the U.S. political system appears far more integrated than Canada's; it also lacks Canada's sharp distinction between regional and national politics. But what is the source of this difference? We can only offer reasoned speculations. The story of the candidate for New York City judge suggests that two institutional differences are critical: First, except for special elections to fill vacancies, local, regional, and national elections occur simultaneously in the United States, whereas in Canada they follow no specific schedule and are generally held at different times. Second, although more than 600,000 offices are filled by election in the United States, the only elections held in Canada are those for the national parliament, provincial parliament, mayors, aldermen, and school boards.

These factors alone do not explain all differences in American and Canadian party systems, but it would be foolish to deny that they are important.[12] Canada's asynchronous local, state, and national elections and smaller number of elections overall can only reduce the value of party labels across levels of government and the symbiotic relationship among political candidates from those levels.

A careful reading of the U.S. Constitution should convince anyone that the formal powers of the president are few: a president cannot sign treaties or make appointments without the consent of the Senate; has no role in amending the Constitution; cannot declare war, despite being commander in chief; has no special authority in emergencies; has no independent source of revenue; has no authority over state or local governments; and has no executive authority except that conferred by the legislature. Nevertheless, the United States is perhaps the most oft-cited example of a strong presidential system.

A U.S. president's authority actually derives from a complex balance of institutional features, most of which are not included in the Constitution. The president is the sole nationally elected figure. Because the office is constitutionally weak as compared with presidents in other countries (e.g., Russia), an American president must influence outcomes by exercising leadership rather than by wielding constitutional authority. And as the sole nationally elected official, the president enjoys one power unique to his office—in Theodore Roosevelt's words, "the power of the bully pulpit."

The bully pulpit would be of little value were it not for another feature of America's political landscape: the election schedule. America's election schedule and the structure of its democracy at state and local levels ensure that every four years, candidates compete for the presidency at the same time that hundreds of thousands of other public offices are filled by direct election in a vast array of local constituencies—states, congressional districts, counties, cities, towns, school districts, and so on. Excluding the U.S. Senate, state legislatures, and state judicial seats, the average number of statewide offices filled by direct election is 12. When entering the voting booth in a typical election year, the average person receives not a single sheet of paper on which to mark his or her vote, but more often than not something that looks like a short manuscript.

The U.S. election schedule and structure, then, turn party labels and an integrated party system into invaluable currency that political elites in every level and branch of government have an interest in cultivating. To do so requires broad and permanent coalitions. Unlike politicians in Brazil or Russia, politicians in the United States do not change their partisan identifications annually. Unlike Canadian labels, U.S. partisan labels carry the same meaning at all levels of government. The ideological character of U.S. parties may be obscure; even the presidential candidates may not read the party platforms so carefully constructed at national conventions. But as coalitions, U.S. parties are among the most permanent features of the country's political landscape.

Sustaining such broad coalitions requires that divisive issues be resolved or banned from political discourse. Political elites in an integrated democracy have no incentive to follow Belgium's example and permit debate of issues such as language. Doing so would undermine party cohesion, reduce partisan labels to little more than indicators of one's position on the issue of the day, and destroy the ability of politicians in different levels and branches of government to help each other achieve their election goals. It may be true, for example, that Democrats today enjoy considerably greater support among blacks than do Republicans. Yet Democrats and Republicans collude to keep race off the political agenda not merely for moral or ethical reasons, but because to do otherwise would disrupt the Democrats' coalition and destroy the Republicans' ability to appeal to middle-class black voters.

Reform in Taiwan

Taiwan faces a number of potentially divisive issues. Although the outside world might regard much of the political maneuvering among elites in Taipei as a harmless game of musical chairs, Taiwan's society does incur a cost: the reduced ability of the political process to resolve or otherwise keep such issues from disrupting normal politics. Unfortunately, there are few signs that the government of the Republic of China is becoming an integrated system:

• There is no guarantee that any resolution of disputes over the powers of the Executive Yuan, the Legislative Yuan, and the National

Assembly will be resolved in such a way that the president will be compelled to exercise U.S.-style leadership rather than Russian-style formal power.

• Barring reunification with the mainland, the office of governor of Taiwan is a second authority who can compete for national visibility. The existence of two such offices can only encourage contentious intraparty bargaining when those offices are controlled by the same party, and contentious interparty bargaining when they are controlled by different parties. (This may be one reason why the Taiwan provincial government and the office of governor have been targeted for abolition in the December 1997 constitutional-reform process.)

• Taiwan's general-election schedule gives the president little opportunity to exercise electoral leadership. Since 1991, Taiwan has held important elections on an annual basis (for the National Assembly in 1991; the Legislative Yuan in 1992; city mayors and county magistrates in 1993; Taipei and Kaohsiung mayors, Taiwan governor, Taiwan Provincial Assembly members, and city legislative council in 1994; the Legislative Yuan in 1995; and the president and the National Assembly in 1996). The current schedule of future elections is equally incoherent.

• Although they vote frequently, voters in Taiwan fill far fewer offices than do their U.S. counterparts—by our count, a total of slightly more than 13,000 offices.[13] If the U.S. model were applied to Taiwan, Taiwan voters, who number approximately one-tenth of U.S. voters, would fill approximately 60,000 offices by direct election.[14]

• Finally, political parties in Taiwan need to decentralize if regional party organizations are to have adequate autonomy. The Kuomintang's and the New Party's nomination of candidates for local offices or for the national legislature are still dictated by a few party leaders.

Despite these problems, Taiwan shows some important positive signs for the further refinement of its democracy. As the result of current election laws, including the island-wide plurality formula employed to elect the president, both the Democratic Progressive Party (DPP) and the New Party are taking a more moderate position on the issue of independence in order to expand their electoral base. Most DPP politicians believe that an extreme position on independence places too low a ceiling on the party's electoral support; therefore, they believe, they must downplay this issue and focus more on traditional public policy issues. As a consequence, a DPP faction has formed a new party—the Taiwan Independence Party (TAIP)—consisting of members who believe the DPP too readily sacrificed its goal of independence "merely" to win elections.[15] This development reveals clearly that Taiwan's election laws are working precisely as they should in a presidential system: they are encouraging the development of two or three primary parties that compete at the center rather than at the extremes of public opinion.

Nevertheless, some specific steps would encourage a more integrated polity and a more decentralized yet integrated party system. Conclusions drawn from the contrast of the United States with Canada above suggest the following:

1) No additional increase should be made in the president's constitutional authority, but his authority in legislation and the appointment of ministerial positions should be clarified.

2) A coherent election schedule should be established—one that minimally requires the simultaneous election of the president, the full Legislative Yuan, and most city and county offices.

3) As many offices as possible, including local judges and prosecutors, should be filled by direct election.

In addition, any move in the direction of implementing proportional representation (PR) election procedures in either chamber of the national legislature should be avoided. Although PR seems an attractive way to ensure representation of minorities, it can at the same time threaten the informal authority of the president to lead. Those who head a party-list ticket can be competitors with the president only for leadership within a party. At the same time, intraparty conflict arises around relative position on the party's list. Party-list PR, then, reinforces conflictual bargaining as the dominant character of intraparty relations. A party should have a single, self-evident national leader, and that person should be the party's candidate for president.

A final suggestion is to maintain the status quo with respect to the office of vice-president. It is true that this position is the target of a great many jokes in the United States. Nevertheless, its existence is an important mechanism of political integration. First, the vice-presidency allows the president to expand his electoral coalition, which can be especially important in a society that might choose to distinguish between "native Taiwanese" and "mainlanders" for the foreseeable future. Second, it facilitates intraparty relations: If a faction of the party fails to secure the nomination of its candidate for president, its loss is mitigated if that candidate is nominated for the second spot on the ticket. Finally, as long as Taiwan retains the position of governor, this second nationally elected official can act as a buffer between the president and the electorate. With a vice-president, the governor of Taiwan loses his identity as the "other" nationally elected official who can claim an island-wide mandate to lead. With a vice-president, the president is more clearly the head of a unique coalition with that mandate.

NOTES

1. For the general academic debate on this subject, see Matthew S. Shugart and John M. Carey, *Presidents and Assemblies: Constitutional Design and Electoral Dynamics* (New York: Cambridge University Press, 1992); Juan Linz, "The Perils of Presidentialism,"

Journal of Democracy 1 (Winter 1990): 51–69; and Emerson M.S. Niou and Peter C. Ordeshook, "Notes on Constitutional Change in the Republic of China on Taiwan," *Chinese Political Science Review* 21 (December 1993): 203–56.

2. John Fuh-sheng Hsieh, "Parliamentarianism versus Presidentialism: Constitutional Choice in the Republic of China on Taiwan," *Chinese Political Science Review* 21 (December 1993): 173–202; Teh-fu Huang and Emerson M.S. Niou, "Party System and Democratic Consolidation: The Cases of Taiwan and South Korea" (unpubl. ms., Duke University, 1995).

3. See, for example, Peter C. Ordeshook, "Constitutions for New Democracies: Reflections of Turmoil or Agents of Stability?" (forthcoming in *Public Choice*).

4. For a more expansive presentation of this argument, see Peter C. Ordeshook, "Russia's Party System: Is Russian Federalism Viable?" *Post-Soviet Affairs* 12 (July–September 1996): 195–217; and Peter C. Ordeshook and Olga Shvetsova, "Federalism and Constitutional Design," *Journal of Democracy* 8 (January 1997): 27–42.

5. For perhaps the clearest statement of the problem, see William H. Riker, *Federalism: Origin, Operation, Significance* (Boston: Little, Brown, 1964).

6. Joseph A. Schlesinger, *Ambition and Politics: Political Careers in the United States* (Chicago: Rand McNally, 1966), 200–201.

7. Roger Gibbins, *Regionalism: Territorial Politics in Canada and the United States* (Toronto: Butterworth, 1982), 141.

8. Yun-han Chu, *Crafting Democracy in Taiwan* (Taipei: Institute for National Policy Research, 1992); John Fuh-sheng Hsieh and Emerson M.S. Niou, "Salient Issues in Taiwan's Electoral Politics," *Electoral Studies* 15 (1996): 219–30.

9. Richard Hofstadter, *The Idea of a Party System* (Berkeley: University of California Press, 1969), 70–71.

10. Samuel Lubell, *The Future of American Politics* (New York: Harper, 1952).

11. Eric L. McKitrick, "Party Politics and the Union and Confederate War Efforts," in William N. Chambers and Walter D. Burnham, eds., *The American Party Systems: Stages of Political Development* (New York: Oxford University Press, 1967), 35–68.

12. One important difference between Canada and the United States is that the U.S. Senate is a legitimate legislative body, whereas Canada's Senate is not. The U.S. Senate is elected directly within the separate states, and its veto power over legislation cannot be overridden by the lower legislative chamber. Canada's Senate is largely ceremonial; its members are appointed by Ottawa and do not represent provincial interests in any meaningful way.

13. Our count includes president and vice-president (2); governor of Taiwan and mayors of Taipei and Kaohsiung (3); county magistrates and city mayors (23); county and city council members (883); Taiwan province, Taipei city, and Kaohsiung city legislators (175); Legislative Yuan members (164); National Assembly members (334); township directors (319); township-government representatives (3,909); and village and district directors (7,564)—a total of 13,376.

14. Comparing the United States and Taiwan on even a per-capita basis is complicated, of course, by the fact that, as a federation, the United States has an additional layer of government. Nevertheless, even if we assume that 100,000 of the 600,000 public offices filled by election are state-level positions (and that number is admittedly an overestimate), U.S. voters still fill four times the number of offices than do voters in Taiwan.

15. So evident are the moderating imperatives of Taiwan's election laws that the TAIP, to "protect itself" against similar pressures, has barred elected politicians from securing outright control of the party. This alone enables us to predict that the TAIP will easily meet its ideological objective; it is unlikely to prove successful at the polls.

III

Civil-Military Relations

10

TOWARD CIVILIAN SUPREMACY IN SOUTH AMERICA

Felipe Agüero

Felipe Agüero is assistant professor of political science at Ohio State University. He has been a senior research associate at the North-South Center of the University of Miami and a fellow at the Institute for Advanced Study in Princeton, New Jersey. He is the author of Soldiers, Civilians, and Democracy: Post-Franco Spain in Comparative Perspective *(1995).*

One necessary condition of democratic governance is that military and police organizations be subject to civilian control.[1] Civilian control, or supremacy, assumes that the military does not occupy leading positions in spheres deemed civilian and presupposes an active presence of civilians in military and defense spheres. This component of democratic government is hard to attain in polities that only recently transited from military-authoritarian rule. All South American authoritarian regimes were militarized—that is, run or significantly controlled by the military. Thus their transitions to democracy were carried out under heavy military supervision. In order to assess the extent to which these new postauthoritarian regimes approach full-fledged, consolidated democracies, we must ascertain the status of civilian supremacy.[2]

This chapter examines the state of civil-military relations in South America in the context of democratization. It traces countries' success in establishing civilian supremacy over the military since their transitions from authoritarian rule and identifies the factors that have contributed to, or hindered, that success. It concludes by naming factors and issues salient to policy making and securing the future of democracy. First, however, we must clarify the concept of civilian supremacy and its relation to the consolidation of democracies.

In a democracy, civilian supremacy is reflected in the ability of a civilian, democratically elected government to 1) conduct general policy without interference from the military, 2) define goals and the general organization of national defense, 3) formulate and conduct defense policy, and 4) monitor the implementation of military policy.[3] In polities that undergo transition from militarized authoritarian regimes,[4] civilian supremacy is reached by first removing military personnel from positions of power outside the defense arena, then appointing and acknowledging civilian political superiors within the defense and military arenas. As the military withdraws from policy areas other than defense, civilian officials gain authoritative capacity in all policy areas, including defense. Because the very boundaries delineating military and nonmilitary matters are subject to debate, civilian and military leaders alike must agree to defined spheres of competence as set by legitimate civilian authorities. In practice, this definition reduces, but by no means eliminates, the military's sphere of autonomous action.

Civilian supremacy involves restricting military roles to assisting in the formulation and implementation of national defense policy. It also involves accepting government decisions in arenas that entail a new delineation of prerogatives and therefore are sensitive: the defense budget, force levels, and promotions of officers to the most senior grades and posts. The transfer of prerogatives in these arenas takes place gradually during—or, more often, after—the transition. Civilian supremacy is unlikely to assert itself in one blow, and it does not necessarily imply a civilian imposition; it may well develop through a process in which the military confines itself to a role more restricted to professional matters. Overt civil-military negotiations and tacit bargaining define the extent and shape of military participation under the new arrangements. It should be underscored that successful arrangements balance expanded civilian prerogatives with appropriate avenues for the military to express professional concerns, and reassure the military that its core institutional interests are reasonably accommodated.

Movement toward civilian supremacy demands that proper governmental structures already exist or be in the making that allow civilians to exert effective leadership over the military. According to Samuel Huntington, the military should be "subordinate to only one other institution possessing effective final authority," which he calls "ministerial control," as it normally comes "in the form of a civilian departmental minister."[5] In the transitions that interest us, civilians have attempted, though not always successfully, to create such an authority structure. A department of defense empowers civilian authorities by providing a unified structure for conducting policy and integrating the military with the rest of the state administrative bureaucracy.

Attaining civilian supremacy does not necessarily require specific attitudinal traits of members of the military. Ideological congruence between civil authorities and the military may eliminate tension in civil-military relations; it is certainly desirable for democratic consolidation. Yet democratization and civilian supremacy can be secured without prior voluntary support of the democratic creed by those in the armed forces.[6]

When the following conditions have been met in a new democracy, one may safely assume that civilian supremacy has been attained: 1) civilian leadership exercised over a number of years reaches habituation (in the sense of repeated practice); 2) prerogatives of civilian political authorities are formalized in the constitution or other major laws; 3) the military as an institution does not overtly challenge the above two conditions for a number of years; and 4) the military manifestly accepts at least one major decision taken by civilian authorities about which military opposition had been previously voiced.[7] Civilian supremacy aids the consolidation of democracy. A new democracy has become consolidated when democratic procedures and institutions—including civilian supremacy—have been set in place and no politically significant group challenges the principal rules of the new regime.[8]

Where the military played an important role in the old regime and in the transition to the new regime, numerous obstacles, many of them formidable, must be overcome to achieve civilian supremacy. A military in retreat from government positions is usually wont to maintain monitoring or tutelary capacities over new authorities, which would affirm authoritarian enclaves within an otherwise democratic regime.[9] Asserting military prerogatives is one way to prevent newly installed, elected civilian leaders from imposing control over the military.[10] Democratic administrations may also face a divided, politicized military that resists the implementation of policies that emanate from the civilian government. Often, military resistance becomes most salient when civilian authorities seek to redress previous injustices or crimes committed by the military, such as human rights violations. Military contestation will threaten new democracies most when it is supported by political parties or influential civilian elites. Political civilian unity in support of civilian supremacy is thus critical to the consolidation of democracy. Gradual subordination of the military to civilian control is more likely when it extends beyond direct, formal government-military interactions to advance simultaneously across all the arenas of democratic governance.[11]

Transitions Under Military Influence

Democratic transitions in South America proceeded under heavy military supervision. Starting in the late 1970s and extending through most of the 1980s, transitions often took off under constitutional frameworks planned by military-authoritarian rulers or under ad hoc rules prepared to oversee change. The military thus significantly influenced the pace and agenda of the transition, affecting the scope and pattern of competition and occasionally banning specific individuals from running for the highest offices. In addition, the military remained mostly unchanged; it often occupied political offices in the administration and cabinets of successor governments.

For instance, in Peru, the military supervised the election in 1978 of a constituent assembly that worked for two years while the military retained control of executive power. Although it was composed mostly of elected civilian representatives who opposed the government, the assembly was nonetheless influenced by the military, which secured prerogatives for itself when power was transferred to an elected civilian president in 1980. These prerogatives haunt the democratic process to this day, particularly in the enforcement of states of emergency in areas of countersubversive activity.

Argentina's military government nearly collapsed after its failed occupation of the Malvinas Islands in 1982. It managed to stay in power for more than a year, during which it passed a law preventing successor governments from trying personnel for abducting and killing thousands of civilians. This amnesty, in the country where South America's most massive human rights violations occurred, created enormous difficulties for successor governments' attempts at justice and retribution, and still troubles civil-military relations there.[12]

The military in Brazil, after monitoring and carefully orchestrating a liberalization process for a decade, allowed the election of a civilian to the presidency in 1985, but arranged to retain six cabinet positions as well as other important positions. In Chile, under a partially reformed constitution, the military presided over the transfer of power to a democratically elected civilian president and a partially elected congress that housed appointees of outgoing president General Augusto Pinochet and the military. A number of clauses allowed the military to continue monitoring the new institutions and denied the president power to enforce crucial decisions. With variations in each case, the military was also powerful in the transitions in Bolivia, Ecuador, and Uruguay.

Despite its position of control, however, the military was rarely able to obtain all that it desired. Once the floodgates of liberalization and democratization opened, the military saw its method of operation transform from imposition of will to negotiation. Actors emerged and mobilized to pursue multiplying demands, which in turn influenced the transition's agenda. The outcome of these complex interactions became unpredictable. The military, often surprised by the unfolding of the transition, had to adjust its strategies to reduce uncertainty and secure guarantees. The military had to cope with a revived civil society and a reactivated and self-assured political elite. The outcomes of the transitions were mixed; neither the military nor its opponents were fully satisfied. Still, all had to coexist within the context of changing guarantees and less-than-pristine democracies.

The Peruvian military, for instance, had to transfer power to Fernando Belaúnde, the former president whom the military had ousted and who had resisted collaboration with the military government during deliberations of the constituent assembly. Voters rewarded Belaúnde and punished the American Popular Revolutionary Alliance (APRA), seemingly the largest party, for its dealings with the military. In Argentina, the military promoted negotiations with Peronist leaders in an attempt to obtain guarantees, but the Radical Party of Raúl Alfonsín, campaigning on promises of retribution, unexpectedly defeated the Peronists in the presidential election of 1983. Following the distinctly calamitous circumstances of the military's exit, Alfonsín's successor government legislated a veto of the military's amnesty and initiated trials against top military officers; they ended up in jail.

In Brazil, despite all the rule changing in its own favor, the military was unable to prevent the election of an opposition civilian in 1985. In Chile, Pinochet's unexpected defeat in the 1988 plebiscite led to the election of a center-left government coalition in 1989. The coalition was made up of opponents and parties the military had treated harshly when it assumed power in 1973.

Despite these setbacks, the military, with the exception of Argentina's, was able to face transitions from initially strong positions and to secure important guarantees for itself. In addition to formal guarantees, the military was powerful enough to use fear as an intangible but effective tool to influence behavior among opponents.[13]

Diverse Post-transition Outcomes

In the years since transitions evolved into imperfect democracies, the civil-military situation has varied enormously from country to country. The initially common look of transitions in South America—strong militaries with significant influence over the transitions—has given way to greater diversity.

Compared with democratic transitions in other parts of the world, especially those of Southern and Eastern Europe, South American transitions appear overmilitarized. Authoritarian regimes in South America that initiated transitions or were forced out of power were military in nature. Military juntas made up of chiefs of the armed services occupied the prevailing ruling matrix; they decided all major appointments in the administration, approved all legislation, and selected the individual in charge of the executive. Only the Brazilian military developed different strategies of maintaining rule. For instance, Brazil allowed a functioning elected civilian parliament; however, it was dependent on executive decrees.

In contrast to the militarized nature of authoritarian regimes in South America, most of the Southern European authoritarian regimes that ended in the 1970s and the East European regimes that crumbled later always were or became civilianized. By the transition, the military in those countries had little say over the transition's agenda and pace (important exceptions were Portugal and Poland). In South America, the military influenced the outcome of the first transition to a far greater extent than in other regions. The first transition outcome—the institutional arrangements under which the new regime takes off and an important initial condition of the ensuing post-transition process—unequally empowered civilians and the military to redress initial arrangements unfavorable to the former's attempts to create a full-fledged democracy.

Transition outcomes influenced predominantly by civilian elites place the burden of redress on the military. Transition outcomes influenced by military pressure and prerogatives place that burden on civilian democratizing elites. In South America, it was the task of successor civilian governments to change the institutional patterns of the first transition outcome and rid it of military influences that ran counter to the norms of civilian supremacy associated with democratic regimes. These governments have been much less successful in this task than were, for instance, Southern European regimes that faced severe military threats to democracy.[14]

Seen against the background of their own initial conditions of a decade ago, however, South American democracies have accomplished a great deal. Their outstanding feature now is diversity. Some of the countries that initiated redemocratization in the past 10 to 15 years have fared much better than others. Countries such as Venezuela that had avoided the authoritarian wave and stood as bulwarks of democracy faced severe threats from the military.[15]

Civil-Military Relations After the Transition

Initial conditions strongly influenced the nature of the power arrangements that ended the transition, but they could not fully constrain subsequent developments. Other factors emerged during the post-transition period that either countered or reinforced the impact of the first transition outcome. Former military disunity, for instance, turned in some cases into more unified support of hard-liners as a result of perceived threats to the military's core interests and mission. Civilian coalescence and the magnitude of public support for successor governments became stronger or weaker in different countries. International political and economic factors, varying capabilities of civilian elites and successor governments to formulate policy, the timing and pace of policy proposal and implementation—all these factors influenced the civil-military balance during the post-transition period in ways that could not have been predicted merely from initial conditions.

Also weighing in are unanticipated events that unexpectedly but decisively benefit one or another set of actors. Coup attempts are a case in point: In Spain in February 1981 and Argentina in December 1990, swift and violent actions of hard-line military groups could have substantially changed the nature of those countries' political processes.

In Argentina, for instance, the rebels could have ousted the civilian government or won greater concessions for the military. Because both attempts failed, those favoring democratization emerged more powerful than before—even able to terminally wound military opponents of democratic change. In hindsight, these events were decisive in the success of democratization. Nowhere, however, can democrats deliberately arrange for these events to take place; it is not just that such events are out of democrats' control; rather, the consequences of such actions are much too uncertain.

In South America, under a combination of formal and de facto arrangements that varied across countries, the military secured prerogatives during authoritarian rule and continued to exert influence over civilian institutions and the political process. Civilian authorities formally reigned over government and administrative matters but were in fact constrained in many policy areas by overlapping prerogatives or fear of military retaliation. Only Argentina and Uruguay managed to overcome some of these difficulties.

Argentina and Uruguay

Following the resumption of democracy in 1983, Argentina's government granted itself prerogatives from the preauthoritarian order and some new ones, but often failed in practice to impose its authority on an unyielding military. The administration of President Raúl Alfonsín (1983–89) redefined the military mission, reassigned prerogatives, restructured the central organization of defense, and increased the number of civilians in charge of defense agencies. Accompanying these reforms were initially impressive reductions in military expenditures and force levels, and attempts to hold the military accountable for past crimes that led to the incarceration of former junta leaders—a feat unprecedented in Latin America. Halfway through the Alfonsín administration, however, the military reasserted its power, reacting against budget cuts, organizational reform, the "hostile media," and legal actions against hundreds of officers for human rights offenses—all of which were seen as parts of a concerted "attack." In retaliation, middle-level officers staged revolts in April 1987, December 1987, and December 1988 against both government policy and "obsequious" senior military leaders. President Alfonsín yielded to demands of the rebels by submitting a bill—the *ley de punto final*—that set a deadline for the initiation of judicial action against military officers and limited the number of such actions, and then submitted another bill—the *ley de obediencia debida*—that restricted responsibility for human rights crimes to senior officers, relieving hundreds of officers from court action.[16]

The partial success of the revolts weakened government leadership and encouraged army factions to seek further concessions. President

Carlos Menem, seeking to appease the military, started out his term in 1989 by granting pardons to all officers who had participated in military revolts during the Alfonsín administration, as well as to senior officers prosecuted for human rights offenses. Then, in 1990, and against the wishes of public opinion, Menem went much further to pardon former junta members who were sentenced during Alfonsín's term.

In December 1990, several hundred army men, mostly noncommissioned officers, surprised the government with a bloody uprising. The uprising, however, received no support among commissioned officers, who felt satisfied with the government's previous concessions. The rebellion failed and its leaders were repressed by the army leadership. Their failure substantially strengthened the government and reduced the chances of a new rebel plot.[17]

From that point, the government concentrated on further civilianizing central defense structures and rationalizing military policies and budgets—including privatizing defense industries and substantially reducing and reallocating forces. In accordance with new foreign policy priorities, projects previously dear to the military, such as the development of intermediate-range ballistic missiles, were arrested. Argentina committed itself to the principles of nuclear nonproliferation and negotiated safeguards with Brazil and international agencies.

The government promoted several other measures with implications for the military: reaching understandings on pending border issues with Chile, agreeing with Brazil and Chile to ban chemical weapons, and participating in international peacekeeping efforts. Argentina's contribution to international peacekeeping was emphasized; it included the inauguration of an international training school.[18] Breaking with long tradition, the military ceased to be spoken of as a political resource for domestic disputes and began to be seen more as a service of the national state.[19]

Uruguay successfully restored traditional civilian prerogatives, but not without first overcoming major roadblocks. During the civil-military negotiations of the Naval Club Pact, which opened the way to the first democratic elections in 1984, the military demanded that special prerogatives be incorporated into the constitution. After the inauguration of democracy, however, these demands received no serious consideration; during the tenure of President Julio María Sanguinetti (1985–90), civil-military relations approached traditional patterns of civilian supremacy. And, in a rare event in Latin America, President Luis Alberto Lacalle (1990–95) appointed new service commanders in the navy and air force, against the wishes of top military commanders.[20]

The military nonetheless retained autonomy in most internal matters and succeeded in wresting defense intelligence from the direct control of the new civilian minister of defense. Later, with the appointment of former junta chief General Hugo Medina as defense minister, the ministry itself became more of a buffer between military and civilian authorities than the government's instrument for conducting military policy. The most sensitive issue facing the ministry involved past human rights violations. In dealing with these matters, Minister Medina assumed the role of protector of the armed forces and, in open defiance of judicial authority, instructed military officers not to appear in court for crimes committed during the dictatorship. The situation forced President Sanguinetti to urge Congress to approve the *ley de caducidad*, which in practice granted amnesty to human rights violators. Opponents of the amnesty, invoking a clause in the constitution, succeeded in collecting the required number of signatures (one-fourth of the electorate) to call a national referendum. They were defeated, however, in the referendum held in 1989, and the *ley de caducidad* was upheld. The dark spots on Uruguay's human rights record, military pressure for the law that exempted officers from legal responsibility, and military involvement with domestic political dynamics separates Uruguay from successful European transitions to democracy. The referendum did, however, go a long way toward laying to rest the most sensitive issue in civil-military relations, opening the way for normalization and progress in civilian control.[21]

The Case of Brazil

In Brazil, the accession of a civilian to the presidency in 1985—the first time in two decades—did not lead to a reduction of the military's political power. During the five-year term of President José Sarney, six active-duty officers sat in the cabinet; the military controlled its own services and the national intelligence and defense systems and had an expanded presence in the presidential and general government bureaucracy. The military continued to act on its own initiative in social and political affairs: for example, it mobilized against striking workers without prior authorization from appropriate civilian officials. The armed forces also organized the country's largest and most efficient lobbying team; officers were assigned full time to influence Congress on the new constitution that would replace the authoritarian document of 1967. The team succeeded: the assembly voted to oppose agrarian reform, defeated proposals in favor of a parliamentary form of government, and opposed a move to shorten Sarney's presidential term.[22] Although the 1988 Constitution progressed in bringing the military under civilian control, the military remained largely autonomous.[23]

Upon assuming the presidency in 1990, however, President Fernando Collor de Mello implemented his campaign promise to reduce the number of military ministers. He appointed a civilian to head national intelligence and disciplined officers who verbally challenged Collor's authority. Collor took other steps that would have been unthinkable a few years earlier: he denounced a secret military program to build a nuclear bomb, worked with Argentina to set up a system of international safeguards, and created a reserve in the Amazon for imperiled Yanomami Indians. Furthermore, during the protracted political turbulence that led to Collor's removal by Congress in October 1992 on corruption charges, the military, visibly breaking with a long tradition of intervention in crises of this nature, stayed on the sidelines.

Despite its relative decline in influence, the military still had recently challenged decisions by elected officials, prevented the creation of a defense ministry, and kept civilian officials from effectively controlling intelligence and other strategic domains.[24] Also, because salaries remained meager and modernization plans came to a halt as a result of budgetary constraints dictated by Congress and a poor economy, agitation in military circles resurfaced in the early 1990s. The military overtly clashed with Congress and civil courts on policies on salaries and raises for civil servants that affected military personnel directly. Declining salaries, constitutional clauses, and lack of presidential restraint in entangling the military in disputes among civil powers continued to feed the military as an autonomous domestic political force.[25] Over time, however, the military's influence tended to decline even though the military occasionally exhibited clout in bargaining for its interests.[26]

Chile and Peru

In Chile, democratically elected authorities assumed office in 1990 under a constitution that had been originally devised to perpetuate Pinochet and his authoritarian regime. This design was thwarted by Pinochet's defeat in the 1988 plebiscite, which led to partial reforms of the constitution agreed upon by the government and the opposition and to a viable transition. Before leaving the presidency, however, Pinochet used his constitutional powers to appoint members to a partially elected Senate and other official agencies. During the successor administration, Pinochet-appointed senators played a critical role in hindering reforms in Congress and precluding any chances of major constitutional revisions.

The constitution also granted the military diffuse oversight through the National Security Council and limited the president's powers to appoint and dismiss military chiefs. General Pinochet, for instance, remained commander in chief of the army (and stayed on after the first democratic president ended his term in March 1994) and could choose to keep the post until 1998, while the president had no power to remove him. Legislation passed during the final days of the Pinochet regime limited the power of government to significantly affect the military budget or to appoint senior officers, and kept military officers immune to judicial action for crimes against human rights.

The inauguration of elected authorities was accompanied by a massive transfer of state facilities and resources—in particular, those associated with previous intelligence activities—to the army, which greatly empowered the army and weakened the new government. During the first years of the successor democratic government, however, officials were able to affirm some civilian prerogatives and to fend off military noncompliance, although significant reforms remained conditioned by the constitutional requirement of a large congressional majority, which the government did not have.[27]

In Peru, democracy was officially established by a new constitution approved in 1980 by an assembly that, although under military supervision, had been freely elected in 1978. The cohesion of APRA and its plurality in the assembly led the military to reconcile with its old foe. APRA entered into agreements that secured a smooth transfer of power following a two-year coexistence of a military government with an elected assembly whose jurisdiction was restricted to constitution making. Under the skillful leadership of the octogenarian APRA helmsman Víctor Raúl Haya de la Torre, the assembly resisted pressures from the military, maintained its independence, and produced a democratic constitution, while simultaneously letting the military govern.

In the 1980 presidential election, however, the electorate rewarded APRA's adversary Fernando Belaúnde's refusal to participate in the military-supervised 1978 elections and punished APRA's collaboration with the military during the transition. Belaúnde, the former president whom the military had overthrown in 1968, made sure that this time he would preside over peaceful coexistence by appeasing the military, respecting its ample sphere of autonomy, and rewarding it with generous budget increases. Civil-military relations were clouded, however, by the dramatic escalation of violence by the subversive Sendero Luminoso (Shining Path). The role assumed by the army in countersubversion highlighted the significant emergency powers that the military had secured through laws passed in the final days of the military government. These powers expanded further in 1985 with the creation of political-military commands in geographic areas placed under states of emergency. In these areas, the military's control was total and outside political control. Violations of human rights skyrocketed in this period; in contrast to other South American cases, they occurred only after the termination of military-authoritarian rule.[28]

President Alan García (1985–90) attempted to restrain military autonomy and enforce presidential prerogatives over the armed forces. Part of his strategy involved creation of a ministry of defense—a move supported by the army but strongly opposed by the air force, whose chiefs staged a mutinous mobilization when the ministry was finally created. The fears of the air force were confirmed when the new ministry was placed under the control of an army general instead of a civilian. The escalation of the Sendero Luminoso's war, entangled with the problems of drug trafficking, massive violations of human rights, and the loss of legitimacy of the national government, rendered ineffectual the efforts to enhance civilian control.[29] Finally, President Alberto Fujimori's unconstitutional coup against Congress and the parties in February 1992, supported by the military, moved this country further away from democratization.[30] Subsequent normalization of Fujimori's rule under formally democratic elections continues to be troublesome given the near-total elimination of opposition in Congress and concessions given the military—including amnesty for military officers condemned for massive killings of opponents and expanded jurisdiction for military courts.[31]

Explaining Different Paths of Change

Argentina and Uruguay stood out for their relative accomplishments. In both cases the previous democratic constitutions were restored, including clauses on military subordination to elected officials. None of the "institutional acts" passed by the former juntas remained in place, and new national-security legislation specified restricted military roles. In Argentina, after the stormy years of the Alfonsín administration, civilianization of the defense ministry and the military's acquiescence to democracy began to gel at the same time that important reforms in the military were promoted. In Uruguay, the military's hopes for change in the constitution after the transition were not realized. And since the referendum on the *ley de caducidad* ended the turmoil on the prosecution of human rights abuses, civilian prerogatives also began to take hold. In Brazil, Chile, and Peru, on the other hand, institutionalized or de facto prerogatives for the military endured, clashing with and limiting the powers of civilian authorities; continuing episodes of military challenges to civilian authority precluded the advancement of effective civilian control.

It is certainly possible that the South American cases, whose transitions were initiated much later than those of the successful Southern European cases, may succeed in due course. In Chile, for instance, democratically elected presidents will be free to alter the composition of the Senate and thus create a majority for constitutional reform when the tenure of Pinochet-appointed senators expires in 1998. Most of the South American cases, however, have already had as much time (about ten years) as the Southern European cases to develop the conditions for civilian supremacy. Attention should thus be paid to the particular conditions surrounding the processes of democratization in these two regions rather than to time differences per se.

What were these conditions? Initial conditions of militarization were common to all South American cases. The extent of control by the military varied, however. As a result of defeat in an international conflict, control by the military was weaker in Argentina. Despite this near collapse, the military managed to occupy controlling positions throughout Argentina's transition. The only legacy of this control was the military's staunch refusal to collaborate on prosecuting human rights violations, evidenced by its issuing of an amnesty. When the successor democratic administration assumed power, Argentina's legal structure reverted to that of the previous democracy, which made no special allowances for the military; the human rights amnesty was nullified. But without this near collapse, military control of the transition would have had greater and more favorable consequences for the military.

Beyond these initial conditions, other factors emerge during the post-transition period that influence the position of the military and its level of unity vis-à-vis the advancing new democracy. For instance, the intensity of the military's reaction to policies ensuing from new democratic institutions is affected by its perception of threats to the core interests of the military organization—including corporate integrity and its view of the essential aspects of nationality, or the national "soul." In Argentina, military reaction was awakened by indictments of large numbers of officers for human rights violations. The military perceived the combination of indictments, reductions in budgets and forces, and the civilianization of defense structures as a concerted attack from traditional domestic adversaries disguised as democrats. In Chile, reactions of the military against civilian authority were triggered by similar perceptions. In Peru, a large and violent subversive movement emerged at the same time democracy was inaugurated, prompting the government to implement rules and procedures inherited from the previous regime that enhanced the military's autonomy.

In different ways and with varying intensity, reaction of the military to perceived threats strengthened the military and severely limited or delayed the reformist initiative of democratic civilian elites. These cases also vividly illustrate the tensions inherent in the choice between reducing military contestation (civil-military conflict) and reducing military prerogatives.[32] Faced with this dilemma, civilian leaders have no standard formula other than to reduce military power and strengthen and unify their own bases of support, even at the price of conflict, if it is deemed temporary and short-term.

Civilian Military and Defense Policies

What factors, then, helped strengthen or weaken the ability of civilian elites to counter military resistance, develop democratic arrangements, and advance civilian supremacy?[33] In the successful cases of Southern Europe, civilian elites during the post-transition period advanced policies on defense and the military that provided an orientation for restructuring and streamlining military forces and substantiating civilian claims to leadership. Often, civilian leaders were urged to advance policy in response to international crises (Greece) or in anticipation of decisions on European or Atlantic structures such as the European Economic Community, the North Atlantic Treaty Organization (NATO), or the European Union.

In South America, only in Argentina were civilian elites forced to deal with an international crisis. With the military leadership fully discredited from the Malvinas debacle, the successor civilian government initiated policies aimed at peaceful resolution of controversies with both England and Chile, as the referendum on the Beagle dispute called by President Alfonsín showed.[34] These policies and the dismal state of Argentina's economy led to sharp reductions in military spending and forces. The military's reaction to—indeed, rebellions against—government policies and court action on human rights cases, however, forced the civilian leadership to concentrate on resolving domestic turmoil. After several concessions by the civilian leadership and a failed military revolt that took place in December 1990, the Menem administration resumed direction of military and defense policy. Reduction and modernization of the forces, participation in international missions, termination of weapons-development projects, institutionalized military cooperation with Brazil, civilianization of the defense ministry and defense industries—all these initiatives attested to incipient policy formulation by civilian elites in these areas.

Brazil, Chile, Peru, and Uruguay fared much worse in this dimension. No international crisis immersed civilian elites in defense and military matters; the military enjoyed greater continuity of its control and prerogatives. In Peru, defense and military matters were absorbed by the insurrection of the Sendero Luminoso and by drug trafficking; civilian involvement was not encouraged.

In Brazil during the Sarney administration, civilian leaders did not attempt to formulate policy or dispute the heavy presence of the military in these areas. On the contrary, the military advanced positions on civilian domains. President Collor did attempt to advance policy in defense and military areas, but his effort, lacking sustained participation of a wider array of civilian elites, was short-lived.

In Chile, the civilian leadership during President Patricio Aylwin's successor administration remained preoccupied with episodes of military contestation and, unsuccessfully, with attempts to reform legislation on civilian prerogatives. Only marginally could the administration begin to address national defense policy, which, excepting a few important foreign policy initiatives with military implications, remained within the confines of the military.[35]

Civilian policy initiatives in military and defense areas are essential for the assertion of civilian supremacy. Disengagement of the military from politics is an important condition, but it is not tantamount to civilian supremacy. In Spain, for instance, democrats could have remained perfectly content with terminating military contestation without initiating any major changes in military and defense structures. Democrats could have allowed the military an ample sphere of autonomy in exchange for the military's implicit agreement not to challenge civilian governance. Instead, democrats deemed changes in the military and defense structures indispensable to the long-term stability of democracy.

If civilian governments do not generate policy, the military has no choice but to develop its own orientations.

Spain and Portugal, however, tackled problems one at a time. Development and implementation of genuinely civilian policies had to wait for the elimination of domestic military contestation. Particularly in Spain, this strategy allowed time for previous foes to learn to trust each other. By the time the Socialists came to power intent on military reform, the army's fear of them as "reds" had substantially subsided. The Socialists were then promoting more moderate policies and the most hard-line leaders had been removed from the army. Reforms conceived and implemented in this way were likely to endure.

In Argentina, on the contrary, the Alfonsín administration tried to progress on several fronts at the same time. Military personnel were tried for human rights violations at the same time that the government tackled numerous reforms: reductions in military budgets and forces, elimination of the national-security doctrine, and changes in legislation. The strategy backfired: the military mounted a series of intimidating rebellions. In the end, Alfonsín compromised, reversing some of the legislation that banned the armed forces from domestic security problems. In hindsight, civilian military policies that were implemented more gradually seemed to have attained greater success.[36]

Gradual timing of policy implementation, however, should not be misconstrued as indefinite postponement of civilian initiative, which might lead to abdication of civilian responsibility.[37] If civilian governments do not generate policy, the military has no choice but to develop its own orientations. Civilians are then faced with the more difficult task of redirecting those policies. In Brazil, for instance, lacking substantive guidelines from the government, the military set its own goals. With the end of rivalries with Argentina and the demise of domestic threats, the military turned to protecting sovereignty in the Amazon and redeployed accordingly. Whether or not this was a sensible course of action, civilians were left only to react to policies advanced by the military.[38]

Civilians sometimes merely develop and affirm instruments to control the military without providing more substantive guidance regarding the new role and mission of the armed forces. Civilian governments may flex their muscles by reducing military budgets and forces, but reductions without clearly defined goals ultimately work against the objective of depoliticizing and professionalizing the military. A military left with few resources becomes demoralized. Without budgets to replace obsolete materiel and carry out training and military exercises, pilots do not fly, ships do not sail, and tanks rust in depots. Personnel devote less time to the profession; low salaries and fewer working hours drive many officers to take second jobs. Without clearly prescribed roles, military personnel grow restless and contestation is likely to revive.[39] These problems were faced in South America by Argentina and Brazil.

An economy capable of sustaining civilian defense and military policies is thus helpful in preventing a military reaction. Economic difficulties of post-transition Argentina and Brazil affected these countries' modernization drives and, more dangerously, lowered salary levels.

Support for Civilian Governments

A government's capacity to promote democratic policies regarding the military is affected by its ability to maintain high levels of public support. A military finds it harder to push for nondemocratic prerogatives and to resist government policies when the government is visibly backed by a wide array of electorally strong political forces. Thus, critical for the advancement of civilian supremacy are governments that, because of their popular backing and the unity of forces supporting them, can persuade the military to desist from further opposition.

The ability of a government to maintain high levels of public support is often the result of its success in handling the economy. All the cases considered here were tested by austere economic conditions, especially at the time of regime change and during the first years of democratic government. Overall, conditions facing governments in Southern Europe were less harsh. In South America, social demands accumulated over years of social inequity compounded the severe economic constraints already facing governments.[40]

The Southern European cases never reached the level of economic disruption encountered by most of the new South American democracies, where inflation skyrocketed to triple-digit levels. Economic hardship and uncertainty nurture the feeling that governments lack control and a sense of direction—that, essentially, they cannot be trusted. While the public may still prefer democracy to military rule, extreme economic hardship may lead the public to withdraw its support from the government, leaving the civilian regime in a weak position vis-à-vis the military. Lacking popular support, incumbents in the presidential systems of South America were left to sit out their terms merely awaiting the inevitable electoral defeat that would throw them out of office. In this scenario, governments become incapable of meeting the great challenges posed by the military.[41] The parliamentary systems of government in Southern Europe—which in most cases ensure that the government will enjoy majority support in parliament—avoid the lame-duck syndrome that often afflicts South American presidents.[42]

The cases of Argentina and Peru illustrate the problems of government support. President Alan García (1985–90), in the second postmilitary administration, began his term with immense popularity and far-reaching plans. Reversing the passive style of his predecessor, Fernando Belaúnde (1980–85), in military affairs, García pursued reforms to strengthen civilian control and reduced the levels of military spending, which Belaúnde had substantially raised. By 1987, however, the situation had dramatically changed. Challenged from within his party and from the left, García embarked on erratic policies—including nationalizing all major banks—that provoked a reaction from the right and increased his isolation. GDP fell abruptly and inflation skyrocketed to over 1,000 percent; the president's approval rating fell from over 70 percent in June 1987 to below 30 percent in October of that same year, to under 10 percent in 1989.[43] Paralyzed by these economic difficulties and lack of popular support, the initially activist president quickly turned into a lame duck, inhibiting the government's ability to solidify civilian control.

In Argentina, President Alfonsín also started out with immense popularity and even more far-reaching plans. The government set out to restructure labor relations, promote broad constitutional reforms, implement unprecedented policies that would bring the military under civilian control—even create a new capital city. The government's initial strength and popular support were ratified later in midterm congressional elections and in a referendum on resolving the Beagle dispute with Chile convoked by the president. But failure in the battle against inflation and a sharp decline in the standard of living of most Argentines led Alfonsín's government to electoral defeat in the 1987 congressional elections and further failures in economic policy.[44] Optimistic plans had to be shelved; severe military challenges to presidential authority—which a strongly supported government could have eventually overcome—acquired self-sustained impetus for increased military assertiveness.

In both cases, significant sectors of the public found ways to express their preference for democracy whenever a serious threat from the armed forces emerged. The calculation made by the military, however, does not consider the general preferences of the public as much as its own assessment of the strengths and weaknesses of a specific administration and its leader.[45] Leaders and governments with waning support among the elites, the public, and parliament found it difficult to appease or maintain ascendancy over discontented militaries in conflict-laden post-transition situations.

In Brazil, President Sarney lost support shortly after his inauguration in 1985 when most members of the coalition that brought him to power shifted to the opposition. Much of Sarney's support came, in fact, from the military, whom he used to pressure Congress on several occasions. His successor, Fernando Collor, supported by an ad hoc party created for his campaign, lacked consistent support in Congress.[46] Despite initial attempts to check military autonomy, Collor's loss of support and ultimate removal hampered the government's democratic progress.

Problems of government support were better overcome in the new Southern European democracies, where parliamentary or semipresidential electoral and government systems tended to facilitate working government majorities. The early Union of the Democratic Center (UCD) and the Socialist governments in Spain, and the Conservative and Socialist governments in Greece, for instance, were incomparable with the awkward position in which Alan García, Raúl Alfonsín, and José Sarney were placed as lame-duck executives in the presidential systems of their countries. Having lost support in parliament because of midterm elections or shifting loyalties of undisciplined party members, these three presidents, unable to implement policy or recover popularity, were forced to wait out their terms in minority status while retaining only formally the powers granted the executive branch. These institutional rigidities compounded government weaknesses in dealing with the military.

Yet when governments secured significant electoral support and a majority in parliament, they were able to move boldly in the area of military reform. President Menem in Argentina secured such a majority during his first term. After crushing the military uprising of 1990 and exchanging pardons of military chiefs for an end to military contestation, he was able to pursue the military reforms mentioned earlier.

In Chile, a center-left coalition based on the stable and disciplined parties, which emerged from the resumption of democracy, created a government with a strong electoral basis and vast support in Congress. Still, the authoritarian legacy of Pinochet-appointed senators denied democratic governments sufficient majority for constitutional reform on military issues. The parties of the right, while reaching agreement with the government on numerous important issues, relentlessly opposed any reforms that would give the government power over the military. Civilian unity, an indispensable ingredient in a successful strategy for the attainment of civilian supremacy, had simply not been achieved.

Civilian Unity

Peru and Ecuador adopted new constitutions to inaugurate democracy in processes that did not unify civilian elites and that also were conducted under the shadow of military influence. In the remaining countries of South America, the transition resumed competition with no accord (Argentina), or was channeled through agreements that failed to include all players (Uruguay) or failed to include all relevant domains (Chile, Brazil).

Among the South American cases, Argentina's collapse-triggered democratization kept contending political groups from reaching the kind of accords that characterized the transitions of better-entrenched militaries.[47] Peronist groups tried, before the elections, to reach accord with the military on guarantees against prosecution, and then presented stiff opposition to President Alfonsín's administration. Later, during Menem's administration, the end of major civil-military tensions on human rights issues—and the end of military contestation—created room for incipient collaboration among political elites on defense and military matters. A similar situation evolved in Uruguay.

In Brazil, aside from the troubled circumstances of José Sarney's rise to the presidency and Fernando Collor's tenure and exit, the formation of unified coalitions was made difficult by the very nature of the political system. The combination of presidentialism, multipartism, and federalism with specific regulations that discouraged party discipline inhibited stable coalitions among the various and shifting sources of political power.[48] Peru did not fare any better, especially after the divisive administration of President Alan García and the confrontational policies that were pursued by President Fujimori, which combined substantial popular support with deepening divisions among the elite. In Chile, despite consensus on numerous matters, particularly on economic and foreign policy, no accord developed on constitutional issues regarding presidential powers over the military.

Military Divisions, International Opportunities

All militaries face transition with internal divisions, although in South America doctrinal developments and a shared concern with the threat of retribution tempered those divisions. Only in Spain, where differing views of the impact of Francoism on the armed forces developed in the army, could those divisions sustain possible joint efforts with civilian democratic reformers. In the other cases, divisions resulted mostly from the experience of military rule or, as in Portugal, from different views on the course that the revolution begun in 1974 should take.

With the end of transition and advancement of democracy, divisions dissolved in some cases and developed in others. Argentina's military followed a complex path. The interservice divisions that so visibly surfaced during the transition subsided later in reaction to the civilian-led human rights "offensive" during the Alfonsín administration. Vertical divisions subsequently developed as midlevel officers complained that military leadership yielded too much on the human rights issue and did not assume full responsibility for the disastrous Malvinas crisis. Top brass was also criticized for tolerating the excessive budget and force reductions that curtailed the professional capacity of the armed forces. Defeat of the last rebellion in 1990, exit of formerly rebel-prone officers to the political electoral arena, and serious, though modest, attempts to partially rebuild the military ended the most visible divisions. Whereas in Portugal post-transition divisions meant the gradual strengthening of moderate groups, which favored resumption of professionalism and discipline, in Argentina post-transition divisions severely challenged the stability of civilian government.[49]

While the Peruvian military became absorbed in the fight against the Sendero Luminoso, the remaining militaries in South America displayed an increasingly uniform interest in modernization. Catching up technologically and enhancing military capacity with appropriate research, organizational change, and weapons procurement characterized Chilean and Brazilian military attempts to accommodate themselves to changed domestic scenarios. Contrary to the case in Spain, South America's modernization drive did not originate from negative evaluations of the authoritarian experience, and, except in Argentina, it was not accompanied by defense reform. The goal to modernize was set by more autonomous militaries. Contrary to the coalitional opportunities with civilians that modernization had opened up in Spain, in South America modernization risked creating a dangerous gap between the military's aspirations and the civilian elite's willingness and ability to support them.

External factors provided Southern Europe with a strongly democratic regional environment that offered the benefits of economic integration. This type of international influence—"democratization through convergence"[50]—was distinctive to Southern Europe. International conditions in the area made it possible for civilian governments to direct the military away from domestic politics. NATO, for instance, provided an opportunity to redirect military missions to external professional concerns.[51]

In South America, international condemnation of military regimes and support for the democratic opposition, especially from Western Europe and, more erratically, the United States, played an important role in democratization. On the whole, however, the international context of democratization in South America was much less auspicious than it was in Southern Europe, especially in regard to the military dimension. The Interamerican Treaty of Reciprocal Assistance, created in 1947, was a poor imitation of NATO that had long lost its initial dynamism; it was perceived by most of its members as rather moribund.[52] The alliance was not prepared, therefore, to provide the kind of framework for military renovation that NATO provided for the Southern European democratic governments.

In addition, many features of the military component of the inter-American system were less openly supportive of the goals of civilian supremacy than NATO was. NATO had a clear structure of political and military participation, with preeminence of the political level, whereas the political and military components of the inter-American system existed side by side. Thus military participation in inter-American military activities did not presume a prior strengthening of the civilian political connections. Inter-American army conferences often ended with statements on policy orientations that had a great impact on domestic affairs but had little to do with the stated goals of national governments.

Despite the United States' support of democratization since President Ronald Reagan's second term, security concerns in the hemisphere led the United States to emphasize domestic concerns of the Latin American countries, which did not allow their governments to reorient the military away from domestic politics. The orientation of U.S. policy circles shifted to using Latin American armies in the war against drug trafficking. Also, a renewed emphasis was given to a vaguely described nation-building mission, which stood against efforts to disengage the military from domestic concerns.[53] In sum, civilians in Southern Europe could use international structures to their own advantage in ways that were not available to civilians in South America.

Brazil, Chile, and Peru have made the least progress, while Argentina and Uruguay have moved further ahead. The weight of negative initial conditions was felt in all these cases in the form of surviving prerogatives of the military or the gloomy legacy in the area of human rights. Military control of the transition, abruptly shifting levels of government support, lack of civilian policies and coalescence, and, in some cases, institutional incapacity to produce the conditions necessary for stable policy formulation and implementation, impeded progress.

Among the South American cases, Argentina followed the most complex path. It combined military-regime collapse with a military-controlled transition; impressive early achievements by a successor civilian administration were followed by mighty military reaction and civilian concessions; a succession of military rebellions and their final exhaustion were followed by the resumption of civilianization, modernization, and reform.

That the full impact of initial conditions may change over time bodes well for countries whose transitions began under unfavorable conditions. Progress, however, depends on the ability of civilian elites to support themselves with the will, policies, and instruments to promote change. At the same time, elites will set off on uncertain paths of military accommodation to democratization and momentous international political and economic changes.

Challenges for the Future

Given the history of South American countries, it is remarkable that no military interventions have succeeded since the transitions ended.

Progress in democratization, however, requires more than the absence of intervention. Although this absence is a necessary condition, the affirmation of long-lasting democratic regimes demands effective civilian supremacy. That is, governance must be free of undue interference from the military, and democratically elected authorities must control defense and military matters, guaranteeing the subordination of all state institutions to a common framework and rule of law.

If no further societal gaps develop, South America has no profound structural factors that would prevent the establishment of a democratic framework for civil-military relations. Still, four significant tasks must be accomplished if progress is to take place.

1) Resolution of human rights issues. The consequences of human rights violations during the period of military rule have been a permanent obstacle to the affirmation of a democratic framework for civil-military relations. Compromise between justice and stability has satisfied few of the victims, punished even fewer of the perpetrators, and inflicted serious ethical wounds on the nation. Problems stemming from these kinds of violations do not go away, even after compromises have been reached and amnesties granted.

Recent revelations in Argentina about the procedures used to eliminate opponents have made wounds and uneasiness resurface. In Chile, the army's reluctance in June and July of 1995 to abide by a Supreme Court sentencing of a senior general and close collaborator of Pinochet made observers and practitioners rethink the extent to which the transition is complete. The military feels unduly attacked by these sentences. Victims and concerned citizens feel compromises consistently fail to address the core issue: information on the whereabouts of the thousands who were abducted and made to "disappear."

The problem is not, however, confined to those cases in the Southern Cone where violations were most massive. It relates more generally to notions about the worth of human life and the effective prevalence of the rule of law. Violations continue to occur in countries that did not experience the kind of repression that, for instance, took place under military rule in Argentina or Chile. In Peru, Colombia, and Brazil, for example, police officers have used reprehensible and illegal practices in the control of common crime.[54] The solution of pending problems in this area, the avoidance of new human rights violations, and the affirmation of a widespread regard for individual rights and the rule of law are critical components of an improved role for the military in democratic regimes.

Because of conflict with the military over these issues, democratic governments can pursue justice and retribution only so far before they put the affirmation of democratic rule at risk. Also, they must often wrestle with dynamics created by the independent activities of the judiciary. Matters of such complexity, which are constrained by the effective power held by the military, cannot be captured by simple formulas. Governments can, however, make sure that human rights violations are investigated and publicized and reparations made. In addition—perhaps most importantly—governments who cannot pursue justice for past abuses and crimes should ensure that military or police organizations commit no further violations under the democratic administrations. Punishment for past abuses may be difficult, but continuing violations under democratic government are unacceptable. Putting an end to such violations depends largely on democratic officials' initiative in controlling the public agencies involved; such officials cannot continue to rely on the excuse of "constraints" on their power. Recent legislation in Brazil on the subject of torture is a case in point.

2) Promoting civilian control. Since the demise of military-authoritarian regimes, the ball has been in the civilians' court: the administration, parliament, the judiciary, parties. Although the military is responsible for managing its own problems and generating its own contribution to democratic accommodation, the fundamental responsibilities of government lie with civilian elites. It is they who must conceive and implement mechanisms to promote civilian control and higher democratic standards in government relations with the military. This is, on one hand, a question of overcoming civilians' historical lack of concern with these matters and of promoting policy development not within just any group of civilian technocrats but specifically within political parties—those entities that develop platforms for governance and select individuals who will occupy office and congressional seats. On the other hand, the civilian leadership must develop an outlook on defense and military matters common among all relevant civilian elites. This is now possible in many countries where it was not in the past (Brazil, Argentina). It is harder in cases where this issue still is the source of a deep cleavage (Chile).

3) Establishing instruments of institutional policy. Institutional-policy instruments, such as a ministry of defense, are essential for the advancement of enduring policies in military matters and defense. Where such an instrument is lacking, it ought to be created. Where it already exists, it must be appropriately structured and endowed; effective civilian government policy instruments must be integrated with the rest of the state administration. Other agencies and instruments of policy must be developed as well, including think tanks to support government and legislative policy and independent agencies to monitor and criticize state performance. Institutional-policy instruments also involve centralization of intelligence under civilian coordination. There has been some progress in this field, but little of it has been institutionalized.

4) Redefining the military's role. Finally, civilian elites and policy makers must tackle the question of military roles in an era of economic globalization and trade integration. The Latin American region will continue to promote economic integration within its own borders. This integration occurs amid all other changes that stemmed from the disappearance of the communist bloc and that are relevant to the military. The civilian leadership must promote plans for military reorganization and modernization while taking these changes into account, lest those plans be made entirely in the military domain. Civilian democratic governments must also understand that the military continues to think in terms of traditional roles in domestic containment—or, in some cases, developmental roles—none of which are naturally harmonious with the goals of further democratization.

With the end of the Cold War, the advancement of domestic democratization, and recent developments in economic globalization and regional trade integration, military roles are undergoing a transition. For instance, international peacekeeping activities have involved several of the Latin American militaries in recent years. Latin America's larger presence in the war on drugs has been encouraged from abroad but has also resulted from domestic pressures. Military cooperation among Southern Cone Common Market (MERCOSUR) countries engaged in the expansion of trade and economic integration is increasingly entertained in the region. Political leaders in these countries ought to assess the new roles of the military with an eye to minimizing the threat of armed conflict and engaging the military in the goals of democratic consolidation.

As with any transition involving complex organizations such as the military, this is a slow transition. However slowly the new mission emerges, civilian political leaders should begin by eliminating autonomous domestic military roles in repression or in the "safeguarding" of political institutions. Also, although this is an issue over which domestic political elites are divided, the military's role in economic development—however broadly conceived—should be eliminated. The military should also be removed from the fight against drugs; this work should be reassigned to specialized agencies. All of these current roles engage the military in domestic affairs at a time when democratization demands the contrary.

With regard to international roles, the military should continue to contribute to international peacekeeping efforts and regional cooperation on collective security. These efforts, combined with efforts to redefine the military's mission in a new regional context that requires smaller but more modern armies, should not detract from what remains the military's core mission: guaranteeing the territorial integrity of the state. This may not sound daring, but is realistic and fully compatible with the goal of democratization and civilian supremacy—more so than "new" missions under consideration, which would expand the role of the military into such areas as fighting drug trafficking or engaging in developmental efforts.

NOTES

1. For an excellent presentation of this seemingly simple statement, see Robert A. Dahl, *Democracy and Its Critics* (New Haven: Yale University Press, 1989), 245.

2. As Adam Przeworski put it, "the institutional framework of civilian control over the military constitutes the neuralgic point of democratic consolidation." See his *Democracy and the Market* (Cambridge: Cambridge University Press, 1991), 29. See also Leonardo Morlino, "Consolidación democrática: Definición, modelos, hipótesis," *Revista española de investigaciones sociológicas* 35 (July–September 1986): 7–61. For an excellent treatment of "the military dimensions to the obstacles to democratic consolidation," and the major issues involved in "articulated military contestation," see Alfred Stepan, *Rethinking Military Politics* (Princeton: Princeton University Press, 1988) (quotations from xiv).

3. For a more thorough discussion, see Felipe Agüero, *Soldiers, Civilians, and Democracy: Post-Franco Spain in Comparative Perspective* (Baltimore: Johns Hopkins University Press, 1995). This formulation is in line with previous ones advanced by Claude E. Welch and J. Samuel Fitch. See Welch, "Civilian Control of the Military: Myth and Reality," in Welch, ed., *Civilian Control of the Military* (Albany: State University of New York Press, 1976); and Fitch, "The Theoretical Model Underlying the Analysis of Civil-Military Relations in Contemporary Latin American Democracies: Core Assumptions" (unpubl. ms., Inter-American Dialogue, Washington, D.C., 1987).

4. For a discussion of the notions of militarized and civilianized authoritarian regimes, see Agüero, *Soldiers, Civilians, and Democracy*, 44.

5. Samuel P. Huntington, *The Soldier and the State* (New York: Vintage Books, 1957), 86–88.

6. Juan J. Linz and Alfred Stepan argue that the general public must voluntarily support democracy as well, although attitudes fully favorable to democracy may develop only gradually. See Linz and Stepan, *Problems of Democratic Transition and Consolidation: Southern Europe, South America, and Post-Communist Europe* (Baltimore: Johns Hopkins University Press, 1996), 143–47. In the case of the military this has practical implications. Democratic reformers often devise policies based on the desire to make the views and ideologies of the military more democratic. This may be an unnecessary and strenuous effort, and often a counterproductive one. If the military adhered to democracy at the outset of the transition, democratization or civilian supremacy would be much less of a problem than it actually is. Yet transitions have succeeded without the military becoming committed to democratic values overnight.

7. Civilian supremacy in emerging democratic regimes should be approached differently than that in long-consolidated democracies. When, for instance, there is evidence of a surge in military influence in consolidated democracies, regime stability is not threatened in any real way, whereas similar evidence has greater repercussions for civilian efforts in new democracies. Differences over NATO or related policies, for instance, have often been voiced by top-ranking military officers in countries like France, Germany, and the Netherlands. These dissenting views do not threaten or question the routine practice of civilian supremacy in consolidated democracies. Similar events, however, would be seen as detrimental to the effort to assert civilian control in a new democracy. As a result, much less freedom to voice different views may be granted in these cases. For a recent commentary on the silence forced on the Spanish army, see Jesús Ignacio Martínez Paricio, "Defensa nacional y militares en el umbral del nuevo siglo," in José Vidal Beneyto, ed., *España a debate: La política* (Madrid: Editorial Tecnos, 1991), 111.

8. For a view of consolidation that emphasizes actual compliance with democratic procedures by all politically significant groups, see Richard Gunther, Hans-Jürgen Puhle,

and Nikiforos Diamandouros, "Introduction: The Politics of Democratic Consolidation," in Gunther, Diamandouros, and Puhle, eds., *The Politics of Democratic Consolidation: Southern Europe in Comparative Perspective* (Baltimore: Johns Hopkins University Press, 1995), 1–32.

Other views of consolidation emphasize the extension of democratic procedures to all significant political domains. See Linz and Stepan, *Problems of Democratic Transition and Consolidation;* J. Samuel Valenzuela, "Democratic Consolidation in Post-transitional Settings: Notion, Process and Facilitating Conditions," in Scott Mainwaring, Guillermo O'Donnell, and Valenzuela, eds., *Issues in Democratic Consolidation: The New South American Democracies in Comparative Perspective* (Notre Dame, Ind.: University of Notre Dame Press, 1992), 54–104; and Guillermo O'Donnell, "Transitions, Continuities and Paradoxes," in Mainwaring, O'Donnell, and Valenzuela, eds., *Issues in Democratic Consolidation,* 17–56.

In *Democracy and the Market,* Adam Przeworski argues that democracy is consolidated when, by evoking generalized compliance, it becomes self-enforcing. This is possible when institutions guarantee that no substantive interests will be denied advancement. A similar view is maintained in Giuseppe Di Palma, *To Craft Democracies* (Berkeley: University of California Press, 1990). Other notions underscore regularity of interactions, group and regime structure, and rule formalization. See Philippe C. Schmitter, "The Consolidation of Political Democracy in Southern Europe and Latin America" (unpubl. ms., Stanford University, June 1988).

The notion of consolidation has received much criticism from different quarters, principally for hindering a focus on the actual problems of seemingly enduring postauthoritarian regimes. See, e.g., Frances Hagopian, "After Regime Change: Authoritarian Legacies, Political Representation, and the Democratic Future of South America," *World Politics* 45 (April 1993): 465; Ben Ross Schneider, "Democratic Consolidations: Some Broad Comparisons and Sweeping Arguments," *Latin American Research Review* 30 (1995): 222; and Felipe Agüero, "Fault Lines of Democratic Governance in the Americas" (paper prepared for the conference "Fault Lines of Democratic Governance in the Americas," North-South Center, University of Miami, 4–6 May 1995).

Guillermo O'Donnell faults consolidation theory for directing attention exclusively to formal institutionalization and away from the real gap between formally prescribed institutions and informal institutionalization, a point at which seemingly enduring polyarchies in Latin America are found (see his chapter in this collection). The notion of consolidation and its emphasis on formal institutions, however, is effective in the study of the military in new democracies precisely because of the formal nature of the military establishment and the importance of legal-formal norms in civil-military relations.

9. For discussion of the notions of authoritarian enclaves and "reserve domains," see Valenzuela, "Democratic Consolidation in Post-transitional Settings," 64–66.

10. Alfred Stepan defined "the dimension of military institutional prerogatives" as "those areas where, whether challenged or not, the military as an institution assumes they have an acquired right or privilege, formal or informal, to exercise effective control over its internal governance, to play a role within extramilitary areas within the state apparatus, or even to structure relationships between state and political or civil society." Stepan, *Rethinking Military Politics,* 93.

11. Juan Linz and Alfred Stepan identify five major arenas of modern democracy: civil society, political society, economic society, state apparatus, and the rule of law. See Linz and Stepan, *Problems of Democratic Transition and Consolidation,* ch. 1.

12. James W. McGuire presents an excellent interpretation of the Argentine case as one in which the interim transition government is an authoritarian incumbent caretaker government with medium-to-low control over the transition, rather than as a case of regime collapse. See McGuire, "Interim Government and Democratic Consolidation: Argentina in Comparative Perspective," in Yossi Shain and Juan J. Linz, eds., *Between States: Interim Governments and Democratic Transitions* (Cambridge: Cambridge University Press, 1995), 179–210.

13. A more detailed presentation of these cases is found in Felipe Agüero, "The

Military and the Limits to Democratization in South America," in Mainwaring, O'Donnell, and Valenzuela, eds., *Issues in Democratic Consolidation*, 153–98.

14. A fuller comparison appears in Felipe Agüero, "Democratic Consolidation and the Military in Southern Europe and South America," in Gunther, Diamandouros, and Puhle, eds., *The Politics of Democratic Consolidation*, 124–65.

15. See Felipe Agüero, "Debilitating Democracy: Political Elites and Military Rebels," in Louis W. Goodman et al., eds., *Lessons of the Venezuelan Experience* (Washington and Baltimore: Woodrow Wilson Center Press and Johns Hopkins University Press, 1995), 136–62.

16. See David Pion-Berlin, "Between Confrontation and Accommodation: Military and Government Policy in Democratic Argentina," *Journal of Latin American Studies* 23 (October 1991): 543–71; Deborah L. Norden, "Democratic Consolidation and Military Professionalism: Argentina in the 1980s," *Journal of Interamerican Studies and World Affairs* 32 (Fall 1990): 151–76; and J. Samuel Fitch and Andrés Fontana, "Military Policy and Democratic Consolidation in Latin America" (Working Paper No. 58, CEDES, Buenos Aires, 1990).

17. Despite evidence of substantial progress, concessions on human rights issues, reversal of legislation on the military's role in internal security that had been advanced under the Alfonsín administration, and persistent internal problems in the military still worked in the early 1990s against full normalization. See Rosendo Fraga, "Permanente inestabilidad: Frágiles relaciones cívico-militares en Argentina" (unpubl. ms., March 1991).

18. See Deborah L. Norden, "Keeping the Peace, Outside and In: Argentina's UN Missions," *International Peacekeeping* 2 (Autumn 1995): 330–49; and Rosendo Fraga, "La política de defensa Argentina a veinte años del último golpe," *Fuerzas armadas y sociedad* 11 (April–June 1996): 15–18.

19. See Paul W. Zagorski, "Civil-Military Relations and Argentine Democracy: The Armed Forces Under the Menem Government," *Armed Forces and Society* 20 (Spring 1994): 423–37; Andrés Fontana, "Más entendimiento entre civiles y militares," *El cronista* (Buenos Aires), 18 June 1992, 17; Rosendo Fraga, "El debate sobre la cuestión militar," *La nación* (Buenos Aires), 20 July 1992, 9; Rut Clara Diamint, "Cambios en la política de seguridad: Argentina en busca de un perfil no conflictivo," *Fuerzas armadas y sociedad* (Santiago) 7 (January–March 1992); and Ernesto López, "Argentina: Desarme de hecho y cooperación para la paz," *Fuerzas armadas y sociedad* 7 (January–March 1992).

20. *Latin American Weekly Report: Southern Cone*, April 1990, 7. For the negotiations on the transition, see Charles G. Gillespie, *Negotiating Democracy: Politicians and Generals in Uruguay* (Cambridge: Cambridge University Press, 1991).

21. Juan Rial, *Las fuerzas armadas en los años 90* (Montevideo: Peitho, 1990).

22. Proposals to shorten President Sarney's term were based on his accidental and unexpected accession. Under a compromise arranged by the moderate opposition to the military government, Sarney ran for vice-president but president-elect Tancredo Neves died shortly before he was to assume office. At the time of his inauguration, Sarney had the support of the military and a civilian coalition dominated by former supporters of the military regime. Frances Hagopian and Scott Mainwaring, "Democracy in Brazil: Problems and Prospects," *World Policy Journal* 4 (Summer 1987): 485–514.

23. Eliézer Rizzo de Oliveira, "O papel das forças armadas na nova constituição e no futuro da democracia no Brasil," *Vozes* 82 (July–December 1988): 21–27.

24. Jorge Zaverucha, *Rumor de sabres: Tutela militar ou controle civil?* (São Paulo: Editora Atica, 1994); Wendy Hunter, "Back to the Barracks? The Military's Political Role in Post-authoritarian Brazil" (paper presented at the 1992 meeting of the Latin American Studies Association, Los Angeles, 24–27 September 1992).

25. On institutional conflicts over salaries, see "Itamar chama a guarda," *Istoe*, 30 March 1994, 34–39. On lack of presidential restraint, especially Sarney's relations with the

military, see Scott Mainwaring, "Dilemmas of Multiparty Presidential Democracy: The Case of Brazil" (Working Paper No. 74, Helen Kellogg Institute for International Studies, Notre Dame, Ind., n.d.).

Domestic involvement was further complicated by the military search for a new mission, which included the battle against poverty. For an excellent presentation of these dilemmas, see Wendy Hunter, "The Brazilian Military After the Cold War: In Search of a Mission," *Studies in Comparative International Development* 28 (Winter 1994): 31–49.

26. See Wendy Hunter, "Politicians Against Soldiers: Contesting the Military in Postauthoritarian Brazil," *Comparative Politics* 27 (July 1995): 425–43; and Scott D. Tollefson, "Civil-Military Relations in Brazil: The Myth of Tutelary Democracy" (paper presented at the 1995 meeting of the Latin American Studies Association, Washington, D.C., 28–30 September 1995).

27. Felipe Agüero, "Chile: South America's Success Story?" *Current History* 92 (March 1993): 130–35; Brian Loveman, "*¿Misión cumplida?* Civil Military Relations and the Chilean Political Transition," *Journal of Interamerican Studies and World Affairs* 33 (Fall 1991): 35–74; Rhoda Rabkin, "The Aylwin Government and Tutelary Democracy: A Concept in Search of a Case?" *Journal of Interamerican Studies and World Affairs* 34 (Winter 1992–93): 119–94; and Alicia Frohmann, "Chile: External Actors and the Transition to Democracy," in Tom Farer, ed., *Beyond Sovereignty: Collectively Defending Democracy in the Americas* (Baltimore: Johns Hopkins University Press, 1996), 238–56.

28. Peru's preceding military regime had been a case of "inclusionary corporatism," which did not rely on the kind of brutal repression that characterized authoritarian rule in Argentina, Brazil, Chile, and Uruguay. See Alfred Stepan, *State and Society: Peru in Comparative Perspective* (Princeton: Princeton University Press, 1978); and Angela Cornell and Kenneth Roberts, "Democracy, Counterinsurgency and Human Rights: The Case of Peru," *Human Rights Quarterly* 12 (November 1990): 529–53.

29. See Marcial Rubio, *Ministerio de defensa: Antecedentes y retos* (Lima: APEP–Friedrich Ebert, 1987); Sandra Woy-Hazelton and William A. Hazelton, "Sustaining Democracy in Peru: Dealing with Parliamentary and Revolutionary Changes," in George A. Lopez and Michael Stohl, eds., *Liberalization and Redemocratization in Latin America* (New York: Greenwood, 1987); and Cynthia McClintock, "El gobierno aprista y la fuerza armada del Perú," in Heraclio Bonilla and Paul W. Drake, eds., *El APRA: De la ideología a la praxis* (Lima: Nuevo Mundo EIRL, 1989).

30. In a blatant display of autonomy, Peru's military reacted to Congress's investigations of human rights abuses by mobilizing tanks in the streets of Lima in 1993. See "In Peru, a 'Second Coup' Reveals the Upper Hand," *New York Times*, 2 May 1993, E6.

For Bolivia and Ecuador see Raúl Barrios and René Antonio Mayorga, *La cuestión militar en cuestión: Democracia y fuerzas armadas* (La Paz: Cebem, 1994); Anita Isaacs, *Military Rule and Transition in Ecuador* (Pittsburgh: University of Pittsburgh Press, 1983); and Catherine M. Conaghan and James Malloy, *Unsettling Statecraft: Democracy and Neoliberalism in the Central Andes* (Pittsburgh: University of Pittsburgh Press, 1994).

31. Carlos Iván Degregori and Carlos Rivera, "Perú 1980–1993: Fuerzas armadas, subversión y democracia" (Working Paper No. 53, Instituto de Estudios Peruanos, 1994).

32. See Pion-Berlin, "Between Confrontation and Accommodation"; and Pion-Berlin, "To Prosecute or to Pardon: Human Rights Decisions in the Latin American Southern Cone," *Human Rights Quarterly* 16 (February 1994): 105–30.

33. This and the following three sections draw heavily from chapter 9 of my *Soldiers, Civilians, and Democracy*.

34. Chile and Argentina made competing claims regarding border demarcation around the Beagle Channel on the Atlantic end, south of the Strait of Magellan. The Argentine military junta had ignored the ruling of arbitration by the British Crown that favored Chile. Quick international pressure prevented the likely initiation of hostilities by the Argentine junta (prior to the Falklands/Malvinas war) and led General Augusto Pinochet of Chile and

General Jorge Rafael Videla of Argentina to request a new arbitration by Pope John Paul II. Alfonsín's referendum was meant to support this peace process.

35. See Jorge Zaverucha, "Civil-Military Relations During the First Brazilian Post-transition Government: A Tutelary Democracy" (unpubl. ms., n.d.); and Louis W. Goodman, Johanna S.R. Mendelson, and Juan Rial, eds., *The Military and Democracy: The Future of Civil-Military Relations in Latin America* (Lexington, Mass.: D.C. Heath/Lexington Books, 1990).

36. This argument is developed more extensively in Agüero, "Democratic Consolidation and the Military in Southern Europe and South America."

37. J. Samuel Fitch, "Toward a Democratic Model of Civil-Military Relations for Latin America" (paper presented at the annual meeting of the International Political Science Association, Washington, D.C., 31 August 1988); and Stepan, *Rethinking Military Politics*, 139.

38. Wendy Hunter, "The Brazilian Military After the Cold War."

39. As J. Samuel Fitch put it, "the democratic professionalist alternative is difficult to sustain where military officers cannot practice their profession for lack of operating funds or where military salaries do not permit officers a minimum standard of living commensurate with other skilled professions." Fitch, "Military Role Beliefs in Latin American Democracies" (Interim Performance Report No. 3, United States Institute of Peace, Washington, D.C., 1993), 15.
An interesting comparative presentation of this argument is found in Wendy Hunter, "Contradictions of Civilian Control: Argentina, Brazil and Chile in the 1990s" (unpubl. ms., Department of Political Science, Vanderbilt University, n.d.). See also Lars Schoultz, William C. Smith, and Augusto Varas, eds., *Security, Democracy and Development in the Western Hemisphere* (New Brunswick, N.J.: Transaction, 1994).

40. New democracies, however, are not evaluated solely on the basis of economic efficacy. Based on a study of Spain, Linz and Stepan argued that democracy can be valued as the best political system even if its socioeconomic efficacy is negatively assessed: "The political perception of desired alternatives has a greater impact on the survival of democratic regimes than economic or social problems *per se*." Juan J. Linz and Alfred Stepan, "Political Crafting of Democratic Consolidation or Destruction: European and South American Comparisons," in Robert A. Pastor, ed., *Democracy in the Americas: Stopping the Pendulum* (New York: Holmes and Meier, 1989), 46.
Linz and Stepan maintain that memories of atrocities and violations of liberties that took place under the previous authoritarian regime provide new democracies with additional public confidence and support. This theory would not apply to cases that were regarded as less politically repressive and more economically successful, as was argued for the case of Brazil in O'Donnell, "Transitions, Continuities and Paradoxes." The extent to which this "system-" or "regime"-tied confidence is in fact transferred without losses to specific administrations is unclear, especially in the face of extreme economic distress and perceived failure of government policy.

41. A vivid, and perhaps extreme, example of a government's incapacity to meet challenges from the military was President Alfonsín's decision to resign in order to allow Carlos Menem to assume the presidency of Argentina four months earlier than dictated by law.

42. See Juan Linz and Arturo Valenzuela, eds., *The Failure of Presidentialism in Latin America* (Baltimore and London: Johns Hopkins University Press, 1994).

43. Carol Graham, "Peru's APRA Party in Power: Impossible Revolution, Relinquished Reform" (paper presented at the 1989 meeting of the Latin American Studies Association, Miami, December 1989).

44. Gary W. Wynia, "Campaigning for President in Argentina," *Current History* 88 (March 1989): 133–36, 144–45; and William C. Smith, "Políticas económicas de choque y transición democrática en Argentina y Brasil," *Revista mexicana de sociología* 2 (April–June 1988).

45. While support for Alfonsín's government declined dramatically in Argentina, attitudes toward democracy remained basically unchanged. See Edgardo Catterberg, "Attitudes Towards Democracy in Argentina During the Transition Period," *International Journal of Public Opinion Research* 2 (1990): 158, 165–66.

In Peru, the combination of the disastrous economy, inherited from the policies of Alan García, and escalation in the subversive war led to substantial public support for nondemocratic solutions such as President Fujimori's decision to break with the constitution.

46. Kurt Weyland, "The Rise and Fall of President Collor and Its Impact on Brazilian Democracy," *Journal of Interamerican Studies and World Affairs* 35 (Spring 1993): 1–37.

47. Marcelo Cavarozzi, "Patterns of Elite Negotiation and Confrontation in Argentina and Chile," in John Higley and Richard Gunther, eds., *Elites and Democratic Consolidation in Latin America and Southern Europe* (Cambridge: Cambridge University Press, 1992), 208–36.

48. See Scott Mainwaring, "Brazilian Party Underdevelopment in Comparative Perspective," *Political Science Quarterly* 107 (Winter 1992–93): 677–709; and Mainwaring, "Politicians, Parties and Electoral Systems: Brazil in Comparative Perspective," *Comparative Politics* 24 (October 1991): 21–43.

49. For a general discussion of military division in Argentina, see Deborah L. Norden, *Military Rebellion in Argentina: Between Coups and Consolidation* (Lincoln: University of Nebraska Press, 1996).

50. Laurence Whitehead, "Democracy by Convergence and Southern Europe: A Comparative Politics Perspective," in Geoffrey Pridham, ed., *Encompassing Democracy: The International Context of Regime Transition in Southern Europe* (New York: St. Martin's, 1991).

51. Although the presence of NATO was generally beneficial for accommodating the military in democratization, it certainly was not a panacea. NATO unquestioningly accommodated authoritarian Greece and Portugal, and Alexander Haig, NATO commander at the time, dismissed the 1981 coup attempt in Spain as "an internal affair."

52. Heraldo Muñoz, "The Rise and Decline of the Inter-American System: A Latin American View," in Richard J. Bloomfield and Gregory F. Treverton, eds., *Alternative to Intervention: A New U.S.-Latin American Security Relationship* (Boulder, Colo.: Lynne Rienner, 1990); and James R. Kurth, "The Rise and Decline of the Inter-American System: A U.S. View," in Bloomfield and Treverton, eds., *Alternative to Intervention.*

53. See Felipe Agüero, "The Latin American Military: Development, Reform and 'Nation-Building'?" in Lars Schoultz, William C. Smith, and Augusto Varas, eds., *Security, Democracy, and Development in U.S.-Latin American Relations* (Miami: North-South Center, University of Miami; New Brunswick, N.J.: Transaction, 1994), 243–64; and J. Samuel Fitch, "Democracy, Human Rights, and the Armed Forces in Latin America," in Jonathan Hartlyn, Lars Schoultz, and Augusto Varas, eds., *The United States and Latin America in the 1990s: Beyond the Cold War* (Chapel Hill: University of North Carolina Press, 1992), 181–213.

54. See Teresa P.R. Caldeira and James Holston, "Citizenship, Justice, Law: Limits and Prospects of Democratization in Brazil" (paper presented at the conference "Fault Lines of Democratic Governance in the Americas," North-South Center, University of Miami, 4–6 May 1995).

11

CIVIL-MILITARY RELATIONS IN SOUTHEAST ASIA

Harold Crouch

Harold Crouch *is a senior fellow at the Australian National University's Research School of Pacific and Asian Studies. Previously he taught political science at the University of the Philippines, the University of Indonesia, and the National University of Malaysia. Among his publications are* The Army and Politics in Indonesia *(1978) and* Government and Society in Malaysia *(1996).*

During the last two decades, military involvement in government has receded significantly in only two Southeast Asian countries—the Philippines and Thailand. A major challenge faced by "third wave" democracies is the need to prevent the military, displaced from its privileged position under authoritarian rule, from reasserting itself. This chapter focuses on the experiences of the Philippines and Thailand, but comparisons are made with Malaysia and Singapore, which have remained under civilian rule since obtaining independence, as well as with Indonesia and Burma, where the military has been the dominant political force since the 1960s.

Direct participation in government by the military in the Philippines was limited mainly to the period of authoritarian rule under President Ferdinand Marcos between 1972 and 1986. After the United States granted the country independence in 1946, the Philippines had a democratic political system until President Marcos declared martial law in 1972. Marcos's authoritarian regime relied on the military to repress opposition, and officers were rewarded with appointments in government administration and in state enterprises. But the government was largely civilian in composition; nearly all cabinet positions were occupied by civilians. Popular opposition to the regime culminated in February 1986 in massive protests against a manipulated election. In a dramatic showdown, military dissidents sided with the "people's power revolution" that forced Marcos to flee into exile. The restoration of democracy under President Corazon Aquino, however, was not fully accepted by the military, some of whom felt that their services in bringing Marcos down had not been sufficiently recognized. During the next four years the Aquino administration survived no fewer than six coup attempts launched by various disgruntled military groups. In 1992 the first presidential election under the new democratic constitution was held. General Fidel Ramos, a former chief of staff of the armed forces who had formed his own political party after retirement, won a narrow victory and ushered in a period of democratic consolidation.

In contrast, the military in Thailand dominated the government for much of the period following the overthrow of the absolute monarchy in 1932. Occasional interludes of civilian rule were brief and normally ended in military coups. The military, however, was sharply divided into factions that sometimes attempted coups against one another. In 1973 a popular uprising in Bangkok felled an internally divided military regime, but a coup in 1976 ended a short-lived attempt to establish a democratic system. Another coup in 1977 resulted in the appointment of the supreme commander of the armed forces as prime minister. A new constitution guaranteed the military a role in government and elections were held under military supervision, but rivalries within the military continued. In 1980 the prime minister was replaced by the army commander in chief, General Prem Tinsulanond, who, like his predecessor, was not an elected member of parliament. During the 1980s, however, the parliament became more important and the prime minister included party representatives in his cabinet. Meanwhile, a dissident military faction launched unsuccessful coup attempts in 1981 and 1985. Although Prem survived the coup attempts, he finally resigned in 1988 rather than face likely defeat in parliament.

Prem's resignation in the face of a loss of parliamentary support was a milestone in Thailand's democratic transition, but democracy was by no means consolidated. The elected civilian government that took office soon gained a reputation for unbridled corruption. Its overthrow by the military in 1991 did not attract widespread public protest, but massive demonstrations broke out in Bangkok when the architect of the coup, General Suchinda Kraprayoon, installed himself as prime minister following an election in 1992. The military, however, was disgraced when troops fired on the demonstrators, killing dozens. Suchinda was forced to resign and the discredited military adopted a low political profile. A fresh election later in 1992 saw the formation of a civilian government, which remained in power until a new civilian government was elected in 1995. Another civilian government was elected in November 1996. Democratic consolidation in Thailand, however, proceeded under the shadow of the military and the possibility of another military intervention.

Before discussing the process of democratic transition and consolidation in the Philippines and Thailand, it is necessary to take into account "given" economic and social conditions. Such "givens" can change over time but are not subject to short-term manipulation by political actors. These factors may either impose limits on the democratization process or provide opportunities to be exploited by democratizing forces.

Economic Development and Democracy

It is frequently argued that economic development is positively associated with democratization. Democracy, according to such arguments, is more likely to be consolidated in relatively wealthy countries and less likely to emerge in poor countries. Civilian rule, too, is more likely to be entrenched in wealthy countries than in poorer countries, while military forces tend to participate in government more often in poorer countries than in wealthy ones. In Southeast Asia, a rough correlation can be found between level of economic development, measured in terms of per-capita national income, and the nature of civil-military relations.

Specifically, Brunei and Singapore were classified by the World Bank in 1994 as high-income countries and Malaysia as an upper-middle-income country.[1] Although Brunei is a monarchy and neither Singapore nor Malaysia could be considered to be more than semidemocratic, all three have civilian governments and have never experienced military intervention. On the other hand, the five Southeast Asian countries classified as low-income countries—Indonesia, Burma, and the three countries of Indochina—have been ruled for several decades by military-dominated or communist governments. Democratic movements have either failed to appear in these countries or have been too weak to bring about significant progress toward democratization. The two countries that were classified as lower-middle-income countries—the Philippines and Thailand—have both experienced significant democratization during the last two decades. The democratization process was by no means smooth and was interrupted in both cases by coup attempts, including one in Thailand that succeeded.

The correlation between high income and democratization is, of course, not simple and automatic, as the cases of Singapore, Malaysia, and Brunei show. But Southeast Asian experience suggests that military-dominated or military-influenced authoritarian regimes are more likely to become vulnerable to democratic pressures after the economy has graduated from low-income status.

While the Philippines and Thailand both belong to the lower-middle-income group, the Thai economy has grown at a much faster rate than that of the Philippines, which stagnated throughout much of the 1980s and has grown only slowly in the 1990s. Indeed, in terms of purchasing power parity the Philippines not only is now far behind Thailand but has also fallen behind Indonesia.[2] Despite their common categorization in terms of per-capita income, it might, therefore, be expected that the dynamics of democratic consolidation and military intervention would be different in the two countries.

Class Structure and Ethnicity

It is plausible that military domination is less likely in societies where economic development has produced class structures in which the business, middle, and working classes are well entrenched. In such societies, policy making is complicated by the need to consult with the representatives of major social forces who are strong enough to force governments to take their interests into account. Military domination is also more difficult to achieve where regional elites have local roots strong enough to resist central domination. Such class structures encourage negotiation and favor democratic consolidation.

In fact, the class structures of the two democratizing countries developed in significantly different ways. In contrast to the other Southeast Asian countries, the Philippines saw the emergence of a class of large, regionally dispersed landlords in the nineteenth century, while the central bureaucracy was historically weak under Spanish and then American colonial rule. Powerful local landlord families formed alliances that dominated politics after independence in 1946 until President Marcos introduced martial law and disbanded the Congress in 1972. But Marcos's campaign against the "oligarchs" did not destroy their social power. They remained in a good position to reemerge politically after the restoration of democracy in 1986. Since then they have continued to dominate the political parties and the Congress.[3] A substantial indigenous business class also developed in the Philippines, in contrast to the situation in most of Southeast Asia, where domestic business is still largely in Chinese hands. The regionally dispersed "feudal" class structure of the Philippines makes centralized military domination difficult because of the presence of entrenched local political forces whose interests cannot easily be ignored. Although Marcos's authoritarian regime succeeded in subduing—and to some extent incorporating—the regional elites for more than a decade, they were not destroyed. Rather, they now constitute an obstacle to the restoration of authoritarian rule. In this regard, the Philippines is quite different from such military-dominated countries as Indonesia and Burma, where countervailing forces against the centralized state are far less strong. Even during the period of martial law under President Marcos, authoritarian rule in the Philippines was considerably less repressive than in the Southeast Asian countries where the military was dominant.

The class structure of Thailand, on the other hand, remained relatively undeveloped and dominated by a centralized bureaucracy until the 1970s. The state had taken the form of a "bureaucratic polity" in which the military was the strongest element.[4] Unlike in the Philippines, regional elites consisted of bureaucrats appointed by the central government, while small peasant holdings predominated in agriculture. Economic growth since the 1960s, however, resulted in growing business, middle, and working classes, which gradually undermined the military-dominated "bureaucratic polity" by providing social bases for political parties.[5] During the 1980s, regional businesspeople became influential in the main political parties and began to play a countervailing role not dissimilar to that of regional landlords in the Philippines, although the central bureaucracy in Thailand remained much stronger. The increasing complexity of the class structure in Thailand has facilitated the gradual consolidation of a relatively democratic system, making it difficult, though not impossible, for the military to contemplate taking power again.

The class structures of the Philippines and Thailand, therefore, have evolved in quite different ways; in both, however, relatively autonomous classes constituted significant checks on the power of the state. While changing class structures certainly did not provide immunity against military intervention, an evolving balance made it more difficult to rule by authoritarian means and thus facilitated democratization.

Southeast Asian countries are ethnically diverse. It is perhaps not a coincidence that both Indonesia and Burma, the two states where the military has been dominant during the past three decades, are ethnically very heterogeneous and experienced major military interventions in the context of regional rebellion.[6] In the two democratizing countries, on the other hand, the Thai Buddhist and Catholic Filipino communities constitute more than four-fifths of the population. Although linguistic and cultural differences are found within these majorities, their political salience has been limited compared with the situation in other Southeast Asian countries. In both cases, however, the central government has faced limited Muslim rebellions as well as communist-led hill-tribe resistance, but the ethnic minorities are too small to have ever posed the kind of threat to the integrity of the state that regional rebellions posed in Indonesia and Burma and therefore did not provide the same opportunity for the military to intervene. It can therefore be suggested that the absence of severe nation-dividing ethnic cleavages facilitates democratic consolidation in both Thailand and the Philippines.

Military Culture and Ideology

The armed forces of the countries of Southeast Asia have different histories, military cultures, and ideologies. These differences are reflected in military forces' organizational structures, which vary according to the extent to which the military's primary role is concerned with defense or internal security. Military culture and ideology in the Philippines and

Thailand are quite different. In one, doctrine inhibits military intervention, while in the other, military involvement in government is considered by military officers to be legitimate and normal.

The armed forces in the Philippines were established during the colonial era and inherited the American doctrine of civilian supremacy. The longstanding belief of many officers in the legitimacy of civilian rule and constitutional processes has been an obstacle to military intervention. Although some officers were attracted to the idea of intervention in the mid-1950s, their plans did not win the support of their colleagues, who continued to recognize the legitimacy of civilian rule.[7] It was only under the authoritarian regime of President Marcos after 1972 that military officers were drawn systematically by the president into government administration, though only as junior partners.[8]

The experience of martial law brought about changes in military culture, especially among younger officers. During the 1970s counterinsurgency operations increased against communist and Muslim rebels. Similar to the "new professionalism" adopted by Latin American armies, counterinsurgency doctrines that emphasized the importance of political, social, and economic, as well as military, measures made younger officers more aware of the inadequacies of government policies, with the result that they were reluctant to give blind loyalty to the civilian government.[9] Many of these officers later supported coup attempts in the late 1980s against Marcos's successor, Corazon Aquino. A survey of the views of officers who had participated in such coup attempts showed that many "(1) view politicians with disdain; (2) complain about graft and corruption in government; (3) perceive President Aquino as a weak President; (4) are dissatisfied with the present government because it is unable to deliver basic services to the people; and (5) favor a bigger decision-making role for the military in areas pertinent to it such as counterinsurgency, U.S. bases, human rights, military organization, and trial of rebel soldiers."[10]

Despite increasing interventionist sentiment within the military, the military leadership sided with President Aquino and accepted the 1987 Constitution, which declared unequivocally that "no member of the military shall engage directly or indirectly in any political partisan activity, except to vote."[11] The failure of the series of coup attempts launched by disaffected officers after the 1986 restoration of democracy indicated that belief in civilian supremacy and the democratic constitution still had many adherents among military officers, though they often sympathized with the rebels in their criticisms of the government.[12]

Military culture and ideology in Thailand, on the other hand, are no barrier to military intervention. Thailand was never directly colonized by a European power, and its military never adopted the Western notion of civilian supremacy. The reigning Chakri dynasty was, in fact, established by a military commander in the eighteenth century. Moreover, military officers were involved in the coup in 1932 that imposed constitutional limits on the monarchy. Thai officers believe that their highest allegiance to "nation, religion, and king" overrides any loyalty they might have to a particular government, and could therefore justify military intervention. Since 1932 there have been ten successful coups and seven unsuccessful coup attempts. That is an average of one coup attempt every four years.

By the 1980s, the Thai military was also influenced by "new professional" doctrines and had formulated a strategy requiring military involvement in rural development and political reform in order to combat communist insurgency. Although the military promoted the idea of "true democracy" to oppose communism, officers believed that the existing political parties prevented the attainment of that goal.[13] Military officers continue to be openly contemptuous of political parties, which they perceive to be corrupt, self-serving, and incompetent.[14] A book on democracy in Thailand, published in the mid-1990s by the military, claims that "most political parties in Thailand come into being as a means to support and sustain influence of certain individuals or group of individuals." It goes on to say that "most people join political parties with hope to gain financial support for campaigning or support from those who are already in the parties." The book concludes that Thai parties "are like heads without bodies."[15] Military officers therefore have little confidence in party politicians and believe that the military has a responsibility to intervene whenever civilian rule is deemed harmful to the higher interests of "nation, religion, and king."

Organizational Structure and Size

The ideological inclinations of the military are reflected in, and reinforced by, its organizational structure. In some countries, the organizational structure of the armed forces facilitates political intervention and control. In military-dominated Indonesia, for example, the army is organized primarily as an internal-security force and the distinction between military and police roles is blurred. Its "territorial" structure runs parallel to the civilian administration and enables the army to oversee political activity down to the village level.[16] In civilian-ruled Singapore and Malaysia, on the other hand, the emphasis is on defense against an external enemy, while internal security is primarily a police responsibility. Although the military in both the Philippines and Thailand enhanced their internal-security functions in response to communist and Muslim insurgencies during the 1970s and 1980s, neither developed organizational structures with the reach of the Indonesian "territorial" system. The military's capacity to intervene is, however, greater in Thailand than it is in the Philippines.

In the Philippines, the alliance with the United States and the presence of American bases initially relieved the armed forces of the need to devote resources to external defense. In response to the communist Huk revolt in the late 1940s, the military, encouraged by the Americans, gave priority to counterinsurgency; after the defeat of the Huks, however, primary responsibility for internal order returned to the paramilitary police constabulary. Following the introduction of martial law in 1972, both communist and Muslim revolts intensified, with the result that both the constabulary and the army were regularly involved in counterinsurgency operations. The security forces were also used by President Marcos under martial law to detain and sometimes assassinate political opponents as well as to manipulate the results of elections. At the local level, the military organized the Civilian Home Defense Force (CHDF), the local units of which were mobilized against both rebels and political dissidents while often falling under the effective control of local landlords as semiprivate armies.[17] Civil rights activists regarded the CHDF as a major perpetrator of human rights abuses.

Yet the Philippine military lacked the permanent institutionalized structures of control found in Indonesia's "territorial" system. Following the overthrow of the Marcos regime, the military remained engaged in counterinsurgency operations, but eventually the government initiated negotiations with the communists and Muslims as well as with rebel military groups. Meanwhile, the notorious CHDF was dissolved in 1987, although the military insisted that new Citizen Armed Forces Geographical Units be formed to assist them in local operations. In 1991, the potential for military intervention was reduced when the constabulary, which had hitherto been part of the armed forces, was separated and amalgamated with local police forces in the new Philippines National Police under the Department of the Interior and Local Government. Responsibility for internal security was thus transferred in principle to the police, while the armed forces concentrated on external defense. In practice, however, implementation of the transfer was slow, and in the mid-1990s the army continued to be in charge of internal security in the southern island of Mindanao and the Cordilleras in northern Luzon, where Muslim and communist guerrillas were still active.

Like the Philippines, Thailand had been allied militarily with the United States, but its proximity to potential communist threats from Vietnam and China led it to devote more of its own military resources to defense. Until the mid-1960s, internal security was a police responsibility, but the rapid expansion of communist insurgency resulted in the army's taking control of counterinsurgency operations.[18] The Communist Suppression Operations Command was established in 1965; it was renamed the Internal Security Operations Command (ISOC) in 1974 after diplomatic relations were established with China. Although structurally separate from the military, the ISOC was headed by the army commander in chief, and its personnel overlapped with that of the army's Civil Affairs Center, which was headed by the army's assistant chief of staff for civil affairs, while regional army commanders headed the ISOC at the regional level. The Civil Affairs Center was concerned with political work in areas where the Communist Party was active. Among its tasks was the organization of paramilitary National Defense Volunteers at the village level. It also established the Volunteer Development and Self-Defense Villages program, which was engaged in rural development, and the Military Reservists for National Security, whose members were given political indoctrination and were expected to participate in local government as well as provide intelligence for the military.[19]

Through the ISOC, the Thai military had a more institutionalized capacity for maintaining control and mobilizing political support in the rural areas than did the Philippine military. For example, the army often mobilized votes for military-backed candidates in elections. Nevertheless, the ISOC's operations were concentrated primarily in areas of communist activity, unlike the Indonesian "territorial" structure, which covered every subdistrict in the country. Moreover, the local organizations under the ISOC were formally under the authority of the Ministry of the Interior through the regional governors, who exercised some influence over their operations. Another important counterinsurgency body, the Village Scouts, had been established by the police in 1972 and was structurally part of the Ministry of the Interior.[20] Following the defeat of the communist insurgency in the early 1980s, the role of village-level paramilitary organizations declined, and the ISOC was restructured in 1987. Although military officers continued to staff the ISOC, the prime minister replaced the army commander in chief as its director-general.[21] Apart from its role in the ISOC, the army also exercises political influence through two television channels and many radio stations.

The capacity of the military to dominate the government is also affected by its size. In Thailand, where the military has often intervened successfully, the current size of the armed forces together with paramilitary forces is more than 300,000. In the Philippines, where the population of 65 million is slightly larger than that of either Thailand (58 million) or Burma (44 million), the military is much smaller. The Philippine military numbered only 54,000 in 1972, but it grew under martial law to 157,000 before falling back to 106,000 today, following the transfer of the 40,000 members of the paramilitary constabulary to the police. Besides its lack of organizational capacity, the relatively small size of the Philippines' armed forces may have contributed to a lack of confidence on the part of many officers in their ability to carry out a coup, let alone establish a military-dominated government.

Participation in Government and Business

The willingness of the military to withdraw from government and permit democratic consolidation is also affected by the degree to which military personnel have participated in authoritarian regimes. The extent of such participation varies considerably across different regimes.

In the Philippines, military officers did not normally play a significant role in government during the pre–martial law era. In the mid-1950s, however, President Ramón Magsaysay appointed military officers to various civilian posts, including several in the cabinet, but their participation declined under later presidents until the introduction of martial law by President Marcos in 1972.[22] Under martial law, 349 military officers were appointed to positions outside the armed forces, although many served in the Department of National Defense. After martial law was lifted in 1980, the number dropped to 115. Of 12 Presidential Regional Officers for Development, six were military officers, while two military officers were appointed as governors in southern provinces where Muslim insurgents were operating.[23] Although military participation in government under Marcos rose sharply, the military was by no means the dominant element. Throughout the entire period of authoritarian rule, the Department of National Defense was headed by Juan Ponce Enrile, a civilian, and only rarely did ministers, such as Romulo Espaldon, the minister for Muslim affairs in the early 1980s, have military backgrounds.

The role of the military in government in Thailand was far more extensive. Military officers dominated most administrations until the 1980s, and many served as cabinet ministers. Even during a democratic interregnum between 1973 and 1976, military officers were prominent in civilian-led governments. Unlike in Indonesia and Burma, however, where military officers hold important bureaucratic positions and often serve as regional governors, Thai officers were not normally appointed to positions in the bureaucracy or regional administration. Referring to the 1970s, John Girling noted that "broadly, the military does not interfere with administrative functions; nor do civilian officials (including those in the Ministry of Foreign Affairs) trespass on the field of security."[24] During the period of communist insurgency, military officers were sometimes appointed as governors in "sensitive" provinces, but governors are now civilian officials appointed by the Ministry of the Interior. It has therefore been easier for the military to relinquish control of the government in Thailand than it would be in Indonesia or Burma, where the military is deeply entrenched in the central and regional bureaucracy.

The involvement of military officers in business also creates vested interests in the continuation of military participation in government. Military officers have often obtained lucrative appointments in state enterprises and have won favors for private companies with which they were associated. Removing these officers from state enterprises and reducing special privileges flowing to military-connected private companies causes considerable resentment among officers directly affected by these measures as well as among middle-ranking officers whose expectations of future access are threatened. On the other hand, such reforms do not necessarily alienate professionally oriented officers and may indeed be welcomed by them as a way of improving the image of the military in society.

In the Philippines, the involvement of military officers in business was minimal until the martial-law era, when President Marcos cultivated military support by appointing military officers to head many state enterprises and agencies. Military officers took control of important public utilities, including electricity, railways, airlines, waterworks, and sewerage, as well as several private corporations in the steel and shipping industries. Military officers were also appointed to the boards of some of the companies previously owned by political opponents of Marcos.[25] Two military-affiliated investment corporations were also established.[26] After the fall of Marcos, Corazon Aquino's administration removed many of these officers. Their removal, however, contributed to the military's alienation from her administration.[27]

In Thailand, it had been common before 1973 for senior military officers to head public enterprises and to join the boards of private companies, which were often managed, in practice, by Chinese businessmen.[28] During the 1980s, the economy grew rapidly while the government became gradually more civilianized, making it less necessary for businesspeople to cultivate military patrons. Nevertheless, military interests continued to control many state enterprises, and it was only in 1992, after the military had further discredited itself by firing at demonstrators in Bangkok, that senior military officers were finally removed from the boards of several major state enterprises.[29] It has also been common for military officers in the provinces to cultivate links with regional businessmen.

Civilian Institutions

The military was therefore much more inclined toward intervention in Thailand than in the Philippines. Thai military officers had no commitment to the concept of civilian supremacy, and the army's long engagement in counterinsurgency operations had created an organizational structure that could be mobilized to back military intervention. The military in the Philippines, on the other hand, acknowledged civilian supremacy and in the 1990s was transferring responsibility for internal security to the police. The Thai military's propensity to intervene was reinforced by its long tradition of deep involvement in government and business, whereas the Philippine military's experience in these areas had been limited largely to the Marcos era.

Military withdrawal from government, however, does not depend on the behavior of the military alone but also requires the development of effective civilian institutions, particularly the bureaucracy and political parties. The circumstances of the bureaucracy and political parties under authoritarian regimes are by no means uniform. In Indonesia and Burma, for example, where military domination is entrenched, the central bureaucracy and regional government are deeply penetrated by the military, while the scope for nongovernment political parties is very limited. In the two democratizing countries, on the other hand, authoritarian rule was not accompanied by extensive military penetration of the bureaucracy. Moreover, in both the Philippines and Thailand, independent political parties had some leeway to organize themselves, although they lacked the enduring organizational networks found in such countries as Malaysia and Singapore, where civilian rule is entrenched.

The Thai bureaucracy is strong and centralized, but it has never succumbed to extensive military penetration.

The bureaucracies of the Philippines and Thailand are very different from each other but are similar in that military influence in each was minimized. The Philippine central bureaucracy's weakness, more than its strength, contributed to democratization, especially at the provincial level, where governors are not appointed by the central government but are elected. In addition to 73 governors, there are 60 mayors and some 17,000 other officials who are elected at the municipal and lower levels. Even during the authoritarian rule of President Marcos, local elections continued to be held, and opposition candidates occasionally won. The long history of provincial and municipal elections has created strong interests in maintaining civilian rule and has been an important barrier to military intervention.

In contrast to the Philippine bureaucracy, the Thai bureaucracy is strong and centralized, but it too has never succumbed to extensive military penetration. Its strength is particularly evident in regional administration, which is controlled by the central government through the Department of the Interior. While the centralized bureaucracies of Indonesia and Burma are penetrated by the military, regional governors in Thailand are normally drawn from the professional, civilian civil service. Although regional military commanders are by no means without influence in regional and local government, authority remains in the hands of civilian bureaucrats. The presence of an entrenched civilian bureaucracy sets an important limit to military influence and facilitates the consolidation of civilian rule. It does not necessarily promote democratization, however, as indicated by the central bureaucracy's successful resistance to demands in 1994 for the election of regional governors.[30]

The development of political parties, too, followed different paths in the Philippines and Thailand. In both, however, parties are still far from being fully institutionalized and continue to lack entrenched grassroots networks. They are usually formed around personalities whose rivalries regularly lead to party splits and the formation of new parties. Party membership is fluid and motivated largely by patronage considerations.

The history of political parties in the Philippines goes back to the early part of the century, when the American colonial rulers held nationwide elections. After independence in 1946, a two-party system based on the American model was established; the two parties were essentially landlord-dominated coalitions competing for patronage opportunities. The parties virtually collapsed following the declaration of martial law in 1972, but the long tradition of party activity was not extinguished entirely by the authoritarian regime. The restoration of democratic elections after the overthrow of Marcos in 1986 saw the emergence of new parties, which, like the old parties, were mobilized to support personalities rather than policies. Parties rose and fell with each new aspirant for political leadership, while mergers and alliances between hitherto rival parties were common. At the regional level parties were controlled by landlord families and other local bosses who relied on patronage distribution and sometimes coercion to maintain political support.[31] Parties in the Philippines are thus still far from being institutionalized in the way that parties are in Malaysia and Singapore. Nevertheless, the long tradition of elections contested by political parties, a tradition that was reinforced by the negative experience of authoritarian rule under Marcos, has given democratic elections and civilian government a relatively high degree of legitimacy. Military intervention is widely, although by no means universally, considered illegitimate.[32]

Political parties in Thailand have been much less influential than they have been in the Philippines. In Thailand, parties were often banned in the past, reemerging temporarily during short periods of political liberalization. The democratic interregnum from 1973 to 1976 was too brief for parties to develop grassroots organizations, and they had no capacity to resist the coups that restored military domination in 1976 and 1977. The new military-dominated government immediately banned political parties, but the faction-riven military soon permitted them to reappear, and elections were held regularly during the 1980s. Initially little more than city-based personal electoral machines, the parties gradually developed electoral and patronage networks in the provinces.[33] By the end of the 1980s, some parties not only had the backing of business groups in Bangkok but also had acquired strong regional bases where local businesspeople looked to parties for commercial advantages. Several parties were backed by military factions, and some were headed by retired military officers.

Party loyalties, however, are weak, and leaders often cross from one party to another with little pretense of standing for distinctive principles and policies. Elections are quite blatant exercises in vote-buying, especially in the rural areas, where it is often said that the only benefits democracy brings to voters are the bribes given to them during election campaigns.[34] Although the military permitted an elected civilian government to take office in 1988, the blatant corruption of many of its ministers made it vulnerable to a military coup in 1991. The extent of popular disenchantment with the government was shown by the absence of widespread protest when it was overthrown. Demonstrations in Bangkok the following year, however, forced the resignation of General Suchinda Kraprayoon as prime minister, suggesting that the public was even less attracted to the restoration of military domination than it had been to the earlier civilian regime. Civilian government was restored and elections held three times. The first government, however, fell after a corruption scandal in 1995. It was succeeded by a government that was widely perceived as extremely corrupt and incompetent. A third civilian government, elected in November 1996, included several parties that had been members of the previous coalition. The reputation of civilian government, therefore, was not good and the possibility of another military intervention could not be dismissed.

Progress toward democratic transition and consolidation is also influenced, sometimes quite decisively, by special institutions peculiar to particular countries. In the two democratizing countries of Southeast Asia, no study of evolving civil-military relations would be complete without reference to the role of the Catholic Church in the Philippines and the monarchy in Thailand.

The Philippines is the only predominantly Christian country in Southeast Asia. In a country where about 85 percent of the people are Catholic, it is hardly surprising that the church wields considerable political influence. The church, however, is not a monolithic organization and has often been divided on political issues. During the Marcos era, a large number of bishops supported, or at least accepted, the authoritarian regime, although a minority were open critics. The Archbishop of Manila, Cardinal Sin, adopted a middle position of "critical collaboration." The government's apparent involvement in the assassination of Benigno Aquino in 1983 turned many priests against Marcos and led them to support Aquino's widow in the rigged 1986 presidential election, which precipitated the massive demonstrations that forced Marcos to flee the country. Cardinal Sin's public support for the demonstrators may have been decisive not only in emboldening them but also in persuading soldiers to abandon President Marcos. Cardinal Sin also provided strong support for Corazon Aquino against the six coup attempts launched during her presidency.

In Thailand, the growing strength of civilian institutions was endorsed by the monarch. In planning their political moves, military leaders could not afford to ignore his reactions, since the outcome of coup attempts normally depended on the king's approval. The present king's attitude toward democratization, however, has been somewhat ambivalent. He endorsed the "revolution" against military rule in 1973 but also endorsed the coups that restored military domination in 1976 and 1977. The king's disapproval seems to have been decisive in the failure of coup attempts in 1981 and 1985, while he apparently approved of the coup against Chatichai in 1991. After demonstrators were fired at in 1992, he admonished both the prime minister, General Suchinda, and the leader of the demonstrations, Major-General Chamlong Srimuang, and then gave his support to the elected civilian government that eventually took office. There is no guarantee, of course, that the king's willingness to endorse democratic governments will be passed on to his heir.

Civilian institutions, therefore, are only partially developed in the Philippines and Thailand. In the capital cities of both countries, popular opinion is strongly against military intervention, but institutional barriers to the extension of military power differ. Although political parties are widely regarded as corrupt and self-serving in the Philippines, a long tradition of competitive elections at all levels of government constitutes a major barrier to military intervention. Moreover, the political parties are largely controlled by, and serve the interests of, a powerful landlord class. In Thailand, on the other hand, the rise of political parties is a recent phenomenon at the provincial level, but the centralized civilian bureaucracy is entrenched and serves to balance military influence, although military and bureaucratic interests in practice often coincide.

The Military and Democratization

It is hardly surprising, given the differences between the military and civilian institutions of the Philippines and Thailand, that the role of the military in democratic transition and consolidation in the two countries has been different. In the Philippines, the military had been a junior partner in a civilian-dominated regime, while in Thailand the military had been the dominant force in previous authoritarian governments. There were, nevertheless, important similarities. In both countries, factional conflict within the military undermined the foundations of authoritarian rule and later contributed to democratic consolidation by preventing military resurgence. In both cases, elements in the military resisted democratization by launching coup attempts, but military disunity ensured their failure. Democratic consolidation, however, required that military officers be persuaded to accept the new order. They had to be convinced that they would not suffer retribution for their earlier behavior and that they would not be excluded from opportunities to participate in politics and business.

The democratization of authoritarian regimes normally follows sharp factional conflict within the regime itself. Factionalism within the military, whether the regime is military-dominated or only military-supported, is an important part of elite factionalism. In both the Philippines and Thailand, disunity within the military was of crucial importance. Not only did factionalism pave the way to democratization, but the failure to restore military unity also prevented military resurgence and may well have been essential for democratic consolidation.

By the early 1980s, the Marcos regime in the Philippines was divided at the top. The economy was in decline and popular opposition was growing. Mass demonstrations followed the assassination of opposition leader Benigno Aquino in 1983, convincing many politicians that it was time to abandon a sinking ship. Although all of the military leaders were in fact protégés of Marcos, the chief of staff of the armed forces, General Fabian Ver, was at loggerheads with his deputy, General Fidel Ramos, who was supported by the civilian minister for national defense, Juan Ponce Enrile. Fearing that Marcos would back Ver and that he might be vulnerable to an assassination attempt, Enrile organized a group of young officers in the semiclandestine Reform the Armed Forces of the Philippines Movement (RAM). Marcos then tried to rig the 1986 presidential election in his favor, but mass demonstrations against his regime followed. Plans for a RAM-led coup against Marcos were leaked. Anticipating a counterblow from the president, Enrile and his protégés withdrew to the military headquarters, where they were joined by Ramos in their challenge to Marcos. In a dramatic confrontation, demonstrators blocked the advance of loyalist forces and prevented them from doing battle with Ramos, Enrile, and their rebel forces. In the end, rather than massacre the civilian demonstrators clogging the road to the military headquarters, and in response to appeals from such church leaders as Cardinal Sin, the loyalists abandoned the president, who was forced to flee the country.

In Marcos's place, Corazon Aquino, the "loser" of the presidential election and widow of the opposition leader assassinated in 1983, took office by acclamation. Supported initially by an awkward alliance of anti-Marcos democrats and dissident military officers, the new government rested on insecure foundations. The new president was suspicious of military officers who had been part of the Marcos regime and who therefore, in her view, bore some responsibility for her husband's long imprisonment and assassination. Moreover, she possessed few political skills and relied heavily on advisors with strong antimilitary sentiments. This alienated many military officers, who were also disappointed by her failure to recognize their services in overthrowing Marcos. During the next four years, no fewer than six coup attempts were launched by various military factions.[35] The coup plotters, who included both Marcos loyalists and RAM officers, were usually as much opposed to one another as they were to President Aquino and were all defeated by the dominant faction headed by General Ramos, whom Aquino had appointed as chief of staff and then as secretary for national defense.

There seems little doubt that a united military could have deposed Aquino, but the divisions within the armed forces between Ramos loyalists, Marcos remnants, and Enrile's RAM group were so deep that the military was not able to cooperate effectively to accomplish this. Continuing military disunity in the Philippines was a vital condition for the consolidation of democracy during this period. By the early 1990s, however, General Ramos had appointed his own men to the top military positions, while the coup leaders had been dismissed, had been imprisoned, or were "on the run." By 1992, when Ramos himself was elected president, although with less than a quarter of the votes, intramilitary quarreling had subsided and the era of coup attempts seemed to have passed.

Factionalism in Thailand

After overthrowing a weak democratic regime in 1976, the Thai military attempted to establish a system that would guarantee it a continuing role in the government. A new constitution in 1978 provided for an elected National Assembly but also ensured military domination of a powerful appointed Senate and permitted a nonelected general to remain as prime minister. General Kriangsak Chommanand, however, was unable to unite the military behind his leadership and, in 1980, lost his Assembly majority when the main military factions, including an increasingly influential group of "Young Turks," turned against him. The commander in chief of the army at the time, General Prem Tinsulanond, was endorsed by the Assembly as Kriangsak's successor but was also unable to establish full control over the military. Conscious of his vulnerability to challenges from one military faction or another, Prem increasingly relied on parliamentary support and made a series of alliances with civilian political parties. On several occasions, he was forced to reconstitute his cabinet in order to maintain his parliamentary majority. In 1986, the Assembly was dissolved and an election held after proposed legislation was defeated. Finally, Prem resigned in 1988 rather than face the prospect of losing a no-confidence motion.

Continuing factionalism within the military prevented it from reasserting itself. The military's declining influence was particularly evident in 1983, when it was unable to block the implementation of constitutional provisions preventing serving officers from being appointed as cabinet ministers or from sitting in the lower house of the National Assembly. Military frustration with the Prem government led to two failed coup attempts in 1981 and 1985, both of which were launched by Prem's former allies in the "Young Turk" faction. In the mid-1980s, Prem also managed to outmaneuver and replace his own supreme commander, General Arthit Kamlang-ek, who seemed to have designs on his office.

Prem's fall in 1988 marked a watershed in the democratization process. When Prem lost support in the Assembly, the divided military did nothing to save him, nor could it agree on a successor from within its own ranks. Yet the army's commander in chief, General Chaovalit Yongchaiyuth, played a major role in the negotiations that led to the appointment of Chatichai Choonhavan as the leader of the Chart Thai party, making him the first elected civilian prime minister since the 1976 coup.

Although Chatichai was a retired military officer, he had no strong military base. In the late 1950s, he had been forced out of the army when his faction found itself on the losing side of an internecine struggle. The Chatichai government, however, soon acquired a reputation for excessive corruption, while its relations with the military deteriorated. Dissatisfaction with Chatichai seems to have made the military more united than it had been during the previous decade, and in 1991 the government was overthrown in a bloodless coup.

The military, however, did not want to provoke popular opposition by immediately forming a military-dominated government. Instead, it established a military-dominated National Peace-Keeping Council, which appointed a new government headed by a nonparty civilian technocrat, Anand Panyarachun, to hold office until elections were held in 1992. In that election, a coalition of parties sympathetic to the military won a majority of seats and eventually proposed the appointment of General Suchinda Kraprayoon, the commander in chief of the army and architect of the previous year's coup, as prime minister. Suchinda's appointment precipitated the massive opposition in Bangkok that was suppressed when military forces fired on demonstrators, killing at least 50 and possibly many more. In response, the king withdrew Suchinda's appointment and reappointed Anand until a new election was held later in the year. This time, a coalition of civilian parties was successful, headed by Chuan Leekpai, who took office as prime minister. In 1995 and 1996, further elections were held that produced new civilian governments.

The democratization process in Thailand was thus very gradual. Factional disunity within the military had forced General Kriangsak and then General Prem to turn to the civilian political parties for parliamentary support. The 1980s had seen the gradual strengthening of the political parties and other organizations to the point where they were strong enough to depose General Prem's government in 1988 and later to challenge and defeat the military in its attempt to regain political power in 1991 and 1992. If a military "strongman" like those of the pre-1973 era had emerged and imposed unity on the military after 1976, it is doubtful that the development of civilian political forces during the 1980s would have been so effective.

The bases of military factionalism in the Philippines and Thailand were various.[36] In both, loyalties were often based on year of graduation from the military academy. In Thailand, Class 5, consisting of officers who graduated in 1958 from the Chulachomklao Military Academy five years after the adoption of a new curriculum modeled on that of West Point, was a particularly cohesive group headed in the 1990s by General Suchinda. The rival group of "Young Turks" was made up largely of officers from Class 7, while General Chaovalit's strongest support came from Class 1. In the Philippines, members of graduating classes from the Philippine Military Academy often felt similar bonds. Thus the main RAM leaders were members of the class of 1971.

Ideological cleavages are harder to identify. In both countries, young reform-minded officers like the RAM group in the Philippines and the "Young Turks" in Thailand banded together. Both groups had become highly politicized by their experience in counterinsurgency operations and were critical of the inadequacies of government-run rural-development programs.[37] In Thailand, the so-called Democratic Soldiers, among whom General Chaovalit was the most prominent, were mainly staff officers with backgrounds in counterinsurgency. In the Philippines, the supporters of General Ramos were usually seen as more "professional" than those aligned with General Ver. Ramos appeared to have had more support from graduates of the Philippine Military Academy, while Ver attracted followers who had joined the military through the Reserve Officers Training Corps. In Thailand, factional rivalry between senior officers was often related to competing commercial interests. For example, the members of the Class 5 group jointly owned a very successful company.

Military disunity, therefore, was important both in undermining authoritarian rule and in preventing the restoration of military power. In the Philippines, the experience of six failed coup attempts seems to have convinced officers that further coups would be unlikely to advance the military's interests. In Thailand, however, the two unsuccessful coup attempts of the 1980s were followed by the coup in 1991 that overthrew the Chatichai government. The military showed that it was still sufficiently united to remove an unpopular civilian government even if it was unable to install a military-dominated regime.

Post-transition Politics

Democratic consolidation is greatly facilitated when military officers can be convinced that their interests, both institutional and individual, will continue to be represented and served under civilian rule. While some officers may welcome withdrawal as an opportunity to concentrate on their professional duties, others will miss the status and material benefits that frequently accompany government appointments. It is therefore likely that democratic government will be more easily consolidated if military officers can participate effectively in the new democratic regime. In both the Philippines and Thailand, retired military officers were appointed to government positions and participated in electoral politics, while active officers in Thailand were directly represented in the Senate.

After the fall of Marcos in the Philippines, the new constitution expressly forbade the appointment of active military officers to civilian positions in the government, although retired generals Rafael Ileto and Fidel Ramos successively served as secretary for national defense.[38] Following the election of General Ramos as president in 1992, several retired officers were appointed to his cabinet, including the post of secretary for national defense. Likewise, others took over government agencies such as those managing airports, railways, ports, and customs. Another was later appointed as ombudsman.

Military officers also turned to electoral politics. Although endorsed by Corazon Aquino as her successor, General Ramos failed to win her party's nomination, so he formed his own party and ran successfully for the presidency in 1992. Ramos was not universally popular within the military but was seen by most military officers as preferable to the civilian alternatives. The presence of a former chief of staff of the armed forces in the presidency enhanced the legitimacy of the democratic regime in the eyes of military officers and thus facilitated democratic consolidation. While six coup attempts were launched against President Aquino, none was launched against President Ramos.

Other middle-ranking officers also contested elections, including several who had participated in failed coup attempts. In 1988 provincial elections, Marcos loyalist Colonel Rolando Abadilla was elected vice-governor in Marcos's home province of Ilocos Norte; one of the RAM officers, Colonel Rudolfo Aquinaldo, won the governorship of Cagayan. In the 1995 congressional and local elections, the dashing RAM leader, Colonel Gregorio ("Gringo") Honasan, won a Senate seat, though several other RAM members failed in their attempts to win elected office.

In Thailand, postcoup constitutions adopted in 1978 and 1991 permitted the appointment of an unelected prime minister, a provision that allowed military officers to hold that office without subjecting themselves to the rigors of electoral contests. Thus neither General Kriangsak, General Prem, nor General Suchinda was elected to parliament. Under the 1978 Constitution, serving military officers could be appointed as senators, but, according to provisions implemented in 1983 despite strong military opposition, they could not be elected to the lower house or be appointed as ministers. These provisions, however, did not prevent many retired officers from being elected to parliament or from serving as cabinet ministers. The defense minister was always a retired general. Serving military officers continued to be appointed to the Senate under the 1991 Constitution, and in 1994, the military defeated a civilian attempt to reduce the Senate's powers.

It is customary in Thailand for military officers to enter politics by joining existing parties or setting up their own parties upon retirement.

When Prime Minister Prem succeeded in blocking General Arthit's plans to replace him, the outmaneuvered general established a party and, as a "civilian" politician, eventually joined the Chatichai government as a deputy prime minister. Arthit's successor as army commander in chief, General Chaovalit, also served briefly as a deputy prime minister in the Chatichai government before forming the New Aspiration Party. The general then held the position of deputy prime minister in successive civilian governments headed by Chuan in 1992 and Banharn in 1995 before taking office as prime minister in 1996. One of the "Young Turk" leaders, Major-General Chamlong Srimuang, was elected governor of Bangkok. In the election that restored party rule in September 1992, two of the three main parties in the successful coalition were headed by retired generals—Chaovalit's New Aspiration Party and Chamlong's Palang Dharma. In the Banharn coalition government elected in 1995, two of six deputy prime ministers were former military officers.

In both Thailand and the Philippines, therefore, democratic politics provided opportunities for military officers to pursue their political ambitions by nonmilitary means. In both countries, former top military officers eventually won the top position in government, with General Ramos becoming president of the Philippines and General Chaovalit becoming prime minister of Thailand. In the Philippines, some retired officers won seats in national and provincial legislatures. In Thailand, active officers were appointed to the Senate, while retired officers were prominently represented in the cabinet and the National Assembly. As retired officers attained some success in democratic processes, the chance that the military would undermine such processes was reduced.

Post-transition Economic Interests

The transition from authoritarian rule in the Philippines and Thailand led to the replacement of military officers by civilians in patronage-dispensing offices in the government. Military officers lost lucrative appointments in public corporations as well as the opportunity to provide benefits to private companies with which military officers were associated. In contrast to Malaysia and Singapore, where the military has never intervened in politics, military salaries in both the Philippines and Thailand are very low, with the result that officers often seek to supplement their incomes by engaging in extramilitary activities. While it is not possible to raise military salaries generally to the levels prevailing in Malaysia and Singapore, newly democratic governments in the Philippines and Thailand have been tolerant of the endeavors of individual officers to supplement their salaries.

In the Philippines, senior military officers were never part of the national commercial elite, as they often are in Thailand and Indonesia. Moreover, the post-Marcos constitution prevented the appointment of active military officers to managerial positions in government-controlled corporations.[39] Many officers, however, are associated with small-scale private business ventures, while those in the regions often maintain links with private businesspeople. Kickbacks regularly accompany military purchases, and it is not uncommon for military equipment to be resold for profit. The police are especially notorious for protecting illegal gambling, prostitution, and criminal activities.[40] Military officers have also been involved in smuggling and illegal logging. It should be noted, however, that military involvement in these activities is usually minor compared with the activities of civilian politicians.[41]

In Thailand, military officers were part of the national business elite in the past. Although they are no longer as prominent as they were in the 1960s and 1970s, there are still many opportunities to engage in business. Thus, for example, former army commander in chief General Suchinda joined the board of one of Thailand's largest private companies, the CP Corporation, following his forced resignation as prime minister. Moreover, under the Banharn government, serving officers were again appointed to head state corporations such as Thai Airways. It was not unusual for serving officers in both Bangkok and the provinces to maintain close associations with local businesspeople, especially in border areas where officers have been involved in border trade with the Khmer Rouge in Cambodia, the "supervision" of trade with Laos, and trade in timber and gems with Burma.[42] One major source of funds for military officers has been corrupt payments by suppliers of military equipment. Thai military hardware is purchased from diverse sources, often reflecting compromises between rival factions rather than rational choices according to military criteria.

Economic growth in Thailand during the 1980s and 1990s has been much faster than it has been in the Philippines and has contributed to the ease of the transition to civilian rule. In the Philippines, on the other hand, the withdrawal of military officers from state enterprises and agencies took place when the economy was still suffering from the effects of the Marcos years. The problem, however, was perhaps less severe than it might have been because Philippine military officers had been less deeply involved in business than the Thai military was.

The Issue of Retribution

A major issue facing new democracies is what to do about abuses committed by the military under previous military or authoritarian regimes. Another question is what to do with the participants in failed coup attempts. In Thailand and the Philippines, members of displaced regimes have usually not suffered severe retribution, and those who have participated in failed coup attempts have been treated leniently.

In the Philippines, General Ver, Marcos's chief of staff of the armed forces, was forced in 1986 to flee with his master. Many other Marcos loyalists, however, remained in the military, although most were gradually sidelined. Officers directly involved in the Aquino assassination were tried and convicted, but little was done to bring soldiers involved in human rights abuses to court. In an attempt to restore unity within the military in 1991, Corazon Aquino appointed General Lisandro Abadia as chief of staff of the armed forces, although he had been among the troops preparing to attack General Ramos at the military headquarters during the 1986 crisis. Abadia, however, was a professional officer who could not be considered a committed Marcos loyalist.

The six failed coup attempts against President Aquino posed more dilemmas for the government. On one celebrated occasion following the failure of a coup attempt in July 1986, Ramos declared participants "free from liability of any crime" and ordered them to do 30 push-ups.[43] Following the failed "God Save the Queen" plot in late 1986, the RAM plotters were not charged but were simply given new assignments. Eventually, Marcos loyalists and RAM officers who posed a threat to the Aquino government were detained, although many were eventually released without being tried. The mercurial Colonel Honasan, who had been captured in late 1987, managed to escape from jail, or, more likely, was allowed to "escape" by sympathetic jailers. Honasan and his colleagues were charged with involvement in two coup attempts, but the charges were suspended when "peace talks" opened with the government in 1992. Eventually the charges were dropped. Meanwhile, as mentioned above, Honasan and some of his associates contested the 1995 elections.

In Thailand, coups and countercoups were almost routine affairs in the past. Members of overthrown regimes were often treated in much the same way that members of governments defeated in elections are treated in other countries. Occasionally, however, the leaders of overthrown governments and of unsuccessful coup attempts were sent into exile for a few years. Most coup attempts were bloodless, with the abortive coup of 1985 an exception.

After the failed "Young Turks" coup of 1981, 52 participants were detained, but they were pardoned five weeks later; in 1986, 28 of these participants, who had been dismissed from the army without pension rights, were reinstated.[44] In 1987, charges against 33 officers who had participated in the 1985 coup attempt were withdrawn; eventually, charges of involvement against seven senior officers, including General Kriangsak, were also dropped.[45] In 1992, the last act of General Suchinda as prime minister was to grant an amnesty to himself and to the officers who ordered troops to fire on demonstrators. The amnesty issue was a difficult one for the new civilian government, which was faced on one side with demands for justice and on the other with the risks of provoking the military. In the end, the government decided to revoke the amnesty but refrained from pressing charges against the generals.[46]

In both countries, governments have been wary of taking strong measures against military officers responsible for coup attempts or abuses. In some cases, offending military officers have been detained for short periods. In other cases, officers have been dismissed from the armed forces, while others were merely reassigned to new posts where they would not have direct control over troops. In both the Philippines and Thailand, lenient treatment has averted the kinds of crises that might have undermined democratic consolidation, but such treatment has disappointed civilians involved in the democratic movement.

The Future

By the mid-1990s, there were signs of democratic consolidation in the Philippines and Thailand. Democracy had lasted long enough for both countries to experience changes in government resulting from elections. Moreover, the elections were vigorously contested, and—unlike in all other Southeast Asian countries—confident predictions about outcomes could not be made in advance. In 1992, Fidel Ramos was narrowly elected president of the Philippines; he succeeded Corazon Aquino, who had managed to complete her six-year term despite the six coup attempts. Following the 1991 coup in Thailand, successive civilian coalition governments were formed after elections held in 1992, 1995, and 1996. By the mid-1990s, the Philippines had not seen a violent military intervention since the failed coup attempt of December 1989. Meanwhile, in Thailand, the military had not resorted to violence since the shooting of demonstrators in Bangkok in May 1992.

The quality of elected governments and legislatures in both countries, however, did not win universal admiration. Political parties were widely perceived as vehicles for self-interested politicians to win power by promising patronage. Party affiliation remained fluid, and improbable alliances between former rivals were often formed. Vote-buying in elections was standard practice in rural areas and sometimes in cities as well. In Thailand, many members of the educated middle class in Bangkok believed that the two unelected governments headed by the technocrat, Anand, were the best that Thailand had ever had.

The survival of democratic governments was favored by economic circumstances in the 1990s. The Thai economy, which had grown at an average rate of 7.6 percent in the 1980s, continued to expand during the first half of the 1990s. On the other hand, the political upheavals of the 1980s in the Philippines had resulted in economic stagnation, with the average growth rate during that decade just 0.9 percent. The economy grew faster in the 1990s, but 1993 per-capita income in the Philippines remained below $1,000 and was less than half of Thailand's $2,110.

Despite its relatively poor economic performance, the Philippines' democratic rule seemed less likely to be challenged by the military than

Thailand's. Whatever the inadequacies of civilian politicians and political parties in the Philippines, the practice of democratic elections at all levels of government is entrenched, while military intervention is widely regarded as illegitimate, a view that was reinforced by the military's involvement in the authoritarian Marcos regime. Although many military officers have little respect for civilian politicians, they do not see themselves as an alternative political elite, in part because military doctrine upholds civilian supremacy. Moreover, the military's organizational structure has limited its capacity to intervene, especially after responsibility for internal security was largely transferred to the police in 1991. The election of General Ramos as president in 1992 and his appointment of retired officers to head various government agencies further strengthened military acceptance of elected and constitutional government.

While few Filipinos anticipate further military attempts to overthrow the government, few Thais dismiss the possibility of another coup. Thailand's limited experience with democracy has yet to produce strong, effective governments. The coalition governments formed after elections in the 1990s consisted of rival parties tied to one another by little more than a common interest in controlling patronage networks. The immediate cause of the fall of the Chuan government was a corruption scandal that gave several of its coalition partners the excuse to seek a better deal with the opposition parties. The new Banharn government achieved immediate notoriety when it included several former ministers in the Chatichai government who had been investigated for their unusual wealth. Further, two leading members of Banharn's own party had been refused visas to enter the United States because of suspected involvement in drug trafficking.[47] The Banharn government was succeeded after a 1996 election by a new coalition headed by General Chaovalit, who had been a deputy prime minister under Banharn and included several parties from the Banharn government in his own coalition.

Unlike in the Philippines, military culture in Thailand endorses military intervention when it is seen to be in the interests of "nation, religion, and king." In recent years, however, military officers seem to have lost confidence in their ability to manage an increasingly complex society and economy; as a result, they have been willing to reduce their role in government. In the final analysis, however, democratization took place less because military officers believed in civilian rule than because they were too divided to prevent it. Although retired military officers hold cabinet posts and are members of the National Assembly, they are often not so much representatives of a common military interest as rivals of one another. While it is not impossible for the military to exploit civilian disaffection to overthrow an elected government, it seems unlikely that officers would be able to form a military-dominated government. Although the legitimacy of democratic government is not strong, neither is support for military rule, especially in Bangkok.

What can be done to make military reintervention less likely in the Philippines and Thailand? In the Latin American context, Alfred Stepan has suggested that democratic leaders adopt a "politically led strategy toward the military" aimed at gradually persuading military leaders to accept reduced privileges. At the same time, Stepan continues, the democratic leaders should promote civilian expertise in military matters in order to "empower" legislatures to monitor military activities.[48] Also writing about Latin America, Larry Diamond has warned against direct confrontation with the military and proposes a step-by-step approach to gradually removing the military from police functions, state corporations, and the mass media. Eventually, he says, a civilian should be appointed as defense minister and the military restricted to responsibilities involving defense and security. As part of the program, he wants to see the size of the military reduced, military doctrine depoliticized, and respect for civilian supremacy inculcated by changing curricula in military colleges.[49] More bluntly, in his "Guidelines for Democratizers," Samuel P. Huntington advises democratic leaders "to make clear that the civilian head of the government is the commander of the military" and to "reorient your military forces to military missions." He also advises them to "ruthlessly punish the leaders of attempted coups against your new government."[50]

Many of these proposals have already been implemented in the Philippines, where circumstances favor military withdrawal in any case. But it is hard to see how civilian leaders in Thailand could persuade their generals to abandon long-established traditions. In contrast to various Latin American cases in which civilian leaders replaced the military in a relatively clean break, the democratic transition in Thailand took place over a period of more than a decade and resulted in a political order in which the military continues to play a major role. As leaders of unstable parliamentary coalitions, Thai prime ministers are in no position to sack their defense ministers, deprive the military of their television stations, or order military colleges to contradict established military doctrines.

In the Philippines and Thailand, government leaders, both civilian and ex-military, have avoided measures that might provoke the military. Instead of appointing civilians as ministers of defense, they have usually appointed former military commanders, who continue to wield some influence among their former subordinates. They have also found it too risky to follow Huntington's advice to "ruthlessly punish the leaders of attempted coups." In both countries, democratic leaders have instead tried to incorporate military officers into the political process. That the military has been subordinated to civilian government more successfully in the Philippines than in Thailand is not due so much to superior policies in the Philippines as to the inherent differences in civil-military relations in the two countries.

NOTES

I am indebted to several people for their helpful comments on various versions of this essay: Noel Adams, Amy Blitz, Michael Connors, Paul Fenoglio, Dan FitzGerald, Carolina Hernandez, Ben Kerkvliet, and Thaveeporn Vasavakul.

1. The data for this section are from World Bank, *World Development Report 1994* (New York: Oxford University Press, 1994).

2. The concept of purchasing power parity (PPP) is often used to supplement conventional per-capita income statistics. PPP estimates are believed to provide a more accurate measure of living standards.

3. Benedict Anderson, "Cacique Democracy in the Philippines: Origins and Dreams," *New Left Review* 169 (May–June 1988): 3–31; Harold Crouch, *Economic Change, Social Structure and the Political System in Southeast Asia: Philippine Development Compared with Other ASEAN Countries* (Singapore: Institute of Southeast Asian Studies, 1985).

4. Fred W. Riggs, *Thailand: The Modernization of a Bureaucratic Polity* (Honolulu: East-West Center Press, 1966).

5. Anek Laothamatas, "From Clientelism to Partnership: Business-Government Relations in Thailand," in Andrew MacIntyre, ed., *Business and Government in Industrialising Asia* (Sydney: Allen & Unwin, 1994), 195–215.

6. The 1962 military coup in Burma was a response in part to ethnic rebellion. The imposition of martial law in response to regional rebellion in Indonesia in 1957 resulted in direct military participation in government.

7. Viberto Selochan, "The Armed Forces of the Philippines and Political Instability," in Selochan, ed., *The Military, the State and Development in Asia and the Pacific* (Boulder, Colo.: Westview, 1991), 83–119.

8. Carolina G. Hernandez, "The Philippines," in Zakaria Haji Ahmad and Harold Crouch, eds., *Military-Civilian Relations in Southeast Asia* (Singapore: Oxford University Press, 1985), 157–96.

9. On "new professionalism" in Latin America, see Alfred Stepan, "The New Professionalism of Internal Warfare and Military Role Expansion," in Stepan, ed., *Authoritarian Brazil: Origins, Policies and Future* (New Haven: Yale University Press, 1973), 47–65.

10. Fact-Finding Commission, *Final Report* (Manila: Bookmark, 1990), 111. The Fact-Finding Commission was appointed by President Aquino to investigate the failed coup of December 1989.

11. Constitution of the Republic of the Philippines, art. 16, sec. 5(3).

12. Felipe B. Miranda and Ruben F. Ciron, "Development and the Military in the Philippines: Military Perceptions in a Time of Continuing Crisis," in J. Soedjati Djiwandono and Yong Mun Cheong, eds., *Soldiers and Stability in Southeast Asia* (Singapore: Institute of Southeast Asian Studies, 1988), 163–212.

13. The army commander in chief, General Arthit Kamlang-ek, went so far as to argue in 1983 that the appointed Senate was more democratic than the elected, albeit party-dominated, House of Representatives. See Suchit Bungbongkarn, *The Military in Thai Politics 1981–86* (Singapore: Institute of Southeast Asian Studies, 1987), 71–72 and ch. 5.

14. Chai-anan Samudavanija and Sukhumbhand Paribatra, "Thailand: Liberalization Without Democracy," in James W. Morley, ed., *Driven by Growth: Political Change in the Asia-Pacific Region* (Armonk, N.Y.: M.E. Sharpe, 1993), 132.

15. Armed Forces Information Office, Supreme Command Headquarters, *Democracy in Thailand* (Bangkok, n.d.), 53–56.

16. Ulf Sundhaussen, "The Military: Structure, Procedures, and Effects on Indonesian Society," in Karl D. Jackson and Lucian W. Pye, eds., *Political Power and Communications in Indonesia* (Berkeley: University of California Press, 1978), 45–81; Richard Tanter, "The Totalitarian Ambition: Intelligence and Security Agencies in Indonesia," in Arief Budiman, ed., *State and Civil Society in Indonesia* (Clayton, Victoria, Australia: Monash University, 1990), 215–88.

17. According to Richard Kessler, "the I[ntegrated] CHDF were employed as bully boys by the local elite to intimidate the populace and were outside the military's direct chain of command." See Richard J. Kessler, "Development and the Military: Role of the Philippine Military in Development," in Soedjati and Yong, eds., *Soldiers and Stability in Southeast Asia*, 213–27.

18. Multhiah Alagappa, *The National Security of Developing States: Lessons from Thailand* (Dover, Mass.: Auburn House), 183–86.

19. Suchit, *The Military in Thai Politics*, ch. 4.

20. Alagappa, *National Security of Developing States*, 184.

21. Kusuma Snitwongse, "Thailand's Year of Stability: Illusion or Reality?" in Institute of Southeast Asian Studies, *Southeast Asian Affairs 1988* (Singapore: Institute of Southeast Asian Studies, 1988), 275.

22. Kessler, "Development and the Military," 218.

23. Fact-Finding Commission, *Final Report,* 47–49.

24. John L.S. Girling, *Thailand: Society and Politics* (Ithaca, N.Y.: Cornell University Press, 1981), 135–36.

25. Fact-Finding Commission, *Final Report,* 47.

26. Hernandez, *Military-Civilian Relations,* 187.

27. As the Fact-Finding Commission pointed out, "The drastic reduction of such business-related benefits under the present administration may have led to heightened feelings of relative deprivation among many military officers" (*Final Report,* 102).

28. Riggs, *Thailand,* ch. 9.

29. Surin Maisrikrod, "Thailand 1992: Repression and Return to Democracy," in Institute of Southeast Asian Studies, *Southeast Asian Affairs 1993* (Singapore: Institute of Southeast Asian Studies, 1993), 343.

30. Medhi Krongkaew, "The Political Economy of Decentralization in Thailand," in Institute of Southeast Asian Studies, *Southeast Asian Affairs 1995* (Singapore: Institute of Southeast Asian Studies, 1995), 343–61.

31. See, for example, the essays in Benedict J. Tria Kerkvliet and Resil Mojares, eds., *From Marcos to Aquino: Local Perspectives on Political Transition in the Philippines* (Honolulu: University of Hawaii Press, 1992), and in Jose F. Lacaba, ed., *Boss: Five Case Studies of Local Politics in the Philippines* (Manila: Philippine Center for Investigative Journalism/Institute for Popular Democracy, 1995).

32. According to public-opinion surveys conducted in 1987 and 1990, the percentage disagreeing with the military's right to intervene was always less than 50 percent but still greater than the percentage agreeing. The percentages disagreeing and agreeing were 44 and 37, respectively, in March 1987; 46 and 24 in October 1987; and 37 and 21 in November 1990. Many people were apparently indifferent. Mahar Mangahas, *The Philippine Social Climate* (Manila: Anvil, 1994), 75.

33. See Suchit Bunbongkarn, "Elections and Democratization in Thailand," in R.H. Taylor, ed., *The Politics of Elections in Southeast Asia* (New York: Woodrow Wilson Center Press and Cambridge University Press, 1996), 184–200.

34. See Anek Laothamatas, "A Tale of Two Democracies: Conflicting Perceptions of Elections and Democracy in Thailand," in Taylor, ed., *The Politics of Elections in Southeast Asia*, 201–23.

35. Detailed analysis of these coup attempts can be found in Fact-Finding Commission, *Final Report*. The report lists seven coup attempts, but one was hardly more than a plot.

36. On the Thai factions, see Chai-anan Samudavanija, *The Thai Young Turks* (Singapore: Institute of Southeast Asian Studies, 1982). See also Suchit, *The Military in Thai Politics*. On Philippine factions, see Francisco Nemenzo, "A Season of Coups," *Diliman Review* 34 (1986): 1, 16–25.

37. According to Alfred McCoy, "the socialization of Class '71 in the Philippines was also shaped by the experience of arresting, interrogating and torturing civilians or serving as combat officers in a civil war against Muslim and tribal Filipinos." As quoted in Alfred W. McCoy, "Ram Boys: Superstars in the Theater-State of Terror," in Dolores Flamiano and Donald Goertzen, eds., *Critical Decade: Prospects for Democracy in the Philippines in the 1990s* (Berkeley: Philippine Resource Center, 1990), 7.

38. Fact-Finding Commission, *Final Report*, 57.

39. Ibid., 57.

40. It is widely believed that soldiers and police are heavily involved in crime. Vice-President Joseph Estrada was expressing a common view when he claimed that 80 percent of "heinous crimes" like kidnapping and robbery were perpetrated by "hoodlums in uniform." *Philippine Daily Inquirer*, 4 September 1995.

41. In a conversation with the author in 1995, a young Philippine army officer told of how he had been under pressure from both the local congressman and the mayor after he seized illegally felled logs.

42. Following the visit of a military delegation headed by the army commander in chief, General Chaovalit, to Rangoon in December 1988, it was reported: "On the Thai side major logging, fishing, gem, export-import, and other concessions have been received from Myanmar by business concerns with close interlocking military ties." A month earlier, Chaovalit had led a delegation to Laos, following which "the Thai military has become the agency for public and private dealing with Laos and the 'fees' associated with this." Donald E. Weatherbee, "Thailand 1989: Democracy Ascendant in the Golden Peninsula," in Institute of Southeast Asian Studies, *Southeast Asian Affairs 1990* (Singapore: Institute of Southeast Asian Studies, 1990), 352, 354.

43. Fact-Finding Commission, *Final Report*, 141.

44. Chai-anan, *The Thai Young Turks*, 64; Suchit, *The Military in Thai Politics*, 80.

45. Kusuma, "Thailand's Year of Stability," 274.

46. Surin, "Thailand 1992," 342.

47. Michael Vatikiotis and Gordon Fairclough, "The Spoils of Victory," *Far Eastern Economic Review*, 27 July 1995, 16–17.

48. Alfred Stepan, *Rethinking Military Politics: Brazil and the Southern Cone* (Princeton: Princeton University Press, 1988), ch. 8.

49. Larry Diamond, "Democracy in Latin America: Degrees, Illusions, and Directions for Consolidation," in Tom Farer, ed., *Beyond Sovereignty: Collectively Defending Democracy in the Americas* (Baltimore: Johns Hopkins University Press, 1996), 55–59.

50. Samuel P. Huntington, *The Third Wave: Democratization in the Late Twentieth Century* (Norman: University of Oklahoma Press, 1991), 251–53.

IV

Civil Society

12

CIVIL SOCIETY EAST AND WEST

Philippe C. Schmitter

Philippe C. Schmitter is professor of political science at the European University Institute in Florence. Previously, he taught at Stanford University and served as director of Stanford's Center for European Studies. He has also served as vice-president of the American Political Science Association. He is the coauthor of Transitions from Authoritarian Rule: Tentative Conclusions About Uncertain Democracies *(1986).*

Except for "democracy" itself, no concept has attracted as much attention as "civil society" in the recent discussions about contemporary regime changes and their probable outcomes. The collapse or self-transformation of so many authoritarian regimes in such a wide range of cultural settings and geographic locations has carried the notion of civil society far beyond its *pays d'origine* in Western Europe. No one disputes that the practices of civil society initially emerged during the first centuries of this millennium in the "city-state belt" that ran from London to Florence and Siena by way of the Low Countries, the Rhine valley, the Swiss plains, and the Po valley—and then diffused gradually and unevenly to the northern, eastern, and southern regions of the European peninsula. Granted, colonialism successfully transplanted some of the practices of civil society to those parts of the world where emigrating Europeans established themselves as the dominant group, but what about those places that only suffered the effects of European imperialism? More important, what about those few peoples that escaped direct subjugation to such foreign powers and thus retained more continuous control over their own institutions and values during the nineteenth and twentieth centuries?

Is it not, therefore, stretching the concept of civil society too far to expect it to play an analogous role in influencing the outcomes of democratization in the former British, French, Dutch, and Belgian possessions of Africa, the Middle East, and Asia? And is it not even more preposterous to imagine that it could have a similar effect on

Persia, China, Thailand, or Japan—not to mention Taiwan and Korea, which were colonies of Japan?

Ten General Propositions

First Proposition. Before venturing into this hazardous terrain —hazardous especially for one who has no expertise on these parts of the world—let me first make explicit what the relationship between civil society and democracy is supposed to be: *The presence of a civil society (or, better said, of some degree, distribution, or type of civil society) contributes positively to the consolidation (and, later, to the persistence) of democracy. Nota bene,* civil society contributes to—but does *not* cause—the consolidation of democracy. It cannot unilaterally bring about democracy. Nor can it alone sustain democratic institutions and practices once they are in place. *Ergo,* civil society acts along with other institutions, processes, and calculations in the democratic process.

Civil society can be defined as a set or system of self-organized intermediary groups that: 1) are relatively independent of both public authorities *and* private units of production and reproduction, that is, of firms and families; 2) are capable of deliberating about and taking collective actions in defense or promotion of their interests or passions; 3) do not seek to replace either state agents or private (re)producers or to accept responsibility for governing the polity as a whole; and 4) agree to act within preestablished rules of a "civil" nature, that is, conveying mutual respect.

Civil society, therefore, is not a simple but a compound property. It rests on four conditions or, better, behavioral norms: 1) dual autonomy, 2) collective action, 3) nonusurpation, and 4) civility. Moreover, these behavioral norms must be practiced within civil society by most of its intermediary units *and* respected by both public authorities and private (re)producers. While the presence of intermediary organizations is necessary evidence for the existence of a civil society, it alone is not sufficient proof. These units can be manipulated by public or private actors; they can be mere facades masking actions by social groups that intend to usurp power from legitimate state authorities or to exert domination over other social groups in "uncivil" ways.[1]

Consolidation of democracy can be defined as the process of transforming the accidental arrangements, prudential norms, and contingent solutions that emerge during transition into relations of cooperation and competition that are reliably known, regularly practiced, and voluntarily accepted by those persons or collectivities (i.e., politicians and citizens) that participate in democratic governance. If the democratic regime settles in, it will have institutionalized uncertainty in some roles and policy areas, but it will also have reassured its citizens that the competition to occupy office or to exercise influence will be fair and circumscribed to a predictable range of outcomes. Modern representative democracy rests on this "bounded uncertainty" and the "contingent consent" of actors to respect the outcomes it produces.

The core of the consolidation dilemma, then, lies in coming up with a set of institutions that politicians agree upon and citizens are willing to support. Arriving at a stable solution is no easy matter, especially in the climate of exaggerated expectations that tends to characterize the transition. Not only are the choices *intrinsically conflictual*—with different parties of politicians preferring rules that will ensure their own reelection or eventual access to power, and different groups of citizens wanting rules that will ensure greater accountability of their professional agents—but they are also *extrinsically consequential*. Once they are translated, via elections with uncertain outcomes, into governments that produce public policies, institutional choices will affect rates of economic growth, willingness to invest, competitiveness in foreign markets, distributions of income and wealth, access to education, perceptions of cultural deprivation, racial balance, and even national identity. To a certain extent, actors anticipate these substantive matters and incorporate them into compromises made with regard to procedures, but there is much room for error and unintended consequences. In the short run, the consolidation of democracy depends on actors' and citizens' ability to come up with a solution to their intrinsic conflicts over rules; in the long run, it will depend upon the extrinsic impact that policies made under these rules will have upon groups within a civil society.[2]

This is *not* to say that civil societies do not differ in significant ways from one another. The degree, distribution, and type of civil society can have an enduring impact on the consolidation of democracy.

Degree of civil society implies that civil society never completely monopolizes the interactions between the state and individuals, firms, and clans, but operates alongside these interactions in differing mixes of efforts to influence the course of public policy. The more these efforts are channeled through intermediary organizations, the greater is the degree of civil society and, by implication, the easier it will be, *ceteris paribus*, to consolidate democracy.

Distribution of civil society implies that the attributes of civil society may be more applicable to some subsets of interests or passions than to others. Standard academic treatments focus on the intermediation of functionally based lines of cleavage in society—classes, economic sectors, and professions—and the desirability that the particularly salient conflicts of these functional groups be processed through the organized channels of civil society. As bases of conflict shift within a given society, however, it may become equally imperative that "other" types of interests—and even passions—be represented in this fashion.

Type of civil society implies that the norms of autonomy, collective action, nonusurpation, and civility can be embodied in quite different ways to produce different general configurations or "systems of intermediation." The most widely discussed of these involves the ideal-typical distinction between *pluralism* and *corporatism*. The additional implication is that both of these configurations (as well as several intervening points on the continuum between them) are compatible with the consolidation of democracy, but that their presence will have a significant impact upon the performance, distribution of benefits, and "quality" of the democracy that emerges.[3]

Second Proposition. *The existence of civil society is not a prerequisite either for the demise of autocracy or for the transition to democracy, nor is it ordinarily sufficient to bring about such a change in regime.* Yet the transition to democracy is almost invariably accompanied by what Guillermo O'Donnell and I have termed the "resurrection of civil society," which usually occurs *after* and *not before* the transition has begun.[4] Much of the original impetus takes the form of relatively spontaneous movements, but, with the convocation of elections during the transition, attention eventually shifts dramatically toward political parties.[5] After the founding elections, however, as the polity settles into the trenches of more routinized conflict, the process of consolidation tends to enhance the role of interest associations and other forms of civil society.

This dynamic can lead to a certain confusion about the nature of civil society in neodemocracies because there may be a temptation initially to identify its presence or strength by the spontaneity of social movements and the enthusiastic participation of citizens in them. This "primacy" accorded to social movements is bound to decline once the regime change has occurred because: 1) the mere advent of democracy satisfies some of the most passionate revindications of movements; 2) the process of consolidation encourages individuals and social collectivities to pursue more "private-regarding" interests and to "free-ride" on the efforts of others; and 3) the mechanisms of modern democracy tend to privilege territory- and function-based interests (hence political parties and interest associations) over theme-based causes (i.e., single-issue movements).

The most important point to keep in mind is that civil society is composed not of a single type of intermediary organization but of a variety of types, and that this mix should be expected to shift over time in response to changes in the substance and intensity of conflict, as well as the stage of democratization.

Third Proposition. *The presence of a stable and functioning party system (of whatever type) is not alone direct evidence for the existence of a civil society since political parties are not likely to be able to* *monopolize the organized intermediation between individuals or firms and public authorities.* No doubt, the functioning of a viable, competitive party system benefits from the presence of a civil society, but such a system can hardly be expected to reflect all of the interests and passions of civil society—least of all during the often lengthy period between elections. Political parties will seek to penetrate and even to subordinate the core institutions of civil society (i.e., its associations and movements), but there are several reasons to suspect that parties have lost much of their capability for aggregating civil society's interests and passions through party programs, platforms, and ideologies.

Very substantial changes have taken place in the nature and role of parties in well-established Western democracies. It would be anachronistic to presume that parties in today's neodemocracies will have to go through all the stages and perform all the functions of their predecessors. Today's citizens—even those in polities that have long suffered under authoritarian rule and have no prior history of civil society—have quite different organizational skills, are less likely to identify so closely with partisan symbols or ideologies, and defend a much more variegated set of interests. Moreover, the new regimes are emerging in an international environment virtually saturated with different models of successful collective action. All this may not preclude a hegemonic role for parties in the representation of civil society, but it does suggest that they will face more competition from interest associations and social movements than their predecessors. We should revise our thinking about democratization accordingly.

Fourth Proposition. *Modern democracy is a complex set of institutions involving multiple channels of representation and sites for authoritative decision making.* Citizenship, democracy's most distinctive property, is not confined to voting periodically in elections. It also can be exercised by influencing the selection of candidates, joining associations or movements, petitioning authorities, engaging in "unconventional" protests, and so forth. Nor is the accountability of authorities guaranteed only through the traditional mechanisms of territorial constituency and legislative process. Much of the activity of citizens can circumvent these partisan mechanisms and focus directly through functional channels and bargaining processes on elected or appointed officials within the state apparatus. For these reasons, *modern democracy should be conceptualized not as "a regime" but as a composite of "partial regimes," each of which has been institutionalized around distinctive sites for the representation of social groups and the resolution of their ensuing conflicts.* Parties, associations, movements, localities, and various clientele compete and coalesce through these different channels in efforts to capture office and influence policy. Authorities with different functions and at different levels of territorial aggregation interact with representatives of these interests and legitimately claim accountability to different interests and passions.

Constitutions, of course, are an effort to establish a single, overarching set of "meta-rules" that would render these partial regimes coherent by assigning specific tasks to each and enforcing some hierarchical relation among them. But such formal documents are rarely successful in delineating and controlling all these relations. The process of convoking a constituent assembly, producing an acceptable draft, and ratifying it by vote or plebiscite undoubtedly represents a significant moment in democratic consolidation, but many partial regimes will be left undefined. For it is precisely in the interstices between different types of representation in civil society that constitutional norms are most vague and least prescriptive. Imagine trying to deduce from even the most detailed of constitutions (and they are becoming ever more detailed) how parties, associations, and movements will interact to influence policies—or trying to discern how capital and labor will bargain over income shares under the new rules.

If political democracy is not a regime but a composite of regimes, then the appropriate strategy for studying the relationship between its consolidation and civil society would be disaggregation. Not only is this theoretically desirable, but it also makes the effort more empirically feasible. In Figure 1, I have attempted to sketch out the property space that would be involved and to suggest some of the specific partial regimes that are likely to emerge. The vertical axis describes the space in terms of the institutional domain of action, ranging from authoritatively defined *state agencies* to *self-constituted units of civil society*. The horizontal axis describes the range of power resources that actors can bring to bear on the emerging political process: *numbers* in the case of those actors relying primarily on the counting of individual votes; *intensities* for those actors whose power depends on weighing the contribution of particular groups of citizens. Competing theories of democracy—liberal and statist, majoritarian and consociational, unitary and federal, presidential and parliamentary—have long argued the merits of particular locations in Figure 1. All are potentially democratic, provided they respect the overarching principle of citizenship and the procedural minima of civil rights, fair elections, free associability, and so on.

Fifth Proposition. In response to the opportunities (and threats) that come with democratization, individual associations already existing under the old regime are likely to have to change their internal structures and operative practices significantly. Some will make every effort to retain the organizational advantages they have always enjoyed; others will seize upon the chance to establish a new relationship with their members and insert themselves independently into the policy-making process. Here,

Figure 1
Sketch of the Property Space Involved in the Consolidation of Whole and Partial Regimes in Modern Democracies

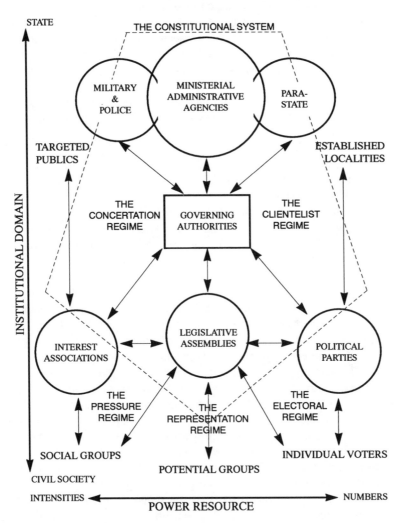

there is a deep-seated irony since those groups in civil society that are in greatest need of collective action—those whose potential members are numerous, dispersed, and relatively impoverished—are the least likely to succeed in recruiting these members on a rational and voluntary basis. The small, concentrated, and privileged groups should have less difficulty in capturing resources under democratic conditions. Not only do they need them less (since their members may have adequate resources to act individually), but these groups were usually the privileged interlocutors and beneficiaries of the old regime. Left to its own devices, then, the new "liberal" associability could produce a systematically skewed overrepresentation of dominant class, sectoral (i.e., clustered according to the specificities of producing different goods and services), and professional interests. Subordinate groups have, of course, the new resource of voting as a means of pursuing their general interests, but they may have to rely on the state recognition, licensing, and subsidization characteristic of the *ancien régime* in order to participate effectively in the democratic game when it comes to advancing their more particular interests. The practical temptations of neocorporatism, in other words, may outweigh the ideological attractions of pluralism.

Sixth Proposition. *Where polities acquire class, sectoral, or professional associations with both strategic capacity[6] and encompassing scope,[7] these units of civil society play a more significant role in the consolidation process than where a great multiplicity of narrowly specialized and overlapping organizations emerge with close dependencies upon their members or interlocutors. Thus pluralist associations weaken the role of interest intermediaries; corporatist ones strengthen it.* This difference also affects the probability of establishing stable partial regimes and, hence, the type of democratic regime. For example, the creation of viable "concertation" regimes—which link associations directly to one another or to state agencies in the bargaining over economic or social politics, either at the macro or the meso level —seems contingent on the development of strategic capacity and encompassing scope. Once concertation is initiated, it tends to encourage "participant associations" to acquire even more autonomy from members and party interlocutors and to extend their scope to bring ever wider domains of interest under their control. At the extreme, the neodemocracy could become populated with a series of "private-interest governments" in sensitive policy areas, with profound consequences for political parties and local clienteles, as well as for the legislative process and the overall governability of the political order.

If strategic capacity and encompassing scope are the two composite, emergent properties of individual associations that seem most relevant for predicting outcomes, the two that best define the nature of interorganizational systems within civil society are *class governance* and *congruence.*

Class governance involves the capacity to commit an entire comprehensive social category—for example, owners of productive property, workers in all industries, self-employed people in all sectors—to a common and long-term course of action as well as to ensure that those bound by such a policy do indeed comply with it. Theoretically, this could be accomplished by a political party, although the logic of continuous electoral competition tends to undermine this for manual workers by forcing them to choose between their narrow class interests and the broad partisan appeals that are required to win elections, and parties have almost never performed this function for capitalists. In practical and contemporary terms, if class governance is to become a reliable property of civil society, then monopolistic, hierarchically coordinated, and nationally focused interest associations (usually culminating in a single peak association) will have to do the job. If the emerging system(s) of intermediation are multiple and overlapping or if they remain localized and dispersed, then civil society will be less capable of delivering and enforcing social peace between conflicting classes. It will, however, be more open, competitive, and innovative.[8]

Congruence refers to the extent to which the coverage, monopoly status, and coordinative capacity of different types of interests within civil society are similar to one another. One could postulate an underlying trend in this direction toward congruence, especially between clusters of associations that represent conflicting interests. Nevertheless, some associations may experiment with (and, occasionally, borrow from abroad) novel forms of self-organization that subsequently diffuse to their opponents or imitators. Given the high degree of uncertainty that characterizes the transition period, some degree of incongruence would seem a rather normal outcome. The question is whether it persists and impedes the consolidation of a mutually agreed upon set of democratic rules.

Seventh and Eighth Propositions. *The presence of civil society contributes (positively) to the consolidation of democracy through the following processes:*

1) It stabilizes expectations within social groups and thereby presents authorities with more aggregated, reliable, and actionable information with which to govern.

2) It inculcates conceptions of interest and norms of behavior that are civic—that is, mindful of the existence of the unit as a whole and respectful of the democratic process.

3) It provides channels for self-expression and identification that are more proximate to individuals and firms, hence less likely to alienate actors from the political system when making demands, especially of remote central-national officials.

4) It governs the behavior of its members with regard to collective commitments, thereby reducing the burden of governance for both public authorities and private producers.

5) It provides important, but not unique, reservoirs of potential resistance to arbitrary or tyrannical action by rulers, whether they be illegitimate usurpers or intolerant majorities.

Civil society is not, however, an unmitigated blessing for democracy.

It can affect the consolidation and subsequent functioning of democracy in a number of negative ways:

1) It can make the formation of majorities more difficult, lengthy, and precarious, thereby lowering the legitimacy of democratic governments.

2) It may build into the policy-making process a systematically biased distribution of influence, especially where its formative principles are strictly liberal, that is, individualistic and voluntaristic. (As E.E. Schattschneider put it, the problem with the interest group chorus in the United States is that it sings in an upper-class accent.)[9]

3) It tends to impose an elaborate and obscure process of compromise upon political life, the outcome of which can be policies no one wanted in the first place and with which no one can subsequently identify.

4) It can reinforce the tendency toward pork-barrel solutions whereby individual associations or movements satisfy their interests or passions at the expense of the whole, which results in an inefficient and inflation-prone economy.

5) Most dangerously, "it" may prove to be not one but several civil societies—all occupying the same territory and polity but organizing interests and passions into communities that are ethnically, linguistically, or culturally distinct—even exclusive. (The historic solution in Western Europe to this "pillarization" of civil society has been consociationalism, or *Proporz-demokratie*. This is not an option for all neodemocracies, which might, therefore, have to face the undesirable prospect of secession.)

Any given civil society will produce a mixture of the positive and negative effects noted above. Nothing a priori guarantees that the positive effects will always outweigh the negative ones, although that has been the European experience over the long run. Unfortunately, actors in contemporary neodemocracies are much more likely to be guided by short-term calculations and hence may be unwilling to gamble on the eventual advantages of an active and viable civil society.

If the above conceptualization of the problem has any validity, it should be possible to assess the probable outcome by monitoring the properties of *strategic capacity, encompassing scope, class governance,* and *congruence* that emerge during the process of regime change. These properties, in turn, depend on the more discrete characteristics that individual associations and movements acquire—that is, their *numbers, densities of membership,* and *domains of representation*—and on the emergent macrocharacteristics of the system of intermediation—its *coverage of interests and passions,* its *extent of monopoly,* and its *degree of coordination.*

Ninth Proposition. *Civil society is not an automatic or unreflexive product of capitalism, urbanization, literacy, social mobilization—that is,* *of development—although it is encouraged by all of the above. Rather, its emergence requires explicit policies by public authorities and implicit practices by private (re)producers.*

Public policies that foster civil society involve a complex mix of rights and obligations. This mix has varied considerably throughout history and hence it is difficult to generalize about which policies will be followed. Nevertheless, such policies include 1) freedom of association, petition, and assembly; 2) legal recognition and immunity; 3) special fiscal treatment; 4) established arenas for functional representation; 5) guarantees of access to decision making; 6) protection from state intromission in internal affairs; 7) subsidization with public funds; 8) obligatory membership or contributions; 9) legal extension of contracts (*Allgemeinverbindlichkeit*); and 10) devolved responsibility for policy implementation.[10]

The private practices that contribute to greater reliance upon the intermediaries of civil society are even more difficult to pin down, although they would include the following: 1) class, sectoral, professional, or group consciousness; 2) willingness to contribute to collective action; 3) "moral sentiments" or self-restraint in the pursuit of group interests; 4) satisfaction derived from interacting with one's peers, that is, sociability; 5) trust in group leadership and in the conformity of one's peers; 6) some degree of "other-regardingness" for the society as a whole; 7) propensity to accept group discipline; 8) willingness to forgo opportunities for special access due to personal attributes, that is, resistance to clientelistic temptations; 9) sense of personal efficacy; and 10) sufficient organizational skills.[11]

Tenth Proposition. As we have seen, *the emergence of civil society can assume a wide variety of organizational configurations; the range that is viable in any given polity, however, is likely to be considerably more restricted.*

Variations in type—especially along the continuum from pluralism to corporatism—can be expected to produce significant differences in the distribution of benefits, the aggregate economic performance, and the governability of the democracy that may eventually emerge. Especially significant for understanding these differences are the two summary properties of individual associations or movements—that is, *strategic capacity* and *encompassing scope*—and the two summary properties that describe the emergent systems of intermediation—that is, *class governance* and *congruence.* The higher the values of these four dimensions—and they tend to be higher in corporatist than in pluralist systems—the greater will be the positive contribution of civil society to the consolidation of democracy.

This is not to say that it is easy to predict or understand why a given polity will adopt one or another configuration. One obvious factor is likely to be the legacy of institutions from the previous autocracy and the extent to which the mode of transition ensures some degree of continuity. Pacted transitions from *anciens régimes* with well-entrenched state-corporatist practices may provide the most favorable context, whereas abrupt or violent changes from personal autocracies based on patrimonial or clientelistic relations ("sultanistic" is the term that Juan Linz has proposed to cover such cases, even if this may do some violence to the orderly and highly bureaucratic rule of the Ottoman Empire) would seem to be the least likely context for the emergence of anything but a very weak civil society.

Many other factors, no doubt, conspire in the background to incline emergent civil societies toward one or another configuration. High levels of preindustrial urbanization, small size of country, delayed but relatively rapid capitalist development, conservative political oversight of the "Great Transformation" to a market economy, persistent artisanal modes of production, policies of agricultural protectionism, and especially strength of social democracy have all been associated with more corporatist outcomes in Western Europe during the nineteenth and early twentieth centuries. It is by no means clear, however, whether these variables still pack the same punch, or even whether they push in the same direction.

A Potentially Novel Contribution

A relatively new and potentially significant development is the emergence of something approaching a "transnational civil society." These networks of nongovernmental organizations—most of which are headquartered in established civil societies and funded and staffed by their citizens—have created a rather formidable capacity for intervening in neodemocracies. Each successive case of democratization since 1974 has furthered the development of formal nongovernmental organizations and informal informational networks devoted to the promotion of human rights, protection of minorities, monitoring of elections, provision of economic advice, and fostering of exchanges among academics and intellectuals. When the first cases of Portugal, Greece, and Spain emerged in the mid- to late 1970s, this sort of infrastructure hardly existed. Indeed, some of the key lessons learned from these experiences have been subsequently applied elsewhere. By now, there exist an extraordinary variety of transnational parties, associations, foundations, movements, and networks ready to intervene to promote or to protect democracy. To the extent that international support for the consolidation of democracy has shifted from public, intergovernmental channels of influence to increasingly direct involvement of private, nongovernmental organizations, it can help to foster the development of national civil societies in countries where they might not otherwise have emerged, or where they might have been absorbed by either public authorities or private (re)producers.

Nine Reflections on Asian Societies

Let us begin with a blatant act of conceptual stretching: *While its historical origins are unequivocally rooted in Western Europe, the norms and practices of civil society are relevant to the consolidation of democracy in all cultural and geographic areas of the world,* provided *that the generic type of democracy that the actors seek to consolidate is modern and liberal—that is, constitutional, representative, accountable via multiparty competitive elections, tolerant of social and ethnic diversity, and respectful of property rights.*

Whether by imperial fiat, actions of resident European colonists, or processes of international diffusion, the norms and practices of civil society have spread beyond the core area in which they were first developed. Admittedly, this has been an uneven process and it has been superimposed upon quite different native traditions. Some extra-European societies may have had analogous institutions in the past—for example, the guild systems of China or the Ottoman Empire—but it is debatable whether such legacies have any contemporary relevance.

Whether there exist other generic forms of democracy that are viable and can better reflect the cultural norms and popular expectations of particular national societies is also a matter for discussion, although I would like to interject a personal note of skepticism. Not only has this notion of a more "authentic" African, Asian ("Confucian"), Latin American ("Iberian"), Middle Eastern ("Islamic"), or just plain non-Western democracy repeatedly been used as a cover-up for autocratic practices, it has rarely been accompanied by any evidence that citizens in the specific society in question actually possessed such distinctive values or political cultures that would require them to hold their rulers accountable in some different fashion.

Moreover, it is worth remembering that area specialists with a fixed investment in the culture of a particularly exotic part of the world have an inherent tendency to assume that the culture they study is especially distinctive, immutable, and hence resistant to the temptations of secularization, development, and Westernization. Remember that it was not too long ago that distinguished American experts concluded that Confucianism was psychoculturally incompatible with capitalism and that totalitarian systems could not possibly mutate into anything else—least of all into the politico-economic institutions of Western societies!

First Reflection. My brief and hurried reading of the literature on contemporary Asia has, first of all, convinced me that *Asian societies are probably too diverse to permit any valid, nontrivial generalizations for the region as a whole.* Even if one excludes the Muslim-dominated countries of the southeast—Indonesia, Malaysia, Bangladesh, and Brunei—and quietly exiles the Catholic Philippines to Latin America, where it belongs socioculturally, the range of variation in belief systems, class structures, levels of development, center-periphery relations, and modes of insertion into the world economy is still very great.

The variation is even greater when one samples on the dependent variable, that is, on each country's situation with regard to democratization. Thailand is frequently cited as a classic case of perpetual alternation between autocracy and democracy, although there are recent indications that it may have broken the cycle. Taiwan and South Korea have entered into transitions "imposed and controlled" from above, although in the latter case strong indications of mobilization from below may have forced the hand of ruling elites. China and Vietnam are firmly entrenched in the "economic transition must precede political transition" mode, while North Korea seems to be stuck in a time warp. Singapore has institutionalized a *democradura sui generis* with virtually no uncertainty about the outcome of elections and, hence, no realistic prospect of a consensual rotation in power.

Second Reflection. As far as I can tell, *all Asian societies have been affected by the diffusion of Western conceptions and practices of civil society.* Needless to say, this was most intense in those countries that were submitted to direct colonial rule. One can hypothesize that the magnitude of the effect in these cases was roughly proportional to the historical strength of civil society in the mother country. Whether this applies, *mutatis mutandis*, to those cities of China that suffered the presence of foreign enclaves is another matter, although the work of Joseph Fewsmith would seem to indicate that Shanghai was a particularly important site of associability.[12]

Even where the impact of such foreign influences was mediated by native rulers and institutions, it seems to have become imperative to copy Western associational practices—at least in those sectors of economic life that were in close contact with foreigners. Merchants and their chambers of commerce were the forerunners, followed by various professional groups such as engineers, lawyers, doctors, and schoolteachers. Western missionaries seem also to have been an important source of inspiration for new forms of voluntary collective action, although native religious organizations had their own repertoire of congregations, associations, societies, and foundations. Everywhere, the impetus toward self-organization of urban workers and the policies of authorities with regard to working-class–based associations, unions, movements, and the like followed a different logic and pattern—something which, incidentally, was also characteristic of the development of European civil societies.

Today, foreign penetration of conceptions and practices has greatly intensified, led by the efforts of transnational nongovernmental organizations and facilitated by new communications technologies such as the fax machine and the Internet. Not only have these developments diversified the sources of inspiration and made them more difficult for authoritarian rulers to control, but they have also sponsored a much wider substantive expansion of the bases of associability. From a relatively narrow range of class, professional, and sectoral *interests* in Asian societies—virtually all of which were in direct contact with foreign traders and investors—it has now become possible for an extraordinary variety of *passions*—for human rights, protection of the environment, resource conservation, women's emancipation, neighborhood improvement, and so on—to find ideas and even financial support from outside (and unofficial) sources.

Third Reflection. As far as I can tell, *all Asian societies (with the possible exception of the Philippines) possessed an indigenous tradition of societal self-organization.*[13] Whether organized as guilds, foundations, religious brotherhoods, temple societies, village associations, familistic lineages, or secret societies, these organizations seem to have intermediated between individuals and localities and higher "national" authorities from time immemorial—certainly from before the accelerated Western penetration of the nineteenth century. What is not clear to me is 1) whether these traditional institutions have persisted to the present day and hence continue to have a major influence upon the forms of self-organization that are being imported from abroad, and 2) whether traditional institutions have succeeded in attaining a significant degree of autonomy from the state and therefore been even potentially capable of resisting the blandishments and threats of autocratic rulers. Given the variety of national experiences in the region, I will not be surprised to be told that the answer to both questions is "it varies from country to country" (or even from region to region).

Fourth Reflection. Virtually all of the sources that I consulted (admittedly, this was not a complete survey of the literature) insisted that whether their origin was native or foreign, *the organizations of Asian civil society have been dependent—at least in their functioning—upon public authority.*[14] Very few of the units of these civil societies could have been organized without the "benevolence" of the state and only in exceptional moments of political disruption could they provide a basis for resistance to arbitrary or tyrannical state power.[15] The clear implication is that, even though they might often have the appearance and nomenclature of Western associations, clubs, unions, societies, foundations, and the like, Asian organizations cannot reliably fulfill the positive functions for democracy outlined above in my eighth proposition. Nor, *par contre,* can they be held responsible for the negative ones.

At first glance, this would seem to contrast dramatically with the literature on Western Europe and North America, which stresses the high degrees of both autonomy from the state and spontaneity in group formation, as well as voluntarism in group membership. It is simply presumed that only units with that history and practice of independent self-organization could possibly stabilize expectations, aggregate reliable information, inculcate alternative conceptions of interests and values, provide proximate channels of identification and expression, govern legitimately the behavior of their members, and sustain a potentially significant reservoir of resistance to either tyrannical rulers or overbearing majorities.

What this inconveniently overlooks is the simple historical fact that on the European continent, in Scandinavia, and occasionally in the United States and Great Britain, many contemporary class, sectoral, and professional associations owe their existence to past state benevolence of one kind or another. It is too often presumed that civil society must be *pluralist* in its origin and functioning, when this is more the exception than the rule. Precisely because it is not an automatic or unreflexive product of capitalism, urbanization, literacy, social mobilization, or development (ninth proposition), civil society in the West has frequently depended on state protection, public subsidization, monopolistic recognition, exemptions from fiscal charges, guarantees of access, obligations to contribute, extensions of contract, concessions for policy implementation, and so on. Many prominent organizations in European civil societies have benefited from several or most of these corporatist devices—and they nevertheless continue to make a very significant contribution to democratic stability.[16]

In sum, Asianists should be careful not to accept a version of the history of European civil society that is too retrospective and cleansed of its diverse origins and practices. There is no a priori reason why initially state-dependent organizations might not develop greater autonomy if offered the opportunity—for example, in the course of democratization.

Fifth Reflection. In a related fashion, the literature on civil society in Asia stresses that, contrary to the Western experience, *there has been less structured and persistent antagonism between a distinctively private and a distinctively public domain.* The line between the two, which has been so crucial to liberal thought, may have been easier to cross—indeed, almost impossible to distinguish—during the early modernization of Asia. From what little I know of traditional political or social philosophy in Asia, I cannot recall the notion that the world is divided first into a private realm of purely individual rational choice, self-interested behavior, and voluntary contracts, and second into a public realm of group identity, collective responsibility, and compulsory obedience to authority. Needless to say, foreigners must have brought these notions with them and behaved according to their contrasting imperatives, but it seems to have been difficult for Asians to assign radically different meanings to one's behavior in families, clans, villages, firms, associations, foundations, provincial governments, central state agencies, and so on. Hence I frequently encountered not only the theme that particular institutions were very difficult to classify empirically as private or public, but also the idea that in normative terms actors did not expect there to be any clash between the two.

Again, Asianists should be careful not to assume too great a contrast with continental—as opposed to Anglo-Saxon—countries. The numerous artisan guilds, professional *ordres*, and sectoral chambers of Austria, Germany, France, Italy, and the Low Countries all had mixed private-public identities and functions in the past and are still difficult to classify today. Moreover, it would not be easy to discern a consistent pattern of antagonism between them and their state sponsors or regulators. At times, intermediary institutions have served as relatively passive agents of public policy and at other times as units of resistance against what was considered unwarranted interference in their affairs.

Sixth Reflection. One thing that I, as a Europeanist, did find particularly puzzling was the assertion that *in Asia, the predominant site for the historical emergence and subsequent development of intermediary institutions was not large metropolitan centers but small towns, villages, and even the countryside.* Now that is a contrast, since in Europe civil society is virtually synonymous with urban society. Granted, there were some instances in Europe of the collective devices of civil society being used in rural and village settings—for example, communal pastures and woodlots in the Alps and Pyrenees, land-reclamation projects and dikes in the Netherlands, irrigation systems in river valleys such as the Po, sheep-raising in the Meseta of Spain, and artisan guilds in small cities. But it was a bundle of distinctive characteristics of the major trading cities in late medieval Europe that opened up the sociopolitical space for such a historic development: internal complexity, strong sense of local identity, participation in extensive networks of economic interdependence, control over the immediately surrounding countryside, ability to play off against one another competing feudal lords and aspiring kings, formation of defensive intermunicipal alliances, and, especially, capacity for self-governance. The Germans even had an apposite expression for this unique situation: *Stadtluft macht frei!* (The air of the city makes one free!)

Nothing that I have read (and, I admit, it is not much) suggests similar developments in large Asian cities, most of which seemed to have served primarily as centers for imperial control. It was precisely the failure of efforts to assert overarching supremacy by the Papacy or the Holy Roman Empire (and the fierce competition between them) that provided the context for greater municipal autonomy in Europe. Hence those in quest of something resembling an Asian civil society have tended to shift their focus to smaller towns and the countryside—where whatever self-organization that did take place was always precarious and contingent upon events taking place at the imperial level.[17] I suspect that it was only with the "pluralistic" situation imposed upon certain cities by the foreign concessions and the creation of such colonial *entrepots* as Hong Kong, Macao, and Singapore that these large metropolitan centers could begin to develop into something more akin to European urban civil societies.[18]

Seventh Reflection. One thing that I was unable to detect in the literature on Asia was any awareness of what I have called above "the condition of dual autonomy" (first proposition). Much attention is paid to civil society's (limited) degree of autonomy from the state and its agents, but *virtually nothing was said about the autonomy of the units of Asian civil society from such primary and ascriptive social groups as the family, the clan, the village, or the firm.* By my reading—influenced in this matter, no doubt, by Hegel—it is equally important that these self-organized groups be capable of operating instrumentally and purposively without being controlled behind their formal organizational facades by the basic units of social production and reproduction. To have those potentially democratic virtues outlined in my eighth proposition, these groups must be able to govern themselves civically, not instinctively or traditionally. This does not necessarily mean they must govern themselves "democratically"—indeed, the social-scientific literature on associations and movements since Roberto Michels has been replete with examples of well-entrenched oligarchy. But it does mean self-organized groups must display a degree of collective deliberation and decision making in which the participants have at least some putatively equal interest or passion. If the so-called members are members of the group ascriptively, by birth or social designation, and if they unreflexively obey its commands out of family, clan, ethnic group, or other traditional forms of loyalty, then it would be a mistake to call that organization a unit of civil society.

Reading between the lines (and limited by my inability to find much monographic literature on how specific associations have operated in different Asian polities), I think I detect a strong undercurrent of dependence upon primary units of production and reproduction. I wonder how many business associations reflect only the domination of a particular ethnic lineage or village of origin, and how many neighborhood or village organizations owe their existence and clout to a single person or extended family. To what extent is it possible for individuals to overcome the tissue of hierarchical, interpersonal, and interfamilial relationships that surround them and treat one another as equals having equivalent interests or passions? Again, I will not be surprised to learn that "it varies," that is, that it is more possible, say, in South Korea than in Taiwan. Or perhaps some ethnic minorities—say, the Chinese in Indonesia or Malaysia—are able to sustain high levels of collective action by relying heavily on family, lineage, and village ties while the natives in these countries are more civilly but weakly organized and depend more upon the support of the state.

Eighth Reflection. *All of the modernizing capitalist societies of Asia have resorted at one time or another to state-corporatist arrangements in order to control the political consequences of such a transformation.* This is hardly surprising since, as Mihael Manoilescu predicted some time ago, all peripheral countries in the emerging world capitalist system would at least be tempted to resort to such devices in order to catch up with their economic and political forerunners. In my review of his prophesy about the "Century of Corporatism," I explored the changes that took place in Southern Europe and Latin America beginning in the 1920s and 1930s when various types of authoritarian regimes sought to use the public sponsorship of monopolistic, hierarchically structured, and officially mandated interest organizations to mobilize and control designated sectors and professions—and to prevent the assertion of class-based movements whose conflictual behavior might have inhibited the regimes' projects for modernization from above.[19] Only later, through the work of students that I shared with Tang Tsou at the University of Chicago, did I become aware that similar tendencies were present in the ideological tenets of the Republican China of Sun Yat-sen and the Kuomintang, tendencies that were later to guide the associational practices of the exiled republic on Taiwan. Moreover, post–World War II South Korea, Indonesia, and Thailand also experimented with analogous arrangements for state corporatism.[20]

In the process of their more recent liberalizations, a number of Asian countries, including the People's Republic of China (PRC), have instituted new systems for registering (and presumably monitoring) social organizations. Apparently, these do not all involve classic state-corporatist provisions, which allow for the recognition only of one organization per category,[21] compel organizations that are recognized to join a similarly approved (and even more tightly controlled) national peak association,[22] and force all potential beneficiaries to contribute as if they were members.[23] What is not clear from the accounts I have read is whether these same systems can also be used to "deregister" those associations that exceed certain bounds in their opposition to official policies.[24] In the case of Taiwan, where, until the 1980s, quite rigid party-state controls were imposed upon virtually all categories of interest representation, these controls appear to have been irreversibly removed.[25]

The subsequent results would seem to testify amply to the willingness of individual Asians—at least those in mainland China, Taiwan, and South Korea—to form and join associations that are intended to promote their collective interests independently—even aggressively—when state officials decide to tolerate such behavior. That should dispel any lingering doubts about cultural inhibitions against behaving in such a Western fashion—as if the activities of overseas Chinese and Koreans were not already sufficient proof of their respective skills in exploiting what Tocqueville called "the art of association"!

Ninth Reflection. I have left the most difficult questions for last: *Will civil society become an enduring component of the regime changes that have already begun to occur in Asia? Will these changes make a significant contribution to the eventual consolidation of democracy in this part of the world?* Even more challenging: *Will the emergence of civil societies in those Asian countries that have so far resisted democratization make a difference in their eventual outcomes?*

I have no credentials of regional specialization for answering any of these questions. I can, however, on the basis of comparison with those parts of the world that I know better and which, fortuitously, have preceded the countries of Asia in the process of democratization, offer some suggestions about where to look for the answers.

1) How do state corporatist systems transform themselves? It would seem that there is (so far) no direct route from party-state control over associability to a "societally" corporatist system in which monopolistic and hierarchically structured interest associations, which represent large categories of citizens, voluntarily bargain with one another and the state in the "concertation" of major policy issues. In short, there is no continuous institutional path from Southern Europe to Scandinavia or Austria. Brazil, Greece, and Turkey demonstrate that it is possible to democratize the territorially based systems of party representation and electoral competition without formally changing the state-corporatist arrangements of the previous regime. Italy, Portugal, and Spain show that if and when these arrangements are changed, a period of intensely competitive pluralist associability will follow that may only gradually and eventually give way to societal corporatism. Mexico at present is in the midst of an ambitious attempt to "change without changing" its previous state-corporatist system in the course of democratization—my hunch is that it will fail.

2) What is the capacity for associations and their leaders to exploit opportunistically the relatively fleeting balances of power that emerge in the course of a transition between contending forces? Although civil society is rarely in a position to determine the timing or even the nature of regime change,[26] its role can be crucial in pushing authoritarian rulers to go beyond their original limited intentions to liberalize a regime. Associations may be conjuncturally better placed than political parties to exploit the uncertainties of the transition because their leaders may be perceived as less threatening to incumbents, they may be more capable of withholding strategic resources needed to accomplish specific tasks of government, and they may have more control over their members than do party leaders. Consequently, associations may emerge from the consolidation with relatively secure rights and privileges.

3) What is the status of the rule of law? The long-term prospects for civil society in Asia are also connected with a gradual and unobtrusive process that may be proceeding independently of regime change and democratization: the assertion of the rule of law. It was immensely important to the outcomes in Southern Europe (at least, Italy, Spain, and Portugal) and in part of Latin America (Chile and Uruguay) that the independence of the judiciary and respect for certain general legal principles was not completely destroyed by authoritarian rulers and could recover quickly upon authoritarianism's demise. The units of civil society depend on legal definitions and protections for their very existence, and they can be very skillful in exploiting legal loopholes and subtleties for the benefit of their members. As Minxin Pei observes in his essay in this collection, there may be quite independent reasons why autocratic rulers engaged in an economic transformation develop an interest in the effective and fair implementation of laws, especially those dealing with property rights and the settlement of commercial disputes.[27] To some extent, the organizations of civil society can "free-ride" on this objective, but they can also seek to extend it to cover a wider range of objectives.

I am aware that the ten general propositions put forth here have been articulated with a great deal more confidence than the nine regionally specific speculations. My hopes are that the former will attract efforts at empirical falsification on the part of scholars throughout the world and that the latter will inspire critical reconceptualization by those specializing in Asia.

NOTES

An earlier version of the first part of this essay was published as "Some Propositions About Civil Society and the Consolidation of Democracy" (Research Memorandum No. 10, Political Science Series, Institute for Advanced Studies, Vienna, September 1993).

1. I apologize to the reader for not being able to provide specific citations to justify this particular definition of civil society. It condenses my reading of classic writings such as those of the two Adams (Ferguson and Smith) on the importance of rational autonomy and the limits imposed by moral sentiments; Montesquieu on the notion of *corps intermédiaires*; Burke on "little platoons"; Hegel on the necessity of dual autonomy; Tocqueville on the role of internal deliberation and political learning; Durkheim on the emphasis on specialization and norm-generation by associations; von Gierke on the

possibility of legal personality and self-administration; and Gramsci on the centrality of the state in relation to class, sectoral, and (especially) professional associations.

I have also taken much from contemporary treatments of these issues, especially Antony Black, *Guilds and Civil Society in European Political Thought* (London: Methuen, 1984); and John Keane, *Democracy and Civil Society* (London: Verso, 1988).

As a participant in the Real Utopias Project on associations and democracy (built around a series of workshop conferences sponsored by the A.E. Havens Center for the Study of Social Structure and Social Change at the University of Wisconsin), I had the opportunity to talk (and, sometimes, to disagree) with some of the best theorists currently attempting to improve the quality of thinking on civil society: Joshua Cohen, Paul Hirst, Jane Mansbridge, Claus Offe, Joel Rogers, Wolfgang Streeck, and Iris Young. Our essays have been compiled in Joshua Cohen, Joel Rogers, et al., *Associations and Democracy*, ed. Erik Olin Wright (London: Verso, 1995).

2. This approach to the process of consolidation of democracy is developed conceptually and explored empirically in chapters 5 and 6 of my forthcoming book, tentatively entitled *Essaying the Consolidation of Democracy*.

3. For a more complete development of the contrasting implications of the pluralist-corporatist distinction, see my "Consolidation of Democracy and Representation of Social Groups," *American Behavioral Scientist* 35 (March–June 1992): 422–49; and my article "Corporatism," in Joel Krieger, ed., *The Oxford Companion to Politics of the World* (New York and Oxford: Oxford University Press, 1993), 195–98.

4. Guillermo O'Donnell and Philippe C. Schmitter, *Transitions from Authoritarian Rule: Tentative Conclusions About Uncertain Democracies* (Baltimore: Johns Hopkins University Press, 1986).

5. The first assertion—that normally the mobilization of civil society takes place *after*, not before, the transition and hence cannot be credited with bringing the transition about—has accumulated so many exceptions that its descriptive status is doubtful. South Korea, the Philippines, and perhaps Peru are cases in which "people power in the streets" probably determined both the timing and the nature of the subsequent transition. E. Gyimah-Boadi suggests in his chapter in this collection that, in Africa, organizations of civil society have been more prominent in motivating regime change. As a nonexpert in that area, I accept the correction—although I cannot help but observe that most of these civil-society–generated transitions proved to be abortive, as was the case in Chile in the early 1980s.

The second assertion—that normally the resurrection of civil society is followed by a demobilization of its units once credible elections are convoked and political parties take over—has proved to be even more controversial. I owe to Tracy Fitzsimmons's doctoral research on Chile the corrective that many organizations of civil society do not so much demobilize as *remobilize* themselves around other objectives, such as the provision of direct services to their members, once the transition is under way. Fitzsimmons, "Paradoxes of Participation: Organizations and Democratization in Latin America" (Ph.D. diss., Stanford University, 1995).

6. *Strategic capacity* is defined as the ability of new or recently renovated organizations (with sufficient resources and autonomy) to define and sustain over the long run a course of action that is neither linked exclusively to the immediate preferences of their members nor dependent upon the policies of parties and agencies external to their domain.

7. *Encompassing scope* is defined as the breadth of the interest domain as defined by each association and accepted by relevant authorities.

8. The positive relation between pluralism and democracy has always been taken for granted; that between corporatism and democracy has always been more contested. For the contrast between these modes of intermediation, see my "Democratic Theory and Neo-Corporatist Practice," *Social Research* 50 (Winter 1983): 885–928.

9. E.E. Schattschneider, *The Semi-Sovereign People: A Realist's View of Democracy in America* (New York: Harper and Row, 1960).

10. For the record, I should note that all of these "public" facilitating conditions involve the exercise of power relations that are subject not only to discretionary implementation but also to eventual changes in government and party in power.

11. For the record, I should insert the caveat that all of these "private" facilitations stem from cultural factors that are notoriously difficult to measure *ex ante* and to impute *ex post*.

12. Joseph Fewsmith, "From Guild to Interest Group: The Transformation of Public and Private in Late Qing China," *Comparative Studies in Society and History* 25 (1983): 617–40.

13. At the conference on which the present book is based, I was corrected by a participant from the Philippines who affirmed that her country does have distinctive and traditional modes of societal self-organization. What is not clear to me is whether these groups are sufficiently corporate in nature and whether they have a minimum degree of those features we earlier identified with civil society: dual autonomy, deliberative capacity, nonusurpation, and civility.

14. I am especially indebted to Hal Kahn for calling to my attention the symposium "Public Sphere/Civil Society in China?" *Modern China* 19 (April 1993). This publication had a major impact on my thinking about this issue. Needless to say, the research reported in this source is confined to China, although its generalizations presumably could be extended to overseas Chinese communities and other countries strongly affected by Chinese culture and practices. As I observed above in my first reflection, however, this is a diverse region. Recent events in South Korea and the Philippines certainly suggest a greater autonomy of associations and movements from state authority.

15. What I did not find, however, was a phenomenon that appears frequently in the background of the few writings on Islamic civil society—namely, the role of apparently spontaneous outbursts by urban marginal populations unstructured by professional or neighborhood organizations but manipulated in a clandestine fashion by shadowy elite conspiracies. This impression may be just a function of my limited knowledge of modern Asian history (what about the Boxer Rebellion?), but my hunch is that Asian cities may have been more internally structurated and hence not as vulnerable to insurrection as were the large agglomerations of the Arab world.

16. Just think of Germany, a country that pioneered new forms of societal self-organization. Many of its most important business and professional groups owe their origin to state promotion during the *Grunderjahre* of the Second Reich. Even in advance of the *Machtergreifung* and subsequent *Gleichsaltung* of the Third Reich, some of the groups had voluntarily gone over to National Socialism before 1933. Today, under admittedly different management and laws, these groups are resourceful and reliable bulwarks of a stable democracy. Similar observations could be made about many of the basic organizations of French, Dutch, Belgian, Italian, Spanish, and Portuguese civil societies.

17. See Minxin Pei's chapter in this collection. Perhaps not coincidentally, he emphasizes changes at the grassroots level of self-government in villages and small cities—and barely mentions any comparable changes in the large cities of the PRC.

18. This reflection makes it even more puzzling to me that the discussion of civil society among Asian specialists should be so impregnated with assumptions about a so-called public sphere. Not only is there some difficulty in applying Habermas's notion to Europe (like Marx, he seems to have fabricated a European model by combining the socioeconomics of the continent with the politics of Great Britain), but such an application would seem to be a complete nonstarter in Asia, where *Stadtluft* did not make people free!

19. See my "Still the Century of Corporatism?" in F.B. Pike and T. Stritch, eds., *The New Corporatism* (Notre Dame, Ind.: Notre Dame University Press, 1974), 85–131. See also Robert Bianchi, "Interest Group Politics in the Third World," *Third World Quarterly* 8 (April 1986): 507–39.

20. Belatedly, I would like to thank Joseph Fewsmith, Dwight King, Jang Jip Choi,

Marc Blecher, and Montri Chenvidyakarn, whose respective work on republican China, Indonesia, South Korea, communist China, and Thailand brought these state-corporatist temptations to my attention. James Babb's work at Stanford University on associability and party strategies in postwar Japan has also convinced me of the validity of this generalization for that country.

21. Actually, the "Management Regulations on the Registration of Social Organizations" of the People's Republic of China (Document No. 43, October 1989) does contain a provision that limits recognition to one social organization per interest category. Jude Howell in his case study of Xiaoshan argues that this is widely circumvented by the artful use of more specialized titles. See Howell, "Interest Groups in Post-Mao China: Civil Society or Corporatism?" (paper presented at the Sixteenth World Congress of the International Political Science Association, Berlin, 21–25 August 1994), 21–22.

22. The formation of national-level associations in the PRC is more carefully policed and restricted than the formation of branch organizations. Howell, "Interest Groups in Post-Mao China," 22.

23. Two very interesting exceptions where membership is compulsory in Xiaoshan (and presumably elsewhere in the PRC) are the Association of Individual Laborers and the Association of Private Entrepreneurs. Ibid., 23.

24. The one source I have relied upon for the PRC hints that proliferation may have peaked during the "tumultuous year of 1989"—just before the registration system was instituted in October of 1989. Ibid., 9.

25. For a very convincing interpretation of this process, I am indebted to Ngo Tak-wing, "Civil Society and Political Liberalization in Taiwan," *Bulletin of Concerned Asian Scholars* 25 (January–March 1993): 3–12.

26. Asia does offer at least two cases so far in which widespread mobilization by civil society did have a quite significant impact upon the initiation of regime change: the Philippines and, even more so, South Korea. I am particularly indebted to Sun-hyuk Kim's recent Stanford dissertation on civil society in South Korea for clarifying this issue. Sun-hyuk Kim, "From Resistance to Representation: Civil Society in South Korean Democratization" (Ph.D. diss., Stanford University, 1996).

27. Ibid., 6–12.

13

FROM OPPOSITION TO ATOMIZATION

Aleksander Smolar

Aleksander Smolar *is chairman of the Stefan Batory Foundation in Warsaw and senior research fellow at the Centre National de la Recherche Scientifique in Paris. He has served as chief political advisor to Tadeusz Mazowiecki, the first postcommunist prime minister of Poland, and foreign policy advisor to Prime Minister Hanna Suchocka. Among his publications is* L'Europe de l'Est 1989–1990 *(1991).*

The peaceful revolutions of 1989 in Central and Eastern Europe were carried out in the name of "civil" society, and the related word "citizen" was one of the most frequently used terms in the public discourse of that time. Citizens' committees, citizens' movements, citizens' assemblies, citizens' initiatives, citizens' parliamentary clubs, and citizens' parties all sprang into being. Today, just a few years later, talk of "civil society" is no longer much heard in the streets, and the idea seems to have gone back whence it came, to discussions held among intellectuals on the changing shape of postcommunist countries. The remarkable rise and fall of the concept of civil society is itself worth examining.

As used in Central and Eastern Europe, the notion of civil society never had much to do with the grand theoretical debates that one may trace across two centuries in the works of Locke, Adam Ferguson, Adam Smith, Hegel, Tocqueville, Marx, and Gramsci, among others. To speak of civil society was instead to express a twofold opposition. The first dimension was opposition to authority. Civil society was "us"; the authorities were "them." The second dimension was one in which civil society was held up in contradistinction to "the nation," understood in hereditary, ethnic terms. The potency of ethnic nationalism in Central and Eastern Europe is well known: ethnicity had long furnished the most salient way of dividing "us" from "them," and Marxist class analysis could not rival it for popularity or profundity of influence.

Although the national-patriotic, even nativist, strain of opposition to communism would in time produce its own champions and manifest its own influence, the tone of dissidence during the 1970s and most of the 1980s was set by intellectuals with left-liberal, Western-oriented views. In speaking the language of civil society, they were implicitly challenging the traditionally dominant ethnic conception of the nation with a nonethnic, political concept. By promoting civil society rather than ethnic community, they were not only proposing a wholly different way of defining "us" and "them," but also suggesting a different way of looking at both the past and the future.

The reflections on civil society and the strategy for its self-organization produced by figures such as Czechoslovakia's Václav Havel, Poland's Jacek Kuroń and Adam Michnik, and Hungary's János Kis (to name some of the most prominent) grew out of the oppositionists' reassessment of past failures to overthrow or reform "really existing socialism" in Central and Eastern Europe.[1]

The Hungarian Uprising of 1956 and the Prague Spring of 1968—the former an armed rebellion and the latter a peaceful revolution sparked by the top-down innovations of reform-minded elites—had roused hopes that the communist system imposed on the region by the USSR could be overthrown by force or transformed by nonviolent political change. In both cases, hope was crushed by the tanks of the Red Army. Clearly, any direct challenge to the Soviet empire was doomed.

From 1956 on, there had been numerous efforts to introduce liberalization and democratization by means of gradual reforms. These efforts fell into three categories, each distinguished by its guiding strategy. The first approach, which I call "politics first," was premised on the idea that the reform of party and state institutions was key because, under real socialism, the party-state commanded the economy and society. The reforms begun in Poland in 1956 typified this strategy.

The dominant approach in the 1960s was the "economics-first" strategy. This focused on the economy as the most promising place to start, because economic reform did not seem threateningly political and because officials could more easily be enlisted to support changes designed to increase output and raise living standards. Some proponents of what came to be called "market socialism" hoped that economic change would open the door to social and eventually political change as well.

The third strategy, associated with the era of détente in the 1970s, stressed the influence that economic linkages with the West might come to exert over developments within the Soviet Union and Eastern Europe. The more the countries of the East bloc could be made to depend on flows of Western credit, technology, and trade, went the theory popular in many Western political circles and among some communist reformers, the more they would be induced to respect the human rights guarantees spelled out in the "third basket" of the 1975 Helsinki Agreement, to limit repressive practices, and to liberalize their economies.

The three strategies did help to expand the sphere of social autonomy in the countries of the Soviet bloc, especially Poland and Hungary, but progress was limited and uneven, and gains often precarious. In 1968, armed Soviet intervention against "socialism with a human face" in Czechoslovakia greatly diminished reformist hopes in Eastern and Central Europe. Yet this disillusionment, along with previous progress, paved the way for a fourth strategy, elaborated by independent intellectuals in the region, which I call the "society-first" approach. In the mid-1970s, they seized on what they saw as (to paraphrase Lenin) the weak link of the communist system. Their approach was one of antipolitics, and their discourse was the language of morality.

"Society First"

The "society-first" program, though formulated in scores of articles, can be summed up in a few sentences. Its first postulate, expressed memorably by Solzhenitsyn and Havel, was *living in truth*. This was a genuine moral imperative, and also a way of denying the legitimacy of a public realm that rested on the forced acceptance of an official definition of reality. The second postulate was the value of *self-organization*. Associations formed and acts of solidarity carried out beyond the purview of the party-state were valued in themselves, and as contributors to the reconstruction of authentic social ties. The third postulate was *respect for law*. Hungarian dissident János Kis wrote of the importance of "the conspicuous exercise of rights."[2] The constitutions and laws of the "people's republics" became instruments of the struggle, as did such provisions of international law as the Helsinki Accords.

Under whatever name—"parallel *polis*," "independent culture," or "independent society"—the idea of civil society remained largely restricted to narrow circles of independent intellectuals in every East and Central European country save one. The exception, of course, was Poland. There, committees for the defense of students, religious believers, and peasants sprang up, as did unofficial "flying universities" and what became the seeds of political parties and, most famously, the Solidarity trade union, which grew out of the Lenin Shipyard strike in Gdansk in the summer of 1980. The society-first strategy was supposed to lead to the gradual rebuilding of civil society, which as it grew was in turn expected steadily and quietly to narrow the terrain over which the party-state actually held sway. The communist parties might never be dethroned, but the substance of their power might be hollowed out to the point where, like the queen of England, they would reign but not rule.

The society-first plan to rebuild islands of social independence soon became the vehicle of even higher ideological hopes. In this gloss, the islands came to be seen as the harbingers of a future society beyond not only communism, but also Western-style capitalist democracy. The civil society taking shape in Central and Eastern Europe would respond not only to the crisis of "real socialism," but to the problems of the West as well. The society-first strategy and its antipolitical approach were taken to portend a worldwide change in human civilization itself.

The first congress of Solidarity spelled out something like this vision in its document on the "self-governing republic," which meant civil society emancipated from the tutelage of the state. Such notions had more than one source: one can see in them a trace of Marx's idea of the withering away of the state, but there was also a strong tincture of traditional Polish antipathy to the state (understandable in a country with a history of foreign rule).

The ideology of civil society had ties to the totalitarian paradigm. In the West, this way of describing communism was associated with authors like Hannah Arendt, Carl J. Friedrich, and Zbigniew Brzezinski. Despite its prestige, the totalitarian model had been rejected by most professional Sovietologists and political commentators by the end of the 1950s. In some quarters, to speak of totalitarianism was to risk being thought a right-wing "Cold Warrior" with an unscientific, ideological view of communist reality. In the 1970s and 1980s, some Western experts on the USSR and other communist countries rated the differences between the democratic West and these countries as merely secondary. Rather than speak of communism or totalitarianism, these scholars spoke of modernizing, bureaucratic, or corporatist systems characterized by organizational or institutional pluralism.

At the same time, oddly enough, the totalitarian model began to predominate in the thinking of independent circles within the communist world itself.[3] By the 1970s, conditions in Poland, Hungary, and even Czechoslovakia and the USSR were a far cry from what they had been under Stalinism. So in a sense, the description of "really existing socialism" offered by dissidents in the East was as unrealistic as that offered by most Western Sovietologists. The new popularity of the totalitarian model among Central and East European dissidents reflected their increasing alienation and marginalization, their loss of confidence that the system could be reformed from within.

The socialism of the 1970s and 1980s was obviously different from that of the 1940s and 1950s, when communist parties still had genuine revolutionary aspirations. Society was becoming less totalitarian, but the institutions created during the revolutionary period retained their form. To put it another way, totalitarianism as a millenarian movement had long since died, but the set of institutions that it had created was left behind like the fossilized carcass of some extinct beast—the party-state that controlled and corrupted state, society, and economy alike.

Paradoxically, the opposition owed its continued existence to the tacit tolerance of the very state that the oppositionists denounced as totalitarian. This tolerance was scarcely principled, of course, being due mainly to pressure from the West (economic interests plus the Helsinki process, plus the need for respectability).

Although it left much to be desired as a description of reality, the totalitarian paradigm played an important role in mobilizing and integrating independent circles of dissidents. The stark opposition of truth versus falsity, spontaneity versus command, voluntarism versus compulsion, and liberty versus bondage served to set apart the world of the nascent opposition that called itself "civil society" from the official world of the party-state and all its works.

The educational and standard-setting role that the opposition played during the 1970s and 1980s was key: it popularized civic attitudes and the ideal of a rule of law, and undermined the legitimacy of the existing order. The emerging islands of civil society contributed to the elaboration and articulation of alternative collective identities and values in the several countries of Central and Eastern Europe. With the crumbling of the state's monopoly over news, public discourse, and the formulation of visions for the future, dissidents were able to make major contributions to the opening of an authentic public sphere.

These efforts were part of the Central and East European opposition's overall strategy of creating what might be called a "minimal civil society." The word "minimal" is appropriate because even when the Solidarity era was at its height, civil societies in the East bloc had little in common with what is called civil society in developed democracies with long traditions of social autonomy. Similarly, the terms "defensive" and "moral" civil society might also be used, denoting an entity that defined itself in opposition to the state.[4] But a civil society whose essence was radical opposition to the communist state could not survive the disappearance of that state. As the hour of victory over communism arrived, however, this had not yet become evident.

After 1989

A burst of euphoria followed the defeat of the communist state—a defeat that was widely seen as signaling the victory of civil society. Poland's June 1989 elections were won by the Citizens' Committees that had sprung up like mushrooms all over the country. "We don't need to define [civil society]," said the prominent Polish dissident Bronislaw Geremek in August 1989, "We see it and feel it."[5] Jiri Dienstbier, a future Czechoslovak foreign minister, spoke of "civil society in power" as Civic Forum became the outgoing communist regime's chief negotiating partner during the Velvet Revolution.

Symbolically, the toppling of the Berlin Wall in 1989 played the same role as the taking of the Bastille had in 1789. In an instant, the "revolutionary civil society" came into being. Yet the feeling of triumph, the holiday atmosphere, did not last. The existence of a civil society of resistance was dependent upon the existence of a hostile state that offered no hope for compromise. As soon as this state disappeared, the civil society that opposed it also disintegrated. The revolutionary civil society is by definition a transient phenomenon, even though it remains deeply embedded in the minds of its participants as a myth and an ideal.

The illusion of "civil society in power" and the opposition's antipolitical ideology had certain important, though fleeting, consequences. Dissidents swept into power by the revolutions of 1989 strove vainly to preserve the unity of the amorphous organizations of the moral civil society. Their efforts were spurred by an aversion to parties and partisanship that had its roots in a profound skepticism about traditional political distinctions. Many civil-society activists felt that the division between left and right was an obsolete convention with no relevance to the real choices facing societies emerging from communism. At the same time, they realized that it was no longer tenable to divide their countries' political space into totalitarian and democratic camps. Many of the new leaders' utterances revealed a belief that Central and East Europeans could find new forms of political organization and interest representation that escaped the drawbacks and costs associated with Western-style parliamentary democracy.

The myth of civil society as united, antipolitical, and supportive of radical reform was one of the first casualties of the postcommunist era. As soon as communist authorities showed themselves willing to bargain over the division of power (or even to give it up outright), politics reasserted itself. What had been "moral civil societies" became political blocs—first in opposition, and then, with the decomposition of the old ruling structures, in power. Civil society, it turned out, had been a historical costume; its usefulness disappeared with the times that dictated its wearing. Broad-front organizations broke up when faced with real political decisions, and multiparty systems began to form. Concrete choices and responsibilities cured many of the leaders of moral civil society of their illusory notions about the possibility of a "third way" beyond capitalism and socialism or dictatorship and democracy. What replaced these fancies was the decision to imitate Western arrangements like constitutional democracy, the market, and the rule of law. "Returning to Europe" or "becoming a normal society" became the watchwords of most of the leaders who came from the ranks of the democratic opposition to communism.

Moral civil society suffered blows from all sides. Its activists moved *en masse* into government and business, leaving a plethora of associations, human rights groups, independent publishing concerns, and informal educational institutions without enough people to keep them going. One especially poignant example was the mass recruitment into the Polish Ministry of Home Affairs, including the political police, of young activists from the pacifist group Freedom and Peace.

The greatest shock for civil-society activists, however, was their discovery of society's real condition. The "revolutions" of 1989 happened not because civil society was tremendously strong, but because Gorbachev's policies of *glasnost'* and *perestroika* had created a deepening international crisis for the Soviet Union's satellite regimes in Central and Eastern Europe. It soon became clear that the former oppositionists could command only limited social support, even where there was profound discontent with the old order. All of civil society's weaknesses had been blamed on the crippling effects of the *ancien régime*. With the crumbling of the party-state, the hobbles were removed and the test was at hand. Would the virtues attributed to civil society—a supposedly greater bent toward idealism and resistance to Western-style materialism, for instance—come to the fore?

After 1989, leading ideologists of civil society like Václav Havel and Adam Michnik became severe critics of their own societies. They painted dark portraits of countries teeming with intolerance, xenophobia, undemocratic tendencies, materialism, and so on.[6] An outpouring of literature detailed the ravages that the *ancien régime* had left behind. Just a few years before, many of the same authors had been writing about popular aspirations for independence, the strength of traditional values, the signs of passive and even active resistance; now their favorite subject became the peril that postcommunist society posed for political and economic reform. A host of writers detected and decried attitudes and behaviors inconsistent with the values of civil society. Much ink was spilled describing *homo sovieticus*—the stunted, distrustful human type produced by real socialism. As one astute observer noted with a touch of irony: "Somehow, imperceptibly, a magnificent society, admired by the whole world, has turned into an unpredictable mass posing a danger to its own existence; it can be said in its defense only that, for a long time, it was subjugated under communism."[7]

Limiting the State

In the 1980s, when there were still no signs of the coming implosion of real socialism in Central and Eastern Europe, oppositionists used to ask a waggish question that could not quite conceal the deep anxiety which lay behind it. "We know that you can make fish soup out of an aquarium," they would say, "but can you make an aquarium out of fish soup?" In other words: Can we rebuild a civil society, a viable democracy, and a developed market economy in countries seared by decades of communist rule? Today, one can risk giving a positive answer, which implies that the "aquarium," even when communist terror was at its apogee, never quite became "fish soup." At the same time, the experiences of recent years have laid bare enormous differences among countries that had long been subject to similar institutions and mechanisms of control. Differences rooted in remote history and variegated traditions came to the fore, though the great influence of choices being made today is also evident. Thus the current situation and future prospects of the Central European countries (Poland, the Czech Republic, Hungary, Slovenia, Slovakia, and probably Croatia) and the Baltic republics (Lithuania, Latvia, and Estonia) look very different from those of the other former Soviet republics or of the Balkan countries (Romania, Bulgaria, Albania, Serbia, and the other ex-Yugoslav republics aside from Croatia and Slovenia).

Eradicating the communist legacy required action in two main directions: a radical separation of the economic, social, and political realms, and a limitation of the role of the state. Under communism—even in its softer and shrunken version—there was no society, economy, or even state in the strict sense: these domains were strictly integrated and subordinated to a single power apparatus. This was true not only "at the top" but also "at the bottom": in addition to their economic role, enterprises also performed important social, cultural, and other functions. Once communism fell, then, it was necessary to make a clean break with totalitarian indistinction; to separate political parties from the state; to divide power within the state; and to peel the economy, politics, and social life away from one another.

The powers of the state were limited in varying degrees in different postcommunist countries, but it was everywhere streamlined and decentralized. "Public space" was reopened through the abolition of censorship, the provision of greater access to the mass media, and so on. The political police were put on a shorter leash. Old constitutions were replaced or heavily amended. Legislation began to conform to international standards. Political competition became the order of the day. A third sector, nonprofit and nongovernmental, came into being as a result of changes in the laws governing associations, foundations, and social organizations.

Economic life was revolutionized. In many postcommunist countries, including Russia, the private sector now accounts for half or more of GDP. Trade and investment barriers were removed, and extensive privatization and reprivatization has occurred. Real banking sectors and capital markets are taking shape throughout most of the region.

The years after 1989 saw liberal thought become intellectually—if not always politically—predominant in the countries that lead the region in development. Leading liberals like Prime Minister Václav Klaus of the Czech Republic maintained that if artificial restrictions were removed, the totalitarian state was dismantled, and basic rules of the game were promulgated, markets and democracy would follow as a matter of course. In the transformation that he successfully conducted, Klaus's avowed emphasis was on "passive" policies (conscious self-limitation by the state, liberalization, and far-reaching deregulation). Klaus was not rigid about this: in carrying out voucher privatization, for instance, he pursued a more active course. (His government also carried out a highly active policy to protect jobs, delaying enactment of a law on enterprise bankruptcy for two years.) As Klaus himself summed up the work of his government:

> During the last two years, we completed the creation of a pluralistic democratic system that guarantees basic civic liberties and enables every one of us to benefit from these freedoms. . . . A market economy was also instituted, with a small and constantly diminishing role for the state. . . . In the political, economic, and civic domains every one of us has adequate space for taking decisions freely and for individual initiative.[8]

The liberal approach displays a broad streak of optimism about people's adaptive capacities. Change is initiated from the top, but success depends on setting in motion the creative forces of society. The market is a source of strong negative stimuli—the threat of bankruptcy, unemployment, or downward mobility—and of positive incentives—the lure of riches, power, and social prestige. A voucher system neutralizes much of the potential social opposition to privatization. Mythical ownership by the whole people gives way to the aggregate of individual ownerships. The socialist ideology of equality yields to the liberal ideology of enrichment, and the idea of collective advancement to that of individual prosperity.

The liberal vision of spontaneous social reconstruction is antipolitical. The transformation of economies and societies is described in largely technical terms: the rules of the market and the open society must be grafted into place as quickly as possible so that the patient cannot reject the transplant. Questions are never raised about the social groups at which the reforms are aimed and the social forces on which they rely. Sometimes the "middle class" is mentioned, but with little or no acknowledgment that in Central and Eastern Europe this group remains a spirit seeking a social body.

Initially, the liberal program enjoyed wide social support, mostly because it represented the absolute antithesis of the *ancien régime*. Yet this support waned daily in virtually every country of the region (though it remains highest in the Czech Republic). In fact, the real base of the economic and social revolution lay in government circles (especially the executive branch and its advisors), the new business class, and small groups of intellectuals.

Central and Eastern Europe's liberal reformers have doubts concerning the concept of civil society. Prime Minister Klaus spoke freely of the "aberrant idea of civil society," obviously referring to Margaret Thatcher's famous statement that "there is no society, only individuals and their families." He seemed to regard civil society as a stalking horse for collectivism, new bureaucracies, and quixotic searches for the "third way."[9] Clearly alluding to President Havel, Klaus scored critics who were not satisfied with "free citizens" but wanted "better citizens" in the bargain, and warned of "moralizing, elitist, and perfectionist ambitions [that] would create a Huxleyan 'Brave New World.'"[10] Liberal reformers seem especially averse to the idea of interest representation in the economy, seeing it as a potential source of stifling corporatism and a threat to market-based reforms.

Lost in Postcommunism

The ideology of the moral civil society placed its hopes in self-organization, self-help, and citizens' activities. These hopes stemmed from the belief that "totalitarian" restraints had bound potent social forces which were yearning to operate freely. Apart from the sphere of the economy and, to a certain degree, of local government (especially in Poland), however, levels of autonomous social activity have been disappointing.

Of the many reasons for this, the most important (at least at first) was the severe economic recession of the early 1990s. People beset by joblessness and falling real incomes are preoccupied with survival and are unlikely to plunge into social, cultural, scientific, political, and philanthropic activities. State budgetary crises prompted a trimming of all "unnecessary" expenditures, including those that might have supported activities independent of the state. Under pressure from such constraints, and sometimes also for doctrinal reasons, some governments in the region tried to shift a large share of the responsibility for health care, schooling, scientific research, and social welfare to society.

Flight from the public to the private sphere may be regarded as a natural reaction to years of forced participation and mobilization. Everyday life under socialism taught people to survive as individuals and to fear any association with independent collective action. Far from creating a "new socialist man" free of egotism and greed, communism actually bred atomized, amoral cynics good at doubletalk and "working the system," but not at effective enterprise. The shakiness of independent organizations, including political parties, suggests the lack of a culture of free collective activity.

The societies of disintegrating communism were places where civil society, traditions, moral norms, the rule of law, and voluntary organizations had been destroyed or greatly weakened. The more intensely totalitarian the regime, the more dramatic were the consequences of its collapse. In many parts of the Balkans and the former Soviet Union, where communists had ruled traditionally patriarchal societies with an iron hand, the collapse of official control mechanisms had disastrous consequences. As a Russian journalist put it, "In the past there were rules to the game, good or bad or whatever. And there was fear. Now there are no rules, good or bad, and there is no fear."[11]

The countries of Central and Eastern Europe have seen the collapse of much of the network of state-run or formal social institutions that performed functions ordinarily belonging to civil society. In the moribund phase of socialism, numerous social-welfare and income-redistribution tasks were handled by state enterprises rather than by specialized public or private agencies. Today, economic rationality dictates that enterprises relinquish these tasks. The whole system of housing subsidies, employee vacations, sports clubs, health and child care, and so on has disappeared.

The collapse of many social organizations associated with the communist party also helped to weaken social bonds. Although these bodies unquestionably aided the regime's efforts at social control and indoctrination, they also often became the basis of useful social networks. Sports clubs, community centers, summer camps, youth groups, pensioners' clubs, and so on filled a certain void, albeit one that the communist system itself had created by suppressing all autonomous versions of such institutions. Today, tight state budgets, skepticism about old ties of power and subordination, and the conscious liquidation of communist-run institutions have conspired to eliminate this network.

Establishing new institutions for civil society takes time, will, skill, and funds. In the meantime, one gets the paradoxical impression that society today is no less—indeed, perhaps even more—atomized than it was in the final years of communism. People seem to feel "lost" in the new reality of postcommunism. As Elemer Hankiss explains:

> By now, millions of people have lost, or fear that they may lose, their traditional roles and positions in the sphere of production and distribution. They have lost their way in the labyrinths of social and industrial relationships, which are in the midst of a chaotic transformation. People do not know anymore, or yet, what are the rules of the new games, what are their duties and rights, what they have to do for what, what is the cost and reward of what. There is no authority to tell, there are no values to refer to.[12]

Not all the communist-affiliated organizations disappeared from Central and Eastern Europe after 1989, and the ones that remain—including political parties, labor unions, and enterprise associations—are among the strongest influences in the terrain between the state and the individual or family. In the new conditions, to be sure, these organizations have different programs, and often new names and leaders as well. Sometimes they take an ideological line radically opposed to the one favored by their communist-era predecessors, but organizationally they are continuous.

Supporters of radical decommunization cite the failure to break cleanly with the old order as the reason for the institutional strength of the ex-communists. The *nomenklatura* managed to turn its political power into financial capital and retain control over a large part of the mass media and the work of nongovernmental organizations. The successors of communist parties and front groups also succeeded in hanging on to a considerable part of the assets of their predecessors.

It goes without saying that ex-communist parties, unions, and the like had an organizational head start over their newly formed democratic rivals. Still, the decommunizers' argument seems insufficient. The ex-communists adapted themselves ably to democratic conditions because even under communism their organizations had a double role: they not only represented the "authorities," but also filled real social needs. Today, for various reasons, alternative organizations that could fill these needs remain weak. The ex-communists have financial as well as human capital, plus the advantages of continuity; their organizations bring together hundreds of thousands of people who have lost (or not yet found) their bearings in the new postcommunist world.

The New Socialist Civil Society

Real socialism, which has disappeared as a political system and to a lesser extent as a form of economic organization, lives on in the minds of people and in the institutions of civil society. Without delving into the psychological, moral, and attitudinal legacies of real socialism, I would like to point out two of its remnants that have had a direct effect on the formation of new civil societies. One is the surprisingly durable social structure and set of interest groups that formed under it; the other is the similarly durable ensemble of informal social ties (the "shadow society") that people created in order to defend themselves against and cope with the demands of real socialism.

The years just after 1989 were a period of high hopes for independence, democracy, and the "return to Europe"; these made it possible to carry out costly reforms. As reform began to pinch and enthusiasm started to wane, the "politics of values" speedily gave way to the "politics of interests." Faith in a "better future" dwindled, and people focused on protecting their own. In fighting for their interests under postcommunism, the social groups formed under the old system unconsciously fight for the restoration of nonmarket, political mechanisms of shaping the social structure.

The mechanism that produces "socialist civil society" works as follows: anxiety over the liberal dismantling of the *ancien régime*, plus the awareness—thanks to the free mass media and the network of political and trade-union organizations—of real group interests, spurs protests against reform and support for those identified with the idealized past. This process goes on even after ex-communist parties like those in Poland and Hungary find out, once elected, that they have little choice but to forget their campaign rhetoric and stick with reform.

Some institutions left over from real socialism, like the communist-satellite Polish Peasant Party (PSL), have become truly independent since 1989. Formally autonomous but quiescent under communism, the PSL today staunchly guards peasant interests—a significant role in a country where more than a quarter of the population engages in small-scale agricultural production and where farming was never collectivized.

The historical joke in all this is that just when it lost political, economic, and spiritual power, real socialism found a refuge in the sphere that it had always tried to suppress: civil society. When real socialism held sway, the "shadow society" was a product of the official world's internal contradictions, ineffectiveness, and red tape—all weaknesses that enterprising individuals exploited in order to gain security, income, or social position. These "operators" fought the system, to be sure, but they cooperated with it as well. In mirror-image fashion, the communist authorities attempted to suppress such "informal" behaviors, but began to tolerate them as well, in part because they increased the system's own adaptive capacity, bringing it more into sync with the needs of society. The best example is the "parallel economy." This helped the official economy to function, but only because labor, capital, and raw materials were undergoing de facto (and illegal) privatization.

In the 1970s, as repression diminished in some East and Central European countries, informal networks began to form out of family ties, friendships, and intimate social circles. These arrangements not only provided practical benefits, but also helped to satisfy needs for belonging and a purpose in life. Society seemed to have two levels: one of artificial official institutions, and another of spontaneous connections formed as a defense against and an adaptation to the official world. In time, this mutual adaptation resulted in the integration and corruption of both worlds. Informal society undermined the logic of the official institutions, while the official world intensified the pathological narrowness of informal social bonds. Private and public gradually became intertwined: the state became privatized, while private life became collectivized.

The official society of real socialism disintegrated. The shadow society—its antithesis—has survived in various forms. Even today, studies reveal more confidence in informal ties that are based on circles of relatives and close friends (or officials who can be bribed) than in the anonymous world of institutions, legal norms, and complicated mechanisms such as those of democratic politics.[13] Although one can hardly say that the shadow society is "civil" or "civic," it does form one of the concentric circles of social autonomy inherited from the old system. As such, it influences the chances and nature of civil society proper.

Relegitimizing the Open Society

The vision of civil society that the anticommunist opposition in Central and Eastern Europe used in its fight for liberty has lost out as a social program. The moral civil society, an antipolitical, anticapitalist, anticommunist community, could endure as a viable ideal only so long as it remained unencumbered by the need to make real choices. Actual postcommunist civil society, which is rising atop the ruins of the old system, is composed partly of elements left over from this system and partly from the heritage of a more remote past. Civil society is being created in an unfavorable atmosphere of economic recession, withdrawal from public affairs, egotistic individualism, mistrust, and lack of a legal culture. It is arising from expressions of social autonomy that often are far removed from civility, if not their complete opposite. Its rise is also challenging the egalitarian outlook that numerous opinion surveys have shown to be deeply rooted in the minds of Central and East Europeans.

Citizens in Central and Eastern Europe can now form associations, publicly express opinions, vote, run for office, and so on. Yet as far as "social" and "economic" rights are concerned, the situation is different. Many think that liberalization and privatization have dramatically changed social relations and the composition of citizens' rights. The major problem facing postcommunist societies is how to relegitimize private property and the open society, with all the uncertainty that accompanies them. The moral foundations of private property—especially when its ownership is highly concentrated—have always been weak, and have needed support from values associated with religion, tradition, democracy, and human liberty. We cannot assume that this support will be present to legitimize private property and the market economy under the conditions of postcommunism.

Political, social, and economic change means a redistribution of costs and benefits among groups and individuals. The upper and middle classes, old and new alike, stand to benefit from the new shape of citizens' rights. Their biographies and the way they acquired their wealth evoke moral outrage—hardly a boon to legitimation. Meanwhile, those of a humbler sort, whose participation in public life is necessarily limited and who thus benefit less from the recovery of civil and political rights, are also the most affected by the new economic hardships. They do not stand to gain much from privatization, and it is costing them more now in terms of lost jobs and reduced living standards, even if in the long run they too will benefit from joining the modern world.

The civic principle is not just a principle of equality; it also creates the normative basis for the inner integration of civil society as well as its integration with the political system. The development of civil society, the consolidation of democracy, and the closer identification of citizens with state institutions—all these require counteracting the atomizing tendencies that the huge changes of recent years (however necessary and ultimately salutary) have set in motion.

NOTES

1. Václav Havel, "The Power of the Powerless," in John Keane, ed., *The Power of the Powerless* (New York: M.E. Sharpe, 1985), 92, 95; Jacek Kuroń, *Polityka i odpowiedzialnosc* (London: Aneks, 1984); Adam Michnik, *Letters from Prison and Other Essays* (Berkeley: University of California Press, 1985) and *Penser la Pologne* (Paris: La Découverte, 1983); and János Kis, *Politics in Hungary: For a Democratic Alternative* (Highland Lakes, N.J.: Atlantic Research and Publications, 1989).

2. G.M. Tamás, "The Legacy of Dissent: How Civil Society Has Been Seduced by the Cult of Privacy," *Times Literary Supplement*, 14 May 1993.

3. Jacques Rupnik, "Le totalitarisme vu de l'Est," in Guy Hermet, Pierre Hassner, and Jacques Rupnik, eds., *Totalitarismes* (Paris: Economica, 1984), 43–75.

4. Pierre Hassner, "Les révolutions ne sont plus ce qu'elles étaient," in Jacques Semelin, ed., *Quand les dictatures se fissurent . . . Résistances civiles à l'Est et au Sud* (Paris: Desclée de Brouwer, 1995).

5. Quoted in Flora Lewis, "Civil Society: Its Limits and Needs," *International Herald Tribune*, 30 September 1989. See also Bronislaw Geremek, "Civil Society Then and Now," *Journal of Democracy* 3 (April 1992): 3–12.

6. See, for example, Václav Havel, "Paradise Lost," *New York Review of Books*, 9 April 1992.

7. Jerzy Szacki, "Polish Democracy: Dreams and Reality," *Social Research* 58 (Winter 1991): 712.

8. Address of 6 December 1994 to the parliament of the Czech Republic, quoted in Václav Havel, Václav Klaus, and Petr Pithart, "Rival Visions," *Journal of Democracy* 7 (January 1996): 17.

9. *Lidove noviny* (Prague), 7 March 1994, quoted from Jiri Pehe, "Civic Society at Issue in the Czech Republic," *RFE/RL Research Report*, 19 August 1994.

10. Address of 17 November 1994 on the occasion of the anniversary of the Velvet Revolution, quoted in Havel, Klaus, and Pithart, "Rival Visions," 14.

11. Yuri Shchekochikhin, quoted in Margaret Shapiro, "Corruption Threatens to Spill Russia's Economic Brew," *Washington Post*, from the *International Herald Tribune*, 14 November 1994.

12. Elemer Hankiss, "Our Recent Past: Recent Developments in East Central Europe in the Light of Various Social Ideologies and Schools of Scholarly Thought" (address delivered at the Institut für die Wissenschaften vom Menschen, Vienna, Austria, 1994). See also Chris Hann, "Philosophers' Models on the Carpathian Lowlands," in John A. Hill, ed., *Civil Society: Theory, History, Comparison* (Cambridge, England: Polity Press, 1995), 158–83.

13. See Lena Kolarska-Bobińska, *Aspirations, Values, and Interests: Poland, 1989–1994* (Warsaw: IFiS Publishers, 1994); Winicjusz Narojek, *The Socialist "Welfare State"* (Warsaw: PWN, 1991); B. Paqueteau, "La société contre elle-même: Choses vues en Roumanie," *Commentaire* 59 (Autumn 1992): 621–28; and Mira Marody, ed., *What Has Remained from Those Years: Polish Society on the Threshold of Systemic Change* (London: Aneks, 1991).

14

CIVIL SOCIETY IN AFRICA

E. Gyimah-Boadi

E. Gyimah-Boadi, a Ghanaian political scientist, is director of the Governance Unit at the Institute of Economic Affairs in Accra, Ghana. Previously, he was assistant professor in the School of International Service at the American University and professorial lecturer at the School of Advanced International Studies, Johns Hopkins University, both in Washington, D.C. He has also taught at the University of Swaziland and the University of Ghana.

Among the forces that dislodged entrenched authoritarianism in Africa and brought about the beginnings of formal democracy in the early 1990s, the continent's nascent civil societies were in the forefront.[1] Although external influences such as the fall of communism and pressure from foreign donors were important, it was often the resourcefulness, dedication, and tenacity of domestic civil society that initiated and sustained the process of transition. The opening of once-forbidden debate on new political directions; the decriminalization of dissent and the acceptance (however grudging) of pluralist politics; the convening of sovereign national conferences and constituent assemblies; preparations for competitive elections; and, in a significant number of cases, the eventual installation of elected governments—for all these things, civil societies can take a large share of credit. Thanks to their efforts, a number of African countries have become part of what Samuel P. Huntington calls democracy's "third wave."[2]

With the first phase of democratization nearing completion, attention is shifting to the problem of consolidation.[3] Expectations regarding civil society's contribution are running high. Unfortunately, they are likely to be disappointed. Civil society remains too weak to be democracy's mainstay, not only in Nigeria and Zaire (where transitions have become stalemated), and in Burkina Faso, Cameroon, Ghana, Kenya, and Togo (where transition outcomes are still ambiguous), but also in Benin, Malawi, and South Africa (where outcomes have been more clearly successful). In nearly all cases, the ability of civil society to help deepen democratic governance and put it beyond reversal remains in serious doubt.

Why do civil society and its contribution to democratic consolidation remain so weak despite the much-touted vibrancy of African associational life? Why do African countries' prolific networks of associations and clubs not make for dense and interconnected civil societies? And what, finally, are the prospects that this will change? Can African civil societies become capable of assisting democratic consolidation?

The third wave hit Africa in late 1989, when civil servants, teachers, and traders in the small French-speaking republic of Benin demonstrated to demand an end to autocracy and economic mismanagement. As similar phenomena became commonplace in other parts of Africa in the early 1990s, similar domestic forces were found leading them. In Zambia, the Congress of Trade Unions and its chairman, Frederick Chiluba, successfully challenged the three-decade incumbency of President Kenneth Kaunda and his United Independence Party; union activism was also pivotal in Mali and Niger. In Ghana, Kenya, and Togo, middle-class associations of lawyers, college professors, and students were highly active in the service of democratization. Student protests against economic mismanagement and the accompanying economic crises in Benin, Mali, and elsewhere were important in setting the stage for prodemocracy activism in those countries.

Significant contributions to democratization have also come from Christian churches and their national organizations. The National Council of Churches of Kenya (NCCK) has been in the forefront of opposition to the authoritarianism of President Daniel arap Moi and his Kenya African National Union. The NCCK was an early and vocal critic of the lack of a secret ballot. Anglican bishops Mnasas Kuria, Alexander Muge, and Henry Okullu earned a reputation as advocates of political change when they disagreed publicly with the conclusions of a government investigation into the causes of July 1990 riots in Nairobi and urged the release of two opposition politicians who had been detained for their alleged involvement in them. A 1992 pastoral letter from Malawi's Catholic bishops, openly criticizing both political repression and the government's mismanagement of the economy, was a seminal event in a country that had long been a bastion of autocratic rule. Christian groups and episcopal conferences in Ghana, Nigeria, and Zambia have also actively fought authoritarianism and supported democratization in their respective countries.

These religiously based civil-society groups, and in particular the ecumenical bodies, played key roles not only in starting but also in guiding the process of political opening. In several groundbreaking cases, the success of the transition to democracy owed much to the broad credibility, political skills, and commitment of Christian organizations and their leaders. In many cases, they served as "honest brokers" in bitter political conflicts between intransigent autocrats and impatient democrats. Roman Catholic prelates such as Bishop Ernest Nkombo of the Congo and Monsignor Laurent Monsengwo of Zaire have been pivotal in the transitions and national conferences of their respective countries. In Togo, when long-ruling President Gnassingbé Eyadéma agreed to convene a sovereign national conference to chart the country's political future, he named Archbishop Fanoko Kpodzro to head that body. And in Benin, Bishop Isodore de Souza became head of the interim High Council of the Republic, which presided over the successful multiparty elections of February 1991 and the transition to democratic rule.

A Record of Disappointment

Civil society's weakness as a force for democratic consolidation is most glaring in the crucial area of ensuring public accountability. The relaxation of press censorship has allowed the emergence of independent newspapers with a zest for uncovering official misdeeds, yet these same papers typically lack the resources needed for in-depth analysis and sustained investigation. In Ghana, official corruption and incompetence should have taken a heavy blow from the resumed publication of reports by government auditors and other public-accounting agencies. Yet malfeasance remains rampant. Legislative-oversight committees and public prosecutors are still too vulnerable to political interference, and pressure from civil society has seldom been strong enough to bring wrongdoers to book.

On the whole, civil society is too weak to redress state-society relations in favor of the latter. Despite the return to formal democracy and the promulgation of constitutions with all the usual checks and balances, officials retain enormous power. In all but a handful of Africa's new democracies, the threat of an "executive coup" à la Fujimori is ever present. Vague and illiberal laws, enacted by colonial or authoritarian regimes in the name of "public order" or "national security," have been used to suppress free discussion and activism. Thus in Zimbabwe, senior staffers of the *Financial Gazette* found themselves detained and charged under a preindependence "criminal defamation" statute because they reported on the personal life of President Robert Mugabe. Similarly, the Ivorian newspaper *La Voie* was suspended, and its editor and two reporters given two years in jail apiece, for a story suggesting that the president's presence at a continent-wide soccer championship had brought bad luck to the national team.

Civil society has also failed to transcend ethnoregional, religious, and other cleavages in any lasting way. One African country after another has seen its own particular movement for democracy fracture along ethnoregional and sectarian lines either during or just after the transition from authoritarianism. In Kenya, President Moi remained in control as the Forum for the Restoration of Democracy splintered into three factions based on the Luo, northern Kikuyu, and southern Kikuyu groups. In Malawi, prodemocracy politics aimed at ousting dictator Hastings Kamuzu Banda took on an ethnoregional cast as the southern part of the country became the base of Bakili Muluzi's United Democratic Front, the north became the base of Chakufwa Chihana's Alliance for Democracy, and the Malawi Congress Party dominated the central province. Likewise, the prodemocracy movement in Togo largely pitted the Ewes of the south against the pro-Eyadéma Kabiyes of the north. In Nigeria, opposition to the military regime and support for democracy have become particularly identified with the Yoruba of western Nigeria.

In Africa's multiethnic and multireligious societies, democratic openings are often associated with heightened sectarian conflict and communal violence. This happens, at least in part, because governments determined to stay in power exacerbate such strife as a way of undermining the credibility of democracy and its advocates. It also happens because opposition and prodemocracy groups, often emerging out of ethnically, socioeconomically, or politically marginalized segments of society, use ethnoregionalist or sectarian appeals in order to mobilize sentiment against authoritarian incumbents. Whatever the causes, the inability of African civil societies to coalesce has cost democratic movements dearly in overall effectiveness and credibility.

The contribution of civil society to democratic consolidation is even more disappointing in the key areas of economic reform and development. Hopes that economic renewal would accompany political liberalization have failed to materialize. The new and freer political climate has severely limited the ability of fledgling democratic governments to pursue meaningful economic reforms. Although elected governments in Benin, Ghana, and Zambia, for instance, are notionally committed to neoliberal economic reforms, they must make significant and perhaps fiscally compromising concessions to organized interests and other forces of civil society. In Mali, President Alpha Oumar Konaré's attempt to embark on much-needed educational reforms has been stalled as a result of violent public protests by well-organized and now legalized student groups.

For most of the 1980s, Ghana had both unrelenting authoritarian rule and an impressive record of fiscal prudence and macroeconomic stability. As multiparty elections loomed in 1992, however, the government of President Jerry Rawlings succumbed to popular pressure and granted extrabudgetary salary increases of 70 to 100 percent across the board, and dropped plans to increase tax revenue by raising petroleum prices. After the elections, paralyzing strikes and violent protests by organized labor and other groups compelled the Rawlings government to abandon key economic reforms such as public-sector job retrenchment, a newly introduced value-added tax, and caps on the growth of student allowances and worker salaries.

It is true that in Benin, the sovereign national conference committed itself to neoliberal economic restructuring, and that the Zambian business community was an early and powerful supporter of the Movement for Multiparty Democracy (MMD) as well as the pro-growth economic initiatives of the newly elected Chiluba administration. Moreover, a few business associations (especially those based among younger entrepreneurs not tied to established rent-seeking networks) and reform-oriented think tanks (such as Ghana's Institute of Economic Affairs) have begun to come out in support of an open economic environment. The larger picture, however, reveals the absence of decisive social coalitions in favor of economic reform and what Thomas Callaghy calls a "production-oriented political economy."[4] For the most part, established private business and its associations have no desire to abandon rent-seeking and cronyism, while the popular classes (especially students and unions) are bent on using their new political clout to push for the retention of unsustainable redistributionist and welfarist policies and to frustrate economic reform. The several forces of civil society, each for its own reasons, thus oppose structural adjustment in particular and neoliberal reform in general. Yet none has articulated a viable economic alternative, and a consensus between governments and civil societies remains elusive even on such basic issues of fiscal prudence as the insulation of key aspects of economic policy from direct political pressure, and the institution of independent central banks and other "agencies of restraint."

Sources of Weakness

On the surface, most African countries contain enough associations to constitute at least a putative civil society. To varying degrees, trade unions, traditional Christian bodies, student groups, professional and business associations, and private voluntary and nongovernmental organizations (especially the "civic" ones) do serve as agents of "democratic civil society." By facilitating the development of civic and political skills, many if not all of them do serve as "large free schools for democracy." And as Michael Bratton and others have contended, they do hold at least a latent promise of political pluralism.[5] In addition, many of them combine a modern outlook and transethnic membership with liberal-mindedness, a commitment to the practice of democracy in their own internal affairs, and a keen dedication to the democratization of their countries—a cause to which many have contributed mightily.

Democracy in Africa has received an additional boost from new independent and nonpartisan national and continental nongovernmental organizations (NGOs) such as the Institute for Democracy in South Africa (IDASA) and the Study and Research Group on Democracy and Social and Economic Development–Africa (GERDDES-Afrique). These organizations boast exceptionally energetic and intelligent leaders, and lend powerful assistance to efforts on behalf of multiparty democracy in their own countries and throughout sub-Saharan Africa.

The protracted economic and political crises that have afflicted many African countries since the late 1970s have hit the middle classes and their organizations hard.

Yet a closer look at many civil-society groups reveals serious deficiencies that sap their effectiveness as key agents in the long and difficult process of democratic con-solidation. Trade unions and student organi-zations (which tend the most toward activ-ism or even militancy, and often challenge central authority) are nonetheless highly vulnerable to repression and co-optation by the state. Dependent (whether directly or indirectly) on government for all or most of their funds, and with members recruited mostly from the public sector, African trade unions cannot afford prolonged anti-government protest or prodemocratic activism. Most of Africa's institutions of higher learning and their students are in a similar relation to the state, and are subject to the same strategies of governmental control. In extreme instances, governments have dealt with recalcitrant unions and student groups by simply banning them.

Middle-class professional bodies such as bar, medical, and university faculty associations have relatively complex and cohesive organizations. They tend also to practice a fairly high degree of internal democracy, and evince a strong commitment to liberal democracy. Yet the protracted economic and political crises that have afflicted many African countries since the late 1970s have hit the middle classes and their organizations hard. In many countries, the latter have lost or are losing most of their membership and their organizational capabilities.

Among middle-strata groups, the establishment or "orthodox" Christian churches (both Protestant and Catholic) appear to suffer the fewest organizational and financial handicaps. Their large memberships; strong, complex, and capable national organizations; politically sophis-ticated leaders; considerable financial security and independence; and international contacts allow them to maintain their autonomy from government. These strengths, combined with civic-mindedness and a commitment to political liberalism, make Christian bodies important parts of Africa's nascent civil society, capable of breaking the "culture of silence" imposed by years of authoritarian rule.

Yet in the context of democratic consolidation, religious bodies also suffer underlying weaknesses. Nationalists view them with suspicion because of their colonial origins. They often compete fiercely among themselves (or with other religions such as Islam) for state support and recognition, thus compromising their nonpartisan credibility and moral authority. Moreover, their well-educated and well-traveled leaders tend to be elitist, and ineffective at forging alliances with organized forces of the subordinate classes. And for reasons of innate caution and self-preservation, these established religious bodies tend to prefer ad hoc rather than prolonged involvements in national politics.

Moreover, the explosive growth in Africa of "independent" charismatic or millennial Christian churches and new-age religions appears to present a threat to the political influence of the orthodox Christians and their organizations. The general social and political conservatism of the new groups and their tendency to foster docility toward temporal authority or political apathy among their members stand in sharp contrast to the political liberalism of their establishment counterparts. Ultimately, the willingness of these newer churches and their leaders (especially the social and political "climbers" among them) to align with governments for reasons of nationalism and aggrandizement (as the Kimbanguist movement did in Zaire during most of the postcolonial period) undermines the work that "orthodox" Christian groups do to counter governmental hegemony.

The proliferation of new types of NGOs in recent years has raised expectations that democratic governance might at last thrive in Africa. While their growing presence largely reflects the waning developmental capacity of the African state, they do contribute directly and indirectly to the creation of a socioeconomic and political setting conducive to democracy. Some NGOs engage in social and political advocacy, consciousness raising, and local service delivery (South Africa's apartheid-era township civic associations are an example). Others produce goods and services and provide relief or social welfare at subnational and national levels (like the credit and marketing associations of West Africa). All foster group and individual autonomy from the state.

Yet these sorts of NGOs also labor under structural, material, and legal constraints that hinder their effectiveness as agents of democratic consolidation. Local NGOs in general are poorly funded and have weak organizational capacities; they often turn for support to governments and external donors, a compromising strategy that distorts the accountability owed to members. Still, only a handful can do without outside help. Assistance from Western bilateral agencies, the UN, and a host of international NGOs such as CARE, Save the Children, Catholic Relief Services, and the African Development Foundation has been crucial for the survival of many local NGOs. International NGOs are usually financially and materially well endowed, but their foreign origins render them suspect in the eyes of local authorities, and African governments are not above "hijacking" their resources.

As NGOs have attained prominence in the economic and political life of various countries, governments (including elected ones) have become determined to control them. Since 1991, governments in Botswana, Ghana, Kenya,

South Africa's civic associations, vital in the struggle against apartheid, are undergoing a postapartheid crisis.

and Zimbabwe have proposed or enacted legislation designed to strengthen official authority over NGOs—usually under the guise of developing a national regulatory framework for associations. Under Kenya's NGO Coordination Act of 1990, the board that oversees NGOs was heavily weighted in favor of government representatives, and its decisions could not be appealed to the courts. NGOs also had to renew their registration every five years, and ministerial responsibility for NGOs rested with the Office of the President.[6] A government-sponsored NGO bill put before the Ghanaian Parliament had similar autonomy-reducing features and appeared to be meant to control and cripple NGOs.

Many NGOs, and especially the "civic" subspecies that is most likely to be involved in democratic activism, suffer from low levels of institutional development. Many have sprung up only in the last five years; in numerous instances, they have withered or changed character as key leaders have taken posts in the new postauthoritarian governments, or plunged into party politics. Indeed, many of Africa's new democracy-specific civil associations have turned out to be nothing more than "political-action committees" and protoparties that have more in common with "political" than with "civil" society.[7]

Developments in postapartheid South Africa provide a good illustration of this problem. South Africa's civic associations, vital in the struggle against apartheid, are undergoing a postapartheid crisis. Some of them have lost their leaders to political parties and the state bureaucracy; funding from abroad is in precipitous decline (as such funds are now channeled directly to the government instead of to the NGOs); and they are having trouble defining a role for themselves in relation to the new South Africa and its Government of National Unity, which is led by the NGOs' erstwhile ally, the African National Congress (ANC).[8]

A formidable array of systemic and contextual factors are clearly responsible for slowing the development of civil society in Africa. Chief among them is the African state. Like its counterparts everywhere else in the world, the African state tends to seek hegemony. In the first 35 years of its existence, the postcolonial African state maintained and even expanded the hierarchies of rule inherited from colonialism.[9] Thanks to their control over surpluses from the export of primary commodities, financial and military aid from one side or the other in the Cold War, and widespread international respect for national sovereignty and self-determination, African rulers could fashion their preferred form of statehood and govern their countries as they saw fit. Typically, the African state assumed a neopatrimonial form—in which the extremes of co-optation and repression were the main modes of state control over society.[10] The international community raised few questions as African governments adopted authoritarian ways, routinely repressing citizens and their organizations. Civil associations faced a choice—insist on autonomy and suffer repression, or allow themselves to be co-opted by and subordinated to the state in order to secure inclusion and enjoy patronage.

Additionally, the patrimonialization of political power and its use for private gain make politics a high-stakes, zero-sum game in which incumbents desperately defend and challengers desperately attack. In such a highly charged atmosphere, compromise and moderation are early casualties, and the limited stock of civic competence and democratic capital is easily dissipated.

While neopatrimonialism has become less tenable as the chief means of political control in the late 1980s and early 1990s, new state-society relations have yet to be fully established or take root. Neopatrimonialism and its accompanying attitudes persist, defying efforts to weaken them through economic liberalization and the democratization of political processes. This is true both in countries where the government enjoys oil-export revenues (Angola, Gabon, and Nigeria) and in countries with an improved balance-of-payments picture (Ghana and Uganda).

Decades of authoritarian rule have also left behind a culture of incivility in politics. In Kenya, President Moi reportedly has threatened to "hunt down and kill" his political opponents "like rats." In Ghana, President Rawlings has referred to the leaders of the main opposition parties as "punks," and progovernment elements smeared human excrement in the offices of a leading private newspaper; Rawlings's opponents in turn called him a "murderer" and a "bastard." Neither country is exceptional. Both reflect, at least in part, the lack of opportunity on the part of the first generation of African politicians to observe at close quarters or participate in high-level politics during most of the colonial era (when Europeans dominated the local political scene). But remarks and actions like these also reflect the political culture created by more than 25 years of pervasive and persistent authoritarian rule; the monopolization of political power; and the arbitrary but sharp division of key political players into "good guys" and "bad guys," patriots and quislings, loyalists and enemies.

Currently, the prevalence of a culture of "high-strung" opposition has grown out of the tendency of many incumbent regimes to use physical abuse and repression against opponents. Vengeance and retribution all too easily become the main political passions; possibilities for reconciliation, even after a democratic transition, are diminished. Thus in Togo, the animosity between the Eyadéma government and the opposition was greatly intensified, and the prospects for a pacted political settlement delayed, by the assassination of leading opposition figures (in which the government was implicated) and the attempted assassination of the president (in which the opposition was implicated). Similarly, in Kenya the prospects for reducing tensions between the government and its opponents were blighted by developments before and after the elections, when several opposition figures became targets of government-sponsored assassination attempts, physical attacks, and arson.

Crisis and Co-optation

Without a strong private economic sector, it is difficult to see how civil society and democracy can prevail. Given state dominance in so much of the formal sector of African economies—especially in the areas of investment and employment—key social groups and their organizations are ultimately dependent on government. With vast swaths of the working and middle classes tied to government through employment, and the private sector dependent on government for contracts, subsidized credit, foreign exchange, and protection from foreign competition, the basis for individual and associational autonomy is extremely weak.

Groups, such as unions, whose members come substantially from the public sector are always vulnerable to governmental arm-twisting. For instance, associations of Ghanaian public servants, doctors, and lawyers were active in the popular movement to demand an end to military misrule and authoritarianism until, in mid-1977, the ruling military council threatened the government employees among them with dismissal and ordered them to vacate their government-provided homes. With this episode no doubt in mind, many of Ghana's professional bodies declined to participate openly in the country's prodemocracy movement in the early 1990s. In Nigeria, intermittent proscription of the Nigerian Labor Congress and the Academic Staff Union of Universities, as well as co-optation of their leaders through bribery and other inducements, has hampered the current popular movement against military dictatorship.

The weakness of the private sector and pervasive dependence on the state have induced subservience toward political authority in key social groups throughout Africa. The middle-class professionals and intellectuals who run key public institutions tend to be understandably preoccupied with their own economic survival, which often prevents their institutions from helping civil society to checkmate state hegemony. Judges depend on government for their appointments and for their operational budgets, and have few opportunities for lucrative private practice should they resign. They can scarcely afford to maintain a posture of strict independence. Private newspapers fear losing much-needed revenue from government advertisements, and will engage in self-censorship rather than displease high officials. For fear of losing profitable government contracts, private businessmen may not place advertisements in private newspapers that the government sees as insubordinate.

The weakness of the private sector generally also applies to business groups. To be sure, all African countries have their business chambers (for mining, commerce, and industry) and employers' associations. But some of them, especially in the French-speaking countries, are state-created and state-funded. Business associations throughout Africa, often none too strong to begin with, have become even weaker in the last two decades as national economies have declined. In general, they avoid confrontation with the state or involvement in politics. Afraid of losing their "cronyist" relationship with government, they confine themselves to behind-the-scenes lobbying on behalf of their own interests, narrowly defined. With the partial exception of Zambia, there is not much evidence that the business elite in any African country has played a role in democratization as decisive as that played by analogous groups in Thailand or Taiwan.[11]

Civil associations of all kinds have seen their material bases of support eroded, first by the protracted economic crisis that gripped Africa starting in the 1980s, and then by the stringent neoliberal adjustment measures imposed with a view to resolving it. Many associations have lost so much self-confidence and organizational capacity that they seem but shadows of what they were even a decade ago. The neopatrimonial state, meanwhile, finds them easy targets for co-optation. Faced with the prospect of penury, many leaders of middle-class and professional groups find it hard to resist making personally advantageous deals with incumbent autocratic regimes, even if such deals undermine prodemocracy movements and shore up authoritarian rule.

This phenomenon has reached alarming levels in Nigeria in recent years, and if unchecked could discredit the prodemocracy coalition. Unable to resist the temptation to save themselves from a swift decline into poverty, some civic leaders and prodemocracy activists have become turncoats, accepting bribes and high-level appointments from the military government of General Sani Abacha. The story in Daniel arap Moi's Kenya is much the same.[12]

Some of African civil society's weakness is internal. Associational life is dominated by traditional, ascriptive, and kin-based groups. These include clans, tribes, and ethnoregional formations; their neotraditional urban counterparts such as home-area improvement and cultural-preservation associations; and Islamic and Christian-millennialist religious groups. It is true that such associations are very good at aggregating the interests of large numbers of people and providing relatively viable nonstate networks of social interaction, cultural and emotional expression, and economic subsistence. It is also true that many people who have had to flee the ambit of the improvident and increasingly predatory postcolonial African state have found refuge in kin-based or religious organizations, and that with varying degrees of effectiveness, the myriad of traditional and modern, secular and religious civil associations has directly or indirectly acted to frustrate the hegemonial project of the African state.[13]

Yet these traditional and neotraditional groups tend to be preliberal or illiberal and to subscribe to gerontocratic, extremely hierarchical, patriarchal, and otherwise undemocratic values. Their leaders are socially and politically conservative and often view democratization with indifference or hostility. More disturbingly, the preliberal or antiliberal values of these core associations tend also to pervade the modern and secular civil associations, including some of those involved in prodemocracy work. The undemocratic values that these traditional organizations and illiberal religious groups foster often manifest themselves in the tendencies of some key civil associations (including those involved in prodemocracy work) to refuse to establish "rational" bureaucracies; to "anoint" rather than elect their executives; and to endow their leaders with "life" chairmanships.

Moreover, core societal groups—whether secular, kin-based, religious, or devoted to sports, entertainment, or mutual self-help—all incline toward parochialism. When they do become engaged in national politics, it is typically out of a narrow concern with how the state can serve their interests. Hence they usually either support the state, or can easily be co-opted into doing so.

Additionally, with their ascriptive or nonsecular membership criteria (in the case of the kin-based and religious groups, respectively), these organizations are inherently exclusionary, often chauvinistic, and sometimes jingoistic. Their unwillingness or inability to enter into alliances with other groups is a leading cause of the pervasive fragmentation of civil society in Africa.

Grounds for Hope

Though the outlook for democratization in Africa is sobering, it is not without its bright spots. The first is an effect of neoliberal economic reforms, especially privatization. Economic decentralization and the expansion of the private sector are laying the material basis for civil associations that are fully independent of the state. That should help remove a major source of civil society's weakness in Africa. Indeed, successful rehabilitation of the state and the economy can also bring material benefits to civil associations. General improvements in the economy—making foreign exchange, spare parts, and other supplies available—are indispensable to associational welfare and potential autonomy.

Second, the increasing trends toward political liberalization and pluralism may give civil society its best-ever opportunity to flourish. Thus, instead of the normal historical sequence in which civil society engenders democratization, the introduction of constitutional rule and pluralism "from above" could have an enabling impact on the growth and development of civil society in Africa.

Africa's many civil associations are deepening their collective awareness of the pivotal role that they must play in fostering democratic governance.

Third, multilateral and bilateral donors are increasingly refusing to regard national sovereignty and borders as sacrosanct, which means a greater willingness to give direct assistance to local NGOs and pro-democracy civil associations. In the past, almost all foreign assistance went through the state, with predictably disastrous consequences for the autonomy of civil society. The increasing amounts of aid coming from prodemocratic international NGOs such as the political-party foundations of Germany, the Westminster Foundation for Democracy of Britain, and the National Endowment for Democracy of the United States could help to redress this imbalance. Government donors from abroad now often condition their assistance on the involvement of private-sector and nongovernmental groups, which could give many civic associations a new lease on life.

Fourth, new information and communications technologies present an opportunity to civil society. A fax machine and a computer can help an association handle many organizational challenges (e.g., updating membership lists and improving record keeping) and end state-imposed isolation (by networking through electronic mail). One analyst of Malawi's recent democratization has identified the fax, the photocopier, the personal computer, and desktop-publishing software as keys to the prodemocracy movement's successful campaign to discredit the Banda dictatorship in 1992–93.[14]

Finally, Africa's many civil associations are improving their knowledge of one another and deepening their collective awareness of the pivotal role that they must play in fostering democratic governance. This greater knowledge and deeper insight in turn promise to bear fruit in the form of greater cooperation, assertiveness, confidence, and perhaps efficacy. In Ghana, for example, a coalition of NGOs led opposition to the proposed law, mentioned above, that the central government wanted to use to bring NGOs under its control. Their counterparts in Kenya had shown the way earlier by banding together to secure significant changes in their favor to the NGO Coordination Bill, which had threatened to compromise NGO autonomy. The 1993 creation of a network for NGOs based in the south and east of Africa (called MWENGO) and the 1995 establishment of a newsletter (*PRONET*) for West African NGOs are two recent indicators of increased networking and capacity-building among African NGOs.

All of these developments are encouraging, but taken together they are not enough to change the most likely prospect. African civil society, given the deep-seated and multifaceted problems it faces, is probably not going to lift itself out of its doldrums in time to play a key role as an agent of democratic consolidation. What is imperative now is to build on the "positives": current democratic openings, economic and political liberalizations, donor interest, available information technologies, and, above all, the enthusiasm of the prodemocracy civil associations themselves. The feasible goal, in every case, should be to reduce the severe organizational, financial, legal, and political constraints that presently burden civil society. That is a responsibility for all supporters of African democracy, both foreign and domestic.

NOTES

1. As used in this essay, "civil society" refers to the ensemble of intermediate organizations that lie between the state and the household, that are formed voluntarily by members of society to protect and advance their interests and values, and that are separate from the state and largely autonomous. This usage also assumes that civil society in Africa is an evolving entity. For a definition of civil society, see John Keane, *Civil Society and the State* (London: Verso, 1988). For an evolutionary view of the concept as applied to Africa, see Peter Lewis, "Political Transition and the Dilemma of Civil Society in Africa," *Journal of International Affairs* 27 (Summer 1992): 31–54.

2. See Samuel P. Huntington, *The Third Wave: Democratization in the Late Twentieth Century* (Norman: University of Oklahoma Press, 1991).

3. Democratic consolidation is used here as defined by Larry Diamond—"the process by which democracy becomes so broadly and profoundly legitimate among its citizens that it is very unlikely to break down." See his "Toward Democratic Consolidation," *Journal of Democracy* 5 (July 1994): 4–18; see also Adam Przeworski, *Democracy and the Market: Political and Economic Reforms in Eastern Europe and Latin America* (Cambridge: Cambridge University Press, 1991).

4. Thomas Callaghy, "Civil Society, Democracy and Economic Change: A Dissenting Opinion About Resurgent Societies," in John Harbeson et al., eds., *Civil Society and the State in Africa* (Boulder, Colo.: Lynne Rienner, 1994), 231–54.

5. Michael Bratton, "Beyond the State: Civil Society and Associational Life in Africa," *World Politics* 41 (October 1989): 407–30.

6. The attempt to regulate Kenyan NGOs is discussed in detail in Alan Fowler, "Non-Governmental Organizations and the Promotion of Democracy in Kenya" (Ph.D. diss., University of Sussex, 1994), 197–99.

7. On the distinction between "civil society" and "political society," see Alfred Stepan, *Rethinking Military Politics: Brazil and the Southern Cone* (Princeton: Princeton University Press, 1988).

8. An extensive analysis of problems facing South African NGOs in the postapartheid

period is found in Kimberly Lanegran, "South Africa's Civic Association Movement: ANC's Ally or Society's 'Watchdog'? Shifting Social Movement–Political Party Relations," *African Studies Review* 38 (September 1995): 101–26; see also Wilmot James and Daria Caliguire, "The New South Africa: Renewing Civil Society," *Journal of Democracy* 7 (January 1996): 56–66.

9. Crawford Young, "The African Colonial State and Its Political Legacy," in Donald Rothchild and Naomi Chazan, eds., *The Precarious Balance: State and Society in Africa* (Boulder, Colo.: Westview, 1988), 25–66.

10. Neopatrimonialism is a form of rule that combines legal-rational administration and law with patrimonial forms of sociopolitical domination and elite management. In this form of rule, policies and the ruling apparatus are personalized, rulers rule their countries as extensions of their households, and institutions and regulations become eclipsed by the discretion of rulers and top officials. Key works on neopatrimonial rule in Africa include Patrick Chabal, *Power in Africa* (New York: St. Martin's, 1992); and Jean-François Bayart, *The State in Africa: The Politics of the Belly* (London: Longman, 1993). See also R.H. Jackson and C.G. Rosberg, *Personal Rule in Black Africa* (Berkeley: University of California Press, 1982).

11. A useful discussion of the role of business groups in the democratic opening in Taiwan is found in Yun-han Chu, *Crafting Democracy in Taiwan* (Taipei: Institute for National Policy Research, 1992), ch. 5.

12. Opposition party-switching induced by bribery from the Moi regime is reported in Frank Holmquist and Michael Ford, "Kenya: State and Civil Society the First Year After the Election," *Africa Today* 41 (1994): 5–26.

13. Naomi Chazan, *An Anatomy of Ghanaian Politics: Managing Political Recession* (Boulder, Colo.: Westview, 1983); also Naomi Chazan and Victor Azarya, "Disengagement of Society from the State: Reflections on the Experience of Ghana and Guinea," *Comparative Studies in Society and History* 29 (1987): 107–31.

14. Daniel Posner, "Malawi's New Dawn," *Journal of Democracy* 6 (January 1995): 131–45.

V

Economic Development

15

WHAT MAKES DEMOCRACIES ENDURE?

Adam Przeworski, Michael Alvarez,
José Antonio Cheibub & Fernando Limongi

Adam Przeworski *is professor of political science at New York University.* **Michael Alvarez** *is assistant professor of political science at De Paul University.* **José Antonio Cheibub** *is assistant professor of politics at the University of Pennsylvania.* **Fernando Limongi** *is assistant professor of political science at the University of São Paulo.*

If a country, any randomly selected country, is to have a democratic regime *next* year, what conditions should be present in that country and around the world *this* year? The answer is: democracy, affluence, growth with moderate inflation, declining inequality, a favorable international climate, and parliamentary institutions.

This answer is based on counting instances of survival and death of political regimes in 135 countries observed annually between 1950 or the year of independence or the first year when economic data are available ("entry" year) and 1990 or the last year for which data are available ("exit" year), for a total of 4,318 country-years.[1] We found 224 regimes, of which 101 were democracies and 123 dictatorships, observing 40 transitions to dictatorship and 50 to democracy. Among democratic regimes, there were 50 parliamentary systems, 46 presidential systems, and 8 mixed systems.[2]

Our definition of democracy is a minimalist one. We follow Robert A. Dahl's 1971 classic *Polyarchy* in treating as democratic all regimes that hold elections in which the opposition has some chance of winning and taking office. When in doubt, we err in the direction of calling a regime dictatorial. Our classification is not idiosyncratic, but is closely related to several alternative scales of democracy. The rationale and the rules for classifying regimes are discussed in the Appendix below.

Democracy. It may seem tautological to say that a country should have a democratic regime this year in order to have a democracy next year. We do so in order to dispel the myth, prevalent in certain intellectual and political circles (particularly in the United States) since the late 1950s, that the route to democracy is a circuitous one. The claim is that 1) dictatorships are better at generating economic development in poor countries, and that 2) once countries have developed, their dictatorial regimes will give way to democracy. To get to democracy, then, one had to support, or at least tolerate, dictatorships.

Both of the above propositions, however, are false:

1) While analyses of the impact of regimes on economic growth have generated divergent results, recent econometric evidence fails to uncover any clear regime effect. The average rate of investment is in fact slightly higher in poor democracies than in poor dictatorships; population growth is higher under dictatorships but labor productivity is lower; and investment is more efficiently allocated under democracies. Dictatorships are no more likely to generate economic growth than democracies.[3] Indeed, the 56 dictatorships with annual per-capita income of less than $1,000 when we first observed them simply failed to develop.[4] By the exit year, only 18 of them had made it (whether under democracy or continued dictatorship) to $1,000, only 6 to $2,000, and only 3 to more than $3,000. South Korea and Taiwan are exceptional: they are the only two dictatorships that started under $1,000 in 1950 and had annual per-capita income exceeding $5,000 by 1990. If we consider as "initially poor" those countries with less than $2,000, we find that among 98 dictatorships first observed below this level, by the exit year only 26 had made it to $2,000, 15 to $3,000, 7 to $4,000, and 4 to $5,000. These figures should be enough to dispel any notion that dictatorship somehow promotes economic growth in poor countries.

2) Democracies are not produced by the development of dictatorships.[5] If they were, the rate at which dictatorships make the transition to democracy would increase with the level of development: analyses of the survival prospects of dictatorships, however, indicate that this is not the case. Indeed, transitions to democracy are random with regard to the level of development: not a single transition to democracy can be predicted by the level of development alone.[6]

Since poor dictatorships are no more likely to develop than poor democracies and since developed dictatorships are no more likely to become democracies than poor ones, dictatorships offer no advantage in attaining the dual goal of development and democracy. In order to strengthen democracy, we should strengthen democracy, not support dictatorships.

Affluence. Once a country has a democratic regime, its level of economic development has a very strong effect on the probability that democracy will survive. Poor democracies, particularly those with annual per-capita income of less than $1,000, are extremely fragile: based on our study, the probability that one will die during a particular year is

0.12. This rate falls to 0.06 in the $1,000 to $2,000 range, to 0.03 between $2,000 and $4,000, and to 0.01 between $4,000 and $6,000. These numbers mean that a democracy can be expected to last an average of about 8.5 years in a country with per-capita income under $1,000 per annum, 16 years in one with income between $1,000 and $2,000, 33 years between $2,000 and $4,000, and 100 years between $4,000 and $6,000.

Whatever their theoretical and political differences, both Samuel P. Huntington and Guillermo O'Donnell claim that there is a level beyond which further development actually *decreases* the probability that democracy will survive.[7] Huntington argues that both democracies and dictatorships become unstable when a country undergoes modernization, which occurs at some intermediate level of development. O'Donnell, in turn, claims that democracies tend to die when a country exhausts "the easy stage of import substitution," again at some intermediate level. Our finding, however, is that there is *no* income level at which democracies become more fragile than they were when they were poorer. Only in the Southern Cone countries of Latin America have authoritarian regimes arisen at the intermediate levels of development. Four out of the nine transitions to authoritarianism above $3,000 transpired in Argentina. Adding Chile and Uruguay, we see that the instances in which democracy fell at medium levels of development are to a large extent peculiar to the Southern Cone.[8]

Above $6,000, democracies are impregnable and can be expected to live forever: no democratic system has ever fallen in a country where per-capita income exceeds $6,055 (Argentina's level in 1976). Hence Seymour Martin Lipset was correct to assert that "the more well-to-do a nation, the greater the chances that it will sustain democracy."[9] Once established in a developed country, democracy endures regardless of how it performs and regardless of all the exogenous conditions to which it is exposed.

Why democracies are more durable in more-developed countries has been the subject of extensive speculation. One reason, put forward by Lipset in *Political Man*, is that the intensity of distributional conflicts is lower at higher income levels. Another plausible hypothesis, suggested to us by Larry Diamond, focuses on institutions: political actors in more-developed countries may be more likely to adopt a superior institutional framework at the moment when democracy is established. Later, we will examine this hypothesis with regard to parliamentarism and presidentialism. First, however, we will take up consideration of our third condition for the maintenance of democracy: economic performance.

Economic performance. For some countries, therefore, the story ends here: once democracy is in place, affluence is a sufficient condition for it to survive regardless of anything else. But democracies can survive in poorer countries, if they generate economic growth with a moderate rate of inflation.

While Lipset, economist Mancur Olson, and Huntington all thought that democracy becomes destabilized when a country grows rapidly, they could not have been more wrong.[10] Rapid growth is not destabilizing for democracies (or for dictatorships): indeed, democracies are always more likely to survive when they grow faster than 5 percent annually than when they grow more slowly. In turn, the fragility of democracy at lower levels of development flows largely from its vulnerability in the face of economic crisis.[11] Poor democracies, those under $1,000, have a 0.22 probability of dying in a year after their income falls (giving them a life expectancy of less than five years) and a 0.08 probability (or an expected life of 12.5 years) if their income rises. Between $1,000 and $6,000—the middle range—democracies are less sensitive to growth but more likely to die if they stagnate: they die at the rate of 0.059 when they decline, so that their expected life is about 17 years, and at the rate of 0.027, with an expected life of about 37 years, when they grow. Thus Larry Diamond and Juan Linz are correct to argue that "Economic crisis represents one of the most common threats to democratic stability."[12] Conversely, economic growth is conducive to the survival of democracy. Indeed, the faster the economy grows, the more likely democracy is to survive.

Inflation also threatens democratic stability. A democratic regime has a 0.023 chance of dying and an expected life of 44 years when the annual inflation rate is under 6 percent; a 0.014 chance and an expected life of 71 years when inflation is between 6 and 30 percent; and a 0.064 chance and an expected life of about 16 years when inflation is above 30 percent. Note that these results appear to confirm Albert Hirschman's 1981 hypothesis that a moderate rate of inflation promotes democratic stability.[13]

Economic performance, then, is crucially important for the survival of democracy in less-affluent countries. When the economy grows rapidly with a moderate rate of inflation, democracy is much more likely to last even in the poorest lands.

Income inequality. The study of the political effects of income inequality is hampered by the paucity and poor quality of the available data. The best collection of internationally comparable data, generated by the World Bank, includes 266 observations, scattered over time for 84 countries.

We tried to assess the impact of income inequality (measured by the income ratio between the richest and the poorest quintiles) on the probability that a democracy will survive for three and for five years following the time for which data are available. Unlike Edward N.

Muller, we could find no pattern.[14] Since income inequality tends to be lower in poor countries, where most of the labor force is employed in self-sufficient agriculture, and in wealthy countries, where most workers are wage earners, and since democracy is brittle in poor countries and impregnable in rich ones, no overall pattern emerged from this analysis. The scantiness of our data, moreover, prevented us from controlling for the level of development.

On the other hand, we did find that democracy is much more likely to survive in countries where income inequality is declining over time. For those democratic regimes for which we had more than one observation of income distribution, we calculated the probability that democracy would die should inequality either increase or decrease We found that the expected life of democracy in countries with shrinking inequality is about 84 years, while the expected life of democracies with rising income inequality is about 22 years (these numbers are based on 599 democratic years, with inequality increasing during 262 and declining during 337). Note that these findings contradict any notion that distributional pressures threaten the survival of democracy: people expect democracy to reduce income inequality, and democracies are more likely to survive when they do.

International climate. Economic factors are not the only ones that matter for the durability of democracy. Indeed, international conditions predict regime survival better than does the level of development. While we cannot statistically distinguish different mechanisms by which the international climate becomes transmitted to particular countries, the proportions of other democracies in the region and in the world matter separately for the survival of democracy in any particular country: the larger the proportion of democracies on the globe and in the region during a particular year, the more likely is democracy to survive in any particular country. The global effect is about twice as large as the regional effect, but these findings indicate that contagion operates independently of the direct influence of Western governments and various international institutions.

Political learning. It is frequently argued—Russia is a favorite example—that the absence of democratic traditions impedes the consolidation of new democratic institutions and, conversely, that democracy is more stable in countries (like Chile) that have enjoyed it in the past. What this argument misses is that if a country *had* a democratic regime (note the past tense), it is a veteran not only of democracy but of the *successful subversion* of democracy. Political learning, in other words, cuts both ways. Democrats may find the work of consolidation easier when they can rely on past traditions, but antidemocratic forces also have an experience from which they can draw lessons: people know that overthrowing democracy is possible, and may even know how to do it. If the failed Russian hard-liners' coup of 1991 was more of a *coup de théâtre* than a *coup d'état*, it was perhaps because the coup plotters simply did not know what they were doing—an ignorance for which they were justly ridiculed by their more-experienced Latin American soul mates.

An overthrow of democracy at any time during the past history of a country shortens the life expectancy of any democratic regime in that country. To the extent that political learning does occur, then, it seems that the lessons learned by antidemocratic forces from the past subversion of democracy are more effective than the traditions that can be relied on by democrats.[15]

The effect of institutions. Democracies are not all the same. Systems of representation, arrangements for the division and supervision of powers, and methods of organizing interests, as well as legal doctrines and the rights and duties associated with citizenship, can and do vary widely among regimes that are generally recognized as democratic. These differences, expressed in the details of institutions, generate effects that two millennia of reflection and investigation have still not enabled us to grasp fully. We are far from knowing any clear answer to the question that Rousseau posed in his *Constitution of Poland*: Which institutions have which effects under which historical conditions?

Should we expect democracy to last longer under one institutional system than under another? Our analysis is limited to only one set of institutional features, summarized as parliamentarism versus presidentialism (we leave "mixed" systems aside as presenting too small a sample to yield any robust estimate). We thus test the hypotheses of Juan Linz, who offers several reasons why parliamentary democracies should prove more durable than presidential ones.[16]

One of Linz's arguments is that the stakes are higher under presidentialism, since a race for the presidency can have but a single winner. Linz observes that a defeated presidential candidate has no official role in politics, and most likely will not even be a member of the legislature, while in a parliamentary system the defeated candidate for the premiership will be leader of the opposition.[17] Moreover, it is likely that the fixed term of office under a presidential system is longer than the expected term of office under a parliamentary system. Finally, under presidentialism the chief executive is at the same time the head of state, thus being able to portray the president's partisan interest as the national interest and thereby undermine the legitimacy afforded to the opposition.

The second reason why presidential democracies may be less durable is that they are more likely to generate legislative paralysis. Such paralysis can occur under either system: under parliamentarism when no majority coalition can be formed, and under presidentialism when the legislature is controlled by a majority that is hostile to the president but not large enough to override presidential vetoes routinely. Under presidential systems the executive, by virtue of the fixed term of office, can survive alongside hostile legislatures, leading to stalemates between the executive and the legislative branch. As the great nineteenth-century English political writer Walter Bagehot observed, "when a difference of opinion arises, the legislature is forced to fight the executive, and the executive is forced to fight the legislature; and so very likely they contend to the conclusion of their respective terms."[18] In several contemporary presidential systems the main line of political conflict is between the president and the congress, rather than among political parties. Under such conditions, no one can govern.

Legislative majorities are more frequent under presidentialism than under parliamentarism: 57.9 percent of the time under the former and 49.0 percent under the latter.[19] But in 24.2 percent of the presidential years, the share of the largest party in the legislature was smaller than one-half and larger than one-third. Since the proportion needed to override a presidential veto is typically two-thirds, these figures indicate that the conditions for executive-legislative deadlock are common under presidentialism. The average number of effective parties is about the same under the two systems: 3.10 under parliamentarism and 3.05 under presidentialism. Yet extreme fractionalization—in which no party controls more than a third of the seats—is more frequent under presidentialism (occurring 18 percent of the time) than under parliamentarism (where it occurs only 8.9 percent of the time).

Linz is right about the durability of alternative institutional arrangements. During the period under consideration, 14 democracies (or 28 percent of the 50 cases) died under a parliamentary system. Only one (12.5 percent of 8 cases) died under a mixed system, and 24 (52 percent of 46 cases) died under presidentialism.[20] Among those democracies that died during the period under our scrutiny, the parliamentary systems lasted an average of eight years, while their presidential counterparts lasted nine. But the parliamentary systems that were still around as of 1990 were much older: on the average about 43 years, as compared with 22 for presidential regimes. The probability that a democracy would die under presidentialism during any particular year of our study was 0.049; the comparable probability under parliamentarism was 0.014. If this difference appears small, think in terms of expected lives: democracy's life expectancy under presidentialism is less than 20 years, while under parliamentarism it is 71 years.

This difference in durability is not an effect of the levels of economic development at which parliamentary and presidential regimes operated. While parliamentary systems are on the average found in wealthier countries, presidential democracies are less durable at almost every level. Excluding countries with a 1990 population of fewer than one million (many of which have parliamentary systems) changes nothing: the hazard rates—conditional probabilities that a regime would die given that it survived thus far—are exactly the same. Nor is this difference due to some hidden features of Latin America: in fact, presidential regimes in Latin America live much longer than those in other regions, the United States excepted. Hence presidential democracies are not shorter-lived because they are in Latin America.

Scott Mainwaring, like Alfred Stepan and Cindy Skach, is also correct: democracies are less likely to survive when they combine presidentialism with a fragmented party system.[21] Combining presidentialism with a legislature where no single party has majority status is a kiss of death: such systems can expect to live only 15 years. Presidential democracies in which a single party does have a legislative majority can expect to live 26 years. "Deadlock," a situation in which the share of seats of the largest party is between one-third and one-half, is even more deadly to presidential regimes. They die at the rate of 0.038 (with an expected life of 26 years) when there is no deadlock and at the rate of 0.091 (with an expected life of 11 years) when there is. Furthermore, descriptive information on parliamentarism supports Scott Mainwaring and Matthew Shugart's argument that "Parliamentary systems with disciplined parties and a majority party offer the fewest checks on executive power, and hence promote a winner-takes-all approach more than presidential systems."[22] Single-party majorities are not conducive to the survival of parliamentary democracies: those in which one party had a majority of seats in the lower house of the legislature have an expected life of 55 years, while parliamentary systems without a one-party majority have an expected life of 111 years. Yet this difference is not statistically significant.

How good are the alternative institutional arrangements at coping with economic crises? When the economy declines during a particular year, parliamentary democracies die at the rate of 0.039: they can expect to live 26 years under such conditions. When the economy grows, their death rate is 0.007 and the expected life is 143 years. Hence parliamentary systems are vulnerable to economic crises. Presidential systems are less sensitive, but they die at much higher rates under any conditions. When the economy declines, they die at the rate of 0.064, with an expected life of 16 years. When the economy grows, they die at the rate of 0.042, with an expected life of 24 years. Democracy is vulnerable to economic crisis under either institutional system, but presidential systems are less likely to survive under good economic conditions than parliamentary systems are under bad conditions.

Statistical analyses provide even stronger evidence in favor of parliamentarism. The expected life of presidential systems depends on the level of development, on economic growth, and on the presence of legislative majorities. Perhaps most startlingly, statistical analysis confirms that presidential systems are highly vulnerable to legislative-executive deadlocks. By contrast, in spite of the descriptive numbers cited above, for parliamentary systems neither the distribution of seats nor economic growth is a statistically significant predictor of the survival of democracy.

Statistics confirm as well that presidential regimes are less likely to survive in those countries that were not independent by 1950 (which is another way of saying "outside Latin America"), while parliamentary systems are equally likely to survive in either the "old" or the "new" countries. In turn, only parliamentary systems are sensitive to the ethnic fragmentation of the population. But this effect, while statistically significant, makes little difference for their expected lives. Thus presidential democracies are simply more brittle.

To summarize, the survival of democracies does depend on their institutional systems. Parliamentary regimes last longer, much longer, than presidential ones. Majority-producing electoral institutions are conducive to the survival of presidential systems: presidential systems facing legislative deadlock are particularly brittle. Both systems are vulnerable to bad economic performance, but presidential democracies are less likely to survive even when the economy grows than are parliamentary systems when the economy declines. The evidence that parliamentary democracy survives longer and under a broader spectrum of conditions than presidential democracy thus seems incontrovertible.

The choice of institutions. Since parliamentary democracies last longer, it is puzzling why so many democracies adopt presidentialism. What determines the initial choice of democratic institutions? Much of the answer can be gleaned from a casual glance at history. Countries that had monarchies but experienced no revolution transferred governmental responsibility from crown to parliament, ending up with parliamentary systems. Countries in which monarchy was abolished (France in 1848 and again in 1875, Germany in 1919) and colonies that rebelled against monarchical powers (the United States and Latin America in the late eighteenth and early nineteenth centuries) replaced monarchs with presidents. As Simon Bolívar once put it, "We elect monarchs whom we call presidents." Countries that emerged from colonial domination after the Second World War typically inherited parliamentarism from the colonizers. Characteristically, however, these same countries instituted presidential systems if and when the initial democracy fell. Just as characteristically, democratizing dictatorships tended to retain presidentialism.

According to our count, among the 35 countries that democratized between 1974 and 1990, 19 adopted presidential systems, 13 chose parliamentarism, and 3 opted for mixed systems. If the political stakes are indeed higher under presidentialism, it is hard to see why this system would emerge under conditions in which the political parties are perfectly well informed and not risk-prone. One explanation might be that the parties are unduly optimistic: each projects itself as a winner at the polls and assumes that it will gain the presidency. Still, we suspect that the choice of presidentialism is not just a decision of political parties.

Note that among the countries that were democratic at some time before the current transition to democracy, almost all chose the same system as the last time around.[23] This continuity, particularly in Latin America, may please those who like to find explanations in culture or traditions.[24] Yet it is more likely that it reflects the continuing political role of the military, which appears to have a preference for presidential regimes, perhaps because such regimes offer a clearer hierarchy. This reason is sufficient for the military to bargain for presidentialism when the issue of democratic institutions appears on the transitional agenda. The empirical patterns appear to support this expectation: while 10 of the 17 democratic regimes that emerged from civilian dictatorships went for presidentialism, an overwhelming 22 of the 28 democracies that surfaced from military dictatorships made the same choice. Thus presidentialism appears to be at least partly a legacy of military rule.

Once we learn that presidential systems are more likely to be adopted whenever the previous regime was military, the obvious question is whether all the findings concerning the longevity of presidential democracies are not spurious. Democracy may be more brittle under presidentialism precisely because this set of institutions is chosen where the military plays an active role in politics. To some extent this is the case: while the expected life of presidential democracies that emerge from civilian dictatorships is about 24 years, presidential systems that follow military dictatorships can expect to last only 17 years. Yet parliamentary democracies that follow military rule simply last much longer: 71 years.[25] Hence it would seem to be presidentialism per se that makes democracy more brittle.

Once we exclude the institutions inherited from the colonial rulers, the level of development at which the transition to democracy occurs does appear to have some impact on the institutions that are chosen: between 1950 and 1990, the average levels at which parliamentary institutions were chosen was $2,945, while presidential institutions were chosen at the average level of $2,584. The mode of transition, at least as indicated by strikes and other forms of social unrest (as coded by Arthur S. Banks), appears not to affect the choice of institutions.[26]

We focus on the moment of transition since particular institutional frameworks tend to persist once established, as if "renegotiation-proof." As the recent Brazilian referendum rejecting a proposed change to parliamentarism shows, the difficulty of changing complex institutional arrangements is that the status quo, whatever it happens to be, is favored. If the proponents of change offer only a slogan, "parliamentarism," then the defenders of the status quo can call for details of the new institutional arrangement; if the proponents of change offer such details, then the defenders can always find innumerable faults with the new system. During the entire period from 1950 to 1990, there were only three instances in which democratic regimes passed from one institutional system to another: France changed in 1958 from a parliamentary to a mixed system, while Brazil changed in 1960 from a presidential to a mixed system, only to return to presidentialism in 1963. Both cases occurred under exceptional circumstances. Countries that adopt presidential institutions when they transit to democracy are stuck with them.[27]

Conclusions. Our central finding is the importance of economic factors in sustaining democracies. While the modernization theory was wrong in thinking that development under dictatorship breeds democracies, Lipset was correct to argue that once established in a wealthy country, democracy is more likely to endure. Indeed, we have found that once a country is sufficiently wealthy, with per-capita income of more than $6,000 a year, democracy is certain to survive, come hell or high water. And while international factors as well as political institutions are important for the durability of democracy in less affluent countries, economic performance does matter: indeed, democracy is more likely to survive in a growing economy with less than $1,000 per-capita income than in a country where per-capita income is between $1,000 and $4,000, but which is declining economically. Democracies can survive even in the poorest nations if they manage to generate development, if they reduce inequality, if the international climate is propitious, and if they have parliamentary institutions.

For a variety of reasons, however, this is not an optimistic conclusion. Poverty is a trap. Few countries with annual per-capita income below $1,000 develop under any regime: their average rate of growth is less than 1 percent a year; many experience prolonged economic decline. When poor countries stagnate, whatever democracies happen to spring up tend to die quickly. Poverty breeds poverty and dictatorship.

Institutional choice offers a partial escape from this trap: parliamentary systems in the poorest countries, while still very fragile, are almost twice as likely to survive as presidential democracies, and four times as likely when they grow economically. Yet since it appears that poor countries are more likely to choose presidentialism, little solace is offered by the possibility of institutional engineering. Equally little solace is offered by political learning. Most countries returning to democracy usually go back to whatever constitution they had in the past, even if it never worked, as in Argentina, where the first democratic alternation in office under the revived 1853 Constitution already violated its letter.[28]

Finally, we find no evidence of "consolidation." A democracy becomes "consolidated" if its aforementioned "hazard rate" declines with its age, so that, as Robert Dahl has argued, democracies are more likely to survive if they have lasted for a while.[29] We find some evidence that this is true, but also that democracies are heterogeneous. Once we control for the level of development, the heterogeneity disappears and the hazard rates become independent of age, meaning that for a given level of development, democracies are about equally likely to die at any age. Since democracies are much more likely to survive when they occur in developed countries, these findings would indicate that hazard rates (uncorrected for the level of development) drop because countries develop economically, and not because a democracy that has been around is more likely to continue being around.

Clearly, we do not think that "consolidation" is just a matter of time, of some kind of "habituation" or mechanical "institutionalization."[30] We discovered that democracies are more likely to survive at higher levels of development. But we also found that democracies survive if they generate economic growth and if they control distributional pressures by allowing some inflation and reducing income inequality. This is not to deny that institutions matter: in fact they do, and not just parliamentarism and electoral systems but others that we have left out of consideration because we lack data. Democracy's ability to survive is a matter of politics and policy, as well as luck. Yet, conversely, if democracies become "consolidated" for whatever reasons, then we should observe that at any level of development the mere passage of time makes their demise less likely. This, however, we do not observe, and so conclude that "consolidation" is an empty term.

In sum, the secret of democratic durability seems to lie in economic development—not, as the theory dominant in the 1960s had it, under dictatorship, but under democracy based on parliamentary institutions.

Appendix: Classifying Regimes

We define democracy as a regime in which governmental offices are filled as a consequence of contested elections. Only if the opposition is allowed to compete, win, and assume office is a regime democratic. To the extent to which it focuses on elections, this is obviously a minimalist definition.

This definition has two parts: "offices" and "contestation." In no regime are all governmental offices filled as a consequence of elections. What is essential to consider a regime as democratic is that two kinds of offices are filled by elections: the chief executive office and the seats in the effective legislative body.

Contestation occurs when there exists an opposition that has some chance of winning office as a consequence of elections. We take quite literally Przeworski's dictum that "Democracy is a system in which parties lose elections": whenever in doubt, we classify as democracies only those systems in which incumbent parties actually did lose elections. Alternation in office constitutes prima facie evidence of contestation.

Contestation, in turn, entails three features: 1) *ex ante* uncertainty, 2) *ex post* irreversibility, and 3) repeatability.

By "*ex ante* uncertainty," we mean that there is some positive probability that at least one member of the incumbent coalition can lose office in a particular round of elections. Uncertainty is not synonymous with unpredictability: the probability distribution of electoral chances is typically known. All that is necessary for outcomes to be uncertain is that some incumbent party could lose.

By "*ex post* irreversibility" we mean the assurance that whoever wins elections will be allowed to assume office. The outcome of elections must be irreversible under democracy even if the opposition wins. The practical consequence of this feature is to exclude sham elections as well as periods of liberalization. Liberalization is typically intended by dictatorial regimes to be a controlled opening of the political space. When it fails—that is, when the opposition does win—a clampdown sometimes follows. Hence there is no certainty that the opposition would be able to celebrate its victory.

The final feature of contestation is that elections must be expected to be repeated. Whoever wins the current round of elections cannot use office to make it impossible for the competing political forces to win next time. Democracy, as Juan Linz once said, is government *pro tempore*. All political outcomes must be temporary: losers do not forfeit the right to compete in the future, to negotiate again, to influence legislation, to pressure the bureaucracy, or to seek recourse to courts. Even constitutional provisions are not immutable; rules, too, can be changed according to rules.

Operationally, a regime was classified as a democracy if it did not fail under any of the four rules listed below. (Our timing rules are as follows: We code the regime that prevailed at the end of the year, even if it came to power on December 31, as, for example, dictatorship arrived in Nigeria in 1983. Transitions to authoritarianism are signaled by a coup d'état. Transitions to democracy are dated by the time of the inauguration of the newly elected government, not of the election. In the few cases, like those of the Dominican Republic in 1963, where a democratic regime lasted six months, or Bolivia in 1979, where the situation changed several times, the information about regimes that began and ended within the same year is lost.) A regime is classified as a dictatorship if at least one of these conditions holds:

Rule 1: "Executive Selection." The chief executive is not elected.

Rule 2: "Legislative Selection." The legislature is not elected.

Rule 3: "Party." There is no more than one party. Specifically, this rule applies if 1) there were no parties, or 2) there was only one party, or 3) the current tenure in office ended up in the establishment of nonparty or single-party rule, or 4) the incumbents unconstitutionally closed the legislature and rewrote the rules in their favor. Alternation in office overrides the party rule: Jamaica, where a single party at one time held 100 percent of the seats in the legislature yet subsequently yielded office after losing an election, was classified as democratic during the entire period.

These three rules are not sufficient, however, to classify those regimes that repeatedly hold elections, allow varying degrees of freedom for the opposition, and always win. There are some regimes that cannot be unambiguously classified on the basis of all the evidence produced by history: we have no way of telling whether the incumbents would have held elections if they were not certain to win. In such cases we must decide which error we prefer to avoid: classifying as democracies regimes that may not be ones or rejecting as democracies regimes that may in fact be ones. Err we must; the only question is which way. We decided to err on the conservative side, disqualifying as democracies regimes that pass the previous three rules but not the following:

Rule 4: "Type II Error." The incumbents held office in the immediate past by virtue of elections for more than two terms or without being elected, and until today or the time when they were overthrown they have not lost an election.

Throughout this discussion, we have focused on democracy. We treat dictatorship simply as a residual category, perhaps better denominated as "not democracy." Since we are often told that democracy "is" a continuous variable, here are the reasons we insist on dichotomizing political regimes: 1) While some democracies are more democratic than others, unless offices are contested, no regime should be considered democratic. Kenneth A. Bollen and Robert W. Jackman, in their 1989 *American Sociological Review* essay "Democracy, Stability, and Dichotomies," confuse the argument that some democracies are more democratic than others with the claim that one can distinguish the degree of "democracy" for any pair of regimes. 2) The idea that we should, as Bollen and Jackman suggest in their discussion of "borderline cases," place the cases that cannot be unambiguously classified given our rules into an "intermediate" category, halfway between democracy and dictatorship, strikes us as ludicrous. 3) "Borderline cases" constitute either systematic or random errors. Systematic errors can be treated by explicit rules, such as our Type II Error rule, and their consequences can be examined statistically. Once this decision is made, the classification is unambiguous. 4) In turn, some errors random with regard to the rules will remain and we have to live with them. But there are no a priori reasons to think that a more refined classification will have a smaller measurement error. A finer scale generates smaller errors but more of them, a rougher scale generates larger errors but fewer of them. If the distribution of true observations is unimodal and close to symmetric, a more refined classification will have a smaller error, but in fact observations on all the polychotomous scales tend to be U-shaped, which advantages a dichotomous classification.

Whatever the peculiarities of our rules, the resulting classification differs little from alternative approaches: the Coppedge-Reinecke scale for 1978 predicts 92 percent of our regimes, the Bollen 1965 scale predicts 85 percent, and the Gurr scales of autocracy and democracy for 1950–86 jointly predict 91 percent. The Gastil scale of political liberties, covering the period from 1972 to 1990, predicts 93.2 percent of our classification; his scale of civil liberties predicts 91.5 percent; and the two scales jointly predict 94.2 percent of our regimes. Hence there is no reason to think that our results are idiosyncratic in the particular classification of regimes.

Since the distinction between parliamentary and presidential systems is un-controversial, we state it only briefly. In parliamentary systems, the legislative assembly can dismiss the government, while under presidential systems it cannot. This criterion coincides perfectly with the mode of selection of the government: by the legislature in parliamentary systems, by the voters (directly or indirectly) in presidential systems. Within each type of institutional design there are important differences. Most important among these differences is the electoral system, some varieties of which may or may not be prone to generate legislative majorities.

Some institutional arrangements, however, do not fit either pure type: they are "premier-presidential," "semipresidential," or "mixed," according to different terminologies. In such systems, the president is elected for a fixed term and has some executive powers, but governments serve at the discretion of the parliament. These "mixed" systems are not homogeneous: most lean closer to parliamentarism insofar as the government is responsible to the legislature; others, notably Portugal between 1976 and 1981, grant the president the power to appoint and dismiss governments and therein lean closer to presidentialism.

Among the 135 countries that are included in our sample, there were 50 parliamentary democracies, 46 presidential, and 8 mixed. Outside the Americas, there were nine presidential democracies: Congo (1960–62), Ghana (1979–80), Nigeria (1979–82), Uganda (1980–84), Bangladesh (1986–90), South Korea (1988–present), Pakistan (1972–76), and the Philippines (before 1964 and then from 1986 to the present).

In Latin America, the only parliamentary regimes were the short-lived attempt in Brazil, preceding the 1964 coup, and Suriname. Most West European countries have parliamentary systems, but parliamentary democracies can also be found in most other parts of the world.

NOTES

This work was supported in part by National Science Foundation grant SES-9022605.

1. Most of the political data were collected by the authors, but some are taken from Arthur S. Banks, *Cross-National Time-Series Data Archive* (Binghamton, N.Y.: Center for Social Analysis, State University of New York at Binghamton, magnetic tape, 1993). They are described in Alvarez, Cheibub, Limongi, and Przeworski, "Classifying Political Regimes for the ACLP Data Set" (Working Paper No. 3, University of Chicago Center on Democracy, 1994). Most of the economic data are derived from Penn World Tables, version 5.6; other data are from the World Bank and the International Monetary Fund. We refer to this collection of data as the ACLP data base. Saudi Arabia and the five Persian Gulf states were excluded because oil revenues accounted for more than 50 percent of their GDP most of the time.

2. These numbers add up to 104 democratic institutional systems since there were three democratic regimes that changed their institutional framework without passing through a dictatorial spell.

3. Adam Przeworski and Fernando Limongi, "Democracy and Development" (paper presented at the Nobel Symposium on Democracy, Uppsala, Sweden, 27–30 August 1994). For divergent assessments of how regimes affect growth, see the overview presented in Przeworski and Limongi, "Political Regimes and Economic Growth," *Journal of Economic Perspectives* 7 (June 1993): 51–69. For recent econometric evidence, see John F. Helliwell, "Empirical Linkages Between Democracy and Economic Growth," *British Journal of Political Science* 24 (April 1994): 225–48; and Robert J. Barro, "Democracy and Growth" (Working Paper No. 4909, National Bureau of Economic Research, Cambridge, Mass., 1994).

4. All figures for annual per-capita income are expressed in purchasing-power-parity (PPP) U.S. dollars in 1985 international prices, as given by version 5.5 of the Penn World Tables. In some cases, these numbers differ significantly from the 5.6 release, used in the remainder of this essay to measure the "level of development."

5. The results reported in this paragraph are treated at length in Adam Przeworski and Fernando Limongi, "Modernization: Theories and Facts" (Working Paper No. 8, University of Chicago Center on Democracy, 1995).

6. After the fact, it may appear that development led to democracy. Suppose that we observe a dictatorship with a per-capita income of $2,000 a year in a country that grows at 2.5 percent per year. Assume further that at $2,000 any dictatorship faces each year the same risk of dying, equal to 0.025. If this dictatorship died exactly 28 years after its birth, at $4,000, we would be tempted to attribute its demise to development. But this dictatorial regime would have had a 50 percent cumulative chance of making it all the way to $4,000 *even if the marginal chance of surviving (the hazard rate) was exactly the same at $4,000 as at $2,000.* Conversely, take Spain, which we observe for the first time in 1950 at $1,953 per-capita income and which grew under the dictatorship at the average rate of 5.25 percent per annum, to reach $7,531 by 1976. Suppose that the Spanish dictatorship faced during the entire period a 0.03 chance of dying during each year, so that, assuming an exponential hazard function, it had about a 50 percent chance of not being around by 1974 *even if it had not developed at all.*

7. Samuel P. Huntington, *Political Order in Changing Societies* (New Haven: Yale University Press, 1968); Samuel P. Huntington and Joan Nelson, *No Easy Choice: Political Participation in Developing Countries* (Cambridge: Harvard University Press, 1976); and Guillermo O'Donnell, *Modernization and Bureaucratic-Authoritarianism: Studies in South American Politics* (Berkeley: Institute of International Studies, University of California, 1973).

8. In addition to the transitions in Argentina in 1955, 1962, 1966, and 1976, they occurred in Chile in 1973, Uruguay in 1973, Suriname in 1980, Turkey in 1967, and Fiji in 1987.

9. Seymour Martin Lipset, "Some Social Requisites of Democracy: Economic Development and Political Legitimacy," *American Political Science Review* 53 (March 1959): 56. Our best guess is that the European countries that succumbed to fascism between the wars had per-capita incomes not higher than $2,000 in the 1985 international prices. See Przeworski and Limongi, "Modernization."

10. Lipset, *Political Man: The Social Bases of Politics* (Baltimore: Johns Hopkins University Press, 1981 [orig. publ. 1960]), esp. 27–63, 459–76, and 488–503; Mancur Olson, "Rapid Growth as a Destabilizing Force," *Journal of Economic History* 23 (1963): 453–72; Huntington, *Political Order in Changing Societies.*

11. This finding parallels again the results of John B. Londregan and Keith T. Poole with regard to coups, which they found to be less likely when the economy grows. See Londregan and Poole, "Poverty, the Coup Trap, and the Seizure of Executive Power," *World Politics* 42 (January 1990): 151–83.

12. Larry Diamond and Juan J. Linz, "Introduction: Politics, Society, and Democracy in Latin America," in Diamond, Linz, and Lipset, eds., *Democracy in Developing Countries,* vol. 4, *Latin America* (Boulder, Colo.: Lynne Rienner, 1989), 1–58.

13. Hirschman's argument was that a moderate rate of inflation allows governments to pacify the most militant groups. See "The Social and Political Matrix of Inflation: Elaborations on the Latin American Experience," in Hirschman's *Essays in Trespassing: Economics to Politics and Beyond* (New York: Cambridge University Press, 1981), 177–207.

14. Edward N. Muller, "Democracy, Economic Development, and Income Inequality," *American Sociological Review* 53 (February 1988): 50–68.

15. Note again the parallel finding of Londregan and Poole in "Poverty, the Coup Trap, and the Seizure of Executive Power" that coups breed coups.

16. Juan J. Linz, "The Perils of Presidentialism," *Journal of Democracy* 1 (Winter 1990): 51–69 and "The Virtues of Parliamentarism," *Journal of Democracy* 1 (Fall 1990): 84–91.

17. Juan J. Linz, "Democracy: Presidential or Parliamentary—Does It Make a Difference?" (paper prepared for the Workshop on Political Parties in the Southern Cone, Woodrow Wilson International Center for Scholars, Washington, D.C., 1984). Linz's claim is disputed by Scott Mainwaring and Matthew Shugart, "Juan Linz, Presidentialism, and Democracy: A Critical Appraisal" (Working Paper No. 200, Helen Kellogg Institute for International Studies, University of Notre Dame, 1993).

18. Walter Bagehot, "The English Constitution: The Cabinet," in Arend Lijphart, ed., *Parliamentary versus Presidential Government* (Oxford: Oxford University Press, 1992), 18. Woodrow Wilson's 1884 essay "Committee or Cabinet Government?"—reprinted in the same volume—makes an argument similar to Bagehot's. Also to be found in Lijphart's collection is an analysis of the U.S. political structure done to mark the 1976 Bicentennial by the U.S. Committee on the Constitutional System. The Committee notes that "The separation of powers, as a principle of constitutional structure, has served us well in preventing tyranny and the abuse of high office, but it has done so by encouraging confrontation, and deadlock, and by diffusing accountability for the results."

19. Note that throughout we refer only to the share of the largest party in the legislature, whether or not it has been the same as the party of the president. In the United States, since 1968, the control of at least one house of the Congress has rested in the hands of the party other than that of the president 80 percent of the time.

20. Mainwaring counted democratic breakdowns since 1945, finding 27 under presidentialism, 19 under parliamentarism, and 4 under other types. "Presidentialism, Multipartism, and Democracy: The Difficult Combination," *Comparative Political Studies* 26 (July 1993): 198–228.

21. Mainwaring, "Presidentialism in Latin America," *Latin American Research Review*

25 (Winter 1990): 157–79. Alfred Stepan and Cindy Skach, "Meta-Institutional Frameworks and Democratic Consolidation," *World Politics* 46 (April 1993): 1–22.

22. Mainwaring and Shugart, in "Juan Linz, Presidentialism, and Democracy," take issue with Linz: in their view it is majoritarian parliamentarism, rather than presidentialism, that increases the political stakes. Yet even if majoritarian parliamentary systems last shorter than minoritarian ones, parliamentary democracies of any kind last longer than presidential regimes. Whether this difference is due to the intensity of political conflicts, however, we do not know.

23. Only Pakistan went from parliamentarism in 1950–55 to presidentialism in 1972–76 and back to parliamentarism in 1988. Only Ghana, Nigeria, South Korea (which was a parliamentary democracy for one year in 1960), and Turkey chose a presidential system after having experienced parliamentary democracies. Lastly, only Suriname opted for a mixed system after having experienced democratic presidentialism.

24. This is the argument of the Nigerian Constitution Drafting Committee of 1976: "The tendency indeed of all people throughout the world is to elevate a single person to the position of ruler. In the context of Africa the division [of powers] is not only meaningless, it is difficult to maintain in practice. No African head of state has been known to be content with the position of a mere figurehead." See the Committee's report in Lijphart, *Parliamentary versus Presidential Government*.

25. Only two parliamentary democracies emerged from a civilian dictatorship and died before 1991. Their expected life is 22 years, but the tiny number of countries involved greatly diminishes confidence in this number.

26. See Banks, *Cross-National Time-Series Data Archive*. Among the 35 transitions that occurred after 1973, parliamentary institutions were chosen in 13 cases at the average level of $3,414, and presidential institutions in 19 cases at the average level of $2,591, making the effect even more pronounced.

27. This is not to argue that countries that have adopted presidential institutions during recent transitions to democracy should immediately attempt to move to parliamentarism. Whenever institutional choice is present on the political agenda, substantive conflicts, even minor ones, tend to spill over to institutional issues. Such situations are dangerous for democracy, since they signify that there are no clear rules by which substantive conflicts can be terminated. Hence having a clear and stable institutional system is more important than having a perfect one. We owe this observation to Hyug Baeg Im.

28. The 1853 Constitution sets the period between the election and the inauguration at nine months because that is how long it took electors to travel from the interior to Buenos Aires. The transfer of office from President Raúl Alfonsín to the president-elect, Carlos Menem, was shortened as a result of a mutual agreement under the pressure of an inflationary crisis.

29. Robert A. Dahl, "Transitions to Democracy" (address delivered to the symposium on "Voices of Democracy," University of Dayton, Center for International Studies, 16–17 March 1990).

30. Guillermo O'Donnell, in his chapter in this collection, implies that "institution-alization" can be understood in two ways: either as a process of gradual stabilization of expectations that a particular institutional system will orient political actions or as an increasing fit between formal institutions and real practices. If "institutionalization" is taken in the first sense, it is tautologically related to "consolidation." But whether democracy can survive when the formal institutions do not describe real practices is an empirical question.

16

THE MIDDLE CLASSES AND DEMOCRATIZATION

Hsin-Huang Michael Hsiao & Hagen Koo

Hsin-Huang Michael Hsiao *is director of the Program for Southeast Asian Area Studies (PROSEA) at Academia Sinica in Taipei, as well as a research fellow at Academia Sinica's Institute of Sociology. He is also professor of sociology at National Taiwan University.* **Hagen Koo** *is professor of sociology at the University of Hawaii at Manoa.*

Recent experiences of democratic transition in South Korea and Taiwan seem to confirm the well-known thesis linking the growth of the middle class to the establishment of democracy. In both countries, economic growth has greatly expanded the size of the middle class, which became increasingly discontented with authoritarian rule and demanded greater political freedom and participation. Increasing middle-class alienation and the associated social pressure for change eventually led to political liberalization in the late 1980s and the subsequent process of democratic transition. While democratic transitions in Latin America and Eastern Europe were often caused by economic failures, the East Asian cases of transition resulted from economic success and efficient economic management by authoritarian regimes. In these cases, the middle class seems to be a key element in explaining this ironic relationship between economic success and the demise of the authoritarian state.

The thesis that economic growth is linked, first, to the rise of a middle class and, second, to democratic transition is valid in broad terms; nevertheless, it requires elaboration. In particular, we must understand when, how, and under what conditions a democratic transition can occur, and how exactly the middle class plays a role in such a transition. As the recent literature on democratic transitions stresses, structural conditions such as level of economic development, class structure, and economic conditions are usually insufficient to bring about a transition to democracy. Moreover, we have seen in recent years that democratic transitions can occur in societies where the usual structural conditions are absent, as in formerly communist countries.[1] Indeed, the relationship between economic development and democratic transition is complex and is contingent on a variety of factors. Specifically, while economic development does invariably enlarge the middle class, this does not automatically bring a political transition to democracy.

This essay examines the role played by the middle class in both South Korea and Taiwan in effecting and later shaping processes of democratic transition. While both the Korean and Taiwanese middle classes played critical roles in those countries' recent transitions from authoritarianism, their approaches and methods differed significantly. Specifically, the Korean middle class has generally been more vocal and active than the Taiwanese middle class. Moreover, the Korean transition involved a much higher level of political conflict and social mobilization. Comparatively speaking, the Korean democratic transition was a bottom-up process, while that of Taiwan was a more top-down, elite-controlled process. Nevertheless, in each case, societal pressures were crucial in forcing the authoritarian regime to liberalize.

The democratic transitions that occurred in South Korea and Taiwan were by no means the automatic result of either economic growth or the rise of the middle class. While the rise of the middle class provided an important structural condition for democracy in both cases, the specific political effects of this phenomenon were not predetermined but rather evolved through delicate political processes in which state power and nonclass elements such as regional, ethnic, and generational cleavages played critical roles. This essay investigates how the South Korean and Taiwanese middle classes, and their various segments, have interacted with other political actors to bring forth and shape the democratic transition from authoritarian rule.

In analyzing the role of middle-class politics in democratic transitions, it is important to realize that such transitions do not happen all at once but rather occur in phases involving different agendas, opponents, and coalitions, as well as a shifting balance of power among key groups. The role of the middle class is likely to vary from one phase to another. Here, we follow the conventional division of the democratization process into three phases: liberalization, transition, and consolidation. Using this approach, we analyze the shifting dynamics of middle-class politics in each phase of the transition process.

The middle class is conceptualized here as those who occupy intermediate positions between the capitalist and working classes. Included in this category are professional and managerial workers, civil servants, white-collar workers, small-business owners, and shopkeepers. Sociological analysis conventionally refers to professional, technical, and white-collar workers as the "new middle class," and to small employers and nonagricultural self-employed people as the "old middle class." We follow this distinction here. In addition, we find it useful to treat intellectuals (writers, professors, journalists, religious leaders, lawyers, and the like) as a special subcategory of the new middle class. As the following analysis will show, intellectuals played a significant role in democratic transitions in both countries and, therefore, deserve special attention. Also important is the role of university students. Strictly speaking, students cannot be regarded as members of any particular class, but most come from middle-class families and are likely to be members of the middle class in the future. Thus, while we do not treat students as full-fledged members of the middle class, we pay close attention to their role in the democratization process in relation to the roles played by various segments of the middle class, especially intellectuals.

Given the ambiguity and fluidity of the concept of the middle class, it is difficult to provide an accurate estimate of the size of the middle class in each society. It is indisputable, however, that the middle class has grown rapidly in recent decades. In South Korea, the proportion of workers classified as professional and managerial increased from 2.9 percent in 1965 to 8.7 percent in 1990; other categories of white-collar workers increased from 4.1 to 13.1 percent. In Taiwan, the proportion of professional, managerial, and white-collar workers has increased to about 20 percent over the past three decades. The size of the old middle class is more difficult to estimate from census occupational-distribution tables, but scholars agree that increases in this class parallel those of urban wage-earning populations. One study indicates that the size of the old middle class in South Korea increased from 13 percent of the total employed population in 1960 to 19.8 percent in 1990.[2] In Taiwan, the old middle class experienced some fluctuations yet remained relatively stable; its size was estimated to be 12 percent of the employed population at the beginning of the 1990s.

We first present separate narrative accounts of how democratic transition proceeded in South Korea and Taiwan and how the middle class affected the democratization process in each case. We then examine the contrasting patterns of middle-class politics in the two cases, using the following questions as guides. To what extent was a particular phase of the transition attributable to the middle class? Which segment of the middle class played the most significant role at given junctures? Were different segments of the middle class mobilized at different phases of transition? How did this affect the transition process? What kinds of alliances were forged by the middle class or segments of that class with other classes or groups, including opposition parties, in order to push for change at various junctures in the transition process? How did the ruling elites respond to demands from the middle class for democratic reform? What strategies did the elites use to incorporate the middle class into the dominant coalition in each case, and how did these strategies differ from those used in response to the demands of labor or other subordinate groups? Finally, what were the major goals during each phase of transition, and how did the middle class contribute to the realization of these goals?

The Korean Case

Liberalization (late 1983 to June 1987). Chun Doo Hwan came to power through a military coup in 1980, after ruthlessly suppressing a civil uprising in Kwangju in May of that year. For the next three years, the Chun regime used extraordinary measures to crush opposition groups and to pacify civil society. Yet the regime could not survive on repression alone. In late 1983, Chun decided to boost his political legitimacy through a series of liberalization measures. The government released dozens of political prisoners, allowed activist students and professors to return to their schools, and granted more freedom to civic organizations. Though such liberalization was limited in scope, it greatly intensified the antiregime efforts of students, opposition parties, and all other dissident groups, while stimulating as well horizontal alliances among these opposition groups. In retrospect, Chun Doo Hwan's attempt to liberalize his regime was a mistake. Yet in a sense he did not have a choice. Chun understood that repression alone would not quell opposition or solve his regime's legitimacy problem. Moreover, it is very likely that Chun anticipated strong support from the middle class as a result of his regime's significant economic achievements.[3]

Contrary to Chun's expectations, however, the middle class turned against him during this initial liberalization period by showing broad support for the opposition movement and for student activists. Of course, the vanguard of the democratization movement was composed of highly politicized segments of the middle class, including students, religious leaders, journalists, college professors, and writers. It was apparent, however, that the middle class as a whole was also solidly behind the struggle to end military rule. There seems to have been little differentiation within the middle class, although the new middle class (composed of professional, technical, and white-collar workers) was considerably more progressive politically than the old middle class (composed of small-business owners, shopkeepers, and other self-employed people).

Democratic opening (June 1987). While opposition movements broadened and intensified, great public anger and moral outrage were triggered when it was revealed that one college student, Chong Chul Park, had been tortured to death by the police. A similar scandal broke after another college-student protester was sexually assaulted during a police interrogation. At the same time, Chun arrogantly rejected the opposition party's demand for a constitutional revision that would have provided for direct presidential elections. This further frustrated the middle class. Finally, the students developed an antiregime ideology known as *minju, minjung,* and *minjok*—democracy, people, and nation—which was used to influence the political orientation of the mainstream middle class.

These events convinced the middle class that the regime was not only authoritarian but also morally repugnant. They played a catalytic role in mobilizing growing numbers of protesters; street demonstrations occurred daily, with student protesters now joined by many white-collar workers and ordinary citizens. During this period, several white-collar unions, including unions for teachers, bankers, researchers, lawyers, and pharmacists, actively contributed to the antiregime struggle by issuing statements, organizing rallies, and engaging in other political tactics. Blue-collar labor unions, however, were inactive, mainly because the government exercised particularly tight surveillance over them because of their potential threat to the regime. Industrial labor remained a powerful though latent antiregime force, with the government fully aware of its potential threat.

By June 1987, street demonstrations had grown too large and were too widespread for the police alone to be able to control them. Chun considered bringing in the army but decided not to for various reasons.[4] Instead, Roh Tae Woo, then chairman of the ruling Democratic Justice Party and Chun's military-academy classmate, issued a surprise statement on 29 June 1987. In it, the ruling group accepted practically all of the opposition party's demands and agreed to hold a direct presidential election at the end of the year. This was a major breakthrough for the democratization movement in Korea, as it clearly resulted from the social pressures generated by grassroots opposition. In fact, the Korean case is unlike other cases of democratization in that it proceeded from the bottom up rather than from the top down. The Korean case is distinct from cases in which divisions within the ruling elite between so-called hard-liners and soft-liners, or between those favoring force and those favoring reform as a strategy for quelling opposition, helped create a democratic opening. In the Korean case, elite disunity did not develop even in subsequent stages of the democratic-transition process.[5]

Among the factors that contributed to democratization in South Korea, the decision by the middle class to join opposition forces was critical. Mainstream members of the middle class actively participated in the democratization struggles not simply because of their inherent democratic impulse against authoritarian rule. The cumulative effects of numerous political struggles of students, intellectuals, and workers, as well as a series of revelations about the regime's brutality, aroused moral anger among the middle class. By June 1987, then, the differences between the mainstream middle class and the more radical dissidents seemed to have largely disappeared, and the broad opposition forces were unified against the common enemy—the Chun regime.[6]

In sum, the Korean middle class played a critical role in bringing about the democratic transition during this period. First, the intellectual segment of the middle class became highly politicized, and was continuously and aggressively engaged in democratization struggles. Second, progressive intellectuals produced an antiregime ideology, which was used to influence the political orientation of the mainstream middle class while also indoctrinating younger members of the middle class attending universities. Third, as the Chun regime's legitimacy became increasingly problematic, and as political crises escalated, the broader middle class actively participated in the democratization struggles. Fourth, the mainstream middle class played a critical role in forcing the Chun regime to surrender to people's demands for a direct, democratic election of the president. Finally, middle-class participation in the antiregime struggle influenced U.S. policy toward the Chun regime, as the United States now urged Chun to take a proreform stance. During a visit to Seoul in June, Gaston Sigur, assistant secretary of state for East Asia and the Pacific, informed Chun that the United States would not support any military mobilization to suppress democratic struggles.

Democratic transition (1987 to 1992). The five-year period from the presidential election of December 1987 to the next presidential election in December 1992 marked the "transition" phase of South Korea's democratization process. Immediately after the 29 June 1987 statement expressing the regime's willingness to hold presidential elections, the country's long-suppressed civil society erupted. The most dramatic manifestations came from the workers. In the fall of 1987, violent labor strikes occurred at every industrial site, and hundreds of new "democratic unions" were formed. The power of the industrial proletariat was amply demonstrated during this period, and state and corporate leaders were unable, at least immediately, to control fierce labor offensives. During this time, several groups of white-collar and professional workers, including journalists, bankers, teachers, telecommunication workers, and others, also organized unions. High on their agenda was "social democracy" (social justice and equitable distribution of resources), in addition to political democracy.[7]

In the highly politicized atmosphere that marked this period, a sense of economic and social insecurity set in and began to affect the prevailing mood of the middle class. The mass media played a critical role in influencing middle-class attitudes as well by fostering negative opinions of the aggressive labor movement. In the first free presidential election, held in December 1987, Roh Tae Woo won. His victory was due mainly to internal divisions within the opposition camp and its resulting inability to field just one candidate. Instead, three Kims—Kim Young Sam, Kim Dae Jung, and Kim Jong Pil—split the opposition vote, delivering a sweet victory to Roh.

At this point, the middle class may have had little to do with Roh's victory, as middle-class votes were divided among different candidates along regional lines. In this and subsequent elections, regional factors were a major determinant of voting behavior. In particular, three major areas of regional ties came to dominate South Korea's electoral politics through regional ties: the Southeast (Kyongsang or Youngnam), the Southwest (Honam), and the mid-central region (Chungchung). Each region is represented by a well-known, old-time politician—Kim Young Sam, Kim Dae Jung, and Kim Jong Pil, respectively. Although pulled by regional allegiances, the middle-class vote nevertheless went disproportionately to Roh; this was particularly true among longtime middle-class residents of Seoul. In the general election held in April 1988, however, Roh's ruling party failed to capture a majority of seats in the National Assembly. Having elected a military man from the former regime as president, voters probably wanted to see more change in the political-power structure at the legislative level.

Subsequently, however, the opposition-dominated Assembly created instability in the political system, rendering uncertain the political future of the ruling party. To solve this problem, Roh made a secret deal to merge his party with two opposition parties: one headed by Kim Young Sam and another headed by Kim Jong Pil. A new "grand conservative" party, called the Democratic Liberal Party (DLP), was thus born in January 1990. Having thus secured political stability, the Roh regime was able to pursue a moderate and limited course of democratic reform.[8]

What role did the middle class play in this phase of transition? It is possible that it was instrumental in creating an opposition-dominated Assembly, given that opposition candidates were disproportionately elected in middle-class districts. On the other hand, the shifting mood among the middle class was responsible for the creation of the grand coalition. The political elites who joined the newly merged DLP must have expected that the broader middle class would support or at least not actively oppose their decision. Indeed, members of the middle class may have expressed cynicism, but they did not express any strong opposition to the merger. Only the students waged protests at this point in the democratization process.

For its first two years, the Roh regime maintained a passive posture toward labor, but it subsequently resumed repressive control over the independent labor movement. Antilabor pressures had been building from the capitalist class and as a more general reaction to the economic slowdown, but another important contributing factor in the regime's policy shift was a change in the attitude of the middle class toward the militant labor movement. The initial middle-class reaction to post-1987 labor unrest was uneasiness; then this group became increasingly critical, especially of violent labor strikes. The mass media, which are sensitive to middle-class attitudes, severely criticized aggressive labor demands for higher wages and the violent methods that labor actions often employed.

Consequently, the decline of the "democratic labor movement" began after substantial organizational growth in 1987 and 1988.

Another interesting development during this period was the rise of social movements. Since the early 1990s, multitudes of new social movements have emerged in the relatively liberal political environment.[9] These social movements had such diverse aims as promoting economic justice, protecting the environment, ensuring fair elections, fighting gender inequality, and raising civil consciousness. The most successful among them was the Citizens' Coalition for Economic Justice (CCEJ). Founded in July 1989 by some five hundred people—primarily professionals such as professors, church leaders, lawyers, doctors, writers, journalists, and the like—the CCEJ targeted "injustice" in wealth formation and income distribution. In particular, it focused on such issues as unearned income, real-estate speculation, and inadequate financial and tax systems in its civil campaigns. From the outset, the CCEJ proclaimed itself a nonviolent and nonpolitical civil movement, in which both the "haves" and the "have-nots" could participate.[10] Three years after it was formed, its membership had grown from about five hundred to seven thousand; by 1993, it had ten regional chapters as well as specialized research institutes, a publishing house, and its own bimonthly magazine. Today, the CCEJ is widely regarded as one of the most influential organizations in Korea.

By and large, these social movements were led by middle-class activists, and their main constituency and social base of support was also the middle class. These movements cannot, however, be narrowly defined as middle class in nature. The movements addressed issues of vital concern to the working class and other lower classes, including distributive justice, transportation, and environmental pollution. This breadth of concerns caused the movements to appeal to many people outside the middle class and proved central to their success. In using the term "new social movements," we do not mean to imply that these movements are either postmaterial or postmodern, like their Western counterparts, but simply that they are newly formed. The new social movements in South Korea are seriously concerned with distributive justice, and their leaders are primarily former student activists from the authoritarian period.

With the rise of the new social movements, there appeared to be a gradual separation between the moderate and liberal members of these movements and the more radical members of the labor and *minjung* movements. During the authoritarian period, the two groups shared essentially the same political and ideological orientation. In the 1990s, however, internal divisions within the various movements became a noticeable trend. Although the leaders of the new social movements were once active in the *minjung* movement, they now maintain some distance from the radical activists. The appeal of the *minjung* movement has been declining steadily, while the new social movements have become more popular.

Consolidation (1993 to the present). With the election of Kim Young Sam as president in December 1992 and the birth of a new civilian government in 1993, a new chapter began in South Korea's political development. The new government was the first nonmilitary regime since 1961, and it marked the end of the perennial problem of legitimacy that had plagued previous regimes. For Koreans, this break with military rule was a significant moment in the transition from authoritarianism to democracy.

Some would argue that South Korean democracy was "consolidated" even during the Roh period from 1988 to 1992, because by this time the threat of a military coup or a reversal to authoritarianism was generally considered extremely slim. For the majority of South Koreans, however, the critical moment was the clean break with the military regime. Although Roh had been democratically elected through a free and fair election, he was clearly heir to the previous military regime, and the old power structure remained largely intact.

After assuming power, Kim Young Sam carried out surprisingly bold reforms. He prosecuted many members of the past military elite, investigated past political corruption, carried out a radical shake-up of the military establishment, and, in August 1993, implemented the "real-name financial system." This system, which required every financial transaction to be conducted in one's real (legal) name, proved the most effective measure for disclosing hidden sources of wealth generation and for curbing the underground flow of money. Kim also appointed as minister of labor a progressive labor lawyer, who attempted to adopt more liberal labor-relations policies. As a result of such drastic measures, Kim was enormously popular during his first year in office.

Later, however, the progressive character of the Kim government gradually waned. In general, his policies became increasingly procapital and antilabor.[11] Further, the progressive labor minister was fired owing to heavy pressure from capitalist groups. Kim's early promise to dissolve many quasi-governmental organizations was withdrawn, and his policies increasingly lacked consistency. As a result, his popularity plummeted. In the most recent local election, the first local election since 1961, his DLP lost by wide margins, particularly in Seoul.

It seems that the political dynamics of this consolidation phase were less affected by class factors or civil society than by the dynamics within the "political society," primarily in the structure and composition of the political parties. In this, Kim's DLP proved an unstable amalgam of politicians, including some who had been affiliated with the previous regimes, as well as some liberals, radicals, and followers of Kim from his earlier opposition period. Thus his party lacked internal unity and coherence. In general, South Korean political parties have been unable to retire past political leaders, such as the well-known three Kims, who have continued to compete for power on a regional basis. In fact, regionalism became more serious as democratic competition intensified.

How can we interpret the role of the middle class during this period of democratic consolidation? It seems that Kim Young Sam's gradual retreat from progressive reforms might have something to do with the inherent conservatism and stability-oriented nature of the middle class, especially in areas related to labor relations. Of course, a more important factor was pressure from the capitalist class. By threatening to not make industrial investments, major capitalists were able to force the Kim government to withdraw many policies that went against their interests. During this period, middle-class support has shifted toward the side of capital.

One possible generalization relates to the imbalance of power between capital and labor in South Korea. South Korea's large middle class, easily pulled to the side of capital, led the Korean democratic transition in a far more moderate reformist, elite-dominated direction than was the case in Taiwan, despite much greater bottom-up pressure for democratization than Taiwan experienced.

The Taiwanese Case

Liberalization (late 1980 to June 1987). Two important sociopolitical developments occurred in Taiwan in late 1980, marking the initial stage of transition from authoritarian rule. The first development was the emergence of new social movements led by the middle class. With these movements, Taiwan's civil society organized itself for the first time in the face of the authoritarian Kuomintang (KMT) state, though the strategy was relatively depoliticized in order not to provoke immediate repression by the state. Nevertheless, the rise of social movements has played an instrumental role in undermining authoritarian rule.[12] Significantly, the new social movements served in this initial liberalization phase to demand greater autonomy and freedom from the state, opening in the process a political space for other social groups to mobilize as well. These demands were taken seriously and were not met with political repression. The social-psychological impact was tremendous, as the voice of civil society was finally heard.

The second important development occurred in the general legislative election in December 1980, just one year after the violent Kaohsiung protest of 10 December 1979. The protest was the largest anti-KMT political rally organized by opposition leaders since the KMT assumed control of Taiwan. In the 1980 election, the opposition gained further support from the public, of which the urban middle class was the most noticeable group, who cast their ballots in favor of the supporters and family members of those convicted in the violent political protest. The election results demonstrated discontent with the KMT experienced by the public, particularly by mainstream middle-class voters, and their support for political reform.

Related to this was the role played by liberal intellectuals, primarily university professors of the new middle class, who promoted prodemocratic assessments of the Kaohsiung protest and the subsequent opposition victory in 1980. They maintained that the Kaohsiung Incident was not planned in advance by the opposition, and that the rally and protest were intended to be peaceful and prodemocratic. The unfortunate violence, they argued, was triggered in part by aggression on the part of the police. The opposition's victory in the 1980 election was further interpreted as the manifestation of the public's verdict on the incident. Moreover, the liberal intellectuals argued that Taiwan could not afford to repeat the tragic mistakes of Korea's bloody May 1980 Kwangju massacre by Chun Doo Hwan and so tried to persuade the KMT elites to grant opposition demands for political relaxation. In other words, moderate and indirect demands for liberalization were first made by various segments of the middle class beginning in the early 1980s.

In May 1983, the hard-liner General Wang Sheng was removed from key posts by then–President Chiang Ching-kuo, signaling the decline of the military and security apparatus. Moreover, Chiang nominated ethnic-Taiwanese technocrat Lee Teng-hui as the vice-presidential candidate in March 1984, accelerating the indigenization and demilitarization of central political leadership within the KMT.[13] In May 1984, a quasi-party known as the Public Policy Research Association was organized by opposition political leaders. Whereas under the previous authoritarian regime such a group would have faced an immediate repressive crackdown, the KMT now responded with indecision and inaction. This encouraged the political opposition to further advance its organizational efforts and, by September 1986, to create the first opposition party in Taiwan's history—the Democratic Progressive Party (DPP).

From 1984 to 1986, the KMT refrained from using repressive measures against the opposition, opting instead for a mediated dialogue. This could be seen as a clear signal from the KMT, especially from Chiang, that political liberalization had been set in motion. During this period, some liberal intellectuals played a crucial role in the dialogues between the KMT and the opposition by becoming actual participants in the mediating process. The liberal intellectuals had long advocated democratic reform and enjoyed the trust and respect of Taiwan's civil society. They were now applauded by many new segments of the middle class for making the unprecedented political dialogue possible. As a result of this dialogue, a political crisis was, for the time being, averted.

Throughout its decades-long rule of Taiwan, the KMT state believed it had controlled and pacified Taiwanese society, and took political stability for granted. The KMT believed that only a few ambitious dissidents and opposition leaders would pose a challenge to the regime, and that the majority of Taiwanese were satisfied with the economic prosperity and political order that had been achieved thus far. Yet these perceptions were critically challenged in the early 1980s when the first wave of grassroots social movements opposing the KMT emerged. These included movements of consumers, environmentalists, women, aborigines, students, and the New Testament church, all making demands on the KMT. The KMT elites, especially Chiang Ching-kuo near the end of his life, felt great pressure and were even puzzled by the growing opposition. It is important to emphasize here that, while each of the movements has its own objectives, all of these early social movements targeted the state, demanding changes in the state-society relations established under authoritarian rule. Such collective support for change was then interpreted by the KMT state as a challenge to its legitimacy.[14]

These organized social movements emerged between 1980 and 1986 and were led in most cases by the new middle class. During this period, they exerted pressure on the authoritarian regime and succeeded in winning concessions from the KMT. In October 1986, Chiang Ching-kuo made a historic statement in which he admitted: "The time is changing, the environment is changing, the tide is changing, and therefore, the KMT has to change." In this statement, Chiang referred not only to the challenges from the political society, but also to the growing demands from the new social movements and other elements of civil society. In this, the middle class was key. New segments of the middle class —including students, professors, other liberal intellectuals, urban middle-income housewives, lawyers, young journalists, and church leaders—organized themselves and demanded change. In the process, they posed an unprecedented challenge to the regime and, together with political opposition, helped force the regime to relinquish some control over society, which in turn set the stage for liberalization.

Chiang Ching-kuo decided to tolerate the social movements as well as the opposition's organizational efforts. More importantly, he officially lifted martial law and other political bans in July 1987. This signified a major concession on the part of the authoritarian state in response to the liberalization challenge from both the political and the social movements. It also represented a watershed in Taiwan's political liberalization, setting the stage for further democratization.

The lifting of martial law further facilitated the second wave of organized civil protests and social movements.[15] These newly emerging social movements included laborers, farmers, teachers, political prisoners, mainlanders, and human rights advocates as well as the handicapped, veterans, and other disadvantaged groups. These social movements were organized by diverse classes, and the issues raised were far more politically sensitive than those raised by the first wave of movements.

The middle class was not necessarily at the core of these second-wave movements, but generally supported their objectives. Again, the authoritarian state did not take any repressive measures against these new, more politically challenging social movements.

The middle class, especially professionals and intellectuals of the new middle class, has organized effective reform-oriented movements that have persuaded the authoritarian KMT state to liberalize.

Democratic opening and uncertainty (July 1987 to July 1988). Between the lifting of martial law in July 1987 and the death of Chiang Ching-kuo in January 1988, Taiwan's politics experienced a democratic opening. With the National Security Law and the Civic Organization Law, however, enacted in 1987 and 1989, respectively, the KMT did manage to limit the scope of liberalization. Lee Teng-hui immediately succeeded Chiang as president, but the hard-liners of the KMT were hesitant to elect Lee to head the party. Between Chiang's death in January 1988 and the eventual election of Lee to chair the KMT in July of that year, political uncertainty prevailed. No one was sure whether political liberalization would continue. During this period, protests from both civil society and the political opposition subsided. Like these social and political movements, the middle class, along with other classes, watched the political climate calmly and cautiously.

The death of Chiang Ching-kuo inspired many liberal middle-class intellectuals and segments of the middle class to anticipate a new era in Taiwan's political structure, breaking even more than before with the paternalistic rule of the Chiang family. The mainstream middle class mourned Chiang calmly and rationally without resenting or retaliating against the Taiwanese. Chiang was particularly remembered as a strong man who terminated his own rule by being sensitive to the rising political and social challenges of the Taiwanese. The new middle class also expressed concern that conservative factions of the KMT might reverse direction in order to counter the liberalization process. The middle class was particularly unsure of whether or not the new president and his reformist followers would be able to carry out the democratic transition within the existing political structures established by Chiang. The watchful stance of the middle class during times of political uncertainty has helped the KMT state under the new leadership of Lee Teng-hui to further prodemocratic reforms.

Democratic transition (July 1988 to December 1994). This period features several important events, including Lee Teng-hui's election as KMT chairman in July 1988, his reelection to the presidency in March 1990, the Council of Grand Justice's ruling in June 1990 to end the tenure of the long-term parliamentarians as of December 1991 and the consequential elections of the three reorganized representative bodies in

1991 and 1992, and the first opposition victories ever in December 1994 elections for the mayors of Taipei and Kaohsiung and for the governor of Taiwan province. During this period, several significant democratic institutional reforms were launched. In particular, the antidemocratic Temporary Provisions of the Constitution were finally repealed, the "Period of National Mobilization for Suppression of the Communist Rebellion" was ended in May 1990, and a constitutional amendment was approved in May 1992. All of these marked a break from undemocratic, extraconstitutional political structures and a restoration of constitutional rights for the nation. Though the constitutional amendment was far from being either complete or satisfactory, with revisions restricted primarily to procedural rather than substantive issues, the state was slowly taking steps toward democratic reinstitutionalization in order to address continuing pressures from the opposition and from the middle class.

During this period, the new middle class, especially the liberal intellectuals and students, played its most significant role yet in pushing for substantive democratic reform. In the spring of 1990, a large-scale demonstration was held to protest military strongman General Hau Pei-tsun's nomination as premier. The demonstrators also protested abuses of power by the National Assembly, which was then still controlled by aging members who were elected on the mainland before the KMT state moved to Taiwan and who had no constituency or social base in Taiwanese society. In such cases, the new middle class has demonstrated leadership in mobilizing other classes to support their democratic cause by staging a series of rallies and demonstrations. Subsequently, the liberal intellectuals and new-middle-class professionals once again took a leadership role in the long fight to abolish Article 100 of the Criminal Law, which was viewed as detrimental to the freedom of speech and democratic expression. This fight was waged in order to protect freedom of speech in Taiwan from any charges of political sedition. This battle was finally won in May 1992, after such strategies as street demonstrations, public lectures, and an alliance with the DPP effectively intensified political pressure on the regime, which finally forced the KMT state to agree to abolish Article 100 of the Criminal Law.[16] Freedom of speech and the "public sphere" of democratic discourse were restored and have been protected ever since; this is a significant step in democratic institutionalization.

Students, university professors, liberal journalists, and legal profession-als had all joined together in the prodemocracy movements described above, and these alliances reinforced their demands for constitutional reform, freedom of speech, structural changes in the parliamentary body, a clear definition of the power of the executive, a guarantee of civilian democratic government without military interference, and support for the development of party politics. In other words, under the leadership of new-middle-class intellectuals and professionals, Taiwan's civil society has indeed taken the establishment of democracy as its primary goal for the 1990s. Moreover, the segments belonging to the new middle class were key in advocating "social democracy" during the liberalization phase of the 1980s, and they have now redirected their attention to "political democracy" during the transition phase of the 1990s.

The old middle class behaved differently during the transition period. In the past 15 years, some of its members—mainly ethnic-Taiwanese small-business owners—secretly supported opposition candidates with campaign donations in various elections. They did not, however, openly take any political stand. During the democratic-transition phase, the old middle class split, with some becoming more vocal in supporting calls for political change and others showing a greater concern for political and economic stability during the seemingly uncertain process of democratic transition. As for marginal elements of the middle class such as low-level clerical workers and the petite bourgeoisie, their ambivalence toward politics has prevented them from engaging in any prodemocracy activities since the beginning of the liberalization phase.

Ethnic divides within the middle class, primarily between ethnic Taiwanese and mainlanders, have also divided the middle class politically. A contributing factor has been an intraparty split within the KMT's ruling bloc between the so-called mainstream faction of the party, led by Lee Teng-hui and other Taiwanese political elites, and the nonmainstream faction, led by the mainlander KMT elites and the New Party (NP). While the former was supported largely by the Taiwanese middle class, the latter gained political loyalty from the mainlander middle class. The ethnic divide was further complicated by the controversy over whether Taiwan should be independent from or unified with China, and this debate has affected the political role played by the middle class during the transition phase. The external "China factor" has indeed complicated the internal middle-class politics of Taiwan.

During this transition, particular segments of the new middle class— liberal intellectuals, professionals, and professors—have continued to play strategic political roles in supporting more substantive democratic institutionalization, as well as more feasible policies in dealing with China's pressure for reunification. In response, the KMT, DPP, and NP have become more sensitive to the political demands of the differentiated middle classes. In particular, the three parties' political agendas concerning Taiwan's national identity and Taiwan's future relations with China have been formulated to respond to various middle-class constituencies.

Prospects for democratic consolidation (January 1995 to the present). The democratic transition in Taiwan is nearing completion. The first direct elections for the mayoral positions of two major cities and for the provincial governorship of Taiwan were held in December 1994 and signified a major step toward completing the transition to procedural democracy. Political elites and the three major political parties then all engaged in intensive political negotiations over the Presidential Election and Recall Bill in the Legislative Yuan. On 20 July 1995, the important 107-clause bill was finally approved; it officially declared that a presidential election would be held on 23 March 1996.

The March 1996 presidential election was seen by many in the middle class not only as an opportunity to exercise their rights as citizens of Taiwan to elect their own president for the first time in Taiwan's history, but also as a significant break with the past. Many of them believed that as long as the 1996 presidential election was carried out in a peaceful and democratic manner, regardless of its outcome, Taiwan was bound to begin a phase of democratic consolidation. Despite China's threatening missile tests in the midst of the electoral campaign, the Taiwanese people courageously participated in their first direct, democratic presidential election. As expected, the major point of contention among competing candidates centered on the controversial issue of Taiwan's future vis-à-vis China. The middle classes were further divided along ethnic lines by this issue during—and after—the election. Over the next few years, the prospects for democratic consolidation will inevitably be determined by the extent of normative and political conflicts regarding Taiwan's national identity and relations with China. China's counterproductive threats, Lee Teng-hui's strong stand through-out the election, and Lee's victory have nevertheless forged the middle classes into a single, stable social base to face pressure from China.

What role will the middle class play in the period from democratic transition through consolidation? There are not yet any definitive answers to this question. It is likely, however, that the split between the old and new middle classes and between the Taiwanese and mainlander middle classes will still be important in post–presidential election years. In terms of Taiwan's ability to achieve democratic consolidation in the next few years, the significance of the March 1996 presidential election has been less the actual outcome of the election than the democratic processes by which it was carried out and civil society's positive response. It is also important to point out that Taiwan's course of democratic consolidation in the years to come will determine how Taiwan, as a de facto independent state, will deal with external pressure from China. At this juncture, the new middle class is most likely to continue to play its dual role as a *demanding force* and as a *stabilizing base* in the future consolidation phase of Taiwan's democracy.

Contrasting Patterns of Politics

The role of the middle classes in initiating political liberalization. Both South Korea and Taiwan began political liberalization in the mid-1980s. In both cases, the authoritarian regimes responded to societal pressures for increased political openness in order to enhance their legitimacy. Both regimes, facing growing opposition, perceived that their legitimacy could no longer be taken for granted. Moreover, in both societies, the main challengers of authoritarian rule were liberal segments of the new middle class, including liberal intellectuals, university professors, students, and professionals, all of whom constituted the vanguard of the liberalization movement.

During this period, both the Chun and Chiang regimes decided not to use repressive measures in order to resolve the social and political conflict. Instead, both regimes allowed the political opposition and social movements some freedom. In South Korea, the dissident movement was much more intense and forceful and the legitimacy crisis more serious and pressing than was the case in Taiwan. In a sense, Chun's authoritarian state was forced to liberalize in order to survive the immediate crisis, whereas Taiwan's KMT regime was persuaded to liberalize less to survive than to enhance its legitimacy. The mediating role played by liberal intellectuals of the new middle class was crucial in convincing the regime to opt for liberalization.

The political opposition in South Korea was stronger and more organized than its Taiwanese counterpart, and its direct pressure on the authoritarian regime was powerful enough to force the regime to liberalize. Politicized segments of the new middle class actively participated in the antiregime struggles, while the broader middle class provided solid support for these struggles. This, in turn, left the regime with very little backing in society, given that broad opposition forces were unified against the common enemy—the Chun regime.

In Taiwan, liberal members of the new middle class took the lead in persuading Chiang to opt for liberalization as an alternative to repression. Whereas South Korea's new middle class joined with opposition groups to press the state to loosen its repressive control over society, Taiwan's new middle class acted relatively independently and was able to exert pressure on the political elites through reform-oriented social movements. In the liberalization phase in both South Korea and Taiwan, the broader middle class merely supported the more active political opposition and social movements. The Korean middle class was more strongly opposed to the regime, and its members were more vocal and daring in supporting the democratization struggles than were their counterparts in Taiwan. In addition, during liberalization, the Korean student movement played a decisive role in bringing about large-scale political liberalization, while the Taiwanese students restricted their activism to on-campus issues.[17]

The role of the middle class in creating a democratic opening. The two countries' middle classes behaved quite differently during the period of democratic opening. In South Korea, students and the new middle class staged huge, uncontrollable street demonstrations, while several white-collar unions demanded political reforms as well. All these activities resulted in a major breakthrough for democratization in South Korea in 1987, when martial law was finally lifted. It was not just the politicized intellectuals and students who aggressively engaged in democratic struggles; it was also the mainstream middle class, including managers, professionals, white-collar workers, small-business owners, and others who became increasingly committed to change. In retrospect, the ideological leadership of the intellectual middle class has been crucial in mobilizing the mainstream middle class into a progressive antiregime movement.

In contrast, Taiwan's middle class played a relatively modest role during the democratic-opening phase, in terms of both its ideological commitment and its organized action. Here, the political uncertainty following the death of Chiang Ching-kuo and the general fear that the conservatives might reverse his reforms prevented the newly established opposition party and the social movements led by the middle class from taking further aggressive steps. A "wait and see" attitude prevailed among the middle class, although the new-middle-class intellectuals and professionals hoped that political progress was still in the making following the breakdown of martial law. The middle class's calm reaction during this phase has helped Lee's leadership proceed with democratic reforms.

In both societies, the labor movement became more active following political liberalization. In Taiwan, the second wave of social movements involving labor and other classes besides the middle class occurred immediately after martial law was lifted. Hence the middle class, especially liberal intellectuals, professionals, and social-movement activists, not only made possible the first move toward liberalization but also, in the case of South Korea, sustained the momentum for further democratic struggle or, in the case of Taiwan, maintained political stability in the midst of political uncertainty.

During the period of democratic opening, the Chun regime in South Korea was under great pressure from the alliance of the middle class and the opposition party. In Taiwan, however, the middle class did not develop an alliance with the opposition party; thus the state was able to control the pace and scope of the liberalization process and the subsequent democratic transition.

The role of the middle class during the democratic-transition period.
The period of democratic transition from authoritarian rule lasted five years in South Korea and six and a half years in Taiwan. The mode and extent of the transition to democracy varied in the two societies. In general, the South Korean experience was much more drastic and

dramatic than the Taiwanese experience, in terms of both the magnitude of the transition and the nature of class politics.

In a strict sense, South Korea's transition to procedural democracy was completed only when former opposition leader Kim Young Sam was elected in December 1992 to serve as the country's first president of a civilian government since 1961. That the election was carried out democratically signaled the success of Korea's transition to democracy. In contrast, Taiwan was near the end of its transition phase when December 1994 elections for the mayoral posts in Taipei and Kaohsiung and for the new governorship of Taiwan province were finally carried out. The opposition DPP even won the mayoral seat in the capital city, Taipei. Democratization in a procedural sense reached a major milestone. Taiwan completed its transition in March 1996, when the Taiwanese people directly and democratically elected their own president for the first time in Taiwan's history.

During the transition period, the Korean middle class became increasingly conservative, and its orientation toward stability gained prominence. To a great extent, this was due to a much higher level of labor strife in South Korea than in Taiwan. The new middle class, which had initially been favorably disposed toward the labor movement during the pretransition phase, became unfriendly, even hostile, toward the aggressive labor movement. The new middle class, along with the old middle class and the petite bourgeoisie, became a force for stability, tacitly supporting the government's renewed efforts to suppress the independent labor movement.

In Taiwan, no such reversal of middle-class attitudes was noticeable. Instead, the middle class was consistent in its orientation toward labor and other subordinate groups, largely because labor had not been mobilized to the same extent that it had been in South Korea, and so did not pose a serious threat to the interests of the middle class. In other words, Taiwan's labor movement, though active and highly mobilized at the local level and within individual firms, has in no way threatened the nation's economic stability. The same is true for the farmers' movement. Therefore, while Taiwan's elite controlled the transition process, the major task of the new middle class was to maintain pressure for a broader and speedier process of democratization. In this, the new middle class, especially its liberal intellectual segment, continued to act as the most progressive agent of change in civil society.

During South Korea's transition period, there was a great deal of social concern about issues of distributive justice and "social democracy" in the workplace. Controlling illicit wealth accumulation and unearned income became a major preoccupation of both the middle and the working classes. Attention was also focused on democratizing the workplace in order to end authoritarian practices in factories and businesses. The active social movements that arose in South Korea in the early 1990s were societal expressions of these and other such concerns. By and large, the new social movements were led by new segments of the middle class, as they had been in Taiwan in the 1980s.

Interestingly, Taiwan's new middle class shifted its focus from "social democracy" to "political democracy," whereas in South Korea the shift was from "political democracy" to more substantive "social democracy." For most of South Korea's new middle class political democratization in a procedural sense was regarded as unproblematic by the early 1990s, and it was generally held that it was now time to move into other substantive areas of democratization. For Taiwan's new middle class, however, the call for social democracy in the form of new social movements in the 1980s was a pragmatic, depoliticized strategy for pursuing democratic reform. Once the democratic transition was under way, the establishment of true constitutional and parliamentary democracy then became the primary concern of the middle class in the 1990s.

In both countries, therefore, the new middle class has continuously acted as a major force for democracy, but its role during the transition and consolidation periods has been to bring stability and moderation to the process. In South Korea, the social movements led by the middle class marginalized radical groups, including the independent labor movement and the *minjung* movement, while keeping social democracy and social justice on the political agenda. Similarly, Taiwan's new middle class helped steer the political-transition process in a moderate reformist direction, while keeping pressure on the state to build more substantive democratic institutions.

The role of the middle class in the consolidation of democracy. During the consolidation period, when electoral politics became more important, significant internal divisions within the middle class appeared in the two societies. While the divisions in Taiwan were linked to ethnicity, in South Korea they were regional in nature. In this phase, class turned out to be a less important factor in predicting an individual's voting behavior than such demographic factors as ethnicity, regional origin, age, and gender. How can we interpret the diminishing role of middle-class politics in the consolidation phase?

First, the democratic transitions in South Korea and Taiwan have already transformed the very nature of state politics and its power relations with civil society. Likewise, electoral politics have become more routinized than they were in the earlier phases of democratization. The democratic agenda that the new middle class advocated in its earlier struggles for liberalization and democratic opening has been gradually replaced during the consolidation phase by other objectives and considerations in succeeding electoral processes.[18] Second, the routinization of democratic politics during the consolidation period revealed the internal disunity and heterogeneity of the larger middle class; consequently, each political party now must woo middle-class voters on the basis of ethnic, regional, or other nonclass criteria.

Finally, in both South Korea and Taiwan, the political role of the middle class was determined primarily by the ways in which its liberal or radical segments were politically mobilized. When the liberal intellectuals and professionals shifted their focus from liberalization and democratic opening to more specific issues of social reform, as in South Korea, or to more concrete political institutional tasks, as in Taiwan, their methods and channels of influence also changed. The shift in focus altered, in turn, the social base of mobilization. Specifically, the early antiregime or prodemocracy agenda successfully mobilized the broader middle class and other classes into a unified political force against the authoritarian state. As the state and political structures became democratic, however, there was no longer a common enemy; thus other issues became more salient in electoral politics.

This does not mean that the political influence of the middle class has diminished in either ongoing electoral processes or the more general process of democratic consolidation in South Korea and Taiwan. On the contrary, the middle class will continue to play a substantial role in both societies by competing with other classes and, in more complex ways, by shaping electoral politics and the ultimate outcome of democratization. The middle class will also carefully manage its demand for democracy in such a way as to ensure political stability throughout the consolidation phase. Moreover, the new middle class of liberal intellectuals and professionals in both South Korea and Taiwan will most likely seek new issues to either expand the scope of democratic institutionalization or deepen the social foundations of the emerging democracy. Finally, the stand that Taiwan's new middle class takes on the issues of national identity and relations with China will determine the shape of Taiwan's democratic course in the near future.

NOTES

1. Samuel P. Huntington, *The Third Wave: Democratization in the Late Twentieth Century* (Norman: University of Oklahoma Press, 1991); Giuseppe Di Palma, *To Craft Democracies: An Essay on Democratic Transitions* (Berkeley: University of California Press, 1990); Larry Diamond and Marc F. Plattner, eds., *The Global Resurgence of Democracy* (Baltimore: Johns Hopkins University Press, 1993); Doh Chull Shin, "On the Third Wave of Democratization: A Synthesis and Evaluation of Recent Theory and Research," *World Politics* 47 (October 1994): 135–70.

2. Doo-Seung Hong, "The Growth of the Middle Strata and Social Change," in *The State and Civil Society in Korea* (in Korean), edited by the Korean Sociological Association (Seoul: Hanul, 1992), 255–76.

3. For more details, see Hagen Koo, "Middle Classes, Democratization, and Class Formation: The Case of South Korea," *Theory and Society* 20 (August 1991): 485–509.

4. Kyung-Ryun Sung, "Social Origins of Korean Democratization," in *Korean Politics and New Social Trends* (in Korean), edited by Institute of Far Eastern Studies, Kyungnam

University (Seoul: Nanam, 1993); Hee-Youn Cho, "Transition to Democracy and Social Movements in Korea" (in Korean) (unpubl. ms., Sungkonghoe University, Seoul, 1995).

5. Sung, "Social Origins of Korean Democratization"; Cho, "Transition to Democracy." Some scholars, however, argue that the elite split appeared in South Korea during this time and contributed to the transition. See Tun-jen Cheng and Eun Mee Kim, "Making Democracy: Generalizing the South Korean Case," in Edward Friedman, ed., *The Politics of Democratization: Generalizing East Asian Experiences* (Boulder, Colo.: Westview, 1994); and Michael Burton and Jai P. Ryu, "South Korea's Elite Settlement" (unpubl. ms., Loyola College, Baltimore, 1995).

6. Chul-Hee Chung, "Social Origin of South Korea's Democratization Movement: Micro-mobilization and Frame Analysis" (in Korean) (unpubl. ms., Yonsei University, Seoul, 1995).

7. Jang Jip Choi, "The Working Class Movement and the State in Transition to Democracy: The Case of South Korea" (paper presented at the conference "East Asian Labor in Comparative Perspective," sponsored by the Institute of East Asian Studies, University of California at Berkeley, Berkeley, October 1993).

8. See Cheng and Kim, "Making Democracy."

9. Su-Hoon Lee, "Transitional Politics of Korea, 1987–1992: Activation of Civil Society," *Pacific Affairs* 66 (Fall 1993): 351–67.

10. Kyung-sok Suh, "Evaluation and Reflections on the Past Three Years of Kyungsilryun" (in Korean), *Sahoe Pyungron* 3 (August 1992): 192–202. See also his English-translated version: "Citizens' Campaigns for the Common Good," *Korea Focus* 1 (1993): 21–28.

11. See Choi, "The Working Class Movement and the State"; and Kwang-Yeong Shin, "Democratization and Class Politics in Korea" (unpubl. ms., Korea University, Seoul, 1995).

12. Hsin-Huang Michael Hsiao, *Retrospects and Prospects of Taiwan's Consumers' Movement* (in Chinese) (Taipei: Jiou Da Cultural Publications, 1987).

13. Yun-han Chu, *Crafting Democracy in Taiwan* (Taipei: Institute for National Policy Research, 1992); Wasashiro Wakabayashi, *Eastern Democracy: An Analysis of Contemporary Taiwanese Politics* (in Japanese) (Tokyo: Tabatashoten Publishing, 1994).

14. For more detail, see Hsin-Huang Michael Hsiao, "The Rise of Social Movements and Civil Protests," in Tun-Jen Cheng and Stephan Haggard, eds., *Political Change in Taiwan* (Boulder, Colo.: Lynne Rienner, 1993), 57–72.

15. Hsin-Huang Michael Hsiao, "The Labor Movement in Taiwan: A Retrospective and Prospective Look," in Denis F. Simon and Michael Y.M. Kau, eds., *Taiwan: Beyond the Economic Miracle* (Armonk, N.Y.: M.E. Sharpe, 1992), 151–67; and "Political Liberalization and the Farmer's Movement in Taiwan," in Friedman, ed., *The Politics of Democratization*, 202–18.

16. San-Tien Lin, *Struggles for Abolishing Article 100 of the Criminal Law* (in Chinese), published by the author, 1992; Pi-Yun Teng, *The History of Taiwan's Student Movement in the 1980s* (in Chinese) (Taipei: Vanguard Books, 1993).

17. See Yun Fain, ed., *The Self-Search of the New Generation: Documenting Taiwan's Student Movement* (in Chinese) (Taipei: Vanguard Books, 1993).

18. For a useful analysis of the Taiwanese case, see Hung-mao Tien, ed., *Taiwan's Electoral Politics and Democratic Transition* (Armonk, N.Y.: M.E. Sharpe, 1996).

INDEX